Contents

Preface

Bringing children and books together is an exciting experience for parents and educators who care about children and who believe that well-written literature has much to offer the developing individual. This book is concerned with children and how they grow, with literature as an art form, and with the ways that literature supports children's development.

This second edition follows the structure used in the first edition, but includes many new books for children and builds on updated research findings. The first two chapters introduce the range of literature for children, demonstrate how standards of literary excellence can be applied, and provide suggestions for day care professionals and teachers for working with parents as they select literature. Chapter three advocates grouping books for presentation so that children discern the interrelatedness of all literature. Chapters four through eight focus on the opportunities books offer for supporting children's language, intellectual, personality, social and moral, and aesthetic and creative development and indicate specific teaching strategies that will enhance growth in these areas. The final chapter shows the many options a day care professional or teacher has in presenting any one book, gives suggestions for determining appropriate approaches, and repeats guidelines for evaluating a literature program.

The book is designed to be used by both preservice and inservice teachers, for day care professionals, for all who work with preschool and primary age children. A brief introduction to each chapter reviews educational theory and research pertinent to the topic and is followed by extensive examples of specific books and strategies. Experienced teachers and day care professionals will find new titles discussed and will see familiar ones presented in a new light. Students preparing for a career in early childhood education will be introduced to both classic and contemporary books for children and will be given an approach to literature that will allow them to select and present high-quality books and poetry effectively.

The writer is indebted to Clyde Slicker of Rhode Island College for his time and effort in reviewing the early form of the manuscript and for his gentle, yet perceptive, criticisms. Thanks also to the children, teachers, and day care professionals of the Henry Barnard School and the Mt. Hope Day Care Center for allowing their photographs to be taken as they went about their daily activities. A special thank you goes to Katherine Scanga, who captured with her camera many of the exciting moments at the day care center. Editor Beverly Kolz has been a joy to work with. And finally, thanks to and a kiss for my husband, Wes Miller, for his constant encouragement, his pride in my work, and his sense of humor about my working hours.

1

Selecting Literature for Children

The three year olds listened intently as a day care professional read to them of D. Plexippus, a caterpillar who was happily eating leaves when a summer storm came up. He was knocked off the leaf and into the "murky" river down below.[1] They stared at the watercolor illustrations showing his travels down the river on a leaf boat. They gasped with delight as they saw that he would soon become a beautiful butterfly. When the reading was completed, they participated eagerly in dramatizing the story, each child on a private leaf boat, tossing and pitching with the current. Later that day, the children prepared for rest time. The sky was cloud covered, and as the lights were turned off, one little girl remarked, "It's murky in here."

It had been apparent during the reading that the children were enjoying the story. Their attention, their smiles, and their pleas to "read it again" proved that. Enjoyment, however, was not all that took place that afternoon. For at least one child, vocabulary enrichment had occurred. The regular sharing of literature with children frequently leads to vocabulary growth, increased reading comprehension, and concept development.

1

Children form attitudes about literature based on their individual experiences with books and with learning to read. One nine year old said that listening to stories was "like being there"; another said that it was nice to have books when the classroom was noisy; a third simply said that books and reading were "punishment." Their encounters with literature had left them with very different opinions about books and reading.

The primary goal of a literature program in the preschool and primary years is the creation of a positive attitude toward literature. Children who enjoy and value literature will continue to read and experience it and will have found a lifelong source of emotional and intellectual enrichment. Teachers of young children, day care providers, and parents are in an ideal position to help create such an attitude.

This book is designed to show the many ways in which literature can and does support the goals of early childhood education and how it can be presented so that children develop and maintain a positive attitude toward literary experiences. Before seeing how literature contributes to the achievement of developmental goals, however, it is essential that you first be aware of the wide range of stories and poems currently available for young children, and that you be able to select from these the best in terms of literary quality. Thus, this first chapter is devoted to defining types of literature and describing criteria for selecting quality literature. In addition, there is a section on helping parents select books.

Chapter two introduces procedures for presenting literature to children. It explains the necessity for, and techniques of, preparation for reading aloud, storytelling, and using audiovisual materials. Following this is a chapter that illustrates how a teacher can group books for presentation so that children can begin to make generalizations about the essential qualities of literature. This chapter also discusses how the imaginative quality of literature contributes to the development, or education, of children's imaginations.

Chapters four through eight show specific ways in which literature supports basic goals of early childhood education and give more information about children's growth in these areas. Chapter nine demonstrates the various approaches that may be used with a single book and presents criteria for evaluating a literature program for young children. You will find teaching strategies and literature suggested in the chapters and in further references at the end of chapters. It is hoped that these suggestions will encourage you to look for ways in which your sharing of literature with young children will aid in their language, intellectual, personality, social, moral, creative, and aesthetic development.

The Range of Literature

There are several categorization systems used to describe and classify books, and within each there are occasional differences of opinion among experts about the placement or labeling of books. Children's books frequently are classified in one of two ways, either by their format or by their genre.

Format

The format of a book is its general makeup. This includes its size, shape, binding, illustrations, cover, paper, typography, and spacing. A description of the format of the picture book *Ox-Cart Man*[2] would include the fact that it is a hardcover book, wider than it is high. The dust jacket shows the New England farmer standing in front of his ox cart, ready to begin the journey to Portsmouth Market. The actual cover of the book depicts the farmer walking off, followed by ox and cart, with wife and child waving good-bye, all shown in silhouette. The end papers are white, with the first small illustration appearing on the title page. Most of the book utilizes full page color illustrations facing a white page on which the text is centered. In a few cases the illustration blends over onto two pages or appears across the entire top half of a double page spread. The text is printed in clear bold type, with ample space between lines. Heavy, high quality paper and a sturdy binding make the book appear durable.

Some books stand out for their unusual format. In *The Grouchy Ladybug*[3] by Eric Carle, an argumentative ladybug approaches one animal after another, asking each if it wants to fight. When each agrees, the ladybug announces that the animal is not big enough and flies off to find someone bigger. The page for the tiny yellow jacket is only two inches wide. As the ladybug progresses to larger animals, the pages also get larger. By the time she gets to a whale, it takes four full-sized double page spreads for her to fly the length of its immense body. One page is cut the shape of the whale's tail. The ladybug's search for a fight is ended when the tail snaps and she is sent flying. Readers snap the tail as they turn the page. In this case, the format helps emphasize the story line.

The Grouchy Ladybug also uses format to provide a chance for the teacher to help children develop or clarify time awareness as related to the position of the sun in the sky. A small clock at the top of each page shows the time of each challenge. The sun rises in the sky, then turns downward. With the pages flat, each extending a half-inch further than the one preceding it, readers can see both the sun's travels and the time.

Format is also a mark of quality. For example, a book with an inadequate binding may resemble a loose-leaf notebook after five readings. Poor paper can dull otherwise excellent illustrations. Even the placement of illustrations on the page is important. If eight Mother Goose rhymes are crowded together on a single page, with illustrations scattered randomly to fill the white spaces, young children may be confused about which illustration goes with which verse. The same is true for counting books, where placement on the page can help or hinder young children as they make the connection between the objects pictured and the numeral representing the number of objects.

Format should be used to make the literature more effective. In *Ox-Cart Man,* the pattern of illustrations on one page opposite the text is broken three times by placement of the illustrations across the top half of a double page spread. These are the three pages that depict the farmer's journey to and from the market. The long horizontal shape of the illustration gives a sense of the length of the journey and allows a panoramic scene of the hills, valleys, streams, and farms which lie between the farmer's home and Portsmouth Market. Thus, the format is used to enhance the presentation of the story.

Many children's books are available in both hardcover and paperback editions. Paperbacks are less expensive, thus making quality literature within the economic reach of more families. However, they are not as durable as hardcover books. Sometimes a paperback edition of a picture book will differ greatly from the original in size. This may be a factor in selecting a book to read to a large group of children. The larger book will give the children a better view of the illustrations.

Some format classifications are used regularly to identify books. The most common are toy and board books, wordless picture books, picture books, and illustrated books.

Toy and Board Books.   Toy books are books with some special device for involving readers. Some have portions that the children can touch to feel different textures. *The Touch Me Book*[4], for example, includes sandpaper, a sponge, and a feather. The text includes adjectives describing how each feels, and, because of their active participation with the book, children will grasp the terms quickly. One very contemporary toy book has the child take money from the "cash machine" outside the bank on one page, then put the paper bills into Daddy's wallet when the page is turned. Some toy books are of the *scratch* and *sniff* type. As the children read the story, they are directed to scratch certain places on the page. When they do so, a fragrance is released. Since it is usually necessary to sniff close to the book to get the scent, the books may give a group of children a chance to share each other's colds as well as the special odors. Still others have pop-up figures that come to life as the page is turned, or various flaps to be lifted or pulled. Eric Hill's stories about Spot,[5] a friendly and inquisitive puppy, are popular with toddlers who delight in answering the questions the text poses, then lifting the flap or pulling the tab to show the answers.

Toy books are generally best suited to use by individual children rather than groups. Many are not sturdy enough for repeated use, and even when durable they require that children take turns. Some, such as flip books, can be used by only one child at a time. In these, the reader must riffle through the pages rapidly to get the effect of animation and thus "see" the story. In one flip book, Martha Alexander's *The Magic Picture,*[6] a boy places a plate of brownies on a table. His dog is curled up underneath it, and a picture of two girls hangs above it. When he walks away, the girls climb out of the picture and help themselves to the brownies. He returns and blames the dog. When the boy leaves the second time, the dog sees that one of the girls still has a brownie in her hand. He barks at the picture until the girl steps out of the frame once more and gives him the last brownie. Only the person holding the book is positioned to see the full effect of changes in the drawings from page to page.

Board books are printed on heavy cardboard, and often they are laminated as well. They are designed for very young children who are just learning to handle books. Because of the stiffness of the pages, they can be grasped and turned more easily than paper pages, and they are also less likely to tear. Board books vary greatly in quality, from those with inaccurate information and overly cute language and characters, to the vast majority of mediocre books, to some very fine ones by authors such as Eric Hill, Helen Oxenbury, Leo Lionni, and Rosemary Wells. The good ones give clear pictures for the child to use in naming,

Max got into the tub.
His orange sherbet sank to the bottom.
BOAT! said Max.

Board books, such as Max's Bath, *can be handled successfully by very young children. (From* Max's Bath, *copyright © 1985 by Rosemary Wells. A Dial Books For Young Readers book. Reproduced by permission of E.P. Dutton, a division of New American Library.)*

have simple direct plots if there is a plot, are accurate in text and illustration, and are appropriate in content for children of one to three years of age.

Some would argue that toy and board books, and those printed on cloth or plastic—they float in the tub—are in fact not books at all. Dorothy Butler, in *Babies Need Books,*[7] acknowledges that for her something becomes a book only if it is printed on paper, and that she can accept board books uneasily at best. One strong point in favor of board books, however, is that they are durable, and thus can be handled successfully by very young children.

Wordless Picture Books.   Wordless picture books are exactly what the name implies. They are books that have no text, but present their message through pictures only. They are also called textless picture books and books without words. Raymond Briggs's *The Snowman*[8] is a wordless picture book that tells the story in a sequence of pictures on each page, somewhat like a comic strip. Some pages have as many as twelve small illustrations, while others vary the size and number of pictures. At one point there is a single illustration covering two pages. The story opens with a little boy waking to a snowy morning, going outside, and building a snowman. During the night that follows, the boy wakes and goes outside to see his snowman. The snowman greets him with a tip of his hat. The two shake hands and the boy invites the snowman into the house, where they explore the marvels of indoor living. The fire in the fireplace is not to the snowman's liking, but he does enjoy cooling his hands before the open refrigerator door and playing with light switches and skateboards. The snow-man returns the boy's hospitality by taking him by the hand and flying him to distant cities. They return before morning, and after a farewell hug and wave, the boy goes back to bed. Morning and the warm sunshine wake the boy, who runs eagerly to see his friend. Morning and the warm sunshine have also had an effect on the snowman. The boy finds a hat and scarf on a small pile of melt-ing snow. *The Snowman* is simple enough to be understood by preschoolers, still enjoyed by second graders, and appealing as well to an adult sharing the literary experience with a child.

Picnic[9] is an even simpler wordless picture book with only a few pictures and a very direct story line, one which a four year old can tell aloud as the pages are turned. The book shows a family of mice heading out for a picnic. As their red truck bounces along the dirt road, one of the nine mouse children falls from the back and is left behind. The pictures then alternately show the lost mouse and the rest of the family. When the family discovers that someone is missing, they begin calling, then all get back in the truck and head toward home in their search. The lost mouse hears the truck, runs out to the road, and all are reunited. Before they can continue, however, the rescued one must retrieve her doll, also a mouse, which she had dropped in the excitement of hearing her family re-turning. Together again, they all can at last settle down for the picnic lunch.

Other wordless books are more complex, with much action in each illustra-tion or with feelings and happenings subtly expressed. *Bobo's Dream*,[10] for in-stance, introduces a dream sequence in which the dog, Bobo, imagines being able to defend his master against other boys who take the football, just as his owner had in reality retrieved Bobo's bone from a larger dog. Preschoolers do not always follow this portion of the plot. Thus, not all wordless picture books are for young children. You must evaluate the understanding level required for these just as you must for books with text.

Picture Books.   Picture books are those books that rely on a combination of illustrations and narrative, with both being integral to the completed work. In *When I Was Young in the Mountains*,[11] the author describes her memories of growing up in Appalachia. Each page tells of both the day-to-day happenings and the special events that characterized her childhood. The family ate corn bread, pinto beans, and fried okra; they spend quiet evenings on the front porch; they went to church in the schoolhouse on Sundays. Sometimes when a snake would come into the yard, her grandmother would go after it with a hoe, and once four of the children had their picture taken with a long dead snake draped over their necks.

The illustrations work with the text to describe this life. When the text tells of the grandfather returning home from the coal mines covered with black dust, and kissing the children on the top of the head, the illustrations show the ac-tion, and also that he will wash on the porch using the bowl and pitcher of water the boy is holding for him. A mood of love and caring permeates both text and illustration, and while the illustrations give more detail than does the text, both are necessary for a complete understanding.

Some authorities differentiate between the general term *picture book* and the more specialized term *picture story book.* A picture story book is a picture book that tells a story with a definite plot. It is not simply a description of everyday events or how a character felt in a particular situation. There is a problem to be solved, an interrelatedness of events. For example, in *Something Special for Me*,[12] Rosa, the little girl who tells the story, describes how she is to use the coins saved by her mother and grandmother to buy a special birthday gift for herself. She and her mother go shopping, and Rosa looks at roller skates, at a dress and shoes, and at a knapsack. Each time she says this is what she wants, and each time changes her mind just before the purchase is completed. She and her mother then stop at the diner where the mother waitresses, and as they leave they hear an accordian player. The mother explains that Rosa's other grandmother had played the accordian for park concerts and weddings, and that people said even the chairs and tables danced to her music. Rosa decides that this is what she wants. With a little extra money from Aunt Ida, they get a second-hand accordian for her, and Uncle Sandy says that he will pay for her music lessons.

The events in this story are related through cause and effect and through the solving of the central problem of selecting a gift. There is a definite chronology to the happenings. *When I Was Young in the Mountains* and *Something Special for Me* are similar in that both are told in first person by a small girl, and both describe events in the life of the family. Both are picture books; however, only *Something Special for Me* can be classified as a picture story book.

Another specialized type of picture book is the concept book, a book that explicates a general idea or concept by presenting many specific examples of it. Thus, a book about shapes might show examples of circles, squares, triangles, and rectangles, sometimes alone on a page, and at other times in combination with other shapes, shown prominently in a drawing or photograph. The many examples help readers understand the concept. Tana Hoban has done many excellent concept books for young children. In *Round & Round & Round*,[13] she demonstrates with color photos the meaning of "round" by showing many common objects that have that shape. Alphabet and counting books are concept books, for they explicate the letter and number systems.

Easy-to-read books are picture books although they are sometimes categorized separately. Publishers use labels such as *I Can Read, Read Alone*, and *Easy-to-Read* to denote books which have a limited vocabulary and regulated sentence length, factors which contribute to the ease of reading material. The books are not written from a standardized word list as are some stories in basal readers, but attention is given to the number of difficult words included. The easy-to-read books are excellent choices for the independent reading of children just learning to read and are used for this purpose rather than for reading aloud to children.

Skilled writers are able to work within the constraints of vocabulary and sentence length restriction to produce interesting and well-written stories. There is no need to limit the topics of easy reading books. In *How Far, Felipe?*[14] Genevieve Gray tells of families who left Culiacan, Mexico, in 1775 under the leadership of Colonel Juan Bautista de Anza, with plans to settle in California. The historical setting and the hardships endured by the settlers are accurately portrayed.

There is no need, either, for writers to use an "Oh! Oh! Look! Look! Look!" style of writing. Arnold Lobel has captured the natural cadence of speech in *Frog and Toad Are Friends.*[15] Frog arrives at Toad's house and knocks on the door:

> "Toad, Toad," shouted Frog, "wake up. It is spring!"
> "Blah," said a voice from inside the house.
> "Toad, Toad!" cried Frog. "The sun is shining! The snow is
>   melting. Wake up!"
> "I am not here," said the voice.[16]

The sentences are short and the vocabulary easy, but the humor shines through.

Illustrated Books. Illustrated books rely more heavily on the text than on the illustrations to convey the story. Generally, the text takes up a greater portion of the page than do the pictures. The illustrations can, and often do, enrich the narrative, but it would be possible to comprehend the story fully without the illustrations. An example of an illustrated book is *Macaroon*[17] by Julia Cunningham. In the first three pages readers learn that Macaroon is a raccoon with a problem. He does not plan to spend the winter outside, holed up in a tree, but he is disturbed by his previous winters. Other falls he has allowed himself to be caught and kept by a child, thus spending the winter indoors as a beloved pet. But in the springs, when he has left, the children have cried, and the memories of their sadness haunt him. Still, Macaroon tells a fieldmouse that he is not going to give up his warm indoor winters.

The illustrations which accompany this portion of the text show the woods where Macaroon lives, and Macaroon talking to the fieldmouse. Thus, the art helps to establish the setting but does not advance the plot. Later illustrations add to the humor of the adventure and capture some of the action. At one point Macaroon is shown lounging in the bathtub, floating in the warm water before washing the cookies he plans to eat. The illustrations are excellent by artistic standards, yet they do not carry equal weight with the text in the telling of the story.

Format alone is not a guide to the difficulty of a book. There are some picture books which are appropriate for toddlers and others which require the maturity of a sixth grader for any real understanding. Look carefully at the content and writing style as well as the format of books as you select ones to share with children.

Genre

Format refers basically to the physical qualities of a book. Genre refers to the content, what is said and how it is said. The major genre classifications are poetry and prose.

Poetry. This division is better understood in practice than by definition. An attempt may be made to differentiate between poetry and prose by saying that poetry rhymes, but blank verse does not rhyme. It may be said that poetry has a depth of emotion and an imaginative quality, but some prose does also. It may be said that the sound of poetry is pleasing, and that the meaning often comes from the sound as well as the sense of the words. However, concrete poetry, shaped like its subject, needs to be seen rather than heard. It may be said that poetry relies on figurative language, yet there are narrative poems without a single simile or metaphor. The best that can be done is to list some of the qualities of poetry, and to recognize that any one poem will not have all of them, and that nearly any one of them may be present in prose as well as in poetry.

For young children, a large portion of their poetry experience will be with Mother Goose rhymes. Also in this genre will be collections of poems and single poems illustrated in picture book format. There will be verse as well, rhymed, but lacking the depth of emotion and compactness of language of quality poetry. Dorothy Aldis, Lucille Clifton, Beatrice Schenk DeRegniers, Aileen Fisher, Lee Bennett Hopkins, Karla Kuskin, Myra Cohn Livingston, David McCord, Eve Merriam, Lilian Moore, Laura Richards, and William Jay Smith are well known poets whose writing is generally appropriate for young children.

Prose.   Prose is divided into nonfiction and fiction, with nonfiction the factual work and fiction the invented work. Each of these is further subdivided.

Nonfiction.   Nonfiction includes informational books and biography. Informational books are designed to tell about a specific subject such as stars, or colonial times, or how to build a doll house. Sometimes the information is told in story form, with child characters sharing their knowledge about the subject, or with the use of *you* and *we* to make it more personal. At other times the information is presented directly, organized by topic. Concept books are related to informational books in that they too deal with facts as building blocks.

Biography is the story of a person's life, or a segment of that person's life. Some biography uses only statements that the person is known to have made and bases all incidents on recorded happenings. Other biography tends to fictionalize incidents and dialogue, having the person say what he or she is likely to have said, and filling in gaps in information with plausible events.

Fiction.   Fiction includes all stories that are created from the author's imagination, even though they may be based on real happenings. If the story could happen now, or could have happened in the past, it is called realism. If the setting is in the past, the genre is historical fiction. *Something Special for Me* is contemporary realism, with a current setting. *How Far, Felipe?*, set in 1775–1776, is historical fiction.

If the story includes any actions that could not happen in the world as we know it today, the book is categorized as fantasy. *Frog and Toad Are Friends* and *Macaroon* are fantasy because, as far as is known, animals do not talk. *The Snowman* is fantasy with its lively snowman who explores a house and gives a flying one-night tour of faraway lands. Of course, if the night adventures of the little boy and the snowman are interpreted to be only a dream the boy is having, then this book could be classified as realism.

Traditional literature—the folk tales, epics, myths, and legends which began in the oral tradition of storytelling—is a rich source of stories for children. The tales themselves were adapted by various storytellers to fit particular audiences. With their quick action and clear portrayal of good and evil, folk tales have survived for generations in a variety of versions. Some have now been told in single picture book editions, while others appear in collections. The title page of the books will often indicate that the tale is "retold by" or "adapted by" an author or illustrator. The original authors are unknown.

Genre and format are two separate systems for categorizing books. *The Snowman, Frog and Toad Are Friends,* and *Macaroon* are all the same genre, fantasy, but they represent three different formats: wordless picture book, picture book, and illustrated book. *How Far, Felipe?* and *Frog and Toad Are Friends* are the same format, picture story books, but they are different genre, the first historical fiction and the second fantasy.

It is useful to know both ways of categorizing books so that you can provide variety of format and of genre for your pupils. It may also be useful as you look for books in a library. Folk tales and poetry are sometimes classified by genre and will appear in the nonfiction section of the library. Other times folk tales and poetry which are in picture book format will be shelved with the picture books. You will need to check the card catalog for the location of specific folk tales and poetry books.

Quality in Literature

Books shared with children should represent the best by both literary and artistic standards. Some help in judging books can be found in reviews of new books which appear in journals such as *The Horn Book* and *Language Arts.* Reading these may help show how criteria are applied, at least by one or two critics. The Caldecott Award, given each year by a committee of the American Library Association to the illustrator of the most distinguished American picture book for children, also shows what one group of people have considered to be outstanding. Libraries most often purchase those books which the librarians judge to be of literary merit. Talking with local librarians may help you learn how they apply standards of literary excellence.

But rather than relying totally on the opinion of others, you should learn to evaluate books for children yourself. This will enable you to be secure in using a book you have not heard about from others and is requisite for you to be able to help children develop taste in literature.

Evaluating Fiction
One way of analyzing fiction is to look at the literary elements that make up the selection. Strengths and weaknesses in plot, setting, characterization, theme, and style of writing can be identified.

Plot.   The plot of a story is what happens in it. In brief form, the plot of *Doctor De Soto* by William Steig is as follows. Dr. De Soto is a dentist who works with his wife as his assistant. Both happen to be mice, and this requires some extra equipment—such as a ladder—when he works on large animals, and also the precaution of posting a sign indicating that he does not accept cats and other dangerous animals for treatment. One day he and his wife look down from the office window to see a fox with a bandaged jaw ringing the doorbell. The fox looks so pitiful, and pleads so mournfully, that they accept him as a patient.

The fox cannot help thinking how good his dentist would taste as Dr. De Soto, wearing rubbers of course, steps into his mouth. The rotten tooth is pulled and the fox is instructed to return the next day for a new tooth. That night, the De Sotos discuss the danger posed by the fox, and they devise a plan.

The fox returns, and after some debate with himself, decides that he will eat Dr. De Soto once the new tooth is in place. However, no sooner is the gold tooth attached than Dr. De Soto steps out and tells the fox about a new preparation that he has developed that will prevent toothaches. The fox agrees to an application. Dr. De Soto paints each tooth and instructs the fox to close his mouth for one minute. At the end of the time, the fox discovers that his teeth are stuck together. Dr. De Soto explains that this will last for a day or two and is necessary for the formula to permeate the dentine. The fox has no recourse but to thank the De Sotos and leave, which he attempts to do with dignity. They smile as he stumbles down the steps, then take the rest of the day off.

A good plot is interesting. It builds suspense so that the reader will want to know what is going to happen next. This story builds from the introduction, which lets the reader know that certain patients can be dangerous to a mouse dentist, to the arrival of just such a patient, to the De Sotos' decision to treat him, through various hints that the fox may well try to eat Dr. De Soto, to the De Sotos' final triumph of outwitting the fox. It is heightened by the fox's thoughts and muttered comments about how good the mice would taste and by the De Sotos' realization of the imminent danger. At one point, the fox even closes his mouth on Dr. De Soto, though he says it is just a joke.

A good plot builds logically. There are causal relationships that connect the events, and these are plausible within the context of the story. Once you have accepted the premise that, in this fantasy, the dentist is a mouse, then it follows that large animals that eat mice would be dangerous to have as patients.

Plots in picture books vary in complexity. There may be only one problem, or several, to be solved. There may be two characters or twenty. Occasionally there will be parallel plots, two story lines weaving together by the conclusion. However simple or complex the plot is, the events should be logically related to one another.

Setting.   Setting, where and when a story takes place, should be an integral part of the story, not just a backdrop that could be changed without affecting the plot. In *Dr. De Soto,* the urban location of their home and office emphasizes the sophistication of the dentist and his wife.

If the story has a specific setting, with the exact time and place identified, the description should be accurate. Other settings may be more generally depicted as being located in a town, or in the country, or "long ago in a faraway land." Even when location is not precisely spelled out, the reader should be given a taste of what life is like at that place and at that time.

Characterization.   Characterization, how the author portrays each character in a book, is often what makes a book memorable. Children know Madeline, Petunia, and Curious George because these characters are clearly delineated.

The reader knows what they like and dislike, how they will behave in a given situation, and what is special about them. They have more than one dimension and so the reader can respond to the many aspects of their personalities. There are some likeable things they do or think, some not so likeable. A good author lets the reader know about characters by showing what they do, what they think, what they say, and sometimes by showing what others say or think about them, or how others treat them. Because of how the De Sotos react to him, readers know that the fox is dangerous even though he displays a deceptively positive, well-dressed appearance. Readers know how much he hates pain from the direct statement made about it, from his begging for help, and by the ease with which he is duped by a promise of freedom from toothaches. They know that he wants to eat the mice as he mumbles while under the anesthetic, "M-m-m, yummy. How I love them raw . . . with just a pinch of salt, and a . . . dry . . . white wine."[19] They know he has a conscience as he wonders to himself if it would be "shabby" of him to eat the De Sotos once his tooth was fixed. And they see him yielding to his nature as a fox when he decides that he will indeed partake of his dentist.

There is contrast between Dr. and Mrs. De Soto. He remains distrustful of the fox. She, who first felt sorry for the suffering fox and said they should risk helping him, also suggests that the fox didn't know what he was saying while under the influence of the anesthetic and will not hurt them since they are help-

The plot, setting, characterization, theme, style, and illustration in a picture book should be mutually compatible. (From Doctor DeSoto *by William Steig. Copyright © 1982 by William Steig. Reprinted with permission of Farrar, Straus and Giroux, Inc.)*

ing him. She is solicitous of her husband as well, and shares his worry about the fox as he describes his own concern.

In some stories the characters change, or develop, as a result of what has happened to them. It is difficult to have much character development in books for young children simply because the stories are fairly short. There is little time to delineate a character fully, then have a believable change take place. None of the characters in *Dr. De Soto* changes. The fox battles his conscience throughout; Mrs. De Soto remains trusting; Dr. De Soto performs his duty but takes no chances.

Theme.   The theme of a book is its underlying idea. It may be a general theme, such as friendship or courage, or be more specific and stated in sentence form such as "Even though persons seem alike, each one is unique," or "We should make our own decisions, and not let others make them for us." A story may have no theme, one theme, or more than one theme. One idea underlying *Dr. De Soto* is that a small but clever character can outwit a larger character; another is that animals will be true to their nature; still another is that self-preservation requires that one be aware of potential danger. None of these themes intrudes on the plot. If there is a theme, it should be an integral part of the story but should not overpower the story. There should be no need for any closing comment by the author to make certain that the theme is understood clearly.

Style of Writing.   The style of writing, which words are chosen and how they are arranged, helps create the mood of the story. Steig uses very expressive vocabulary as he describes actions of the characters. The fox, while still in pain, "wailed," "whimpered," and "yelped" his comments. He "caressed" his new tooth with his tongue.

There is humor in the story, in the concept of a tiny dentist treating larger patients, in the equipment necessary, and in the small events that contribute to the larger plot. When Dr. De Soto enters the fox's mouth, he gasps, not only because of the "rotten bicuspid" he discovers, but because the fox has "unusually bad breath."

Steig employs dialogue to advance the plot. When Dr. De Soto tells his patient that "This tooth will have to come out,"[20] the reader learns what is going to happen next. Other authors may use descriptive passages, which achieve the same end of advancing the plot, but that give a tale a slower pace. The style should be appropriate to the story being told. It should appear so natural that readers are not caught up in it, and are scarcely aware of how it is functioning.

Plot, setting, characterization, theme, and style should be mutually compatible, each complementing the others. In addition to these marks of good writing, books for children should be free of stereotypes and of condescension in tone. Stereotypes generally indicate poor writing as well as being intellectually and socially offensive. They present a person not as an individual, but as a representative of a group, all of whose members are judged to possess the same characteristics. A condescending tone should be avoided because it is an insult to children.

Evaluating Nonfiction

Standards for nonfiction should be applied as rigorously as those for fiction are. And like fiction, nonfiction should be well written and interesting. However, there are other key criteria. Factual accuracy is one of the most important. Nonfiction for any age level should not contain misinformation. Nor should it oversimplify a topic to the point of inaccuracy.

Also, books of nonfiction should indicate when pertinent information about a topic is not known. In a book called *Little Monsters,* M. Jean Craig writes about a star-nosed mole, with its twenty-two tenacles around its nose, "No one knows whether it smells with the tenacles or feels with them."[21] In a less direct statement of the unknown, Craig writes about the coloration of the spicebush swallowtail butterfly larva, "Perhaps the colored spots frighten away the birds or lizards that are the caterpillar's natural enemies."[22] In both instances she shows that there is still more to be learned, that the subject is open. Books can help convey to children the excitement of discovery and an attitude of inquiry. They can show how much is yet to be learned, to be explored, to be reassessed.

Nonfiction should be clear about when a statement is of a factual nature and when it is an opinion or a value position. Jane Goodsell was careful in her biography of Senator Daniel Inouye of Hawaii. She wrote: "He joined the Democratic party. He believed it to be the political party that would help Asians gain rights to the same education and jobs as other Americans."[23] Whether the Democratic party was indeed the one that would help is a value position. She has stated it clearly as his belief, not as a fact. Earlier she had established the difficulty Asian students in Hawaii had in getting the same education as white students.

By contrast, Susan Harris has combined fact with opinion in this paragraph written about beavers in a book titled *Swimming Mammals.* "Beavers were once plentiful. But many have been killed for their fur. This is very sad. Beavers are hard workers. Their dams help stop floods. And they show us we can all work better together."[24] The opinion that it is sad is stated in exactly the same manner as the fact that beavers have been killed for their fur. The reason for the sadness about beavers being killed is unstated. It might be implied from the text that the reason is that their dams are needed for flood control, or that they are role models for cooperation. Others might agree with the sadness but base it on a value position that holds that the killing of animals is wrong. Still others might feel that no animal should be allowed to become extinct. Value positions related to nonfiction need to be included. They are a part of understanding the topic. However, they should be identified.

Harris's writing about beavers earlier in the book exemplifies another problem which occurs in some nonfiction. She writes that beavers "know just the kind of home they want."[25] This giving of human feelings and thoughts to animals, or to inanimate objects, is called anthropomorphism when it occurs in nonfiction writing. The beavers are made to appear almost like humans, deciding rationally what they like and do not like, what kind of home they want. While this is appropriate in a book of fantasy, it is not acceptable in a book of nonfiction. Nor is another outlook which permeates some nonfiction. This is the use of teleological explanations. (All of nature works according to one grand plan. Mother Nature guides it. Whatever happens, it is because that is the way "Mother Nature" works.) There seems to be a greater use of anthropomorphism and teleological explanations in books for young children than in books for older readers. If you find yourself saying, "Isn't that cute?" about a nonfiction picture book, better reevaluate it.

Evaluating Poetry

A reliable choice of poetry for young children is Mother Goose rhymes. The rhythm and rhyme of these verses have lasting appeal. The narrative ones tell intriguing tales and the nonsense ones are filled with humor. A familiarity with Mother Goose, built by listening to and joining in as the rhymes are read, by dramatizing them, by knowing them, is a sound basis for later appreciation and enjoyment of poetry.

Poetry takes careful reading. There is a compactness of language in which every word counts. The sound of the language as it is read aloud is vital. The rhythm should be strong and natural. Even free verse has a rhythm to it. The rhyme, if it is a rhyming poem, should have a pattern. There may be the steady beat of such poems as "The Little Turtle."

> There was a little turtle,
>   He lived in a box,
> He swam in a puddle,
>   He climbed on the rocks.
> He snapped at a mosquito,
>   He snapped at a flea,
> He snapped at a minnow,
>   And he snapped at me.
> He caught the mosquito,
>   He caught the flea,
> He caught the minnow,
>   But he didn't catch me.
>
>   Vachel Lindsay[26]

Here the rhythm seems to sing. There may also be a more varied use of rhythm and rhyme, such as that found in "O Sliver of Liver."

> O sliver of liver,
> Get lost! Go away!
> You tremble and quiver
> O sliver of liver—
> You set me a-shiver
> And spoil my day—
> O sliver of liver,
> Get lost! Go Away!
>
>   Myra Cohn Livingston[27]

In both poems the authors have used language for its sound as well as for its meaning.

CURLY locks, Curly locks,
  Wilt thou be mine?
Thou shalt not wash dishes
  Nor yet feed the swine,
But sit on a cushion
  And sew a fine seam,
And feed upon strawberries,
  Sugar and cream.

A familiarity with Mother Goose rhymes is a sound basis for later appreciation and enjoyment of poetry. (From Mother Goose. *Selected and illustrated by Michael Hague. Copyright © 1984 by Michael Hague. Reprinted by permission of Holt, Rinehart and Winston, Publishers.)*

The rhyme in poems such as these should not take precedence over the meaning. That is, words should not be stated in awkward order just so the last words will rhyme. Nor should there be lines, included because they rhyme, which would not make sense if found in a prose selection.

Language should be fresh. It may show a new way of looking at something, or a new way of telling about it. Poetry often uses figurative language, making comparisons. It relies heavily on imagery, describing how experiences are perceived by the senses. Read poems to see if the comparison and descriptions make sense, and if they are vivid.

Livingston has described liver with words which let the reader not only know how it looks, but also how she feels about it. Children will know what she means when she says that it sets her a-shiver. Some may wish that they too could tell it to go away. The emotional content of poetry helps make contact between poet and reader.

The literary standards by which poetry for children is judged are no less demanding than those for adult poetry. A poem which is poor by adult standards is poor for children as well. Nor is there any need to talk down to children, to make poems cute or easy. Writes English educator Joan Cass, "A poet must write what he believes in, and he must believe in his own maturity: to toss off immature verses in the expectation that they will do for young children is to create something which is false and unconvincing."[28] Teachers have a responsibility to select for children those poems which have literary merit.

Evaluating Illustrations

Charles Keeping, an illustrator of many picture books for children, feels strongly that publishers, librarians, and reviewers of children's books should have some training in art.[29] After all, the art is essential to the book. Yet there are judgments you can make about the effectiveness and quality of illustrations in picture books whether you have had any formal training in art or not.

First, the illustrations should be near the text they depict, either on the same page or on the opposite page. Children look at the pictures as the story is being read or may use the pictures as clues to meanings if they are reading the book by themselves. If the story is to be unified, then text and illustrations must appear together. In books of poetry, the illustration should be tied to the poem by its placement on the page as well as by its content.

Illustrations should match both the action and the description in the text. When the text says that Dr. De Soto fastened an extractor onto the rotten tooth and then, with his wife, began to winch it free until it came out and hung swaying in the air, then that is exactly what should be shown. However, the illustrator is free to add any actions or details that might extend the story, develop the setting, or enhance the characterization. The reader sees not only the tooth being removed, but the ladder that the doctor had used earlier, with his tools resting on the top. The reader also gains perspective in the size differential of the characters through the illustrations, and a look at the clever use of winch and hoist used by the dentist for entry into the mouths of his larger patients. In this story, there are no descriptions of the characters' clothing given, so the illustrator is free to dress them appropriately. Dr. De Soto appears in his white coat, and his wife is in a long dress, but with an apron. The fox, who has been said to be "well-dressed," is rather nattily attired in slacks, dress shirt, tie, vest, and blazer. All the characters appear in fresh clothing on the second day, but maintain their unique styles.

The illustrator may be selective in what is shown; not everything mentioned in the text must be pictured. The basic criterion is that there be no conflict between text and illustration.

Sometimes illustrations can be confusing rather than helpful. *Days With Daddy*[30] is a realistic story of a family in which the father decides to go back to school and the mother goes to work. Most of the book tells about the first day Daddy spends at home with the children. One problem with the illustrations is that they combine realism with fantasy although the text does not. The people are drawn realistically; the dog and the turtle are personified. The dog is pictured sitting at the table with a spoon in its paw, and waiting in line for the bathroom, front legs crossed over its chest. The turtle is able to sit up and to manage a most forlorn expression.

In addition, the setting is supposedly contemporary, and the mother's clothing reflects current styles. The boy, however, is shown wearing suspenders and at night goes to bed wearing a nightcap. The illustrations themselves are inconsistent. Thus, they do not help develop the text.

The medium and the style of the illustrations must be appropriate to the mood of the story. *Dr. De Soto*'s cartoon-style illustrations fit the mood of this light and humorous story. A different type of story requires a different type of illustrations. In *Where the River Begins*,[31] author/illustrator Thomas Locker has created magnificent landscape paintings to capture the sights seen by two boys and their grandfather as they follow a river back to its source. The illustrations are quiet, filled with the grandeur of woods and field and sky. They enhance the simple narrative by illuminating the force and beauty of the natural surroundings. There are other media and styles that might be appropriate for this story, and that might work well, and some that would not. Realistic pen and ink sketches might have been used successfully; the cartoon style of *Dr. De Soto* would have been incongruous with this text. The illustrator must choose a medium and a style that will extend the mood and the meaning of a story.

The purpose for some books helps define criteria for evaluating the illustrations. In alphabet books, used with young children to name objects, the illustrations should be clear and uncluttered. If the alphabet book is designed to emphasize the sound or sounds made by each letter, then the illustrations must be accurate. That is, *c* should not be represented by an object such as a chicken, for although the word does begin with *c*, it is the sound of the *ch* blend that is heard.

If the book is designed to help children learn to count and to recognize numerals, then the illustrations must show the objects clearly. The child should know what is to be counted. There should be no confusing background, no questions about whether it is the bugs or the legs on the bugs to be counted.

In nonfiction, the illustrations must help convey the facts or concepts being presented. Walter Lorraine, both a publisher and an illustrator, writes that "to be effective the artwork must first and foremost do the job it was intended to do. In nonfiction it must indeed communicate the facts, whatever its drawing appeal, color, or composition. If it does not, then that art fails in its function."[32] Of particular interest in nonfiction is the way in which scale is shown, or if it is shown at all. In *Redwoods Are the Tallest Trees in the World*,[33] Kazue Mizumura shows the comparison between a house and a redwood tree, and the final page shows a boy standing in a redwood forest, dwarfed by the size of the trees. Often an artist will include in the illustration something whose size is known, such as a hand or a finger, or may label the size of the object. The illustrations must help the reader visualize not only the subject, but the subject in context.

Illustrations are central to the success of picture books. They should be evaluated carefully, for they are a basic component of young children's literary and artistic education.

The medium and the style of illustrations in picture books should reflect the content and the mood of the text. (From Where the River Begins, *copyright © 1984 by Thomas Locker. A Dial Books For Young Readers book. Reproduced by permission of E. P. Dutton, a division of New American Library.)*

Children's Preferences in Literature

The topic of children's preferences in literature has been more fully researched for intermediate grade children than for primary and preschool children. Looking at what is available, though, several cautions should be kept in mind. First, these research results, and others like them, tell what children as a group appear to like. They do not indicate what an individual child will like. They give the starting point, a suggestion, not an answer. Second, a survey of preferences helps educators judge the content and type of literature children may enjoy, but it is not a guide to literary quality. Teachers must work both with what they know of children and with what they know of literature as they select books.

In general, sex differences in reading interests do not appear strongly until children are around eight or nine years of age.[34] Primary school children, both boys and girls, enjoy stories about personified animals, about nature, about children their age or slightly older, about daily life and familiar experiences.[35] They rely heavily on illustrations in their liking for a book, more so than on content.[36] They prefer illustrations that adults would term representational as opposed to abstract when they are judging pictures apart from text.[37] In general, color is preferred over black and white, and drawings over photographs.[38] However, any one book, a combination of content and type of illustration, may become a favorite. Isolating a single factor has not proven to be a reliable method of predicting children's responses to a specific book. You may want to observe the children you teach to see which books they prefer, what patterns of response they exhibit. Some teachers conduct interest surveys within their own classes, determining what interests the children have in common, and finding individual interests which can be matched with appropriate literature. Many teachers find that books about monsters and books that are humorous are currently very popular with their classes.

You may also want to read each year's "Children's Choices" results. Under the direction of a joint committee of the International Reading Association and the Children's Book Council, a list of books is selected from those published during the current year. They are selected for literary quality and for diversity of types and subjects. The list is then sent to teams of educators who share the books with children. The children vote on their favorites, and each year the list of winners is published in *The Reading Teacher* and is available as a reprint from the Children's Book Council.

Primary grade children, in a pilot study conducted by Carol Fisher and Margaret Natarella, showed a favorable attitude toward both rhyming and unrhyming poetry but preferred the rhyming. Often if they liked the topic of the poem, they liked the poem too. If they disliked the subject, they disliked the poem about it. The children had difficulty in comprehending figurative language, tending to interpret it literally for some rather strange conceptions of what the poem was about. Their favorite poems had strong rhythm and rhyme and frequently were narrative in form.[39]

Perhaps one of the most consistent findings of all the studies is that preschool and primary grade children enjoy literature, both prose and poetry. Teachers and day care providers have the opportunity to extend this enjoyment, to broaden children's taste in literature, and to plan literature experience in such a way that goals of early childhood education are supported.

Individual Children and the Literary Experience

Each individual who reads or listens to a work of literature helps to create for himself or herself the meaning of that work. Whether adults or children, we bring our own expectations and backgrounds to whatever we read. Louise Rosenblatt[40] describes experiencing literature as a transaction, a two-way process between a reader and a text. The reader comes to the work having made a decision, whether conscious or unconscious, about whether the reading is to be done primarily to gain information or primarily for enjoyment. Thus the reader may read a textbook, or a manual, with the express purpose of learning certain facts or how to do something. The reading is a means to an end. At other times, the reader may approach a story or a poem simply for the pleasure of reading. There is no attempt during the reading to remember particular facts, no specific searching for information. Reading and responding are ends in themselves. The literary experience for young children is generally of this second type. They listen to stories and poems, responding to the rhythm of the language, the excitement of the plot, and the feelings evoked. They can express their responses later in art, in discussion, and in drama, but they are not listening in order to engage in the activities. Day care professionals and teachers help reinforce the importance of responding to literature as a pleasurable experience by allowing children to share their interpretations and responses in open-ended activities and discussions. When very specific recall questions about facts within a story are employed regularly following story reading, children begin listening to stories as if they were for information gain only.

In addition to approaching reading material with a preconceived idea of its purpose, the reader also helps to create the meaning of the text by interacting with it. The author contributes the piece of literature, having selected a topic and developed it with conscious choice of style. The reader contributes meaning to that literature by making inferences and generalizations based on his or her own thoughts, feelings, and memories. A story may mean different things to different people or to the same person at different ages. The adults in the day care center where *Down the River Without a Paddle* was read knew that the caterpillar had become a butterfly because they understood the process of metamorphosis. The children said that the character was the same, but they knew that because the caterpillar and the butterfly had the same face in the illustrations.

An author may control some responses by using characters or words which generally evoke a particular reaction. Other responses, however, come from the individual. A child listening to *Dr. De Soto* may have heard enough strories about foxes to know immediately that the fox is dangerous to the dentist and to expect the fox to try some clever trick. Thus the author's use of character matches the reader's expectation. One child may respond to the story with sympathy for Dr. De Soto, who is portrayed as a conscientious dentist who cares about his patients. Another, perhaps having recently experienced pain in a dentist's office, may see Dr. De Soto as the antagonist and secretly hope for the fox to have dentist for dinner.

Choosing books of literary excellence is only half the formula. The other half is being aware of the child as reader or listener. It makes sense to begin choosing books using what we know of children's preferences, and of their developmental levels. Chapters four through eight begin with brief descriptions of developmental sequences in language, intellectual, personality, social and moral, and creative and aesthetic growth. The books suggested follow the general developmental levels of children and the goals for these areas. However, adults also must be aware of the reactions, special needs, and unique interpretations of the children they teach.

Helping Parents Select Books

As a day care professional or teacher, it is likely that you will find yourself being asked many questions by parents who value your expertise. One topic of concern for parents is the selection of books appropriate for their children. There are various ways that you individually, and the school or center where you work, can assist parents.

It is helpful to describe for parents the type of books that are generally appropriate for particular developmental levels, and to show them examples of such books. For infants and toddlers up to two years of age, toy and board books are often good choices. Board books are durable, and young hands can turn the pages. They allow the children, who are in a stage of exploring the world through the senses—they will taste as well as look at a book—to participate actively. The pictures should be clear and uncluttered, ones that can be identified by the child, and discussed by parent and child together. Helen Oxenbury's *Playing*,[41] for example, shows illustrations of a toy on the left page and a baby playing with that toy on the right. Pictured are blocks, a ball, a book, a teddy bear, a pot, and other very common toys. Children of this age also respond to the sounds of language, and this is the time to introduce Mother Goose rhymes and books with patterned language.

Children from two to five can follow simple plots, and are beginning to develop a sense of story. It is a good time to share books that have clear plots, such as *Happy Birthday Sam*[42] in which Sam is too short to open the front door, to brush his teeth at the bathroom sink, and to do various other tasks. On his birthday, his grandfather gives him a stool, and with it Sam can do all of the things mentioned earlier in the book. The story is clear, and it explores relationships that children of this age can understand. Children from two to five are in a period of rapid growth in language. They respond to rhythm and repetition in language. This is a time to present traditional literature which has refrains or a cumulative plot structure, stories such as *The Three Little Pigs* and *The Three Billy Goats Gruff*. Children can repeat the refrains, clap to the rhythm of the words, and participate as they hear the story read or told.

Children from five to eight are able to follow more complex stories that may have subplots. They are beginning to be able to distinguish between fantasy and reality, to generalize, to recognize different points of view, and to read for themselves. They notice details in both text and illustration. This is a time to present a wide variety of picture books, some that are fantasy, some that are realism. Traditional tales are still enjoyed, with ones such as *Snow White* and *Cinderella* being favorites. Beginning reading books such as *Daniel's Duck*[43] give the new reader a chance to feel successful and to use his or her new skills. However, parents should be encouraged to continue reading aloud to their children during this period, for many of the books enjoyed by primary grade children are still above their reading level. In addition, the sharing of literature provides a period of closeness between parent and child.

You, as a teacher or day care provider, will also be in a position to show the parents examples of what is being shared in the school or center. This can be done in a parent conference, where the parent is encouraged to browse through the room library, or by showing the parents books that have special appeal to their child. Children can be allowed to take books home to read with their parents, and some teachers send books home with suggestions of appropriate activities that parents might do with their children, or topics related to the book which they might discuss.

A school or center can provide ways for parents to see what literature is available, either through special workshops or through a book fair. If teachers or day care professionals are present at these functions, they can talk with the parents at this time about appropriate literature. They may also have some input in the selection of which books will be discussed at a workshop or offered for sale at a book fair.

Schools or centers can provide materials for parents which will aid them in selecting books. *The Horn Book Magazine* publishes a short quarterly newsletter for parents titled *Why Children's Books?* The magazine is sold by subscription and gives excellent suggestions for book selection, as well as brief articles about the importance of literature, all written in a conversational tone. (For subscription information, write to *The Horn Book Magazine*, 31 St. James Avenue, Boston, Mass., 02116.) Booklists may be made available for parents to borrow. Those that may prove helpful include *Children's Books of the Year*[44] published each year by the Child Study Children's Book Committee at Bank Street College, *Reading With Children Through Age Five*[45] by the same committee, or *What Books and Records Should I Get for My Preschooler?*[46], a micromonograph published by the International Reading Association. These are all short, easy-to-use lists. More extensive booklists are listed at the end of this chapter, though they are there more for your use than for use by parents.

Encourage parents to use their local libraries. They may find that story hours are presented on a regular basis. They can also find what their children enjoy, and provide a stimulus for reading if they take their children with them to the library and have the children select some books themselves. The parent also may select some books so that there is a variety of types of literature to be shared at home. Young children can learn to browse at bookstores, seeing what appeals to them and handling books carefully. One mother boasts that her four year old can occupy himself with books in a bookstore for thirty to forty minutes. Of course, this is a mother who likes to read herself, who is hooked on bookstores, and who has shared both her love of literature and her interest in seeing new books with the child. When the child becomes restless, they leave the store, so that it remains a pleasant experience for them both.

Let parents know the importance of children's owning books themselves. They might want to see which books are popular with their children, then buy these. They might also begin by purchasing books that are classics, such as Mother Goose and various fairy tales. Certainly a good collection of children's poetry is a necessity, one such as *The Random House Book of Poetry for Children.*[47] They can designate a special place for the books, so that the child knows that these are his or her books, a private library. Paperbacks as well as hard cover books may be purchased. Parents might also look into magazine subscriptions or book clubs, so that new reading material would be arriving on a regular basis. Some parents buy cassettes so that their children can hear favorite stories read again and again. For families who have tape decks in their cars, listening to stories provides a valuable diversion during family automobile trips.

Finally, talk with parents about techniques of reading aloud to children. Because they are reading to only one or two children at a time, they have the opportunity to listen to the children's responses during the story, and to have the children point to objects and words and take part in the reading. They should set the stage for reading by finding a quiet place, helping the child get comfortable, and holding the book so that the child can see the illustrations. They should begin the reading by letting the child look at the cover of the book and make

Let parents know what books their children enjoy at the school or center.

comments about the story within, and during the reading they should encourage the child to respond. The child should have some control over the reading, perhaps turning the pages so that it is the listener who determines when he or she is ready to continue. The child should also have the opportunity to select which books he or she would like to hear. If the child becomes restless, the parent should end the session. Children should be encouraged to talk about what they have heard and to participate as fully as possible in the sharing of books and poetry.

Parents who share literature with their children are providing a base of understanding about the reading process, about human relations, and about the enjoyment that books can bring. You should give them all the help and encouragement you can.

Summary

This book is designed to show the many ways in which literature can and does support the goals of early childhood education. At the center of any literature program for children is the literature itself and its contribution to the development of children's imaginations. Beyond this, reading regularly to children and engaging them in active response to literature supports their language, intellectual, personality, social, moral, aesthetic, and creative development.

To plan a literature program, you need to know what literature is available for children and how to assess its literary merit. Books for children vary in format and in genre. Format refers both to the physical features of a book such as its paper, binding, and typography, and to the ratio and relationship of text and illustrations. Genre refers to the type of literature, whether prose or poetry, fiction or nonfiction, realism or fantasy.

Fiction can be evaluated by assessing the effectiveness of the literary elements of plot, setting, characterization, theme, and style of writing, as well as how the five are integrated to provide a unified whole. Nonfiction can be judged for factual accuracy and clear differentiation between fact and opinion. Poetry for children can be evaluated on its freshness and compactness of language, its use of rhythm and rhyme, and its emotional content. Illustrations can be judged for appropriateness of style and media to the mood and content of the text, and for their extension of the text.

Teachers and day care professionals may want to use research results about children's preferences in literature as a guide to the initial selection of literature to present, but need to keep in mind that any one book or poem is a combination of many elements, and that preferences will vary from individual to individual. In addition, each individual helps to create the meaning of a work through his or her own background which influences that person's interpretation of what the author has written. From the wide range of literature available, teachers and day care providers will select for sharing only that which is of high literary merit.

You will be in a position to provide valuable assistance to parents in selecting books for their children. Information about which books are being used in the school or center, publications for parents, booklists, and techniques for sharing literature with children will help parents give their children a rich literary background.

Extending Your Learning

1. Compare a hardcover and a paperback edition of the same book.
2. Go to both a bookstore and a drugstore or grocery store. Assess the range and quality of books for preschoolers in each of the settings.
3. Make a toy book for children that uses either the sense of touch or the sense of smell.
4. Rank order five wordless picture books by level of difficulty. Tell why each one is placed as it is in your list.
5. Tell how you might use a specific alphabet, counting, or other concept book with a young child.
6. Read collections of poetry by at least three of the poets mentioned in the preceeding chapter. Select two poems by each of the poets that you would enjoy sharing with children.
7. Compare two reviews of the same book. Reviews of children's books appear in such journals as *Language Arts, The Horn Book, The Bulletin of the Center for Children's Books, School Library Journal,* and *The Booklist.*
8. Write your own review of a book. Then find a published review of it and compare the two. See if you and the other reviewer used the same criteria and saw the same qualities in the book.
9. Using the same criteria as were applied to *Dr. De Soto,* evaluate a picture book of your own choice.
10. Compare the illustrations in any two winners of the Caldecott Award. Look at the choice of media, the style of art, and the effectiveness of the illustrations in helping to tell the story.

11. Look at the book that won the Caldecott Award and the Honor Books for a single year. See if you agree with the committee's choice of a winner.
12. Suggest books and activities for three different age levels that a parent and child might do together at home.
13. Develop a booklist for parents.

Notes

1. Robert and Claire Wiest, *Down the River Without a Paddle* (Chicago: Children's Press, 1973).
2. Donald Hall, *Ox-Cart Man*. Illus. by Barbara Cooney (New York: Viking Press, 1979).
3. Eric Carle, *The Grouchy Ladybug* (New York: Thomas Y. Crowell Publishers, 1977).
4. Pat and Eve Witts, *The Touch Me Book*. Illus. by Harlow Rockwell (Racine, Wis.: Western Publishing Co. Inc., n.d.).
5. Eric Hill, *Where's Spot?* (New York: G.P. Putnam's Sons, 1980);
Spot's First Walk (New York: G.P. Putnam's Sons, 1981);
Spot's Birthday Party (New York: G.P. Putnam's Sons, 1982);
Spot's First Christmas (New York: G.P. Putnam's Sons, 1983); and
Spot Goes to School (New York: G.P. Putnam's Sons, 1984).
6. Martha Alexander, *The Magic Picture* (New York: Dial Books for Young Readers, 1984).
7. Dorothy Butler, *Babies Need Books* (New York: Atheneum Publishers, 1982).
8. Raymond Briggs, *The Snowman* (New York: Random House Inc., 1978).
9. Emily Arnold McCully, *Picnic* (New York: Harper & Row, Publishers, Inc., 1984).
10. Martha Alexander, *Bobo's Dream* (New York: Dial Press, 1970).
11. Cynthia Rylant, *When I Was Young in the Mountains*. Illus. by Diane Goode (New York: E.P. Dutton Inc., 1982).
12. Vera B. Williams, *Something Special For Me* (New York: Greenwillow Books, 1983).
13. Tana Hoban, *Round & Round & Round* (New York: Greenwillow Books, 1983).
14. Genevieve Gray, *How Far, Felipe?* Illus. by Ann Grifalconi (New York: Harper & Row, Publishers, Inc., 1978).
15. Arnold Lobel, *Frog and Toad Are Friends* (New York: Harper & Row, Publishers Inc., 1970).
16. Excerpt from *Frog and Toad Are Friends*, by Arnold Lobel. Copyright © 1970 by Arnold Lobel. pp. 4–5. By permission of Harper & Row, Publishers, Inc.
17. Julia Cunningham, *Macaroon*. Illus. by Evaline Ness (New York: Pantheon Books Inc., 1962).
18. William Steig, *Dr. De Soto* (New York: Farrar, Straus & Giroux Inc., 1982).
19. Ibid.
20. Ibid.
21. M. Jean Craig, *Little Monsters* (New York: Dial Press, 1977), 36.
22. Ibid, 6.
23. Excerpt from *Daniel Inouye* by Jane Goodsell. Courtesy of Thomas Y. Crowell Publishers.
24. From *Swimming Mammals* by Susan Harris. All rights reserved. Used by permission of Franklin Watts, Inc.
25. From *Swimming Mammals* by Susan Harris. All rights reserved. Used by permission of Franklin Watts, Inc.
26. Reprinted by permission of Macmillan Publishing Company from *Collected Poems* by Vachel Lindsay. Copyright 1920 by Macmillan Publishing Company, renewed 1948 by Ellizabeth C. Lindsay.
27. "O Sliver of Liver," From *O Sliver of Liver and Other Poems* by Myra Cohn Livingston (A Margaret K. McElderry Book). Copyright 1979 by Myra Cohn Livingston. Used by permission of Atheneum Publishers.
28. Joan E. Cass, *Literature and the Young Child* (London: Longmans, Green & Co., 1967), 52.

29. Charles Keeping, "Illustration in Children's Books," *Children's Literature in Education* 1 (March 1970): 42.

30. Pauline Watson, *Days With Daddy*. Illus. by Joanne Scribner (Englewood Cliffs, N.J.: Prentice-Hall Inc., 1977).

31. Thomas Locker, *Where the River Begins* (New York: Dial Books for Young Readers, 1984).

32. Walter Lorraine, "The Art of the Picture Book," *Wilson Library Bulletin* 49 (October 1977): 145–46.

33. David A. Adler, *Redwoods Are the Tallest Trees in the World*. Illus. by Kazue Mizumura (New York: Thomas Y. Crowell Publishers, 1978).

34. Alan C. Purves and Richard Beach, *Literature and the Reader: Research in Response to Literature, Reading Interests, and the Teaching of Literature* (Urbana, Illinois: National Council of Teachers of English, 1972): 93.

35. Ibid., 70.

36. Dan Cappa, "Sources of Appeal in Kindergarten Books," *Elementary English* 34 (April 1957): 259.

37. Gerald Smerdon, "Children's Preferences in Illustration," *Children's Literature in Education* (Spring 1976): 30.

38. John Stewig, "Children's Preference in Picture Book Illustration," *Educational Leadership* 30 (December 1972): 276–77.

39. Carol J. Fisher, "Poetry Is: Questing," talk given at National Council of English Preconference Workshop on Poetry (Kansas City, Mo., November 22, 1978).

40. Louise Rosenblatt, *The Reader the Text the Poem* (Carbondale: Southern Illinois University Press, 1978).

41. Helen Oxenburg, *Playing* (New York: Simon & Schuster Inc., 1981).

42. Pat Hutchins, *Happy Birthday Sam* (New York: Greenwillow Books, 1978).

43. Clyde Robert Bulla, *Daniel's Duck*. Illus. by Joan Sandin (New York: Harper & Row, Publishers, Inc., 1979).

44. Child Study Children's Book Committee, *Children's Books of the Year* (New York: Bank Street College, 1984).

45. Child Study Children's Book Committee, *Reading With Children Through Age Five* (New York: Bank Street College, 1980).

46. Norma Rogers, *What Books and Records Should I Get for My Preschooler?* (Newark, Del.: International Reading Association, 1972).

47. Jack Prelutsky, *The Random House Book of Poetry for Children*. Illus. by Arnold Lobel (New York: Random House Inc., 1983).

Recommended References

Bader, Barbara. *American Picturebooks from Noah's Ark to the Beast Within*. New York: Macmillan Publishing Company, 1976.

Barron, Pamela and Burley, Jennifer. *Jump Over the Moon*. New York: Holt, Rinehart & Winston, 1984

Cameron, Eleanor. *The Green and Burning Tree*. Boston: Little, Brown & Co. Inc., 1969.

Carr, Jo. *Beyond Fact: Nonfiction for Children and Young People*. Chicago: American Library Association, 1982.

Cullinan, Bernice E. *Literature and the Child*. New York: Harcourt Brace Jovanovich Inc., 1981.

Cullinan, Bernice E. *Literature for Children: Its Discipline and Content*. Dubuque, Iowa: Wm. C. Brown Group, 1971.

Gerhardt, Lillian, ed. *Issues in Children's Book Selection*. R. R. Bowker Co., 1973.

Glazer, Joan I., and Williams, Gurney. *Introduction to Children's Literature*. New York: McGraw-Hill Book Co., 1979.

Huck, Charlotte S. *Children's Literature in the Elementary School*. 3rd ed., update. New York: Holt, Rinehart & Winston, 1979.

Huus, Helen, ed. *Evaluating Books for Children and Young People*. Newark, Del.: International Reading Association, 1968.

Lukens, Rebecca J. *A Critical Handbook of Children's Literature.* 2nd ed. Glenview, Ill.: Scott, Foresman & Co., 1982.

Norton, Donna E. *Through the Eyes of a Child.* Columbus, Ohio: Charles E. Merrill Publishing Co., 1983.

Recommended Wordless Books

Anno, Mitsumasa. *Anno's USA.* New York: Philomel, 1983.

Ardizzone, Edward. *The Wrong Side of the Bed.* Garden City, N.Y.: Doubleday & Co. Inc., 1970.

Carle, Eric. *I See a Song.* New York: Thomas Y. Crowell Publishers, 1973.

DePaola, Thomas Anthony. *Sing, Pierrot, Sing.* New York: Harcourt Brace Jovanovich Inc., 1983.

Felix, Monique. *Another Story of . . . the Little Mouse Trapped in a Book.* New York: Methuen Inc., 1983.

Fuchs, Erich. *Journey to the Moon.* New York: Delacorte Press, 1964.

Goodall, John S. *Shrewbettina's Birthday.* New York: Harcourt Brace Jovanovich Inc., 1971.

Hogrogian, Nonny. *Apples.* New York: Macmillan Publishing Company, 1972.

Keats, Ezra Jack. *Clementina's Cactus.* New York: Viking Press, 1982.

Kent, Jack. *The Egg Book.* New York: Macmillan Publishing Company, 1975.

Krahn, Fernando. *Who's Seen the Scissors?* New York: E. P. Dutton, Inc., 1975.

Mayer, Mercer. *Ah-Choo.* New York: Dial Press, 1976.

———   *A Boy, A Dog, and A Frog.* New York: Dial Press, 1967.

Ormerod, Jan. *Moonlight.* New York: Kestrel, 1982.

Schweninger, Ann. *A Dance for Three.* New York: Dial Press, 1979.

Spier, Peter. *Rain.* New York: Doubleday & Co. Inc., 1982.

Turkle, Brinton. *Deep in the Forest.* New York: E. P. Dutton Inc., 1976.

Wezel, Peter. *The Good Bird.* New York: Harper & Row, Publishers, Inc., 1964.

Winter, Paula. *The Bear and the Fly.* New York: Crown Publishers Inc., 1976.

Young, Ed. *The Other Bone.* New York: Harper & Row, Publishers, Inc., 1984.

2

Presenting Literature

The voice of a young child entreating an adult to "read it again" is proof of the pleasure that can come from literature shared aloud. Much of what children enjoy hearing they are unable to read themselves. Picture story books, usually written on a third grade or higher readability level, are inaccessible to preschool and to many primary grade children without someone to present them. And poetry, even more than prose, needs to be read aloud by a skilled reader. Such a reader can emphasize the meaning and the rhythm of the words, having passed the stage of struggling simply to recognize and pronounce the words. A smooth presentation shows children the power that literature can have.

You may choose to read a story or tell it. If you tell it, you may want to let your voice alone carry the tale, or you may want to use a flannelboard or other visual aid. You may share literature through records, films, filmstrips, or videocassettes. In the course of the school year, you will have the opportunity to share literature in a variety of ways.

Whichever way you choose, however, you will need to prepare. One way of thinking about this preparation is to think of three steps, all beginning with *p: p*review the material, *p*lan the setting, and *p*ractice your *p*resentation.

Reading Aloud

Previewing the Material

As you begin looking through books or poems to choose one to share with children, you will want to consider several factors. One aspect, of course, is the quality of the material itself. Using the criteria presented in chapter one, you will want to assess literary merit, eliminating from consideration any books that are of poor quality.

You will want to have in mind your purpose for reading. Suppose you are working with a group of three and four year olds. It is the beginning of the year and you and the children are just beginning to get to know one another. You decide you will begin story time with them by telling some stories you think they will have heard at home. You want the children to feel comfortable with you, and this will help you establish rapport. You also want the experience to lead into a sharing of other similar stories that the children may not have heard. You decide to work with traditional literature.

The two stories that you will tell are "The Three Bears" and "The Three Little Pigs." Both are folk tales that use a pattern of three in the happenings and that have a repetition of phrases and events. Now you need to select two or three similar folk tales to share on succeeding days. You will want these to have clear action, an appealing repetition of language, and only a few characters. You may begin by looking in the card catalog at the library and talking with the librarian about possible choices. You might look in texts or reference books about children's literature. The textbook *Children's Literature in the Elementary School*[1] by Charlotte Huck has a section on traditional literature which groups tales by motif and by country of origin.

You might look in sources that list books for children. The *Subject Guide to Children's Books in Print,*[2] for instance, lists under subject headings all of the children's books currently in print. There are no annotations, so you would need to find the actual books to get further information about them. The titles may, in this case, jog your memory about appropriate stories.

Other useful references are the *Children's Catalog*[3] and the *Elementary School Library Collection,*[4] both generally available in the children's section of public libraries as well as in school libraries. You may want to purchase reference books that categorize and annotate books for children. *Adventuring With Books,*[5] edited by Mary Lou White, lists books under such headings as Wordless Books, Modern Fantasy, Holidays, Concepts, Social Studies, The Arts, Language, and Traditional Literature. Age ranges are listed for each book as well as evaluative statements. The Bank Street College Bookstore[6] publishes a pamphlet listing the books for sale at the store. Books are classified under headings such as Concept Books and Relationships and Feelings. It is a brief listing with one sentence descriptions of each book, but the list has been compiled by educators at the Bank Street College of Education, and the books are recommended by them. Most of the books are for young children, with some for the two- to four-year-old child as well as for the kindergarten to grade three range.

If you check a variety of listings, you will have many book titles from which to choose. Some teachers keep a card file of books that they have used successfully. They add to it as they learn of new titles and as they explore new areas with their classes. In this way, they have personal listings readily available. New teachers sometimes find it helpful to talk with other teachers and with librarians. They find that colleagues are often an abundant source of information.

Using these sources, you have selected titles and gathered the books to read and preview. You have decided to share *The Little Red Hen* and have found seven versions listed, four of which the library owns. You are also going to look at *Who's In Rabbit's House?,*[7] *The Three Billy Goats Gruff,*[8] and *Deep in the Forest.*[9] You read through the books, keeping in mind your purposes and assessing the literary and artistic quality of each selection. You choose *The Little Red Hen,*[10] illustrated by Paul Galdone, and *The Three Billy Goats Gruff,*[11] illustrated by Marcia Brown. Both are effective retellings of the tales, and both have uncluttered, expressive illustrations. You decide to wait until later in the year to read *Who's in Rabbit's House?* because although it does have a repetition of phrases and of action, it has far more characters and is more complex than the other tales. It will be better appreciated by the children when they have had a little more experience with literature and are able to attend to a story for a longer period of time.

Your last two selections are *The Little Red Hen/La Pequena Gallina Roja*[12] by Letty Williams and *Deep in the Forest* by Brinton Turkle. You plan to read the second version of *The Little Red Hen* for two reasons. First, because it is told in both English and Spanish, you can mention to the children that it is written in two languages and tell them the title in both. If you had Spanish speaking children in your group, you might have read the entire story in both languages—assuming you read Spanish—but since you do not, you will introduce but not emphasize this aspect. Second, you will show how one tale maintains its structure but varies in details with different retellings. The Galdone version has a cat, a dog, and a mouse who watch while the Little Red Hen plants the wheat and finally bakes a cake. The version by Williams has a cat, a dog, and a pig who watch while the Little Red Hen plants the corn and finally makes tortillas. In both, the Little Red Hen enjoys the fruits of her labor, and does eat what she has worked to produce.

Deep in the Forest is a wordless picture book in which a bear cub enters a cabin in the woods to find a table with three chairs and three bowls, in the standard small, medium, and large sizes of *Goldilocks and the Three Bears.* The story reverses the characters, for it is the young girl who returns to find a cub in her bed and her cabin in disarray. You choose this because you think the children will delight in grasping what has happened to the story, and because it will elicit discussion of the structure of the tale as the children point out the changes.

You have chosen carefully, keeping both your purposes and the children's needs and interests in mind. You have also noted that the books you are planning to share with the group are large enough for the children to see the illustrations clearly as you read. If they were not, you would need to share the books with only one or two children at a time, or perhaps use a filmstrip that would allow all of the children to see.

Of course, there are some instances when children may not need to see the illustrations as the story is being read. They may listen to familiar Mother Goose rhymes and only later look at the illustrations. In an illustrated book with few pictures, the teacher may decide to show the illustrations by walking around so that children get a closer view. With only a few pictures, this does not create much of an interruption in the story.

Having previewed and selected the literature, you are now ready to begin the next step in presenting literature.

Planning the Setting

The next step is to plan the physical setting, how you will share the literature, and how you will involve the children. Whether for a small group or the total class, plan the setting so that it will be as easy as possible for the children to pay attention. This means trying to find a quiet place to read. If there is going to be extraneous noise, move so that your voice and the noise are not coming from the same direction, competing with each other. Place yourself so that visual attention can be focused on you and on the book. Put the children's backs to any movement that may distracting. If there is a strong light source, such as a window, have the children's backs to it also. Light shining on you and on the book will make both easily seen; light shining behind you and the book may have children squinting at a silhouette.

If you know the children are likely to be restless, plan how you will help them calm down. Perhaps it will be by saying a few poems together; perhaps by having the children each tell one thing they heard on the playground; perhaps it will be by doing two or three finger plays. Let children know what your expectations are. If story time is to be quiet time for listening, praise such behavior. If you want children to hold their comments until the conclusion of a story, remind them of this when you begin.

A set time for story hour lets children know it is an important part of the day. It also gives them some control over the situation because they know what the pattern is. You may want to have a rule that says they may leave the story circle if they wish, but they are not to make noise or talk or in any way distract those who are listening. Or you may want to establish a pattern where all children stay for all of the story.

Think about the contingencies which may arise. A comment that you are certain to hear at least once is, "I've heard it before." You will want to be prepared to respond with a comment such as, "Don't tell how it ends," or "See if you notice anything in the story this time that you didn't when you heard it before." This acknowledges the child's remark, yet avoids a lengthy discussion about whether he or she wants to hear it again.

Plan how you will introduce the book. Some teachers give the title and author at the beginning, others do it at the end. At some time, however, children should be told the title, author, and illustrator. This helps to establish the idea that books are written by real people.

There are many ways to build interest in a book you are about to read. You might ask children to make some guesses about the story from the title or from the picture on the cover. Before sharing *The Little Red Hen,* you might ask the children to look at the cover and tell what they think the Little Red Hen likes to do. For *The Three Billy Goats Gruff,* children might answer the question, "What

differences do you see among the three goats shown here?" Introductory comments set the stage for the story and can be used to guide children's learning.
Having them listen for special things encourages careful listening. Having them
guess what will happen fosters logical thinking about cause and effect.

You will also need to plan any concluding activities. If you are going to discuss
the book, questions should be developed and written down. If there are to be
follow up activities, you will need to have materials and directions ready. If there
is to be no follow up, then you may simply say, "And that's the story of Dr.
De Soto," or "There are other books by this author. Would you like to hear
another story by him?" If you do ask the children a question about what they
would like to hear, be prepared to honor their response. If they say yes, then
plan to read what they want. If they say no, skip the book for now even though
you may know it is excellent literature.

Many teachers have a special place where they put the book they have just
finished reading. Children then know where to find it if they want to read it
themselves or look at the pictures. This practice also gives the teacher a chance
to judge the reaction of children to particular books. Some may sit unopened;
others may be in constant demand.

Practicing the Presentation

This third step in preparing a literature selection will take less and less time
as you become more experienced. Read the selection aloud. Being familiar with
the material will eliminate any stumbling over unusual words. It will give you
a chance to plan any special voice you may want to use for different characters.
If you are reading poetry, it will allow you to plan where the breaks should be
so that you keep the meaning intact.

It is often useful to get feedback on your skill in reading aloud. One way of
doing this is to tape-record yourself. As you listen to the tape, ask several questions. Am I enunciating clearly? That is, are my words distinct? Is the volume
pleasant, loud enough to be heard without straining, yet not uncomfortably
loud? Am I reading at a speed that allows the listener to comprehend easily?
Does the expression in my voice move the story along, make it more interesting?
If the answer to any of these is "no," then perhaps you will want to practice
the same story several times, concentrating on improving areas of weakness.

Another way of getting feedback is to ask a friend to observe you as you read
to a group of children. Ask the friend to answer the same questions you would
ask of yourself if listening to a tape. In addition, ask the friend to tell you if
you are looking up as you read, making eye contact with the children.

When you practice reading aloud, practice holding the book as you will with
children. Try to hold it so that they can see the illustrations as you read. Some
teachers accomplish this by holding the book to one side as they read. Others
look down over the top of the book, reading the print upside down, but allowing the children to see the illustrations. If there is lengthy text, it may be easier
to read the page, then show the illustrations. If you share pictures in this way,
remind yourself to move the book slowly so that children have a chance to focus
on the picture and see more than a blur of color flash before them.

Being familiar with the content of the book through having practiced reading
it aloud frees you to make more eye contact with the children, to share in their

enjoyment of the story. It allows you to see children's responses, to see what is amusing them, to see if any of them are getting tired of listening.

After each reading, perhaps formally but generally informally, evaluate your presentation. If all went well, be aware of what you did which contributed to the success. If there were problems, try to analyze why they occurred, and what might be done to avoid them in the future. For example, if the fire bell rang in the middle of the story, there is little you could have done to have prevented it. But if the story was interrupted by one child kicking another, perhaps if you had been looking up more often you would have seen the two poking at each other with increasing frequency. A look from you with a shake of your head or your moving one of the children as you showed illustrations in the book might have prevented the incident.

Although reading aloud is probably the most frequently used method of sharing literature with children, other ways are effective also. One of these is storytelling.

Storytelling

Previewing the Material

In selecting a story to tell, either with or without visuals, you will use many of the same criteria which you use in selecting a book to read aloud. You will want it to be good literature. You will want it to match the interest and understanding level of the audience. But there are other criteria as well. A basic one is that the story have a fairly compact plot, with much action. It should have a strong beginning and a satisfying conclusion. Folk tales, originally told orally rather than being read, are excellent for telling because they match these criteria. Other stories for children will meet them also.

If there is extensive descriptive language as an integral part of the story, then perhaps the story should be read. The same is true if exact dialogue is essential to the story. The storyteller tells the tale in his or her own words, so if specific language is more than a refrain that can be memorized, the teller might better choose another.

The story should be one that you like. If you spend the time learning it, you will want to tell it more than once. Therefore, you should enjoy telling it, and it should be one that you think will have appeal for many groups of children. You can build a repertoire of stories by learning three or four each year.

Briggs and Wagner[13] describe children ages three to six years as being in the "age of repetition." They enjoy stories that have repetitious plots, such as *The Three Little Pigs* and *Chicken Little*. Repeated lines keep the children oriented to the sequence of the story. They also enjoy taking part in the telling themselves, saying the refrain with the storyteller, or engaging in motions to accompany the story. You might want to learn stories such as "Here We Go on a Lion Hunt" or "Brave Little Indian"[14] if you are working with preschool children. Both have motions that children perform as the tale is being told.

Children ages six to nine are described by Briggs and Wagner as being in the "age of fancy."[15] From about seven to nine is the period of peak interest in fairy tales. These children are able to distinguish fantasy from reality. They

Whenever possible, hold the book so children can see the illustrations as you read.

can tolerate the violence because they know the story is make-believe. They expect the evil characters to be punished and the good rewarded, a pattern of justice which exists in most fairy tales. You may find that you know many fairy tales now, ones that you might be able to prepare for telling by just a quick review and a little practice.

The most popular visual aid used by classroom storytellers is the flannelboard. This is some type of board, masonite, plywood, or stiff cardboard, which is covered with cloth. Characters and bits of setting are placed on the board as the story is told. To select stories for flannelboard telling, keep in mind the space on the board and how much you can manipulate at one time. There will not be room for a cast of thousands. And if only eight different characters make entrances and exits in the story, but do so in groups of two or three and not in a regular pattern, all your attention will have to be given to finding the right characters at the right time.

Look for stories that have a fairly simple plot. Think about what can be used to give the idea of the story. Neither setting nor characters need be exact in detail. If you were to tell the story of *Sam Who Never Forgets*[16] on the flannelboard, you would need one figure to be Sam, the zookeeper. You could then make each of the animals Sam feeds, and the food he brings them. If you were working with children on color recognition, then you might want to emphasize the colors of the food, as is done in the book. Sam brings green leaves to the giraffe, yellow bananas to the monkeys. The story lends itself to a flannelboard telling because the sequence is clear and the actions take place at a steady pace. Sam feeds the animals one by one. The elephant thinks it has been forgotten; all the other animals sympathize. But Sam, who never forgets, has just gone for a whole wagon full of hay because he knows how hungry the elephant is. At the end, Sam and the elephant can be moved together to show the hug they give one another.

Planning the Setting

In storytelling, as in reading aloud, it is essential that the children be able to see the presenter. One of the rewards of storytelling is that you can maintain constant eye contact with the children. You can adapt the story to their reactions. You can show that you too find the tale amusing, or sad, or quietly beautiful.

Some teachers use a puppet to introduce stories that they are going to tell. It may be a hand puppet that comes to the session with the teacher, hidden in a pocket or a bag. The teacher wakes the puppet, and the two may have a brief conversation about the story, or the puppet may talk directly to the children. It is a way of setting the stage for storytelling.

The puppet is put away during the telling and perhaps recalled at the conclusion. Some stories may be told twice, allowing the children to become familiar with the sequence and to master any refrains so that they can say them with the teacher. The same is true as children learn motions to accompany the telling or if they sing during the telling as a part of the story.

If you are going to use a flannelboard, decide whether you want it to be flat on a table or propped up on an easel or chair. Think about where it will be in relation to the eye level of the children. Will they be able to see it comfortably? Plan also where you will stand or sit. It will need to be a place where you can reach the board, reach the characters, and see the children.

At the conclusion of the story, you may want to encourage the children to retell it placing the characters on the board themselves. At other times, you may want to manipulate the characters yourself and have the children tell what is happening. If the children are taking turns, let them know when the session is about to be ended. Comments such as "Let's hear from two more people before we stop," or "Ted, we'll let you be the last one to tell our story for today," give children a sense of conclusion rather than interruption.

Practicing the Presentation

Preparing to tell a story usually takes more time than preparing to read a story. Teachers may wonder where they will get the time to do this preparation. One educator, Patrick Groff, believes that the problem could be alleviated partially if we recognized that the purposes for telling stories are different for a teacher than they are for an artist. He writes that "instead of referring to what master storytellers do as a model for how teachers telling stories should behave, we need to set different goals for each."[17] He suggests that teachers not spend time on "exceptional efforts at concentration, memorization, overlearning of stories, and speech work."[18]

It is profitable to see how storytellers go about learning a story, then adapt it to individual situations. Few storytellers memorize a story word for word. Most make note of the basic sequences of action, what happens when. They may memorize the opening sentence and the concluding sentence, and any refrains which are part of the story, but the rest they tell in their own words. Some list the action on a sheet of paper, others use note cards. They use these to set the action in their minds and to refresh their memories if they have not told that particular story for a while. They do not use them during the storytelling itself.

Some teachers use a puppet to introduce stories they are going to read or tell.

Suppose you have selected to tell *The Old Woman Who Lived in a Vinegar Bottle.*[19] Your note cards might look something like this: *Opening*— "Once upon a time there was an old woman who lived in a vinegar bottle." The vinegar bottle was a round, stone house that looked like the stone bottles vinegar was made in. The old woman is content. Though poor, she keeps the house spotless. She lives with Malt, a cat who is twice as fat as she is. Looking at her belongings she says, "Little more *would* be good. But taking it all in all, it's enough for the likes of me."

Units of Action

1. Saturday morning, as she is sweeping the walk, she finds a silver sixpence.
2. She uses it to buy a fish from fishermen who are just unloading their nets. It is a tiny fish. She watches it gasp, then tosses it into the lake.
3. She has turned to leave when the fish reappears and calls to her. It tells her if she ever wants anything she need only to call, "Little fish. Little fish," and it will come and grant her wish. She does not want anything.

4. When she gets home, the old woman begins thinking. She returns to the lake and asks the fish for a good hot dinner for herself and for Malt. When she gets home, there is a beautiful table laden with food.
5. There is a storm during the night. The next morning the woman returns to the lake and asks the fish for a cottage.
6. After getting the cottage, she returns to the fish for new furniture.
7. She sees herself in a mirror in her old clothes. She goes to the fish and requests new clothes. At this point she seems so different that Malt will not rub against her skirts.
8. She cannot clean her cottage in such nice clothing. Returns to the fish, requests a maid.
9. The maid makes her nervous so she decides to walk into the village for the afternoon church service. Her new shoes hurt, so she returns to the fish and requests a "conveyance."
10. The conveyance the fish gives is a cart and pony. She goes back and tells the fish she meant a car.
11. The car is small and red. She cannot drive it. She goes to the fish and demands a large car with a chauffeur.
12. The fish now tells her she has become greedy and ungrateful and sends her back to her vinegar bottle.
13. That evening, she tells the fish that she is sorry and ashamed. The fish offers to return everything. She says no, except for a good hot meal now and then.

Conclusion.   She still lives in the vinegar bottle, but she knows it was not a dream because every Sunday at noon a hot meal appears for her and Malt. "Malt is now three times as fat as the old woman."

You might have some additional reminders to help with the story. For this one, you would note that each time she called the fish, the old woman said, "Little fish. Little fish." You would also note that she began as a very humble woman, but with each request became less humble and more demanding, so that by the time the fish refused her wish, she was quite haughty. Also, each gift leads to the need for another gift.

You would probably want to read the story through several times after you had made the note cards. This helps with details which may be added to the skeleton of the story. Then practice saying it aloud. You will be able to identify any rough spots in the telling. Some teachers practice telling stories as they drive or as they do chores around the house. Once you have mastered the story, you can recall it going over your note cards quickly and perhaps saying it once or twice to yourself.

Using a flannelboard to tell the story shortens one part of the practice and lengthens another. Learning the story will probably take less time, for by stacking up the figures in the order they appear in the story you are giving yourself clues to the sequence of the story. If you were telling *The Old Woman Who Lived in a Vinegar Bottle* with a flannelboard, you would see the progression of wishes in each figure which showed them granted. With *Sam Who Never Forgets,* you would see which animal is to be fed by Sam. Some teachers keep the figures face up in a pile; others put them face down so the numbers which mark the sequence will show on the back. A brief synopsis of the story can be kept in the folder with figures. This provides a quick review before each telling.

The preparation would be lengthened by the making of the figures themselves. They can be cut from felt or made from paper with sandpaper or felt pieces glued to the back so that they will adhere to the board. Velcro is also used for sticking figures to the board. The flannelboard itself is covered with cloth, generally a dark solid color which provides a background for many stories. Ramon Ross describes using indoor-outdoor carpeting for this purpose.[20] You can experiment with different backings and different ways of making characters to find the ones that suit you best.

It is necessary to practice using the figures as you tell the story. Set the board up exactly as you plan to use it with children. Find out ahead of time if the angle of the board is such that the characters fall to the floor every minute and a half. Adjust the board or add more backing to the figures so that the story can proceed smoothly when you tell it to the children.

When you have completed the story, take a minute to evaluate your presentation. After you have told three or four stories to a group of children, you might ask them to tell which stories they liked best and why. This will guide them in comparing stories, in seeing how tales are alike and different. It may also give you some insight into your own presentations. If they tell you that they liked *The Three Billy Goats Gruff* because the troll's voice was scary, you know you were effective in expression and voice quality. If they cannot remember any of the events in *The Old Woman Who Lived in a Vinegar Bottle*, then there was a problem either with your presentation or with the selection of the tale for those children. Perhaps there were distractions during the telling of the story. The children may be able to tell about the fight on the playground outside the window instead of the story. Perhaps the story was too complicated or too long for that group. They simply lost interest or were unable to follow what was happening from the beginning. Analyzing each presentation will help you improve future ones.

Using Audiovisual Materials

Previewing the Material

The first step in selecting audiovisual materials is finding out what is available. One source is a list of films, filmstrips, and recordings based on children's books published by the American Library Association. It is titled *A Multimedia Approach to Children's Literature*[21] and is edited by Mary Alice Hunt. There are 568 books, 153 films, 365 filmstrips, and 348 recordings listed and annotated. The materials are rated from acceptable to excellent in literary quality, and all were tested with children. Indices to titles, authors, and subjects make the book particularly useful.

Reviews of new media can be found in a variety of professional journals. Some, such as *Previews,* are devoted entirely to media. Others, such as *Early Years, Learning, Instructor, Language Arts,* and *School Library Journal,* devote a section, or a special issue to media. You might also want to send for catalogs from studios, such as Weston Woods, that produce media based on children's literature.

All of these will let you know what is being produced, and what you might ask the school to order. You will also want to know what is available immediately. Find out what media and equipment the school owns and what can be borrowed from the central administration or other central sources. See if public libraries in your area have films and records for loan or if there is a media cooperative from which you may borrow materials. Check with your state department of education for any media. See also if these sources have any funds for renting media.

Once you know what your choices are, you can begin to select in keeping with the purpose for its use. Perhaps you want to share a book with the total class, but it is so small that they could not see the illustrations. A filmstrip will overcome this problem. If you have been introducing the work of several poets, you may want your class to listen to recordings of these poets reading some of their own poetry. It may be that you want a cassette which the children can play themselves, one that you can leave in the listening center. Children can then elect to hear their favorite stories or poems again and again. If you want to encourage children to follow along in a book while listening to the text being read, then you will probably want a recording that has a sound to mark

The appeal of literature often shows in the faces of young readers.

the turning of each page. This will help beginning readers keep the place. Being clear in your own mind about the purpose for using the media will help you select the most appropriate type.

Preview the material before you share it with the children. Assess the quality of the audiovisual material just as you do print materials. Generally speaking, media cannot rescue a book which was of poor quality originally. If you know that the book version is of literary merit, you will still need to evaluate the media version. The medium should be appropriate to the story. A recording may fit very well for a story which has many descriptive passages, for children can visualize the picture in their minds as they listen to the words. On the other hand, a recording may prove confusing to children if several speakers utter dialogue from a book and the voices are difficult to distinguish.

Check the technical quality of the production. Voices should be clear and easily understood. In live action films, lips and voices should be synchronized. Prints and pictures should be distinct, in focus. Sound effects and music should help establish the mood of the story, not overpower the story.

Check also for authenticity. If there is a dialect, it should be spoken accurately. If the story has a specific setting, it should be realistically portrayed. Note whether a film or filmstrip based on a children's book has the original artwork. If it does not, you will need to judge the quality of the art as well as the technical quality of the filming.

Think about the length of the presentation in relation to the attention span of the children who will be experiencing it. Weston Woods Studios has made a motion picture of *The Snowman*,[22] the wordless picture book by Raymond Briggs. It is exquisitely produced, with smooth animation and a beautiful orchestral score. The story is easier to follow in this format than in the original because only one scene appears on the screen at a time, rather than the progression of small scenes which appear on a single page in the book. A few scenes have been omitted, and several sequences added. It is a superb film, yet it runs for twenty-six minutes, a long time for preschool or primary children, particularly since the film is rather slow paced. To retain the attention of young children, you may want to show the movie in two segments. During your preview session, you can decide where to make the break.

Adapting a story to a new medium does not necessarily change the level of difficulty of comprehension. If five year olds are baffled by the ambiguity and interplay of fantasy and reality in Chris Van Allsburg's haunting *The Wreck of the Zephyr*,[23] it is likely that they will have the same difficulty whether they encounter the story as a picture book, a film, or a record. If the content or presentation is too sophisticated for your group, make another selection, even though the work itself, and its translation into audiovisual format, may be outstanding.

Planning the Setting

When you order nonprint materials, note the type of equipment which will be needed for sharing it. If possible, set up the equipment either before the children arrive or while they are engaged in other activities. They can become restless as they wait for a projector to be threaded, especially if the machine decides to balk. It is also more difficult to set up equipment if you must simultaneously attend to twenty-five children.

Many picture books, such as The Snowman, are available in motion picture or filmstrip format. (From The Snowman by Raymond Briggs, Copyright © 1978 by Raymond Briggs. Reprinted by permission of Random House, Inc.)

Let the children get settled before beginning a film or filmstrip. They can be asked to be sure they can see the screen before the lights are turned out. You may want to tell them a little about what they are going to see to set the mood, or ask them to watch for specific happenings.

Think about the children's reactions to the presentation. The Children's Film Theatre tested films with children ages three to twelve. In their second report, a book listing recommended films titled *More Films Kids Like,* they sometimes list suggestions for preparing children. For the film *Hansel and Gretel, An Appalachian Version,* they write:

> Some adults were reluctant to use it; they thought it would frighten kids. But it was one of our most successful films—most groups ask for it again and again (perhaps in part to tame it). It does require discussion, particularly with young and middle groups, and before we showed it to these children we told them it was a scary film and suggested they sit near someone they like or hold hands if they got scared.[24]

This sort of preparation could make the difference between children's enjoyment of a film and their dislike of a film they found frightening.

Practicing the Presentation

Obviously showing a film or listening to a recording does not require the same sort of practice that reading or telling a story does. Your previewing of the material should give you the practice needed. It should demonstrate whether you know how to use the equipment. It should also show if there is anything special you need to know. For example, some filmstrips are advanced manually. The teacher uses a booklet which shows the text of the recording which accompanies the filmstrip. One first grade teacher found herself at a loss when she began showing the Weston Woods filmstrip of *Rosie's Walk.*[25] There is little text to this tale of Rosie the hen who walks around the barnyard stalked by the fox. Oblivious to the danger, Rosie gets back home safely, while the fox meets disaster after disaster. The record which goes with the filmstrip has Rosie walking to the strains of "Turkey in the Straw." The booklet, which would normally show the text as an indication of when to advance the filmstrip, showed instead the musical notation for the background music. For this teacher, who did not read music, the showing of the filmstrip was as disastrous as the fox's walk. Previewing the filmstrip would have prevented the problem. She could have decided not to show that filmstrip, or could have gotten help in working out when to turn the filmstrip forward.

Teachers have a wide selection of literature they may share with children, and ways in which to share it. Guided by their purposes, their knowledge of children, and their evaluation of the literature itself, they can bring children and books together in a way which will make the relationship a lasting one.

Helping Aides Share Literature

It is likely that you will have either professional or volunteer aides at least part of the time to assist you in your classroom or center work. Some day care centers have a regular schedule of "grandparents" who come once a week to work with the children. Some actually are the grandparents of children in the program, but many others are older community residents who enjoy being with children and want to contribute their time and skills to a meaningful activity.

Having these people share literature with children is an excellent use of their time. They can read to one or two youngsters, letting them select their favorite stories. It is important that children hear some stories over and over, for this helps them gain the concept that print holds a story constant, and that whoever reads the story will use the same words. The words are in the book, not in the adult's head. However, the story that one child wants to hear again may not be the favorite of others. Thus individual and small group sharing of literature is vital.

In addition, when reading to only one or two children, the adult can allow the child to point to objects and to discuss the book in the midst of the reading. This practice can become distracting when done with a large group, for as one child discusses, others may become confused about the story line or lose interest in hearing the book. The adult can focus on left to right progression of words, point to certain words and tell what they say, have the child find words that he or she can recognize, and in general engage in practices that set the stage for the child to learn to read. Those children who can read already might read every other page themselves, or perhaps even read the whole story with the adult as the listener.

When the adult is reading to just one child, he or she can talk with the child about the child's reactions to the story, or let the child retell the story, either from memory or by looking at the illustrations. It is an ideal time for communication and for maximum involvement of the child.

You may need to be very direct in suggesting to the aide those behaviors that contribute to effective oral reading. In a study that compared the oral reading skills of teachers with those of aides, Lamme[26] found that the aides were not as effective as the teachers in oral reading, and that there was no relationship between the way the teacher read and the way the aide read. Even aides who indicated that they read regularly to their own children at home were not necessarily skilled readers. Be certain that aides know what is expected of them. They should practice so that they read with expression, using appropriate volume and speed. They should show the illustrations and involve children with the reading. They should maintain eye contact as much as possible.

If you have an aide who is skilled as a storyteller, by all means make use of him or her in this capacity. Find out if your aide speaks and reads in the language or languages spoken by your bilingual students. This opens up more possibilities for the sharing of literature, as many public libraries have sections of children's books in other languages. Train your aides in the skills they need to have to work effectively, and build on the unique skills they bring to the center or classroom.

Summary

To present literature well, whether by reading, telling, or using audiovisual materials, it is necessary to prepare carefully. One way of thinking about this preparation is to think of three steps, all beginning with *P: p*review the material, *p*lan the setting, and *p*ractice your presentation.

Sharing books individually provides an ideal time for communication and for maximum involvement of the child.

During the previewing process, you find the literature you may share, using selection guides when necessary. You apply the standards of good literature to any story or poem under consideration, with added criteria applied to stories for telling or in audiovisual format. The selection is done with a specific group of children in mind.

The next step is to plan the physical setting, how you will share the literature, and how you will involve the children. Plan so that distractions are at a minimum. A regular time and procedure for the sharing of literature help establish a pattern, and demonstrate that you consider literature an important activity. Know how you are going to introduce the literature, perhaps having children describe what they think the story may be as they look at the book cover and hear the title, or setting the stage for a story you will tell by working with a hand puppet. Know also what concluding statements, questions, or activities will follow the actual sharing of the literature.

Finally, practice your presentation. Read aloud the stories and poems you plan to share; make cards to help you recall the sequence of action in a story you plan to tell; stack the figures for a flannelboard story in the order in which you will use them; preview audiovisual materials both for the content and to make certain you know how to use the equipment.

If you have aides to assist you, have them read to one of two children at a time. Teach them to read skillfully. Careful preparation by you and your aides will help bring children and books together not only for the fifteen minutes it takes to read a story but for the rest of their lives.

Extending Your Learning

1. Ask a friend or classmate to listen as you read a picture book orally, and to evaluate your reading based on appropriate speed and volume, enunciation, expression, and eye contact.
2. Make a tape recording of your own reading of a book for children and evaluate your oral reading skill.
3. Plan how you would introduce three different picture books to a group of children.
4. Read five folktales that are in picture book format. For each, assess whether it would be a good one for telling as well as reading.
5. Make flannelboard characters and use them to tell a story. You may want to use the list of books recommended for flannelboard stories at the end of this chapter to help you find an appropriate book.
6. Read a folktale and divide it into units of action for telling.
7. Preview a film or filmstrip based on a children's book. Assess the quality of the production and describe a potential audience for the material.
8. Compare a children's book with an audiovisual adaptation of it.

Notes

1. Charlotte S. Huck, *Children's Literature in the Elementary School* (New York: Holt, Rinehart & Winston, 1979 update).
2. *Subject Guide to Children's Books in Print* (New York: R. R. Bowker Co., 1984).
3. *Children's Catalog*, 14th ed. (New York: H. W. Wilson Co., 1984).
4. Mary Virginia Gaver, et. al. *Elementary School Library Collection*, 8th ed. (New Brunswick, N.J.: The Bro-Dart Foundation, 1979.)
5. Mary Lou White, ed., *Adventuring With Books* (Urbana, Ill.: National Council of Teachers of English, 1981).
6. Bank Street College Bookstore, 610 West 112th Street, New York, New York 10025.
7. Verna Aardema, *Who's in Rabbit's House?* Illus. by Leo and Diane Dillon (New York: Dial Press, 1977).
8. P. C. Asbjornsen and J. E. Moe, *The Three Billy Goats Gruff*. Illus. by Marcia Brown (New York: Harcourt Brace Jovanovich Inc., 1957).
9. Brinton Turkle, *Deep in the Forest* (New York: E. P. Dutton, Inc. 1976).
10. Paul Galdone, *The Little Red Hen* (New York: Seabury Press, 1973).
11. Asbjornsen, *Three Billy Goats Gruff*.
12. Letty Williams, *The Little Red Hen/La Pequena Gallina Roja*. Illus. by Herb Williams (Englewood Cliffs, N.J.: Prentice-Hall, 1969).
13. Nancy E. Briggs and Joseph A. Wagner, *Children's Literature Through Storytelling & Drama*, 2nd ed. (Dubuque, Iowa: Wm. C. Brown Group, 1979), 36.
14. Joseph Wagner, *Children's Literature Through Storytelling* (Dubuque, Iowa: Wm. C. Brown Group, 1970), 74–75.
15. Briggs and Wagner, *Storytelling & Drama*, 37–38.
16. Eve Rice, *Sam Who Never Forgets* (New York: Greenwillow Books, 1977).
17. Patrick Groff, "Let's Update Storytelling," in *Language Arts* 54 (March 1977), 274.
18. Groff, "Let's Update Storytelling," 274.
19. Rumer Godden, *The Old Woman Who Lived in a Vinegar Bottle*. Illus. by Mairi Hedderwick (New York: Viking Penguin, 1970). Copyright © 1970 by Rumer Productions Limited. Illustrations copyright © 1972 by Macmillan London Ltd.
20. Ramon R. Ross, *Storyteller* (Columbus, Ohio: Charles E. Merrill Publishing Co., 1972), 100.

21. Mary Alice Hunt, *A Multimedia Approach to Children's Literature* (Chicago: American Library Association, 1983).

22. *The Snowman* by Raymond Briggs. Weston Woods motion picture, MP 288.

23. Chris Van Allsburg, *The Wreck of the Zephyr* Boston: Houghton Mifflin Co., 1983.

24. Maureen Gaffney, *More Films Kids Like* (Chicago: American Library Association, 1977), 56.

25. *Rosie's Walk* by Pat Hutchins. Weston Woods filmstrip, FS 125.

26. Linda Leonard Lamme, "Reading Aloud to Children: A Comparative Study of Teachers and Aides." Unpublished research report. University of Florida, 1977.

Recommended References

Baker, Augusta, and Greene, Ellin. *Storytelling: Art and Technique.* New York: R. R. Bowker Co., 1977.

Bamman, Henry A.; Dawson, Mildred A.; and Whitehead, Robert J. *Oral Interpretation of Children's Literature.* 2d ed. Dubuque, Iowa: Wm. C. Brown Group, 1971.

Bauer, Carolyn Feller. *Handbook for Storytellers.* Chicago: American Library Association, 1977.

Briggs, Nancy E., and Wagner, Joseph A. *Children's Literature Through Storytelling and Drama.* 2d ed. Dubuque, Iowa: Wm. C. Brown Group, 1979.

Chambers, Dewey W. *Storytelling and Creative Drama.* Dubuque, Iowa: Wm. C. Brown Group, 1970.

Coody, Betty. *Using Literature With Young Children.* 3rd ed. Dubuque, Iowa: Wm. C. Brown Group, 1983.

deWit, Dorothy. *Children's Faces Looking Up.* Chicago: American Library Association, 1979.

Gaffney, Maureen. *More Films Kids Like.* Chicago: American Library Association, 1977.

Gaffney, Maureen. *What to Do When the Lights Come On.* Phoenix, Ariz.: Oryx Press, 1981.

Hunt, Mary Alice. *A Multimedia Approach to Children's Literature.* 2d ed. Chicago: American Library Association, 1983.

Ross, Ramon R. *Storyteller.* Columbus, Ohio: Charles E. Merrill Publishing Co., 1972.

Sawyer, Ruth. *The Way of the Storyteller.* New York: Viking Press, 1942.

Recommended Titles for Storytelling

Brown, Marcia. *Stone Soup.* New York: Charles Scribner's Sons, 1947.

DePaola, Tomie. *The Legend of the Bluebonnet.* New York: G. P. Putnam's Sons, 1983.

Galdone, Paul. *The Gingerbread Boy.* New York: Seabury Press, 1975.

_____ *The Three Bears.* New York: Seabury Press, 1972.

Ginsburg, Mirra. *The Magic Stove.* New York: Coward-McCann, 1983.

Hogrogian, Nonny. *Carrot Cake.* New York: Greenwillow Books, 1977.

Jacobs, Joseph. *The Three Sillies.* Ed. & illus. by Paul Galdone. Boston: Houghton Mifflin Co., 1981.

Kent, Jack. *The Fat Cat.* New York: Parents Magazine Press, 1971.

Lipkind, William, and Mordinivoff, Nicolas. *Finders Keepers.* New York: Harcourt Brace Jovanovich, Inc. 1951.

Lobel, Arnold. *How the Rooster Saved the Day.* Illus. by Anita Lobel. New York: Greenwillow Books, 1977.

Lobel, Arnold. *Ming Lo Moves the Mountain.* New York: Greenwillow Books, 1982.

Mosel, Arlene. *Tikki Tikki Tembo.* Illus. by Blair Lent. New York: Holt, Rinehart & Winston, 1968.

Williams, Jay. *One Big Wish.* Illus. by John O'Brien. New York: Macmillan Publishing Company, 1980.

Wolkstein, Diane. *The Magic Wings; A Tale from China.* Illus. by Robert Andrew Parker. New York: E. P. Dutton Inc., 1983.

Zemach, Harve. *A Penny a Look: An Old Story.* Illus. by Margot Zemach. New York: Farrar, Straus & Giroux Inc., 1971.

Recommended Titles for Flannelboard Stories

Bailey, Carolyn Sherwin. *The Little Rabbit Who Wanted Red Wings.* Illus. by Dorothy Grider. New York: The Platt and Munk Co., 1945.

Domanska, Janina. *The Turnip.* New York: Macmillan Publishing Company, 1969.

Galdone, Paul. *What's in Fox's Sack?* Boston: Houghton Mifflin Co., 1982.

Ginsburg, Mirra. *Mushroom in the Rain.* Illus. by Jose Aruego and Ariane Dewey. New York: Macmillan Publishing Company, 1974.

Gross, Ruth. *The Girl Who Wouldn't Get Married.* Illus. by Jack Kent. New York: Four Winds Press, 1983.

Hogrogian, Nonny. *One Fine Day.* New York: Macmillan Publishing Company, 1971.

Krasilovsky, Phyllis. *The Man Who Didn't Wash His Dishes.* Illus. by Barbara Cooney. New York: Doubleday & Co. Inc., 1950.

Krauss, Ruth. *The Carrot Seed.* Illus. by Crockett Johnson. New York: Harper & Row, Publishers, Inc., 1945.

Lionni, Leo. *Little Blue and Little Yellow.* New York: Astor-Honor, 1959.

Miles, Miska, *Chicken Forgets.* Boston: Little, Brown & Co. Inc., 1976.

Preston, Edna. *One Dark Night.* New York: Viking Press, 1960.

Roberts, Bethany. *Waiting-for-Spring Stories.* Illus. by William Joyce. New York: Harper & Row, Publishers, Inc., 1984.

Tresselt, Alvin. *The Mitten.* Illus. by Yaroslava. New York: Lothrop, Lee & Shepard Books, 1964.

Wildsmith, Brian. *Python's Party.* New York: Franklin Watts, Inc., 1974.

Zemack, Margot. *It Could Always Be Worse.* New York: Farrar, Straus & Giroux Inc., 1976.

3

The Literature Curriculum

Developing the Imagination

The kindergarten teacher looked around her classroom after the children had gone home. She visualized the church four youngsters had constructed in the block corner; she smiled at her remembrance of the dramatic play in the housekeeping corner, and "mother" Darice's insistence that the "children" take a nap; she looked at the four paintings still drying on the easels and decided to display them on the wall above the bookshelves.

The teacher was actively engaged in using her imagination. She was forming mental images, some based on events that had happened, others on projections of ideas. The children, too, had been using their imaginations as they created pictures and buildings and as they took the roles of other people in dramatic play.

Imagination is central to the competent functioning of independent individuals and of free societies. The ability to construct mental images allows individuals to weigh evidence and explore the possible consequences of particular actions. It allows them to create, and to evaluate, new ideas. Northrop Frye writes that "The fundamental job of the imagination in ordinary life is to produce, out of the society we have to live in, a vision of the society we want to live in."[1] Without an educated imagination, one can only adjust to society as it is. With an educated imagination, one can evaluate and attempt to change society, and exercise what Frye sees as free speech, the capability of using language effectively and having thoughts of one's own to express with that language.

Literature contributes to the development of the imagination. Participating in the literary experience is itself an imaginative endeavor, for readers are projecting themselves into a story. Often they are seeing worlds which they could not, or would not choose to, experience themselves. The confrontation with lives both better and worse than their own and with experiences quite different from their own refines their sensibilities and broadens their perspectives.

Literature exposes for readers the basic wants and needs of other people, the problems they have, the values and attitudes which underlie their decision making. Readers are forced to look at their own values, and their own prejudices, more objectively. Frye writes that as readers experience literature, they gain a kind of detachment in viewing others and themselves. This detachment leads to an ability to accept the existence of differing beliefs and thus to the development of tolerance.[2]

Literature presents readers with a more structured picture of life than does real experience. Authors select for presentation those events which have the most relevance to characters' actions and those feelings which most epitomize the characters' personalities. They impose an order or mode of presentation designed to help the reader grasp the significance of the total happening. Literature thus aids readers in their ability to interpret experiences by narrowing the range of events discussed.

The development of the imagination through literature is particularly vital for children. Aiden Chambers writes in *Introducing Books to Children*:

> All these different ways in which literature functions have enormous value for children, as for adults. Children are forming attitudes, finding points of reference, building concepts, forming images to think with, all of which interact to form a basis for decision-making judgment, for understanding, for sympathy with the human condition. Literary experience feeds the imagination, that faculty by which we come to grips with the astonishing amount of data which assails our everyday lives, and find patterns of meaning in it.[3]

Glenna Davis Sloan, author of *The Child as Critic*, concurs.

> Young people require educated imaginations if they are to cope with the social pressures that confront them. A well-developed imagination is their protection against social mythology in all its forms: entertainment, advertising, propaganda, the language of cliche and stereotype, the abstractions of jargon and gobbledegook. In an irrational world the trained reason is important. But a developed imagination is fundamental to the survival of a sane society.[4]

The basic goal, then, of a literature curriculum is the education of children's imaginations. By listening to a broad spectrum of literature, children participate in the imaginative experiences of many authors and begin to see that all literature is part of a body of interrelated works. Day care professionals and teachers of young children contribute to this basic goal by involving children with literature in ways that establish positive attitudes toward it and by grouping books and structuring presentations so that children begin to perceive the interrelatedness of literature.

Promoting Positive Attitudes

Because literature is more *experienced* than *taught,* if children are to become deeply involved with it, they must choose to do so. This will happen if literature is a satisfying experience for them. You can help children become involved and develop positive attitudes toward literature through regular reading and careful selection of stories and poetry, and through activities which extend books in a pleasurable manner.

Regular Sharing of Literature

Obviously for pre-readers to experience literature, it must be read to them or presented through dramatic or audiovisual means. Even after children have begun to read themselves, however, literature should be shared orally by the teacher on a daily basis. Many books and poems that are appropriate for young children are still too difficult for them to read themselves. Most are more enjoyable when presented by a skilled reader than when deciphered on a word by word basis. The teacher has the opportunity to show children how effectively language can be used and what enjoyment it can bring.

Literature Selection

As suggested in chapter two, you will need to know the children and their backgrounds as you select books to read to them. Most young children like humor, with slapstick being very popular and with the verbal humor of puns and riddles becoming more and more appreciated. Young children respond to exaggeration in words and in illustrations and enjoy being in on pranks and jokes being played on fictional characters. Humorous books should be a basic part of your literature curriculum. So, too, should books whose content has appeal to many young children: books about everyday events, about animals, about the world of "once upon a time."

In a study of the poetry preferences of first, second, and third graders, Fisher and Natarella[5] found that the children liked the poetry presented to them, with 76 percent of the responses to each poem being positive, either "all right" or "great" as a rating. There were strong patterns of preference, but the researchers noted that every poem read had some students who gave it a star as outstanding and some who did not like it at all. For teachers, this means that a wide selection of poetry is recommended. However, knowing the types of poetry that were most popular will allow you to make certain that you include poems with a high probability of being well received. The children liked narrative poetry best, with free verse, lyric poetry, and haiku the least popular forms; they liked rhymed, metered poetry and disliked poetry which was heavily dependent on metaphorical language, even though care was taken to use poems with metaphors children were expected to understand; they liked poems about familiar experiences involving children and animals and rated humorous poetry as their favorite kind. There was evidence that the children tended to like poems they had heard before. Fisher and Natarella conclude their report with the following statement:

> Since the focus for selecting poems is two-fold, extending children's taste and maintaining a positive attitude toward poetry, teachers and publishers should be clear about their purpose for each choice. We do not want to turn off children by too many poems that are not apt to be popular, and yet we should expand the range of well-liked poetry.[6]

Keeping in mind the general preferences of young children, you will also need to assess the difficulty of the poem or book you are considering. Children, and adults too, often dislike what they do not understand. If the literature is beyond the children's comprehension, you are likely to be wasting both your time and theirs by reading it. The following is an excellent poem that builds on a knowledge of *The Three Little Pigs*, and that might make it seem a reasonable choice for young children. However, it uses the characters and the situation to express in subtle fashion an emotion known by adolescents and adults rather than by preschool or primary children.

The Builders

I told them a thousand times if I told them once:
Stop fooling around, I said, with straw and sticks;
They won't hold up, you're taking an awful chance.
Brick is the stuff to build with, solid bricks.

You want to be impractical, go ahead.
But just remember, I told them; wait and see.
You're making a big mistake. Awright, I said,
But when the wolf comes, don't come running to me.

The funny thing is, they didn't. There they sat,
One in his crummy yellow shack, and one
Under his roof of twigs, and the wolf ate
Them, hair and hide. Well, what is done is done.
But I'd been willing to help them, all along,
If only they'd once admitted they were wrong.[7]

Sara Henderson Hay

There are no hard and fast rules for determining *exactly* which book is appropriate for *exactly* which child, nor for saying *exactly* how much of a book a child should understand for the literary experience to be a legitimate one. Still, you will get an idea of the difficulty of a book if you assess the style of writing, the approach to the content, and the complexity of the theme.

Style of writing includes, among other aspects, the choice of vocabulary and the sentence length and structure. Reading and listening comprehension are related to these items. Here are excerpts from two picture books. The first is from *Are You Sad, Mama?,* a story that tells of a little girl's efforts to cheer her mother. She tries singing a song and drawing a picture, but her mother remains sad.

> "I will bring you my bear, Mama.
> Maybe that will make you happy."
> So the little girl sat her fuzzy brown bear
> in her mother's lap.
> "Hello, Bear," said her mother.
> She touched his chewed off ear
> and his button nose.
> But her face looked sadder than ever.
> So the little girl put away her bear.[8]

When the little girl offers to go away, her mother says that will make her cry. The girl hugs her mother and that makes them both happy.

The second excerpt is from *The King's Fountain,* a story about a poor man who stops a king from building a fountain which would have cut off the water supply for the city. He has tried to get others whom he believes to be more qualified than he to speak to the king. The scholar is involved in matters more lofty and is not interested; the merchant gives advice but is afraid to face the king; the metalsmith is strong but unwise. The poor man must plead with the king himself.

> The King started up, ready to call his guards. But he stopped and fell silent for a time, his frowns deep as his thoughts. Then he replied: "You are too simple for clever debate with me; but you have a wiser head than a scholar. Your speech is halting; but there is more true eloquence in your words than in the golden tongue of a cunning counselor. You are too weak to crack a flea; but you have a braver heart than anyone in my kingdom. I will do as you ask.[9]

The vocabulary in the second passage is far more advanced than that of the first. Not only are more difficult words used, "eloquence" and "cunning counselor" for example, but also methaphoric expressions such as "golden tongue" and "frowns deep as his thoughts." Neither passage has sentence structures that are inordinately complex, or which would make comprehension difficult for young children.

There is a similarity of content in that both books are about one person attempting to help another person or persons. *Are You Sad, Mama?* uses content much closer to the experience of young children than does *The King's Fountain* and characters are more recognizable to young children. The approach differs in that the first is more straightforward, telling only of the child's attempts to comfort her mother and making no further observations. The second shows the irony of the ineffectual scholar, merchant, and metalsmith, who, after the success of the poor man, continue writing and telling of his success with no realization of their own ineptitude.

Both books share a theme of the "weak" being able to help the "strong," a child helping an adult, a poor man saving all in his city from thirst. The first, however, has only this direct theme, plus the theme of love being a comfort to one who is sad. The second weaves many themes into the telling of the story: if something is to be done, we must do it ourselves; we should be concerned for others as well as ourselves; the humble who sincerely care may accomplish more than the proud who are unconcerned; the eminent citizens of a community may not be able to accomplish what is needed. Ezra Jack Keats, the illustrator of the book, has said that the theme can be expressed by the words of Hillel:

> If I am not for myself,
>   who will be for me?
> And if I am only for myself,
>   what am I?
> And if not now,
>   when?[10]

Thus, writing style, approach to content, and theme all make *The King's Fountain* a book appropriate for children eight or older, while *Are You Sad, Mama?* can be shared with children as young as three or four. There are, however, a vast number of books which are enjoyed by children from four or five years of age all the way through eight or nine years of age. Use your judgment about the difficulty of a book, then watch the children's reactions as you read and listen to their comments. Use their responses to determine how well you are matching their level of comprehension.

Activities for Response to Books

In addition to careful selection, you can maintain and enhance positive attitudes toward literature by suggesting activities for extending the books that are enjoyable and satisfying for the children. Activities should be such that they encourage further involvement with literature. If second graders must fill in book report forms for each book they complete, they may decide to stop reading. If they are asked to draw their favorite part of every book they hear, they may begin to dread story time. If, however, they are engaged in a variety of creative responses, as suggested in chapters four through nine, have the opportunity to work both with others and by themselves, and make choices about their activities, they are likely to want to hear and read more literature.

Activities serve many purposes. They help children explore the structure of literature. They encourage comparisons of stories, leading to a concept of what a story is. They support growth in many areas of development. They give teachers a measure of their students' comprehension.

Glenna Sloan writes:

> The child's response to the literature he encounters is a central aspect of criticism. The response may come in the form of a question or comment; it may involve sharing a favorite poem or retelling a familiar story; it may be an original composition in words, a drawing, a dramatization, a puppet play, a dance drama, or the story board for a film. In the attempt to guide and foster the child's growth in comprehension and responsiveness, a teacher guides responses, providing assistance in planning and structuring them, and opportunities for developing, sharing, and evaluating them.[11]

*Activities based on books can encourage further involve-
ment with literature.*

Criticism here means the study of literature in which children learn the verbal trappings for talking about prose and poetry. They learn these in a context
in which the terms arise naturally, and they build a foundation for a later, more
formal analysis of literature. It is one more reason for encouraging creative
responses to literature.

Grouping Books for Instruction

Children should be guided to perceive literature as a body of work rather than
as separate and unrelated stories and poems. If you group books for presentation, you set the stage for children to see the relationships among books, to
notice the recurring structural patterns of literature. You give children a data
base from which they can make their own generalizations about literature.

Arthur Applebee analyzed the patterns children used in telling stories and
the responses they gave when asked about fiction and fictional characters to
determine the concept of story held by children ages two through seventeen.
He assumed that young children who might not say directly what they expected
to find in a story would reveal their expectations in the stories they told. He
found that even two year olds distinguished some conventions of story. They
told stories having formal openings or titles, "Once upon a time . . ."; having

formal closings, ". . . and they lived happily ever after" or "the end"; and which were consistently in the past tense. Seventy percent of the two year olds included at least one of these conventions in the stories they told. The use of these three devices rose with age until by age five, ninety-three percent of the children used at least one of them and forty-seven percent used all three.[10] Applebee noted that many of the stories read to young children are based on the oral tradition, and employ these conventions.

The data also showed that as the children matured, they told stories which became more and more removed from the immediate setting of home and family. They used the conventions of story also to explore behaviors unacceptable in terms of general social norms. As the unacceptable behaviors were included, the use of realistic settings dropped. The threat of exploring *bad* actions was lessened by the distance from reality.

Young children often see stories more as histories than as fictions. At age six, nearly three-fourths of the children studied still were uncertain about whether stories were real, though by age nine, all of the children classified stories as make-believe. This interview with Joseph, age six years and three months, shows a process which occurs often. Children combine the events of the story with the rest of their knowledge about the world.

Is Cinderella a real person?	No.
Was she ever a real person?	Nope, she died.
Did she used to be alive?	Yes.
When did she live?	A long time ago, when I was one years old.
Are stories always about things that really happened?	Yes.
When did the things in *Little Red Riding Hood* happen?	A long time ago when I was a baby, they happened. There was witches and that, a long time ago. So when they started witch . . . they saw two good people and they made some more good people, so did the more horrible people. And they made more good people and the bad people got drowned.
Are there still people like that?	Nope, they were all killed, the police got them.[12]

Joseph's knowledge of police is combined with characters from folk tales and with the biblical story of Noah and the flood.

Applebee reasons that "It is only after the story has emerged as a fiction that it can begin a new journey toward a role in the exploration of the world not as it is but as it might be, a world which poses alternatives rather than declares certainties."[13]

One role of the preschool and primary teacher is to guide this emerging realization that fiction presents possible alternatives, that it is of the imaginative world. Children develop a sense of story as they mature intellectually. Realiz-

ing that the world of literature is not factual, but an imaginative way of learning and of knowing is a gradual process. Applebee found that many children
of six said that stories in general did not have to be about real happenings,
but they nonetheless contended that certain fictional characters special to them
were real. Stories might be make-believe, but yes, they could visit Snow White
if only she did not live so far away.

As you share books with children, tell them the names of the authors and
illustrators. This gives them the information that stories were created by people, information that will take on meaning for them when they are ready to
fit it into their schemata for organizing their world. Present examples of many
types of stories, with diverse settings and varied characters, so that the children
have the data to generalize broadly about the conventions of story. Group stories
to help children see that certain events, or images, or story shapes occur repeatedly. They can observe how two stories, with differing characters, settings,
and plots, may still offer the same theme. They can see that one animal
character and one human character may occupy the same role in different
stories as each leaves home for an adventure, is successful, and returns home.
There are many ways of grouping books. During any one school year, you will
want to vary your approach to grouping. At times you will group only two books
for comparison while at other times you may use either the unit or the web
approach to larger groupings.

Book Comparisons

Questions in any one discussion about books usually focus attention on only
a few of the many responses to literature. Some questions help children identify with the characters, others stimulate creative thought. Still others guide
children in their literary understandings. It is particularly useful to discuss more
than one book at a time if the goal of the discussion is the sharpening of
children's awareness of the interrelatedness of literature. Book comparisons
demonstrate that certain patterns, themes, and types of characters appear in
many stories. They show that the elements of literature work together in any
one story, and that these same elements are the core of all literature.

Suppose you read *The King's Flower*[14] to a group of second graders. In this
book, the king wants to have his possessions be bigger and better than anyone
else's. He sleeps in a huge bed, and his knife and fork are so large that they
must be suspended from the ceiling by ropes in order for him to use them. When
he has a toothache, his dentist has gigantic pincers forged for pulling the of-
fending tooth. Later the king orders that the pincers be converted into a mam-
moth birdcage. It proves ineffective for keeping small birds inside, but it does
provide a refuge for them when they are chased by a large eagle. Then the king
has an enormous flower pot filled with soil and a bulb planted. When the flower
finally blossoms, it is not the biggest in all the world, but only an ordinary tulip.
The king stares at it, deciding that it is beautiful and that perhaps biggest does
not necessarily mean best.

There are many possibilities for extending this book., Children might try to
think of uses for the king's giant toothbrush, or his big clock, or the flower pot,
just as the large pincers were converted into a birdcage. To help children develop
literary understandings, however, you would need to ask questions or suggest

activities that focused on the structure of the story. These should be questions which explore the relationship of one part of the story to another, or describe how the author and illustrator created a mood or tone for the tale. Here is a series of questions for discussion of *The King's Flower.*

1. Why do you think the king wanted to have big things?
2. How did his wanting big things affect his life?
3. Were you surprised that the king liked the tulip? Why or why not?
4. What did the king learn?
5. How might the story have ended if the tulip had turned out to be huge?

When children tell how a story might be different if one thing were changed, whether it be a happening, or a character, or a setting, they are seeing how that element fits into the total story, the impact it has on every other part. When they tell what one of the major characters "learned," they are frequently identifying the theme of the story. When they tell whether they were surprised by an event, they are demonstrating their expectations for the story, expectations which are founded on the characterization and plot development.

Questions should be phrased so that they allow children to explain in their own words their understanding of the story. If children answer with only a "yes" or a "no," they miss the opportunity to develop their own ideas and the adult misses the opportunity to see how the child is reasoning. If children are having difficulty with a question, it can be rephrased, perhaps requiring less information or fewer inferences, but still allowing the child to explain fully. For example, if the children had trouble responding to the second question above, it might

Questions that focus on the structure of a story help children develop literary understandings.

be changed to two questions. First, "Describe at least one time when the king used something big," and then, after several children have responded to this, "How did his liking for big things make his life different from what it might have been otherwise?"

Reading a second book on a similar theme, or about a similar situation, or of the same genre, or sharing one that contrasts sharply with the first provides more information for children to process, information about how literature works. After reading *The King's Flower*, you could share *The Biggest House in the World*,[15] another book that offers the theme that the biggest is not always the best. In this book, a small snail tells his father that he wants to have the biggest house in the world when he grows up. The father takes his son aside and tells the story of another snail long ago who said the same thing to his father. The little snail, however, learned to move in such a way that his shell began to grow. It grew larger and larger, and he learned that by moving his tail, he could grow pointed bulges, and that by pushing and wishing, he could make beautiful designs appear all over the house. His colorful shell was admired by all, once even being mistaken for a cathedral by a swarm of butterflies. As his shell grew larger, it also grew heavier, until it was so heavy that the little snail could no longer move. The cabbage leaf the snails were eating was devoured, and when the other snails moved on to other cabbages, the little snail was left behind, eventually starving since he was unable to move. The shell disintegrated and the snail was forgotten. When the father finishes his tale, the little snail decides that a small house is best after all, one that is light enough to be carried easily.

Children could follow this story with an activity such as creating their own exaggerated shell or making their own elaborate houses, using boxes, milk cartons, styrofoam and other building materials. Before beginning such a project with them, you could lead a discussion about the book which would emphasize its literary aspects. Here are questions you might use.

1. Why do you suppose the author made this a story within a story, and had a father snail telling his son what happened?
2. What did the little snail learn from the story his father told?
3. How might this story have ended if the snail had been able to move his "biggest house in the world"?
4. How was the snail like the king in *The King's Flower?* How was he different?
5. How were the two stories alike? How were they different?

Again, the questions focus on the structure of the story and on the interaction of the parts. When the children begin to compare the two books, they have already stated the themes of both books. They may see that for the king, biggest was not always best because he saw something small that was beautiful. For the snail, biggest was not best because he learned of another snail who so encumbered himself with his possessions that he lost his freedom and capacity to cope, and died because of it. They may also see themes of being content with what is natural and of the dangers of materialism. They may realize that while the king's story has a happy ending, and is a comedy in literary terms, the snail's story would be a tragedy were it not for the fact that the snail's demise is told within another story which does end with all well. They will observe that stories with very different characters and plots can still present the same or similar themes.

Having compared books under the guidance of their teacher, they can begin to compare them on their own, working within a framework which includes literary comparisons. Jean Karl, an editor and a writer of books for children, has said that "A good children's book is an experience of events and also an experience of ideas that lie deeper than events. Such a book is a means by which a sensitive adult can give a child an opportunity to deepen as well as broaden his vision of life."[16] Children should have these sorts of books, and should have the chance to talk about that deeper vision.

Units

Books with characteristics in common can be grouped together into units which focus on a single item, describe similar content, or represent literature of a particular genre or by a particular author or illustrator. When you plan a unit, you will consider a variety of titles but will narrow the selection to those books which best fit your purposes and include only those which you actually plan to use. Generally the sequence of books and activities is planned in advance, though modifications may be made based on children's reactions or on new information.

Suppose you are working with five or six year olds. You think about their interests and needs and about the literature you know. You might do a unit on making friends, or being afraid, or on stories about animals which talk. You decide to do a unit on books which show the characters using their imagination in ways which are understandable to young children. You want the children to recognize that people use their imaginations in a variety of ways and for a variety of purposes. You hope to engage the children in activities which stimulate their own imaginations, and you want the children to discern techniques used by authors and illustrators to indicate the imaginative life of the characters.

You list books with which you are familiar, and use the book selection guides available in the library to make a general list. Then you decide on the four or five books, or poems, which you will share with the children. You choose the following books:

Burningham, John. *Come Away from the Water, Shirley.* New York: Thomas Y. Crowell Publishers, 1977.

Shirley and her parents go to the beach where her parents set up their beach chairs and get comfortable. Shirley stands at the water's edge. While her parents, shown on the left page throughout the book, make comments to her about not petting the dog and being careful not to get tar on her shoes, Shirley imagines all sorts of adventures for herself, all shown on the right hand pages.

Keats, Ezra Jack. *The Trip.* New York: Greenwillow Books, 1978.

Louie has moved to a new neighborhood and does not know anyone there. Using an old shoe box, he makes a peep box of an urban neighborhood like the one he left. As he looks in, he pretends he can fly the paper plane he has suspended from the top of the box. He returns to his friends and gives them a ride, and as he waves good-bye, hears his mother calling him and the children outside yelling "trick or treat." He puts on his Halloween costume and goes outside.

Krauss, Ruth. *A Very Special House.* Illus. by Maurice Sendak. New York: Harper & Row, Publishers, Inc., 1953.

A little boy tells about his very special house in which he can draw on the walls, jump on his bed, watch a lion eat the stuffing from the chairs and a giant play a drum. In a continuation of the bouncy language, he explains that this house is right in the middle of his head.

Ryder, Joanne. *The Snail's Spell.* Illus. by Lynne Cherry. New York: Frederick Warne & Co., Inc., 1982.

A small child is pictured crouched in a garden. The reader is told to imagine himself or herself without any bones, getting smaller and smaller. The directions continue as the child in the pictures and the reader imagine what it would be like to be a snail in this lush garden.

Sendak, Maurice. *Where the Wild Things Are.* New York: Harper & Row, Publishers, Inc., 1963.

Max, wearing his wolf suit and making mischief, is called a wild thing and sent to bed without his supper. He fantasizes a forest in his room and sails to where the wild things are. They make him king and at his command take part in the "rumpus," and although they beg Max to stay he sails home. He wants to be where someone cares for him, and when he returns his supper is waiting for him.

To determine the sequence of presentation, you look for ways the books relate to one another and for natural progressions. You plan discussion questions and activities that will help children explore the relationships among the books and that will support their growth in other areas.

You want to begin the unit with the children's experience so you engage them in guided fantasy. They sit comfortably in a group and you tell them that they are going to have the chance to play an imagination game. They are to close their eyes and make a picture in their minds of what you tell them. Your description goes something like this. "See if you can make a picture of a rabbit in your mind. Picture his fur . . . his ears . . . his nose . . . his tail. Whisper the color of your rabbit. Make the rabbit hop around. Now have it take great big leaps. Put a hat on your rabbit. Do his ears stick through the hat? Picture the bed you sleep in. Put the rabbit in your bed. Have the rabbit bounce on your bed. Have the rabbit hop all around your room. Now have the rabbit take a bite out of your door. Have him sniff your shoes. Now make the rabbit hop outside and nibble grass. Take a good look at your rabbit, then open your eyes."

You ask each child to tell one thing about his or her rabbit. After the children have finished talking, you introduce *A Very Special House* by telling that it is a book about a boy who can do just what they have been doing. He can use his imagination. You read the book, showing the illustrations as you read. When it is finished, you show several of the pictures and ask the children why some parts of the pictures are in color and the rest are just pencil drawings. They recognize that this is the technique used to differentiate reality from fantasy. You place the book on a special table, and on the wall behind it you post a huge sheet of paper. Children can draw on this sheet just as the boy draws on the wall in his special house.

The next day you continue with the idea of imagination and imaginative activities by reading *The Snail's Spell.* You read the book twice. The first time you have the children listen with their eyes closed, imagining everything the text describes, and moving in their places as the tiny snail does. They tell what they saw and how they felt. For the second reading, the children observe the illustrations as you read. This time they talk about how the artist viewed what was happening. Finally, you ask them how *A Very Special House* and *A Snail's Spell* are similar.

The third day you read *Come Away From the Water, Shirley.* The children have heard two stories in which the characters use their imaginations. In the discussion that follows your reading, you concentrate on the artist's technique for differentiating the fantasy from the realism in the story.

1. If Shirley's parents told about their day at the beach, what might they say? (You show the illustrations again here.)
2. If Shirley told about her day, what might she say? (You show the pictures.)
3. Do Shirley's parents know what she is doing? What makes you think this?
4. How does the artist let you know what is going on?
5. Would you rather have Shirley's day or her parents' day? Why?

You call the children's attention to the fact that Shirley figures prominently in the stories she imagines. She rows herself out to the pirate ship, engages in battle with the pirates, discovers buried treasure. Then you let two or three children tell an adventure with themselves in the key position. You tape-record their stories for transcription later. The stories will be put with the books and the wall drawings, and the children are encouraged to dictate stories about themselves in an adventure to you or to classroom aides so that the collection grows and so that each child has the opportunity to tell a story.

Now you read *Where the Wild Things Are.* You lead a brief discussion in which your questions are designed to stimulate the children to think about Max's feelings as related to his fantasy, and to see the illustrator's use of increasingly larger pictures to build to a climax. You ask:

1. How did a forest grow in Max's room?
2. Why do you think Max went to visit the wild things?
3. Do you think the wild things are scary? Why or why not?
4. Watch as I show the pictures again. What do you notice about them? Why do you think the illustrator made them that way?
5. How do you think Max was feeling at the end of the story? What made him feel this way?

You and the children look again at the rumpus scenes. The children try to imagine sounds the wild things are making. Then you ask, "What kind of music could the wild things hear as they danced?" Using rhythm instruments, the children develop music for the rumpus. Once the rhythm is established, other children dance to it, having their own "rumpus."

Children can imagine what a text describes. (Illustration from The Snail's Spell *by Joanne Ryder, illustrated by Lynne Cherry. Reprinted by permission of Viking Penguin Inc.)*

You conclude the unit with *The Trip*. You have all five books handy for the discussion that follows the reading. First you ask a few questions about the book just completed.

1. Why is the book titled *The Trip*?
2. How do you think Louie felt when he decided to make the peep box? How could you tell?
3. Do you think Louie's trip made him feel better?
4. If you were going to take a trip like Louie's, where would you go? What would you do?

Then you guide the children in a comparison of the books, holding up the books as you mention them. You begin by asking the children what they remember about each book. You call on several children to respond to each question.

1. As I hold up each book, tell me one thing you remember about it.
2. In what ways are these books like each other?
3. What were some of the ways characters in these books used their imaginations? Why did they use their imaginations?

With the children dictating, you make a chart that lists all the ways they use their imaginations.

You place the books, chart, drawings, and dictations in the same area. You listen to the children's comments during the week, and after a few days, you ask the children to select one of the five books for you to reread. When you move the books back to the regular bookshelves, you inform the children of what you are doing as you prepare the space for a new display and new work.

When the unit has been completed, you look at your purposes to evaluate whether they have been fulfilled. Did the children recognize that imagination was being used for differing reasons, sometimes for the enjoyment of it, other times for escaping loneliness, boredom, or frustration? Were the children stimulated to use their own imaginations? Did they participate in the guided fantasy, tell a story in which they had fantastic adventures, create and move to a "wild thing" rhythm, and contribute to a listing of ways the imagination can be used? Did they notice how the illustrator showed fantasy within a story, using techniques such as a combination of line drawings and colored figures, or reality on one page and fantasy on another? Your purposes should be sufficiently clear for you to assess the effectiveness of specific lessons. Some teachers find it useful to state the purpose, or objectives, for each lesson in behavioral terms, writing exactly what behaviors are expected from the children. A strict behavioral objective gives the condition under which the behavior is to be performed, the observable behavior, and the criteria for how well the behavior must be performed. A general objective for the guided fantasy preceding your reading of A Very Special House is that "The children will take part in a guided fantasy and will use their imaginations in their understanding of the story." A behaviorally stated objective would be that "Given a teacher directed guided fantasy, each child will state one characteristic of the rabbit he or she visualized." The advantage of behaviorally stated objectives is that they are clear and precise, and you know at the end of a lesson whether the objectives were met. The disadvantage is that some objectives cannot be measured easily by observable behavior. In order to evaluate experiences with literature fully, you will need to use your own sensitivity to the children and their responses as well as your clearly stated objectives.

If you are working with three or four year olds, the literature you select will of course be simpler than that you would choose for six year olds. You will plan to involve the children in the language, content, and feelings of the stories, but will spend little time in analyzing the literature itself. You will, however, be aware yourself of the types of literature you are choosing, and will plan to expose children to a variety of genre.

Suppose you are working with three year olds in a day care center. You decide that you will select books with a single kind of animal as the main character. You begin looking at pigs, dogs, and bears, and settle on bears because the children have enjoyed Brown Bear, Brown Bear, What Do You See?[17] so much. Then you realize that you will probably need to choose between bears as animals or bears as toys. There are ample stories in each category. Because you have been talking about seasons, you decide to choose bears as animals, and integrate some discussion about hibernation and seasonal changes. You select the following five books as the core of your unit.

Allen, Pamela. *Bertie and the Bear.* New York: Coward-McCann, 1983.

This story opens with Bertie being chased by a bear. The queen sees what is happening, chases after the bear shouting "shoo," and then a series of other characters join the chase, all making noise. The bear suddenly stops, amazed that it is all for him. He takes a bow, does some cartwheels, and begins to dance. The other characters then dance along after him.

Asch, Frank. *Just Like Daddy.* Englewood Cliffs, N.J.: Prentice-Hall Inc., 1981.

This story is told in first person by a little bear who wakes up and yawns "just like Daddy." Throughout the morning he does everything "just like Daddy" as the family has breakfast and heads out for a fishing trip. On the last page he catches a large fish, "just like Mommy."

Asch, Frank. *Mooncake.* Englewood Cliffs, N.J.: Prentice-Hall Inc., 1983.

This has the same bear as *Just Like Daddy* but the story is told in third person. One summer evening Bear tells his friend Little Bird that he is hungry and thinks a bite of the moon would be delicious. Determined to get a taste of this delicacy, he builds a rocket. When fall comes, the bird flies south, and Bear, still in his rocket, proceeds to fall asleep. Bear awakens once and sees snow for the first time. Assuming he is on the moon, he tastes some snow, then gets back into his rocket and sleeps. When spring comes and the bird returns, Bear awakens and tells him that the moon was delicious, just as he had expected.

Dabcovich, Lydia. *Sleepy Bear.* New York: E. P. Dutton Inc., 1982.

This is a very simple story in which fall activities such as leaves falling and birds flying south are noted. Bear goes into his cave and sleeps through the winter. When spring comes, he awakens and emerges, unfortunately to bugs, but also to bees and the pleasant thought of honey.

McCloskey, Robert. *Blueberries for Sal.* New York: Viking Press, 1948.

Little Sal and her mother go blueberry picking, while on the other side of the hill a mother bear and her cub are also seeking berries. Sal follows her mother, listening to the sound of the berries hitting the bottom of her pail, then eating them, until she finally sits down in a large clump of bushes. The bear cub, tired of trying to keep up with his mother, also stops in a clump of bushes. The two little ones hear sounds ahead, but each ends up following the wrong mother. The two mothers are able to set matters straight, and the two families head for home, Sal and her mother with blueberries to can for winter, and Little Bear and his mother full of food stored up for the winter.

With these five books, you will have exposed children to both nonfiction *(Sleepy Bear)* and fiction. They will have heard several types of plot construction. *Mooncake* and *Just Like Daddy* have progressive plots that advance toward a single climax. *Blueberries for Sal* has parallel plots, with two sets of action occurring simultaneously. *Bertie and the Bear* has a cumulative plot, with repetition and the addition of character after character to the chase. The children will also have been introduced to the idea of a surprise ending in *Just Like Daddy.*

You begin the unit with *Sleepy Bear.* As the children listen to the story and see the pictures, you draw their attention to the bear's contented look in the title page illustration, and ask why they think he is so happy. Some may note the bees and the honey he is eating. At the end of the story, it is the memory of honey that entices him to leave his cave. You introduce the word *hibernate* although it is not used in the book. You encourage the children to describe what happens in fall, in winter, and in spring.

Next you share *Blueberries for Sal.* When the text has the mother bear telling her cub that they must eat berries so they will grow big and fat for the long winter, you mention the similarity to Sleepy Bear, but then continue reading. You talk about the sounds in the story: the berries hitting the bottom of the pail, the rustling in the bushes, the noises that both mothers recognized as belonging to their children. You use an activity that another teacher has done successfully with her group. Each child takes a handful of fresh blueberries and drops them one by one into a pail, listening to the sound. Each child describes the sound either as was done in the book, "kuplink, kuplank, kuplunk," or makes up his or her own words for the sounds. Then the children eat the blueberries.

The third book used in this unit is *Bertie and the Bear.* Because each character makes a sound as he or she joins the chase, you read a page once, giving the sound, then again, allowing the children to make the sound with you. After you have finished the book, you ask them what they think the author meant when he said that all those characters made an "IN-CRED-IBLE" noise. You tell the children, "This story is make-believe," and ask, "What parts do you think couldn't really happen?" Then, looking at the illustrations of the bear, the children first assume some of his poses, then show how they think the bear walked. You put a record on, and this time the children dance, follow-the-leader style, just as Bertie danced after the bear.

When you read *Just Like Daddy,* the children are quick to catch on to the pattern, and they begin chiming in with "Just like Daddy" at the appropriate times. When the story is over, you ask them if they were surprised at the ending. Then you discuss things they do just like their mothers, fathers, grandparents, or siblings. Finally, each child is asked to draw something he or she does just like someone else in his or her family.

As you prepare to read the last book, *Mooncake,* you have the other four with you. You ask the children to look at the covers and describe what they see. They may add what they remember from the stories. You ask them if they know any other stories about bears, expecting them to mention *Goldilocks and the Three Bears* and *Brown Bear, Brown Bear, What Do You See?* and wondering if they will cite any others. You show the cover of *Mooncake* and tell them that this book was written by the author of one of the other four books. Can they tell which one? Let them see that the bears look alike on the two covers. Then ask them to predict what the story may be about based on the cover and title. The cover shows bear eating some "cake" while the bird watches. What do they think "mooncake" could be?

After reading this story, reread *Sleepy Bear* and ask the children how the two bears are alike. See if any remember the term *hibernate* and use it in their discriptions of both bears sleeping. Notice if they talk about what the bears liked to eat. Tell them that one of these two stories is make-believe. Which one do they think it is and why? You then put all the books together on a shelf, the "Books About Bears" shelf. You notice that the children are looking at these books regularly, and you hear one little girl whispering, "kuplink, kuplank, kuplunk" as she drops crayons into a box. From these responses, you know that your literature presentation has been successful.

Children could try following the bear's lead, or doing a dance of their own, (illustration by Pamela Allen reprinted by permission of Coward-McCann, Inc. from Bertie and the Bear *by Pamela Allen, © 1983 by Pamela Allen.)*

Webs

A web is a diagram that charts either the potential within a single book or the possible ways of developing a single topic through literature. Webs differ from units in that they show far more ideas than will be actually used and in that they do not show sequence. They are a form of brainstorming. You think of all the possible extensions of a book, or all the aspects of a topic. You jot them down around the main heading, categorizing as you go. When you have finished, you see many ideas you might pursue with children. Webs can help teachers remain flexible in their use of books because they encourage an exploration of many facets of a book or topic. A teacher may then emphasize one aspect of the book or topic with one group of children, another aspect with a second group.

The web on the next page is on the topic, rain. Stories, poems, and activities are grouped around topics related to rain. If you were using this web, you would select those items from it that seemed appropriate for your group of children. You would develop the ideas more fully before you presented them. For example, if you had been talking about feelings, you might use all the books and activities under the heading *Experiences,* for all of these relate to children's reactions to rain and storms. With another class, you might compare the different retellings of the story of Noah. However, webs are most often used to provide a spectrum of books and activities rather than to concentrate on a single aspect of a topic. Thus, you would be most likely to use the web by selecting one or two books, poems, or activities from each heading.

Evaluating a Literature Program

Work with literature should be evaluated on both a short term and a long term basis. Short term evaluation is keyed to objectives for a specific literature experience. You note whether the children did indeed perform the tasks set out for them, whether their art project reflected their feeling about a story, whether they dramatized four stanzas of the poem. Long term evaluation is more general

STORMS

The Storm Book—Zolotow
Lost in the Storm—Carrick
The Washout—Carrick
Flash, Crash, Rumble & Roll—Branley
—Compare fiction and nonfiction
  books about storms
—Make mural of a rainstorm

POETRY

"Tornado!"—Adoff
"A January Fog Will Freeze a Hog"—Davis
"April Rain Song"—Hughes
"Spring Rain"—Chute
"Galoshes"—Bacmeister
"Spring Rain"—Behn
"Rain"—Livingston
"The Little Rain"—Thurman
"Rain Rivers"—Moore
"Summer Rain"—Merriam
"Rain Rain Go Away"—Mother Goose
"One Misty Moisty Morning"—Mother Goose

EXPERIENCES

Umbrella—Yashima
One Monday Morning—Shulevitz
The Bravest Babysitter—Greenberg
Staying Home Alone on a Rainy Day—Iwasaki
Rain—Spier
All Wet! All Wet!—Skofield
—Measure rainfall
—Role play helping someone afraid of thunder
—Make catalog of rainy day activities

SENSORY AWARENESS

Rain Drop Splash—Tresselt
Rain—Crews
Rain Rain Rivers—Schulevitz
Where Does the Butterfly Go When It Rains?
  —Garelick
Taste the Raindrops—Hines
—Listen to and tape record sounds of rain
—Make onomatopoetic words for rain
—List words that describe different kinds of
  rain—"drizzle" "shower"
—Make rain song using rhythm instruments
  and tone bars
—Take walk following rain—note smells, sights

RAIN

TALES

Mushroom in the Rain—Ginsburg
It All Began With a Drip Drip Drip . . .—Lexau
Tales of Thunder and Lightning—Devlin
The Rain Puddle—Holl
—Use cartoon strip format to tell a rain tale in
  pictures

NOAH

Noah's Ark—Spier
Noah's Ark—Haley
Noah and the Rainbow—Bolliger
Two by Two: The Untold Story—Hewitt
One Wide River to Cross—Emberley
Prayers From the Ark—DeGasztold
—Dictate own prayers "from the ark"
—Compare versions of the ark story

RAINBOWS

A Rainbow of My Own—Freeman
Annie's Rainbow—Brooks
—Make rainbow picture using chalk

HUMOR

Mr. Gumpy's Motor Car—Burningham
Rain Makes Applesauce—Scheer
It's Raining Said John Twaining—Bodecker
Cloudy With a Chance of Meatballs—Barrett
—Dramatize Mr. Gumpy or John Twaining nursery rhyme
—Dictate story as told by a raindrop

and is an assessment of your entire literature program. You would engage in long term evaluation at the end of the year, but would be doing periodic checks as well.

The basic goal of a literature program is to "educate" children's imaginations. This means helping them discover the interrelatedness of works of literature, understand and enjoy the language of literature, and respond to literature in imaginative ways. Because you are concerned for the child as a total person, you will also want to evaluate literature's contribution to other areas of development.

Look first at the program itself: the books you have shared, the groupings of books you have used, the activities in which the children engaged. The books should represent the best available in terms of literary quality. There should be a balance in the program between types of literature—prose, poetry, fantasy, realism—and between the classics with their lasting appeal and the newly published books. The groupings should be such that they help children make generalizations about literature. The suggested activities should encourage individual response to literature and should deepen children's understanding and appreciation of literature.

Look also at the children's behavior. A successful literature program should result in some or all of these behaviors:

- Children reread or look at the illustrations in books you have read them.
- Children choose to read or look at books in their free time or as work choices.
- Children recommend books and book related activities to one another.
- Children choose to respond to literature through art, music, movement, and drama.
- Children talk about book characters and happenings in new situations.
- Children ask you to read to them.

All demonstrate that children are developing favorable attitudes toward literature and are making it an integral part of their lives.

As you evaluate other areas of children's growth, you will also be evaluating the effects of your literature program. Literature contributes to children's language, intellectual, personal, social, moral, aesthetic, and creative development. The next chapters demonstrate how literature supports these areas and give suggestions so that you will recognize and incorporate into your planning the immense potential of literature.

Summary

The basic goal of a literature curriculum is the education of children's imaginations. Teachers of young children and day care professionals contribute to this goal by involving children with literature in ways that establish positive attitudes toward it and by grouping books and structuring presentations so that children begin to perceive the interrelatedness of literature.

Positive attitudes are developed through the regular sharing of literature, through careful selection of high quality literature so that it matches children's interests and understanding, and through activities that allow children to respond to books in a stimulating and satisfying manner.

Children begin to perceive the interrelatedness of literature when books are grouped, either in pairs for comparison, or in units or webs. When books are paired, questions should focus on the structure of the stories so that children see how each is like or different from the other. Books may also be grouped into units that focus on a single theme, describe similar content, or represent literature of a particular genre or by a particular author or illustrator. Generally the books, the sequence in which they will be presented, and the activities are planned in advance, although modifications may be made.

A web is a diagram that charts either the potential within a single book or the possible ways of developing a single topic through literature. Webs differ from units in that they show far more ideas than will be actually used and in that they do not show sequence. Both units and webs present literature so that children see the relationships among several works.

The literature program should be evaluated on both a short term and a long term basis. Short term evaluation is keyed to objectives for specific literature experiences. Long term evaluation looks at children's behavior in relation to literature. Do they choose to read or look at books in their free time? Do they recommend books to one another? Do they choose to respond to books through art, music, movement, and drama? Do they ask you to read to them? Each of these behaviors indicates that the literature program is successful.

One measure of a successful literature program is that children choose to read in their free time.

Extending Your Learning

1. Interview a child between the ages of three and five about whether a particular story or book character is real or not.
2. Develop and sequence a set of questions to guide a discussion about a book. Make the questions ones that will help the child develop literary understanding.
3. Read any two books that are similar in content or theme. Develop and sequence a set of questions that will engage a child in comparing the books.
4. Develop a unit using books on a single topic or theme.
5. Develop a web on a topic of interest to young children.
6. Select a book from the list of recommended references by Carlson, Hopkins, Jacobs, Lamme, Moss, Somers, Stewig, or Whitehead. Apply one of the suggestions given to a book of your own choosing, or read a book they've suggested and develop your own idea for its use.
7. Look at two or three of the bibliographies listed in the recommended references. Describe the criteria that were used for selecting the books and how this might influence your use of the list.

Notes

1. Northrop Frye, *The Educated Imagination* (Bloomington: Indiana University Press, 1964), 140.
2. Northrop Frye, *The Educated Imagination*, 77–79.
3. Aidan Chambers, *Introducing Books to Children* (Boston: The Horn Book, 1983), 28.
4. Reprinted by permission of the publisher from Glenna Davis Sloan, *The Child as Critic* (New York: Teachers College Press, copyright © 1975 by Teachers College, Columbia University.)
5. Carol J. Fisher and Margaret A. Natarella, "Of Cabbages and Kings: or What Kinds of Poetry Young Children Like," *Language Arts* 56, No. 4 (April, 1979): 380–85.
6. Fisher and Natarella, "Of Cabbages and Kings," 385.
7. Hay, Sara Henderson, "The Builders." *The Story Hour* (Fayetteville: The University of Arkansas Press, 1982.) Used by permission of the author.
8. Text excerpt from *Are You Sad, Mama?* by Elizabeth Winthrop. Text copyright © 1979 by Elizabeth Winthrop Mahoney. By permission of Harper and Row, Publishers, Inc.
9. Lloyd Alexander, *The King's Fountain*, Illus. by Ezra Jack Keats (New York: E. P. Dutton & Co., 1971), n.p.
10. Hillel, quoted in Lloyd Alexander, *The King's Fountain*, n.p.
11. Sloan, *The Child as Critic*, 13.
12. Reprinted from *The Child's Concept of Story* by Arthur N. Applebee by permission of The University of Chicago Press. © 1978 by the University of Chicago, 44.
13. Applebee, *The Child's Concept of Story*, 41.
14. Mitsumasa Anno, *The King's Flower* (New York: William Collins Publishers, 1979).
15. Leo Lionni, *The Biggest House in the World* (New York: Pantheon, 1968).
16. Jean Karl, *From Childhood to Childhood* (New York: John Day Co., 1970), 6.
17. Martin, Bill. *Brown Bear, Brown Bear, What Do You See?* Illus. by Eric Carle (New York: Holt, Rinehart & Winston, 1983.)

"Web" Listings

Poetry

Arnold Adoff, *Tornado*. Illus. by Ronald Himler (New York: Delacorte Press, 1977).

Hubert Davis, ed., *A January Fog Will Freeze a Hog*. Illus. by John Wallner (New York: Crown Publishers, Inc., 1977).

Langston Hughes, "April Rain Song," in Langston Hughes, *The Dream Keeper* (New York: Alfred A. Knopf, 1932).

Marchette Chute, "Spring Rain," in Marchette Chute, *Rhymes about the City* (New York: Macmillan Publishing Co., 1946).

Rhoda Bacmeister, "Galoshes," in Rhoda Bacmeister, *Stories to Begin On* (New York: E. P. Dutton, Inc., 1940).

Harry Behn, "Spring Rain," in Harry Behn, *The Little Hill* (New York: Harcourt, Brace and Company, 1949).

Myra Cohn Livingston, "Rain," in Myra Cohn Livingston, *Whispers and Other Poems* (New York: Harcourt, Brace & World, 1965).

Judith Thurman, "The Little Rain," in Judith Thurman, *Flashlight and Other Poems* (New York: Atheneum Publishers, 1976).

Lilian Moore, "Rain Rivers," in Lilian Moore, *I Feel the Same Way* (New York: Atheneum Publishers, 1967).

Eve Merriam, "Summer Rain," in Eve Merriam, *There is no Rhyme for Silver* (New York: Atheneum Publishers, 1966).

Tales

Mirra Ginsburg, *Mushroom in the Rain* (New York: Macmillan Publishing Co., 1974).

Joan M. Lexau, *It All Began With a Drip, Drip, Drip . . .* Illus. by Joan Sandin (New York: McCall Publishing Co., 1970).

Harry Devlin, *Tales of Thunder and Lightning* (New York: Parents Magazine Press, 1975).

Adelaide Holl, *The Rain Puddle*. Illus. by Roger Duvoisin (New York: Lothrop, Lee & Shepard Books, 1965).

Storms

Charlotte Zolotow, *The Storm Book*. Illus. by Margaret Graham (New York: Harper & Row Publishers, Inc., 1952).

Carol Carrick, *Lost in the Storm*. Illus. by Donald Carrick (New York: Seabury Press, 1974).

Carol Carrick, *The Washout*. Illus. by Donald Carrick (New York: Seabury Press, 1978).

Franklyn Branley, *Flash, Crash, Rumble & Roll*. Illus. by Ed Emberley (New York: Thomas Y. Crowell Publishers, 1964).

Noah

Peter Spier, *Noah's Ark* (Garden City, New York: Doubleday & Co. Inc., 1977).

Gail E. Haley, *Noah's Ark* (New York: Atheneum Publishers, 1971).

Max Bolliger, *Noah and the Rainbow*. Translated by Clyde Bulla. Illus. by Helga Aichinger (New York: Thomas Y. Crowell Publishers, 1972).

Kathryn Hewitt, *Two by Two: The Untold Story* (New York: Harcourt Brace Jovanovich Inc., 1984).

Barbara Emberley, *One Wide River to Cross*. Illus. by Ed Emberley (Englewood Cliffs, N.J.: Prentice-Hall, 1966).

Carmen De Gasztold, trans. Rumer Godden. *Prayers from the Ark*. Illus. by Jean Primrose (London: Macmillan, 1967).

Experiences

Taro Yashima, *Umbrella* (New York: Viking Press, 1958).

Uri Shulevitz, *One Monday Morning* (New York: Charles Scribner's Sons, 1967).

Barbara Greenberg, *The Bravest Babysitter.* Illus. by Diane Paterson (New York: Dial Press, 1977).

Chihiro Iwasaki, *Staying Home Alone on a Rainy Day* (New York: McGraw-Hill Inc., 1969).

Peter Spier, *Rain* (New York: Doubleday & Co. Inc., 1982).

James Skofield, *All Wet! All Wet!* (New York: Harper & Row, Publishers, Inc., 1984).

Sensory Awareness

Alvin Tresselt, *Rain Drop Splash* Illus. by Leonard Weisgard (New York: Lothrop, Lee & Shepard Books, 1946).

Donald Crews, *Rain* (New York: Greenwillow Books, 1978).

Uri Shulevitz, *Rain Rain Rivers* (New York: Farrar, Straus, and Giroux, 1969).

May Garelick, *Where Does the Butterfly Go When It Rains?* Illus. by Leonard Weisgard (New York: W. R. Scott, 1961).

Anna Grossnickle Hines, *Taste the Raindrops* (New York: Greenwillow Books, 1983).

Rainbows

Don Freeman, *A Rainbow of My Own* (New York: Viking Press, 1966).

Ron Brooks, *Annie's Rainbow* (Cleveland: Collins-World, 1975).

Humor

John Burningham, *Mr. Gumpy's Motor Car* (London: Jonathan Cape, 1973).

Julian Scheer, *Rain Makes Applesauce* (New York: Holiday House, 1964)

N. M. Bodecker, *It's Raining Said John Twaining* (New York: Atheneum Publishers, 1973).

Judi Barrett, *Cloudy With a Chance of Meatballs.* Illus. by Ron Barrett (New York: Atheneum Publishers, 1978).

Recommended References

Applebee, Arthur N. *The Child's Concept of Story.* Chicago: The University of Chicago Press, 1978.

Bettleheim, Bruno. *The Uses of Enchantment.* New York: Alfred A. Knopf Inc., 1976.

Butler, Dorothy. *Cushla and Her Books.* Boston: The Horn Book, Inc., 1980 (copyright 1975).

Chambers, Aidan. *Introducing Books to Children.* 2d ed. Boston: The Horn Book, Inc., 1983.

Duff, Annis. *Bequest of Wings.* New York: Viking Press, 1944.

Favat, F. Andre. *Child and Tale: The Origins of Interest.* Urbana, Ill.: National Council of Teachers of English, 1977.

Frye, Northrop. *The Educated Imagination.* Bloomington: Indiana University Press, 1964.

Hazard, Paul. *Books, Children and Men.* Trans. by Marguerite Mitchell. Boston: The Horn Book, Inc., 1944.

Karl, Jean. *From Childhood to Childhood.* New York: John Day, 1970.

Meek, Margaret; Warlow, Aiden; and Barton, Griselda. *The Pattern of Children's Reading.* New York: Atheneum Publishers, 1978.

Purves, Alan C. and Monson, Dianne L. *Experiencing Children's Literature.* Glenview, Ill.: Scott, Foresman & Co., 1984.

Rosenblatt, Louise M. *Literature as Exploration.* 3d ed. New York: Noble and Noble, 1976.

Rosenblatt, Louise M. *The Reader, The Text, The Poem.* Carbondale: Southern Illinois University Press, 1978.

Sloan, Glenna Davis. *The Child as Critic.* 2d ed. New York: Teachers College Press, 1984.

Smith, Lillian. *The Unreluctant Years: A Critical Approach to Children's Literature.* Chicago: American Library Association, 1953.

Recommended References—Teaching Ideas and Booklists

Baskin, Barbara Holland, and Harris, Karen A. *The Special Child in the Library.* Chicago: American Library Association, 1976.

Carlson, Ruth Kearney. *Enrichment Ideas.* Dubuque, Iowa: Wm. C. Brown Group, 1970.

Cianciolo, Patricia. *Picture Books for Children.* Chicago: American Library Association, 1973.

Cullinan, Bernice E., and Carmichael, Carolyn W., eds. *Literature and Young Children.* Urbana, Ill.: National Council of Teachers of English, 1977.

Hopkins, Lee Bennett. *The Best of Book Bonanza.* New York: Holt, Rinehart & Winston, 1980.

———— *Pass the Poetry, Please!* New York: Citation Press, 1972.

Jacobs, Leland B., ed. *Using Literature With Young Children.* New York: Teachers College Press, 1965.

Johnson, Ferne., ed. *Start Early for an Early Start.* Chicago: American Library Association, 1976.

Lamme, Linda, ed. *Learning to Love Literature.* Urbana, Ill.: National Council of Teachers of English, 1981.

Lamme, Linda. *Raising Readers, A Guide to Sharing Literature With Young Children.* New York: Walker & Co., 1980.

Larrick, Nancy. *A Parent's Guide to Children's Reading.* 5th ed. Philadelphia: The Westminster Press, 1983.

Montbello, Mary S. *Children's Literature in the Curriculum.* Dubuque, Iowa: Wm. C. Brown Group, 1972.

Moss, Joy F. *Focus Units in Literature: A Handbook for Elementary Teachers.* Urbana, Ill.: National Council of Teachers of English, 1984.

Somers, Albert B., and Worthington, Janet Evans. *Response Guides for Teaching Children's Books.* Urbana, Ill.: National Council of Teachers of English, 1979.

Stewig, John Warren, and Sebesta, Sam L., eds. *Using Literature in the Elementary Classroom.* Urbana, Ill.: National Council of Teachers of English, 1978.

Trelease, Jim. *The Read-Aloud Handbook.* New York: Penguin Books, 1982.

Tway, Eileen, ed. *Reading Ladders for Human Relations.* 6th ed. Washington, D. C.: American Council on Education, 1981.

White, Mary Lou, ed. *Adventuring With Books.* Urbana, Ill.: National Council of Teachers of English, 1981.

Whitehead, Robert. *Children's Literature: Strategies of Teaching.* Englewood Cliffs, N.J.: Prentice-Hall, Inc. 1968.

4

Supporting Children's Language Development

Language Development in Young Children

Linguists have listened to the utterances of children as eagerly as new parents awaiting the first "Da Da" or "Mama." They have identified certain patterns in children's development of language and have attempted to explain just what is happening.

Although linguists do not agree on all aspects of language acquisition, there is consensus that children are born with a natural capacity for oral language, and that youngsters are influenced by the language environment in which they find themselves. Children also go through predictable stages in acquiring the phonology, or sound system, and the syntax, or word order, of their native tongues. Their semantic knowledge increases as they both learn new words and clarify and refine their concepts of words already familiar to them. In a similar manner, their knowledge of the meaning and function of print grows out of their experiences with it.

How Children Learn Language

The process by which children learn language is one in which they construct for themselves the grammar, or rules, of the language they are hearing. However, this construction of the rules is not a conscious effort; a four year old could not state the rule for making a verb past tense. Yet that same four year old could use the rule to tell about yesterday's trip to the dentist. "I played in the waiting room until it was time to go in. I looked at all the things on the tray. Dr. Carroll cleaned my teeth." It is because she *knows* the rules subconsciously that she is able to create new sentences and not simply repeat the exact sentences she has heard someone else say. It is because she is using rules that she will overgeneralize on occasion, apply the rule when the example at hand is irregular and does not follow the rule. She may say, "I runned all the way home," or "That one's yours and this one's mines." As she matures she will include in her language repertoire the exceptions as well as the rule-based word formations.

How Children Become Literate

Marilyn Cochran-Smith, in *The Making of a Reader,*[1] looked at the way adults help children understand and develop the ability to read and write. The process by which children figure out how print works grows out of their experiences with adults in print-related situations. Cochran-Smith describes these literacy events as being with "contextualized print," such as street signs or labels, where much of the meaning can be derived from the context in which it occurs, and "decontextualized print," such as books, where the meaning of the language is independent of the environmental context. Children in the nursery school she observed had many opportunities to interact with print in the environment, learning in social situations where adults acted as "intermediaries" between the children and the print, performing tasks children were unable to do themselves. The children also had wide experiences with storyreading, learning how to use their own knowledge of the world to make sense of the text and illustrations in books.

Adults sharing books with toddlers can see children's growing concept of print as the child listener no longer covers the words with his or her hand, and stops turning pages rapidly when there is print but no picture. These actions show that the child knows that it is the print that is carrying the message. The child may engage in "reading-like" behavior, providing some of the text of stories he or she has heard before, or repeating a phrase immediately after it has been read. Many toddlers absorb a story so thoroughly that they can "read" the book by looking at the illustrations, often maintaining most of the story language, but at times using their own language while retaining the meaning.[2] As children begin to associate the print with the exact word, they go through a time when the number of words appearing on a page does not match the number of words they are using, particularly if they think of each syllable as a word. Knowing a story by heart allows them to go back again and again to a page, work on the problem, and teach themselves that long words have more than one syllable.

Careful observation of and conversations with young children have demonstrated to a series of researchers that children know more about writing than had once been assumed. Harste, Woodward, and Burke contend that adults often confuse product with process and thus overlook what children know. They point out that if children's writing doesn't look like adult writing, this does not mean that the children do not know about writing. If their spelling differs from standard spelling, that does not mean that the children do not know about spelling. These researchers noted that the children they observed could produce writing when asked to, and could tell what their writing said, even though it might appear to be a "scribble," to the adult observer.

> We have found that by the age of 3 all children in our study could, under certain conditions, distinguish art from writing. Their decisions in writing, as in art, are systematic and organized. We found further that all 3-year-olds had developed a marking which to them symbolized their name. This marking acted as any symbol acts, serving to placehold meaning during writing, and to reconstruct that meaning during reading.[3]

Children refine their writing over time, learning to make the letters in standard form. However, their initial understanding of what print is, and how writing functions, comes from their experiences with print and with writing in their everyday lives. Living in a literate society, they expect that reading and writing will be part of their lives.

There are two very basic ways in which adults can nurture the language learning of young children. The first is to provide rich, varied, and abundant samples of both oral and written language. The second is to give children regular opportunities to use their language.

The Need to Hear Rich Language

It is important that children hear rich samples of language, for this is the data base from which they generalize rules for how the language works. It is also their source of vocabulary items. Adults are of more help to children's language growth if they use mature syntax than if they limit their speech to what they perceive to be the child's level. In one study by Cazden[4] twelve children ages twenty-eight to thirty-eight months took part in an experimental study. One group of four served as a control group and received no special instruction. The second group of four received deliberate expansions of their speech. If a child said, "Dog run," the adult would repeat what the child had said in a full sentence, "Yes, the dog is running." In the third group the adult responded to the child's comment with a full sentence, but not one which was an expansion of the child's words. To "Dog run," the adult might say, "Yes, I think he's chasing the cat," or "Yes, but I hope he doesn't run into the street." The adult added new ideas to what the child had said. Contrary to what the researcher had expected, the third group performed better than the other two on measures of language development. This seems to indicate that adults can help children develop mature language by responding to the content of children's telegraphic speech with mature language of their own. Other researchers have reached the same conclusion, finding that adults are most effective in aiding children's language development if they respond with new information or if they encourage the child to add to his or her previous comments.[5]

Literature provides another source of mature and expressive language. Children listening to stories read aloud are being exposed to language which is often more complex than that which they hear in ordinary conversation. They hear new sentence patterns and new words. Chomsky[6] found that there was a positive correlation between the linguistic development of the children in her study and the average complexity level of the books each had encountered, the number of books each named as familiar, and the numerical score each received based on such factors as having been read to during the early years. This positive relationship between linguistic development and exposure to literature was true for prereaders who had listened to books as well as for older children who had read the books themselves. The prereaders in the high linguistic stages had heard more books each week, were read to by more people, and had heard more books at higher complexity levels than had those children at lower linguistic stages.

Hearing books read aloud increases children's competence in other areas of language as well. Cohen[7] tested the reading ability of a group of second graders at the beginning and again at the end of the school year. Some of the children were in an experimental group which heard literature every day. After hearing the stories, the children engaged in follow-up activities. The other group heard stories occasionally, but with no specific plan or follow up. The children in the experimental group showed an improvement in vocabulary, word knowledge, and reading comprehension that was significantly greater than that of the group only randomly exposed to literature.

These studies show the positive results of presenting children with examples of effective language. Note that in all of these the language was used in context. Adults responded to children in light of the situation and with regard to the children's comments. The books described experiences or thoughts as wholes, giving vocabulary and sentence patterns within the total story setting. It is essential that language be tied to experience and that it be presented in context if it is to have optimal meaning for children.

The Need to Use Language

In addition to presenting abundant samples of language, adults can nurture children's language growth by providing opportunities for them to use language. Children form hypotheses about the grammar of the language and then must test their hypotheses. This testing, by using language themselves, provides direct feedback. Children can judge whether or not they have communicated effectively. They may also refine their definitions of particular words as they gather more information about the concept named by the word. "Car" is no longer used for any four-wheeled vehicle but is narrowed down to one type of vehicle.

It seems logical that correcting children's speech would accelerate their grasp of adult language patterns. This is not the case, however. Only when children are ready to assimilate a new pattern will it have meaning for them. McNeill cites the example of a conversation between a parent and child.

Child: Nobody don't like me.
Parent: No, say "Nobody likes me."

Children judge whether they have communicated effectively by the responses they receive.

Child:	Nobody don't like me.
Parent:	No, "Nobody likes me."
Child:	Nobody don't like me. (seven more repetitions of this)
Parent:	No! Now listen carefully. Say "Nobody likes me."
Child:	Oh! Nobody don't likes me.[8]

The form the parent is attempting to teach is not within the child's current rule system; therefore, the child is not able to assimilate this new information. You, as a day care professional or teacher, will want to give children opportunities to use their language in conversations, in discussions, in spontaneous dramatics, in writing. Efforts to encourage extensive use of language will prove far more productive than attempts to "correct" children's grammar. Overcorrecting a child's grammar may result in that child's refusal to talk, the exact opposite of the desired behavior.

You will want to structure your program so that children become more skilled in speaking and listening and develop skill in reading and writing. Work in the first two areas enhances the second two. Comprehension taught through listening is an aid to comprehension in reading, as shown by Cohen's study. In addition, children who have been exposed to literature are familiar with the patterns of written language, patterns they will encounter when they begin to read themselves.

Immersion in literature, which helps children make sense of written language, also helps create a positive attitude toward learning to read. Reading becomes desirable because there are things to be learned and tales to be enjoyed in books. Children are also intrigued by the sounds of language from its poetic beauty to its light-hearted nonsense. Chukovsky[9] observed the speech of three year olds and found that they repeated pairs of rhymed words and played games with repetition and rhyme. Literature builds upon and expands this fascination with language.

A curriculum that abounds in opportunities for children to use oral language provides a foundation for their written language. Children gain experience in composing as they tell stories, give directions, or participate in sharing times. They can dictate stories individually, or work with the group to compose an experience chart, thus seeing their words transcribed into written form.

Children should also be encouraged to experiment individually with print. The child who has used scribbles symbolically, knowing how writing functions if not how letters are formed, moves into more standard writing while maintaining the view of writing as a purposeful activity. Regular writing times in the primary grades, where children know that they will write and that they will usually choose their topic themselves, lets them know that writing is a personal and effective way of communicating.

To summarize, children's language develops best in an environment where mature language is heard, where children have many opportunities to communicate with others, and where language is presented in context.

Goals for Teaching

Teaching goals for language growth can be categorized into long term developmental goals, into general goals for each grade or age level, and into specific goals for individual children. Long term goals describe behaviors or competencies which are developed over time and which are thought of as desired patterns of behavior. One long term goal for language development is that children will enjoy the creative and aesthetic use of language. They will become lifelong readers and lifelong appreciators of literature.

General goals for each grade level are often listed in curriculum guides. At other times they are developed by the teacher or day care professional as he or she plans an outline for the year's learning. A general goal for the preschool level is that children will listen attentively and follow simple directions.

Goals for specific children are even more individualized. Teachers develop them as they come to know each child. A specific goal for a second grader might be, "Roberta will read one book by herself and tell her classmates one incident from the story." The goal reflects Roberta's need, a need that may not be shared by other members of the class. Goals of this type are referred to as "objectives" in some planning schemes.

Your use of books can aid in the achievement of all three types of goals. This chapter focuses on long term developmental goals, ones that are common to the preschool and primary years. Literature offers opportunities for you to help children toward the following goals for language development:

- Children will understand and use the mature syntax of their language.
- Children will expand their vocabularies.
- Children will enjoy the creative and aesthetic use of language.
- Children will become skilled listeners.
- Children will learn to read.
- Children will communicate effectively both orally and in writing.

Opportunities Books Offer

Exposing Children to Mature Language

Children need to hear many examples of mature language if they are to develop an understanding of the more complex syntactic structures of the language and if they are to become users of those structures themselves. Read to children every day, perhaps twice each day. Encourage parents and guardians to share literature with their children at home. Become aware of the kind of language being used in a book.

Listening to Varied Syntax.   Language varies. This is one of the reasons that literature is so beguiling. Some authors present material in a direct manner, yet use more compound and complex sentences than one would hear in normal conversation. This passage is from *Miss Maggie*:

> Miss Maggie tended a garden alongside the old log house. But what with cows, dogs, and boys occasionally passing through, Miss Maggie's garden didn't grow a lot. Still, there was always a potato or two to boil. Nat would see Miss Maggie rising up from the soil, her brown, wrinkled face partly hidden by a faded blue bonnet, and he'd watch while she shuffled back to the house with an apron filled with a few vegetables that had survived.[10]

Children hearing this passage are being given data about standard word order in English, and about ways that several pieces of information can be combined into a single sentence.

Other authors may invert word order and use more poetic language. Theo Gilchrist opens *Halfway Up The Mountain* with:

> Over the green hill and across the blue river, in a shack halfway up the mountain, there lived an old man and an old woman.
>
> Though the old man was slow of movement, the old woman didn't mind. Though the old woman was almost blind, the old man didn't mind. Hand in hand they greeted the sunrise. Hand in hand they greeted the sunset.[11]

Children now are learning that changing the word order maintains the meaning but gives a different mood to a story. "Hand in hand they greeted the sunrise" gives the same information as "They greeted the sunrise hand in hand," but the tone is more gentle. Hearing patterns which occur far more frequently in writing than in speech prepares children to cope with written language when they begin reading themselves.

Enjoying Figurative Language.   Authors often use expressive language, with words chosen carefully, and with figurative language fitting naturally into the text. The girl in Joanne Ryder's *A Wet and Sandy Day* was standing on the beach in her bathing suit when it began to rain. She describes what happened:

> The warm drops trickled down my nose and chin. I had to squint to keep them out of my eyes. "I'm wrinkling up," I said, looking at my pruney fingers. But my arms and legs were wet and shiny like a big slippery fish. "I am a rainy thing now," I thought. There were a million raindrops on me. And I felt cleaner than if I'd taken a hundred baths.[12]

Listening to this story, children are exposed to the flexibility of language and to its creative possibilities. If a prune has wrinkled skin, then "pruney" could describe human skin wrinkled from having been wet over a period of time. If one feels thoroughly clean, it is as though one had "taken a hundred baths."

Children need to hear the language of books such as these three. They do not need to discuss it, for word order and writing style are topics that are too abstract to be appropriate for young children. Your task as teacher is to select books that the children will enjoy and that will, in the process, give them exposure to the mature and effective use of language.

Hearing Different Dialects.   You will find that books give you the opportunity to let children hear a variety of different dialects. Some may give a feel for the language but not follow all the rules of the specific dialect. The books about Obadiah by Brinton Turkle[13] do this by using "thee" and "thou" to help establish that the characters are Quakers.

Walter Dean Myers describes making up the tale *Mr. Monkey and the Gotcha Bird* to entertain his son on a long plane trip, and telling it in what he describes in a foreword to the book as "playful, musical language." The story of how Mr. Monkey tricks the Gotcha Bird has a rhythm and pattern that presents children with a new sound to the language. The dialect is used for both dialogue and narration. Here is a sample.

Long time ago, before you born, Monkey he live in place you don't know about. Monkey like he live there. He drink plenty cool water, eat fruit, and sit in sun.

One day Monkey he thinking how he big stuff. He walking around with nose in air. Got flower in hair. He no see Gotcha Bird come fly low near ginger plant. "Gotcha!" Gotcha Bird grab Monkey by he tail.

"Loose that tail, Gotcha Bird!" Monkey say. "I plenty danger!"

"You no danger to Gotcha Bird. You supper."[14]

Dialect may appear just in the dialogue of characters. Rebecca Caudill uses an Appalachian dialect for five-year-old Charley as he talks with Mr. Champion, the principal of Raccoon Hollow School. Charley has been wearing a large hat all day, and efforts of various teachers to get him to remove it have proved futile.

"We men don't usually wear our hats when we eat, Charley," said Mr. Champion. "Why are you wearing yours?"

Charley sat staring at his plate, saying nothing, eating nothing.

"Can you tell me why you're wearing it?" Mr. Champion asked.

Charley shook his head, no.

"Where did you get your hat, Charley?" asked Mr. Champion.

"Uncle Hawk give it to me," said Charley.

"Is your uncle at your house now?"

Charley nodded his head, yes.

"He isn't working over at the Benham mines?" asked Mr. Champion.

"He got laid off," Charley told him.

"And he's come to live with your family?"

Charley nodded his head, yes. "Till the mines open again," he said. "He's been mighty nigh everywhere looking for work. But nobody wanted a man to work."

"I see," said Mr. Champion. "And so he gave his hat to you?"
"He slung it on the bed and I picked it up and put it on my head, and Uncle Hawk said, 'I believe I'll give you that hat, boy. I reckon I won't need it anymore.' But Mr. Champion, I got to keep it on my head all day. For a special reason."[15]

In this book, the dialect of Charley and his family contrasts with that of the school employees and with the standard English used in the narrative portions of the book.

Sharing books which are written in different dialects shows children even more ways in which the English language is used. In general, the books currently available in dialects other than standard English are for children of school age. Books for threes and fours are direct and simple and are in standard English. The two books quoted would be most appropriate for second or third graders. Children of this age recognize when a dialect differs from their own, though they may not be able to tell how it differs. Let children begin early to hear various dialects and to appreciate the many ways in which English is spoken and written.

Introducing New Vocabulary in Context

Vocabulary expands as children learn new concepts and the words which denote them and as new words are presented for concepts already known. When new words are presented in context, children often can determine the meanings themselves. If they do, they are less likely to forget the word than they would be if its meaning had been explained to them in isolation. Thus, teachers of young children introduce new words as they arise in the course of ongoing activities.

Presenting New Words.   Literature presents new words to children in the context of a complete story or poem. When you call attention to a particular word, look carefully at the section where it appears to determine if the context needed is the entire story, one or two paragraphs, or just one sentence. For example, in *Summer on Cleo's Island*, several paragraphs are needed. The setting, an island off the coast of Maine, is described as Cleo, a cat, roams around exploring. Here is the text from four pages of the book:

> The dory was still there.
> Luke grabbed Cleo and tossed her into the little boat, pushed off from shore, then hopped in.
> The old fishing pole was still under the seat.
>
> Luke baited the hook and tossed the line over the side. Soon a pollack seized the bait. Luke reeled it in and dropped it into a burlap sack to take up to the house.
>
> He placed the fish between two pie tins and baked it in the oven for ten minutes. Cleo could hardly wait to eat it![16]

In this story, both "dory" and "pollack" are explained in the text that follows their initial appearance. After reading the entire story, you could return to the pages that refer to a dory. Show the illustrations, read those two pages again, and then ask the children what they think a dory is. Let them tell you what they think and also how they know. They might point to the boat in the illustration, although other objects in that illustration are prominent enough to be labeled "dory" if that were the only clue. It is important to read the story through so that the children have the full context and to reread the sections under discussion so that they are fresh in the children's memories.

When you ask children to use context to hypothesize about the meaning of a word, make certain that there is indeed context that is explanatory. At one point in *Summer on Cleo's Island* the text reads, "At slack tide she watched minnows dart out from the darkness under the bridge."[17] There is no hint from either text or illustration of what "slack tide" might be. Thus, this would not be a valid example for using context to determine word meaning. You might comment as you show the illustration, "Slack tide means the water was fairly still," and continue with the story.

There are opportunities to evaluate and to reinforce children's comprehension of words that may be new to them by asking them to tell what happened in the story or by using the phrases from the story to elicit personal responses from the children. There are five short stories in *George and Martha Back in Town*. This is the beginning of the story titled "The Book."

> George was all nice and cozy.
> "May I join you?" said Martha.
> "I'm reading," said George.
> "I'll be quiet as a mouse," said Martha.
> "Thank you," said George.
> And he went back to his book.
> But soon Martha was fidgeting.
> "Please!" said George.
> "Have some consideration!"
> "Sorry," said Martha.
> George went back to his reading.
> But in no time Martha was fidgeting again[18]

George goes home, and as he reads his book he finds that it says people may be thoughtless without knowing it. He takes the book to Martha, but as soon as he arrives she apologizes for fidgeting and says she was lonely. George says he never considered that, and he just came over because he was lonely too. The two visit and tell each other stories.

Children might be asked to tell the class about or draw pictures of times when they "fidgeted." They could also be asked to list with the teacher times when people should "have some consideration" for others. After the children have been introduced to words in one context, activities such as these help them apply those words to other contexts.

Unless you are certain that the story will be misunderstood without fully discussing the meaning of a word or phrase, wait until the book is completed before talking with children about it or give only a brief explanation and continue reading. If it is necessary to explain a number of words in order for the children to make sense of the selection, the book is probably too difficult for that group of children and should not be shared with them until they are older.

Martha disturbs George's reading with her fidgeting. (From George and Martha Back in Town *by James Marshall. Copyright © 1984 by James Marshall. Reprinted by permission of Houghton Mifflin Company.)*

Sharing Books That Emphasize Word Meanings. Most books will present the vocabulary as part of the story, as a tool needed to convey the content. There are some books, however, that work directly with vocabulary. Some are concept books, exploring the qualities of the concept as well as the word that names it. An example is *Snake In, Snake Out*[19] by Linda Banchek. The text consists of one word per page, prepositions such as "in" and "out" and "down." The illustrations show an old lady who is given a parrot, and gets a stow-away snake as well. The story line, carried by the pictures, is of her attempts to get rid of the snake. Children can look at the illustrations and tell what is happening, using the word at the bottom of the page. Because each illustration shows several instances of the concept, children could also be asked to find as many instances of the word as they could.

Other books may not fall into the classification of concept book but still present vocabulary directly. *Busy Day*[20] is one of several by Betsy and Giulio Maestro which have only one word per page, a word that applies to the picture. *Busy Day* uses all verbs, so that one sees the elephant and the man, the two protagonists of the story, each engaging in the action described by the verb. For "washing" the man is at a sink, wiping his bald head with a wet washcloth. The elephant is outside, his own pan of water on the grass, giving himself a shower by spraying water into the air with his trunk. Not only do the illustrations supply the context for the verb used with each page, but they also combine to tell the story of the man and the elephant in their jobs as circus performers.

Involving Children with New Vocabulary.   Whether you are working with vocabulary within a story or as part of a book emphasizing new words, involve children as actively as possible with the meanings of the words. You may do this by having them act out the meanings. Suppose you read "Jump or Jiggle" by Evelyn Beyer.

> Frogs jump
> Caterpillars hump
>
> Worms wiggle
> Bugs jiggle
>
> Rabbits hop
> Horses clop
>
> Snakes slide
> Sea gulls glide
>
> Mice creep
> Deer leap
>
> Puppies bounce
> Kittens pounce
>
> Lions stalk—
>
> But—
> I walk![21]

Children can listen to the poem, then on the second reading show how each animal moves. There is the fun of the movement, the enjoyment of the rhyming language, and also the learning of new words for some of the children.

You might involve them by having them tell about experiences they have had that are similar to the ones you are reading about. After reading *The Sick Day*,[22] children could describe times when they have been sick. It is a natural time for talking about words used in the book, such as "thermometer." They may also react to some of the words, such as the little girl saying that she thinks she is going to "swallow up." Is that the expression they would use? Do they think it is a good way of describing the event? You could help the children make props for the play corner so that they could dramatize their own sick days. They could show what their parents do to help them feel better, just as the little girl's father played the recorder for her and told her a story.

Reading Several Books on a Single Topic.   You can reinforce vocabulary by reading several books on the same topic. If you had shared and discussed *Baby Animals*[23] with a group of three and four year olds, you might want to read several more books about animals. *Baby Animals* has no story line, but simply gives the names of baby animals: piglets, ducklings, and the like. Following this, you might read *Whose Baby?*,[24] a book that begins with the baby animal being named, then asks whose baby it is. The book gives the answer, with clear illustrations of the baby and its parents. You might then introduce the book *The Chick and the Duckling*[25] by asking the children what kind of animals they expect to see in the book. After their guesses, this book about the chick who attempts everything the duckling does and succeeds until the duckling decides

Father tries to cheer Emily during a day when she is sick. (From The Sick Day *by Patricia MacLachlan, illustrated by William Pene Du Bois. Copyright © 1979 by William Pene Du Bois. Reprinted by permission of Pantheon Books, a division of Random House, Inc.)*

to go for a swim could be read. Your reading of the story would reinforce the terms, and you might choose to have the children join in the "Me too" refrain of the book or in some other oral activity, rather than once again asking about "chick" and "duckling."

Encouraging Language Play and Demonstrating How Others Have Used Language Creatively

If you listen to young children as they play, you will find that they seem to have a natural enjoyment of language. They repeat nonsense words just for the fun of listening to the sounds; they use jump rope rhymes and other chants in their games; they tell riddles. Literature that exudes this same delight in language appeals to them, and often their favorite books are those that capitalize on the sound of language.

Playing with Language.   Using literature which demonstrates how others have played with language has several benefits for children. First, of course, they enjoy it and thus develop positive attitudes toward literature. It sets the stage for continued enjoyment of poetry, with its reliance on the rhythm, rhyme, and the patterns in language. It shows them that the tone and feeling of a word contribute to its meaning, that words connote as well as denote. It stimulates them to reflect upon the language itself, not just the message being conveyed. Linguists refer to this ability to attend to the forms of language as "meta-linguistic awareness," and suggest that it may be critically important in both reading and writing.[26]

Language play takes on a variety of forms. Some center on the sound of the language, some on the patterns within the language, some on the appearance of written language, some on the meanings of words or phrases. Blatt has looked at how children's books can stimulate word play and has concluded that teachers should follow up on the use of creative language in books. She writes that "The best possible follow-up is an activity in which the class plays with the words themselves."[27]

One nursery school teacher suggested to her group of three and four year olds that they make their own goodnight poem after listening to *Goodnight Moon*. The children followed the book's short couplet format naturally. Here is their poem:

> Goodnight toys,
> Goodnight boys,
> Goodnight book,
> And goodnight hook.
> Goodnight fire,
> And goodnight tire.
> Goodnight flowers,
> And goodnight powers.
> Goodnight rocks,
> And goodnight box.
> Goodnight cradle,
> Goodnight dreydl.
> Goodnight dolls,
> And goodnight balls.
> Goodnight berries,
> Goodnight cherries.
> Goodnight koala bear,
> Goodnight little chair.
> Goodnight Daddy,
> Goodnight Matty.
> Goodnight Mummy,
> Goodnight tummy.
> Goodnight bee,
> Goodnight flea.
> Goodnight everything,
> And goodnight me.[28]

The children explained as they dictated that the "powers" in line eight were space heroes. They also changed the position of the last two lines from the middle to the end after hearing their poem reread.

Playing with the Sounds of Language.   Playing with the sounds of language may take many forms, but those appearing most frequently in books for children are the use of rhythm, of rhyme, of alliteration, and of onomatopoeia. Preschoolers respond to the toe-tapping rhythm and rhyme of *Chicken Soup With Rice*.[29] By the time the narrator has told of the joys of chicken soup in each month of the year, the listener is ready to join in extolling its virtues.

A contrasting rhythm in "Close Your Eyes" has its own appeal, the softness of a lullaby:

> . . . Close your eyes and you can play
> With wooly lambs on a lazy day.
> Or tabby cats in a pile of hay.
> Close your eyes and you can lie
> Hidden deep in a field of rye
> Or on a cloud in a sunset sky. . . .[30]

This book sets a quiet mood if only the text is shared. Children looking at the illustrations will see another story taking place as the words of the song appear. A father is attempting to put his son to bed. Pictured are both the events described by the words and the interaction between the boy and his father. There is a congruence between the two, as when the father is rubbing his son dry with a fluffy towel/sheep skin and helping him into flannel pajamas as the text talks about wooly lambs. For one reading, children might listen to the words and create their own mental pictures to accompany them. At a second reading, they might look at the illustrations to see the story within the story.

Some authors write narratives in rhyme. Their work may be lighthearted and humorous or of a serious and thoughtful mood. If you are working with children in the preschool and kindergarten years, look for the books of Rosemary Wells, Ludwig Bemelmans, Margaret Wise Brown, and Janina Domanska. If you are working with primary grade children, look for the work of Jack Prelutsky, Virginia Kahl, Theodor Geisel (Dr. Seuss), Lucille Clifton, Byrd Baylor, and Aileen Fisher. These will give you a standard of good writing by which you can measure other poetic narratives for children.

Look also at the work of poets Clyde Watson, David McCord, and Eve Merriam. All three have poems that play with the language in various ways. You will need to select poems from their collections that are appropriate for the age of your students.

Alliteration is a technique of writing in which initial consonant sounds are repeated at close intervals. The poem "Godfrey Gordon Gustavus Gore"[31] is popular with children partly because they enjoy hearing and attempting to say the little boy's name. Tongue twisters are based on alliteration. They intrigue children all through the preschool and primary years. Read some of the selections from *A Twister of Twists, a Tangler of Tongues*[32] aloud. After reading several to the children, ask them to make up their own. Kindergarteners can work as a group, dictating their twisters for the teacher to write down. Primary children can work individually, asking the teacher for help in spelling the words as they need it. All can try saying the tongue twisters, then repeating them as fast as they can.

They might also illustrate their twister. Nicola Bayley in *One Old Oxford Ox*[33] uses the pattern of the counting book, but develops the illustrations for each numeral based on a text filled with alliteration. The Old Oxford Ox of the title is sitting under a tree opening oysters. On the next page are two toads who are trying to trot to Tisbury. One group of third graders made their own counting book, with each child responsible for providing the tongue twister and the illustration for one numeral. Their book went to twenty-two. The class favorite was the illustration which accompanied "Fifteen frisbees flying forward" and which showed members of the class engaged in a frisbee-throwing contest.

Preschoolers enjoy the slapstick action and the word play in *Thump and Plunk,*[34] a tale of a brother and sister pair of mice and their two dolls, named Thumpit and Plunkit, who manage to "thump" and "plunk" their way through an entire story. The repetition of sounds delights the young listener.

Onomatopoeia, the use of words whose sound suggests their meaning, is another element of writing popular with children. David McCord's poem "The Pickety Fence"[35] is built on using words so that they make the sound and the rhythm of a stick being run along a picket fence. When Drummer Hoff[36] finally fires the cannon, it goes off with a resounding "KAHBAHBLOOM." In *Umbrella,* Moma listens to the sound of the raindrops on her umbrella.

> Bon polo
> bon polo
> ponpolo ponpolo
> ponpolo ponpolo
> bolo bolo ponpolo
> bolo bolo ponpolo
> boto boto ponpolo
> boto boto
> ponpolo[37]

Children hear how others have used language to describe sounds. They can listen to sounds on the playground, or in the boiler room, or in their own classroom. What word could they make up for each sound? Try having children listen to machines in their homes or in the neighborhood, then make their own words for those sounds. What sound does a vacuum cleaner make? A washing machine? A hair dryer?

As children play with the sounds of the language, they can appreciate when a book character has trouble with those sounds. *The Surprise Party*[38] by Pat Hutchins opens with Rabbit whispering to Owl that he is having a party. Owl repeats the news to Squirrel, explaining that Rabbit is going to be hoeing the parsley. Squirrel repeats it as Rabbit going to sea, and the message continues to be garbled as it passes from animal to animal. The game of Telephone, where each child whispers a message to the next person, saying it only once, would be a natural follow-up to this book.

Playing with the Patterns of Language.   Authors may play with the pattern of language as well as with the sound. *The Little Engine That Could*[39] has remained a favorite with children for over fifty years. Some of its popularity may be attributed to the story itself, that of getting the toys to the children on the other side of the mountain, but equally important is the author's use of onomatopoeia in the sounds of the engine, and the patterning of the language. The engine's pep talk to herself, where she keeps repeating "I think I can," sounds like the rotation of the train wheels, getting faster and faster as she picks up speed. The pattern is established on the way up the mountain and continues after she has made it to the top and started down. The refrain is then "I thought I could."

The use of refrains invites children to join with the teacher as the story is being read. The little old man and little old woman in *Millions of Cats,* who must contend with:

> Hundreds of cats,
> Thousands of cats,
> Millions and billions and trillions of cats[40]

in order to find one cat to be their own, are remembered both for their plight and for the language that tells about it.

Cumulative tales have a patterning of language that is part of the story. As each new event, or each new character, is added, all the earlier ones are repeated. *I Know an Old Lady*[41] can be read or sung and intrigues children as the old lady, who first swallowed a fly, keeps swallowing larger and larger animals in order to catch the animal before. All the while, the spider, which she swallowed to catch the fly, just keeps wriggling and wriggling and tickling inside her.

The patterning may be one of positive and negative, or real and imaginative, or other opposites. In *Fortunately*, first something good happens, fortunately, and then something bad, unfortunately. Children in the primary grades generally see the pattern after about four or five pages and are then thoroughly captivated by the humor. In the story. Ned had been invited to a surprise party, but needed to get from New York to Florida.

> Fortunately, a friend lent him an airplane.
> Unfortunately, the motor exploded.
> Fortunately, there was a parachute in the airplane.
> Unfortunately, there was a hole in the parachute.[42]

Ask the children what they notice about the pages to see if they recognize the use of color on the "fortunately" pages and black and white on the "unfortunate-ly" pages. Let them do short sequences themselves, perhaps giving them the opening statement. This is the sort of composing which could be made into a roll story, where each phrase and a picture illustrating it is drawn on a roll of shelf paper, so that the story unwinds as the paper unwinds.

Playing with the Appearance of Language.   Authors can play visual games with language. Rebus writing is one such game. It is a combination of words and pictures, in sentence form. To read it, one must name the object in the order in which it appears and read the words or parts of words attached to it. *Bunny Rabbit Rebus*[43] is an extended story that uses eighty-five picture sym-bols to tell about hungry Little Rabbit and the things he and his mother do to get more carrots and lettuce. It is for the beginning reader, although it could be used by prereaders working with an adult. *From A to Z: the Collected Letters of Irene and Hallie Coletta*[44] is an alphabet of rebus rhymes. It might best be presented to several children at once, who could work together to decipher the poems. This book is appropriate only for children who are reading and who have a grasp of phonic skills. They must work out such combinations of syllable and picture as *no* plus a picture of a bull to get *noble* and a picture of a slipper plus *y* for *slippery*. Context clues play a part in successfully reading the poems, for some pictures could have several different names, *steps* or *stairs*, for instance. Children who enjoy it could make puzzles of rebus writing to be solved by their classmates.

Another visual game with language is to print the word in a way that signifies its meaning. Karla Kuskin in *Roar and More*[45] shows how the sounds that various animals make look. After a poem about fish talk looking like bubbles, the illustration shows circles of several sizes and shapes going to the top of the page, as though rising to the surface. The sound of the snake is a series of S's going along the bottom of the page and gradually diminishing in size. Children need to see the illustrations closely to appreciate them.

Playing with the Meanings of Language.   One last broad area of language play is based on the meaning of words. This includes puns, riddles, nonsense words that seem to take on meaning, idioms, and figurative language. The books about Amelia Bedelia take a look at the literal interpretation of idioms. Amelia is a maid who believes in interpreting language literally. In the first of the series, *Amelia Bedelia*[46], she does what Mrs. Rogers has told her to in a list of instructions. When the list says to dust the furniture, she sprinkles dusting powder all over the sofas and tables. When it says to change the towels, she does so by cutting them into a different shape. Amelia is not totally unknowing, however. When Mrs. Rogers returns to find all of the mistakes and is about to fire Amelia, she gets a taste of the lemon-meringue pie which Amelia has baked even without instructions to do so. The job is saved, and Mrs. Rogers learns to say things such as "undust" the furniture. Children delight in Amelia's interpretation of idioms they understand and often can think of examples themselves.

A similar approach is used by Fred Gwynn in *A Chocolate Moose for Dinner.*[47] A little girl repeats some of the things her parents have said, with her interpretation of the meaning shown by the illustrations. Some are idioms, such as her father playing the piano by ear. He is shown banging away on the keys with—yes—his ear. Others are plays on homophones, such as the title picture which shows a brown moose sitting at the table with a napkin tied carefully around its neck. This is the "chocolate moose" they had for dinner. The spellings given are for the words as interpreted by the girl. If the book is to be enjoyed by children, they must understand the correct meaning for the phrases. Seeing men in seashells rowing with oars is not funny unless they know what is really meant by "rowing in shells." Thus, this book and ones like it are most appropriate for second and third graders and for even older children.

Preschoolers and kindergarteners enjoy Naomi Bossom's *A Scale Full of Fish and Other Turnabouts.*[48] The book is a collection of turnabouts with language, illustrated with woodcuts. The examples face each other. On one page is "race for a train," with passengers hurrying along, and opposite it is "train for a race,"

Amelia interprets language literally as she follows directions to put the lights out. (Illustration by Fritz Siebel from Amelia Bedelia *by Peggy Parish. Pictures copyright © 1963 by Fritz Siebel. By permission of Harper & Row, Publishers, Inc.)*

with three runners. Once children catch on to the pattern, they can be shown the first illustration and asked to guess what the second one will be.

Children of all ages delight in riddles. There is a vast supply of books with riddles available. Select one or two, let children guess the answers, then let them tell what they think makes a good riddle. They can make up one of their own to try on their classmates. Having them tell you several riddles themselves will give you some insight on how complex the riddles should be in books you select for them. Here are riddles several children offered when asked simply, "Can you tell me a riddle?" You may remember some of these from your own childhood.

Three year old: Why did the bunny cross the road?
                  To get to the other side.
Four year old: What has two eyes and a sheet over it?
                  A ghost.
Four year old: Knock, knock.
                  Who's there?
                  Lettuce

Lettuce who?

Lettuce in, it's cold out here.

Six year old: What is black and white, black and white, black and white and green?

Two skunks fighting over a pickle.

Six year old: What time is it when an elephant sits on a fence?

Time to get a new fence.

Eight year old: What can jump higher than a house?

Anything—houses can't jump.

Eight year old: What is a vampire's favorite holiday?

Fangsgiving.

Understanding Figurative Language.   Riddles are similar to figurative language in that new meanings are often attached to words, and differences and similarities are emphasized. Young children sometimes have difficulty understanding the figurative language that others use even though they may use metaphors that seem very inventive themselves. To see the similarity between a psychological state and a physical entity, as in phrases such as "heart of stone," requires a high level of abstract thinking.[49] Fisher and Natarella, in their study of primary children's poetry preferences, found that none of the children's favorite poems contained metaphors, while the least preferred poems were heavily dependent on metaphorical language. They conclude that it may be because the children did not understand the poems with metaphors, or because the poems with metaphors tended to be descriptive rather than narrative.[50] They note, however, that every poem in the study was given the top rating by some pupils.

It would seem that figurative language can best be presented in a context that provides other clues to the meaning and should not be singled out for "study." If children are to hear the full range of language, they must be exposed to the use of metaphor. It is central to much literature, both poetry and prose, and effective use of metaphor gives the reader new insight into ideas being expressed as well as new ways of looking. Yet it is illogical to stress the discussion of topics that do not appear to be compatible with the developmental level of young children. The inclusion of well-written stories in a literature curriculum will ensure that children hear metaphorical language. Children hearing Lyle's reaction to a birthday party for Joshua will be identifying with his feelings and will at the same time be hearing figurative language such as, "Suddenly, like storm clouds coming down upon a lovely day, Lyle was jealous. . . ."[51]

Enjoying Mother Goose Rhymes.   For encouraging language play, the key source of material for young children is Mother Goose. The verses are catchy and often humorous and certainly display the range of kinds of play with language. For those children who have heard the rhymes at home, hearing you read them provides a link between home and school that fosters a feeling of security. For the increasing number of children who are not read to at home and are not familiar with Mother Goose, it brings to them a part of their literary heritage which nearly all enjoy. Here is just a quick sampling of the kinds of language that appears in Mother Goose.

Rhythm and rhyme—

> Tom, Tom, the piper's son,
> Stole a pig, and away he run.
> The pig was eat, and Tom was beat,
> And Tom went roaring down the street.

> Pease-porridge hot,
> Pease-porridge cold,
> Pease-porridge in the pot,
> Nine days old.
> Some like it hot,
> Some like it cold,
> Some like it in the pot,
> Nine days old.

Alliteration—

> Peter Piper picked a peck of pickled peppers,
> A peck of pickled peppers Peter Piper picked;
> If Peter Piper picked a peck of pickled peppers,
> Where's the peck of pickled peppers Peter Piper picked?

Onomatopoeia—

> This is the way the ladies ride,
> Tri, tre, tre, tree,
> Tri, tre, tre, tree;
> This is the way the ladies ride,
> Tri, tre, tre, tre, tri-tre-tre-tree!

> This is the way the gentlemen ride,
> Gallop-a-trot,
> Gallop-a-trot;
> This is the way the gentlemen ride,
> Gallop-a-gallop-a trot!

> This is the way the farmers ride,
> Hobbledy-hoy,
> Hobbledy-hoy;
> This is the way the farmers ride,
> Hobbledy hobbledy-hoy!

Patterning of language—

> There was a crooked man, and he went a crooked mile,
> He found a crooked sixpence against a crooked stile;
> He bought a crooked cat, which caught a crooked mouse,
> And they all lived together in a little crooked house.

Nonsense—

> Hey diddle diddle,
> The cat and the fiddle,
> The cow jumped over the moon;
> The little dog laughed
> To see such sport,
> And the dish ran away with the spoon.

Riddles—

> Humpty Dumpty sat on a wall;
> Humpty Dumpty had a great fall.
> All the king's horses and all the king's men
> Couldn't put Humpty Dumpty together again.

> "A Candle"
>
> Little Nanny Etticoat
> In a white petticoat,
> And a red nose;
> The longer she stands
> The shorter she grows.

Look through collections of Mother Goose yourself. Plan to read the verses to children on a regular basis. Look also for ways that children can be involved with the rhymes. Which ones lend themselves to dramatization? Which have games that accompany them? Which could children clap to, sway to, move to? Which ones have refrains that could be repeated? Which can be sung? Look for and build upon the strengths of these rhymes, which have enthralled children for generations.

Giving Children Practice in Attentive, Critical, and Appreciative Listening Skills

Educators use a variety of terms to describe and categorize types of listening skills. One such system classifies listening as marginal, attentive, critical, or appreciative. The sort of listening that occurs when one is not really paying attention, but does respond if his or her name is called or if a sound such as a siren intrudes, is often termed *marginal* or *passive* listening. Sharing literature with children is seldom concerned with this type of listening.

Building Attentive Listening Skills.   Attentive listening occurs when the listener can tell the literal meaning of what is heard, can recall sequence, can follow directions. It requires that the listener attend to what is being presented and understand the meaning directly conveyed by the words. One way in which literature can build skill in attentive listening is for the teacher to involve the children with the story during the reading. This can be done by having children repeat refrains in cumulative stories. They must listen to the story and be ready when it is time to say "Hundreds of cats, millions of cats . . . " or "I think I can."

Children can be given special parts in the telling of a story so that they must listen for their time to participate. You could read a story such as *Good-Night, Owl!*[52] in which owl is trying to sleep, but all the other animals are alert and noisy. The pattern of the book is such that as each animal is named, the sound it makes follows. Thus, the bees buzz, "buzz buzz," and jays scream, "ark ark." Read it through once so that the children see the pattern. Then have two or three children take the part of each animal. When you read that the bees buzzed, the two or three will respond "buzz buzz." The story reading becomes a joint project in which the children are providing the sound effects. There is the possibility of expanding upon this, perhaps having all the children make the sounds together to hear what owl heard as he tried to sleep. Many teachers find it useful to have a hand signal that the children recognize when sound effects or musical instruments are being used. For example, teach the children that when you lift your hand in the air, the sound is to begin, and when you lower it to the top of the book, the sound is to end. The higher your hand, the louder the sound; the lower your hand, the softer the sound. This allows you to orchestrate the effects and lets you and the children work together rather than your having to stop their continued buzzing and arking in a voice that rings of reprimand.

A second technique for helping children become attentive listeners is to give them a specific purpose for listening. Most people listen more carefully when they need to know the information being given. Before reading an informational book, ask children to listen for the answer to specific questions, or to listen for one new bit of information. Second and third graders can dictate to the teacher what they already know about the topic, or what they would like to find out. This helps focus their listening. Sometimes teachers will give each child a different question to answer. Sometimes they will ask children to raise their hands when they hear a specific piece of information. All of these set a purpose for listening.

Building Critical Listening Skills.   The kinds of questions you ask about a book direct the kind of listening children are likely to do. If you ask only questions which require direct recall, then children are going to form the habit of listening for detail only. To encourage critical listening, you will need to develop a pattern of asking questions and providing activities which go beyond memory. Critical listening, sometimes called analytical listening, is that in which the listener goes beyond the data as stated directly. The facts are interpreted, generalizations and inferences are made, the material is evaluated. The listener engages in critical thinking about what has been heard.

Responding to *Good-Night Owl!* with the sounds is an activity which promotes attentive listening. If, following the reading, you were to ask, "What did the woodpecker do?" or "What did owl want to do?" you would be reinforcing habits of attentive listening. To encourage critical listening, you would need to plan activities and questions that require thinking that goes beyond the memory level. You might ask questions such as "Do you think the other animals will behave any differently toward owl in the future?" "Why or why not?" or "How do you think owl felt about the other animals? What makes you think this?"

You could have children draw a picture showing one solution to owl's problem of not being able to get his daytime sleep.

In general, memory type questions and activities do not lead children to explore the more important aspects of literature. Thus, you will want to go beyond this level and engage children in critical listening and thinking. Chapter five has a more detailed discussion of questioning and of types of activities that encourage children to interpret, compare, and evaluate literature.

Building Appreciative Listening Skills. The fourth type of listening, appreciative, is that listening that leads to aesthetic enjoyment. This is the sort of listening one engages in when hearing a symphony—or a rock concert—, when hearing poetry, when enjoying the humor in a story. You can encourage appreciative listening by showing that you value it. This means that you listen to a poet read several of her poems on a record as the children listen, and do not succumb to the temptation to fill out the attendance card while the children are listening.

You can encourage the children to make mental images as they listen. How did they picture the dog in the poem? Did they imagine themselves when they had an ice-cream cone melt in their hand? They might later transfer some of their mental images to paper.

For all types of listening, you can help children develop skill by occasionally rereading a story after a discussion. Children can check their own impressions as they hear once again what the author said.

Creating a Foundation for Reading

The best foundation for reading is no doubt the desire to read. Literature shared orally helps instill this desire, for children learn that books give interesting information and contain good stories and poems. In addition, those who have listened to a variety of stories have been introduced to many new words and sentence patterns that they will encounter when they read themselves.

Observing the Reading Process. The oral sharing of literature can be structured in such a way that it helps children understand the process of reading. Simply from watching the adult look at the page, turn the pages, and "tell" a story from it, children begin to realize that the print on the page carries a message. When they hear the same story several times, they learn that somehow the book keeps the story constant. If they watch the print as the adult reads, they begin to associate certain segments of print with segments of speech. At first, this may be the entire sentence or phrase, and later separate words, and eventually the correspondance between letters and sounds.

To help children gain these understandings it is essential that you provide ways for children to hear a story more than once. This may be by your reading it to a group when many of them request it, but more often it should be a rereading for the individual who requests it. Have parents who are willing to help or classroom aides set up an area for reading, an area where a child can come to have his or her special book read again and again. It is through this repetition that children can begin to generalize about print and speech. The adult can point to words as they are read, can reinforce the left to right pro-

Children learn about the reading process from watching and hearing an adult read.

gression that you have demonstrated in your reading to the entire class, can let the child read any words that he or she knows, can let the child turn the page, can talk about ideas or words with the child.

Some teachers invite fifth and sixth graders to their kindergarten and primary classes to read to individual children. This can be a valuable experience for the older as well as the younger child. Older ones have a chance to improve their own oral reading skills, for there is a reason to do so, and they get feedback on how well they are doing. Younger ones get attention and individual help with reading. It may be necessary, however, for you to provide some instruction on oral reading for both older children and parents and aides. Lamme,[53] after video-taping and analyzing the oral reading of a group of teachers and aides, concluded that reading aloud well requires training, and that simply watching someone else read, even if that person is a perfect model, appears to have little transfer value. She was using criteria for oral reading that included involving children in the story through discussion and pointing out words and phrases.

Set up a listening center where children can listen to tapes or records of stories and poems. Have the books there also so that children can follow the story as they hear it, seeing the illustrations and the print as well. Several companies, including Weston Woods, Spoken Arts, Miller-Brody, and Scholastic, sell media packages that include a copy of the book and a tape or record of the text. For those who are not yet reading or are just beginning, a bell or beep on the sound track that indicates that a page is to be turned helps children follow accurately. If you are making the tape yourself, consider using a sound to tell children to turn the page, or simply say "Turn the page." A listening center can be a regular option for children as they make work choices or as you assign tasks to children.

Sharing Familiar Texts in Writing.   Let children see in writing rhymes, chants, or poems which they know. If they can repeat "Mary Had a Little Lamb," make a wall chart of that rhyme and point to the words as they say or "read" it. You could mimeograph copies of the rhyme and let them create the illustration. If you did this for several rhymes, they could make a booklet. Your regular sharing of Mother Goose should ensure that the children will have a repertoire of rhymes, even those children who did not know any when they first came to preschool or school. Select and display for the children's perusal several books of Mother Goose rhymes which have only one rhyme per page and which have illustrations which will help children identify the rhyme, editions such as *Brian Wildsmith's Mother Goose*[54] and *The Baby's Lap Book.*[55]

All of these procedures are designed to help children move into reading naturally by letting them observe for themselves the uses of written language. Emans writes that:

> The process for children learning written language may be similar to the process for learning oral language. Thus children may be able to learn to read naturally when enough repeated examples of written language are presented so children are able to extract necessary generalizations for themselves.[56]

Give children opportunities to read words they see regularly in their environment. Three books by Tana Hoban, *I Walk and Read,*[57] *I Read Signs,*[58] and *I Read Symbols,*[59] have clear and colorful photographs of common signs or symbols. There is no text. Children will readily recognize and read such words as "stop," "exit," and "Don't walk." Because the books show photographs, children see the print exactly as it appears, which helps in recognition and demonstrates that there are many different styles of print.

Encouraging Children to Respond to Books Orally

Activities frequently involve more than one aspect of language development, even though only one may be emphasized. While some children are speaking, others are listening. Children compose as they dictate stories, then read as they go over their own words that the teacher has transcribed. Oral activities for children can help both the speakers and the listeners: speakers to become more fluent and more lucid, listeners to become more attentive and analytical. For example, a child opens a picture book and describes one of the illustrations without showing it to other members of the class. Another child then is given the closed book and asked to find the illustration just described. The speaker needs to be detailed in describing the illustration; the listener needs to be attentive so that the description can be compared with each picture until a match is found. Most oral activities either naturally involve listening activities or can be structured so that they do. The discussion that follows will focus on the oral, but there is a listening component as well.

Dramatizing a Story.   Literature offers many opportunities for creative dramatics, both interpreting and improvising. Children interpret a story when they dramatize it following the plot closely; they are improvising when they create their own plot. A story which has long been a favorite with young children is *Caps for Sale.*[60] In this story a peddler who sells caps walks along with his merchandise stacked on his head. After a morning of calling out "Caps for Sale," and having made no sales, he walks out into the country and sits beneath a tree to take a nap, still carefully balancing the caps. When he awakens, he finds only his own hat on his head and looking up discovers that the tree is filled with monkeys, and on the head of each monkey is one of his caps. He shakes his finger at them and demands that they return his caps. They shake their fingers at him. With each action emphasizing his pleas to return his caps, the monkeys only mimic him. In disgust he throws his hat on the ground—and all the monkeys follow suit. Picking up his caps, the peddler returns to the village to try once again to sell his wares.

This story can be dramatized in several ways. One approach is to narrate the story and have the children do the actions, with one portraying the peddler and the rest being monkeys. This would be a beginning for children who have had no experience with drama. Your telling of the story frees them to respond with actions.

Another approach would be for you to narrate parts of the story, but have the children speak the dialogue. You would tell about the peddler, then the "peddler" would call out his pitch of caps for sale. As you prepare for this, children could take turns saying the peddler's words and trying to make their voices sound the way they thought his might have. They do not memorize lines, but rather say what fits with the progression of the story. The monkeys could work to make their voices reflect a teasing mood.

You might have the children dramatize the story providing all of the dialogue themselves and adding words or phrases that would help move the story along. The peddler, for instance, might mutter to himself about feeling hungry or make some exclamation upon discovering that his hats were gone. The monkeys could talk among themselves as they picked up the hats from the head of the sleeping peddler.

For any of these three approaches, you could use simple props, such as hats for the peddler, or you could have children pantomime. You would not want to get involved in the extensive use of props, which is more appropriate to a production than to a classroom story interpretation.

Role Playing and Improvising.   Literature can provide a stimulus for drama that does not follow the content of the story, but builds upon themes, or characters, or ideas within it. Role play and improvisation both fit into this category. In role play, the child takes on the role of one of the characters and then reacts to a new situation as he or she thinks the character would. A child role playing the peddler might be told that it is the next day and the peddler is once more at the tree where he had rested previously. He must decide what to do. Will he take off the caps to protect them? Will he keep going? The monkeys also must decide what to do. Will they follow the peddler? Will they grab for the caps even if the peddler does not go to sleep?

Role play involves being able to understand the viewpoint of another and for this reason is more appropriate for children who are in the primary grades than for three and four year olds. Often children will be themselves in the situation, giving their own reactions and not those that they think the character might have. Even so, role play encourages children to listen to others and to express ideas clearly in speech.

Improvisation builds an entirely new story, but may use the characters from literature, or may use a problem from literature as its source. Using an idea from *Caps for Sale*, children could be asked to pretend that they are in the painting area, then go out for recess or stop for snack time. When they go back to finish their painting, the paints and paper are gone. The improvisation begins at the point where they go back to the painting area. They discover their paints missing and must decide what to do. When the improvisation is completed, children talk about what happened and how they felt. They often repeat role plays or improvisations, exploring different actions and solutions to problems.

Using Masks and Puppets.   Children who are somewhat reticent to speak sometimes are more verbal if they use a mask or puppets in the interpretation of literature. It becomes less them and more the character who is speaking. Masks can be made by the children to represent characters and are held in front of the face as they speak. Some have a space cut out for the child's face, some just for the eyes. Puppets too can be constructed from various objects which are then attached to a stick or dowel of some kind and manipulated by moving the rod. Paper plates, pictures cut from magazines and mounted on heavy cardboard, figures drawn on heavy paper, and paper cups are all commonly used as puppet heads or bodies. The important thing to remember in helping children make puppets is that the youngsters should be able to manipulate them easily. The children can then concentrate on the action and dialogue of the puppet and the interaction among the characters. If you are interested in more information about mask and puppet construction, check the list of professional references at the end of this chapter for recommended reading on the topic.

Talking About and Telling Stories.   In addition to leading to dramatization, books can also lead to other oral activities. Children can tell parts of stories they liked to classmates, with a period in which they can be asked questions. They can tape-record their opinions of particular books, with the tapes put in the book area for other children to hear. These same tapes can be played for the speakers to hear, not to evaluate, but to know how they sound. They can retell a story using the flannelboard. They can engage in teacher lead discussion. They can explain art activities based on books as they share these products.

Wordless picture books offer many opportunities for children to tell a story. First graders looking at *Pancakes for Breakfast*[61] can add the text by looking at the pictures, giving a sentence or two for each illustration. They would describe the woman who awoke thinking of pancakes, got out her recipe book, began gathering the ingredients for the pancakes, and after collecting eggs from the hen house and milking the cow, still needed maple syrup. They would describe how she returned home with the syrup to discover that her cat and dog had knocked over the batter and ruined her breakfast plans. And finally, they would end by telling how she smelled pancakes from the house next door, went over, and ate her neighbors' breakfast.

They might tell the story by passing the book around a group of four children, each telling about a page when it was his or her turn. One child might tell the

story, making a tape-recording of it, and seeing if other children could understand the book from the tape alone. They might tell the story as if they were
the old woman, beginning with "When I woke up . . ." instead of narrating it
in third person. As you listen to the descriptions children give, you will learn
about their understanding of the story itself and gain some insight into their
language development.

As you preview books and poems, look for ones that lend themselves to choral
speaking. Books with refrains, such as *Millions of Cats*,[62] or with sounds, such
as *Good-Night, Owl!*[63] invite class participation. Short poems can be spoken
in unison or divided so that groups within the class say different lines. All might
recite "Jack Be Nimble" as they act out the rhyme, and jump over an imaginary
candlestick. "Jack Sprat" is divided easily into one line, the first, to be said
by one group—"Jack Sprat" could eat no fat;" then a second for a second
group—"His wife could eat no lean;" and the last two for the entire group—
"And so between them, they licked the platter clean."

Finally, give children the opportunity to talk with one another as they work
on projects that are book related. This informal conversation provides language
practice in a natural situation and gives many children the opportunity to speak
if they are working in pairs or small groups. Their turn to talk comes often,
and they are actively engaged in listening.

If two or three children work on the same project, then their conversation
can be focused, and they must use group interaction skills as well. A book such
as *If the Dinosaurs Came Back*[64] stimulates discussion by posing a problem.
What might change if the dinosaurs did come back? In groups of threes, children
can create murals showing what they envision happening. They would need
to present their ideas to one another and to plan where each result would be
pictured in the mural. When completed, the murals would be shared with other
groups.

Engaging Children in a Variety of Writing Activities

To discuss writing activities, it is necessary to remember that there is often a
gradual transition from the child dictating the material to someone else to the
child writing the material himself or herself. The ideas presented in this section could be utilized by having children compose orally and having an adult
or older child record, by having the children do the actual writing, or by any
of the various intermediate steps in which adult and child work together to get
ideas on paper. The needs and abilities of the children will determine which
approach is used.

Sometimes books seem to lead directly into writing activities. *Would You
Rather. . .*[65] by John Burningham presents a series of choices. Would you
rather get to help a witch make a stew, an imp be naughty, gnomes look for
treasure, or Santa Claus deliver presents? Would you rather live with your dog
in a kennel, gerbils in a cage, or a rabbit in a hutch? Children can answer one
of the questions, giving their choices and the reasons for them in writing. They
might try making up similar questions of their own and asking their classmates
to make choices.

The Mysteries of Harris Burdick[66] by Chris Van Allsburg contains illustrations,
each accompanied by a title and one sentence. The premise of the book is that

one Harris Burdick had come to a children's publisher with the pictures, promising to return the next day with the stories if the publisher were interested. The publisher was, but Burdick never returned. Thus the drawings remained, and one can only imagine the stories they were meant to illustrate. And that is the fascination of the book—what is the story for each picture? Children can select an illustration that interests them and create the story. Perhaps they will complete the story for "Under the Rug," deciding just what it is that is creating the bump between the carpet and floor. Or they might decide what the little girl will do with the two caterpillars that she knows she should "send back," and who are spelling "good-bye" in her hand. Some of the illustrations are fairly sophisticated, but primary grade children will be able to select those with meaning for them.

At times both the content of a book and its form will suggest writing activities. *Patchwork Tales*[67] is about a little girl who listens to her grandmother tell "patchwork quilt stories" at bedtime. Each piece of cloth in the quilt has a history, whose it was and where it came from. Children could find out about

The two caterpillars wiggle to spell "good-bye" in the little girl's hand. (From The Mysteries of Harris Burdick *by Chris Van Allsburg, Copyright © 1984 by Chris Van Allsburg.)*

objects within their own homes, asking parents or grandparents to share origins or special memories, then writing what they've learned. They might decide to make up stories about things within their homes, the center, or classroom, and put these together as their own "quilt" of stories. The book suggests that there are interesting things to find out and to tell about belongings. *Yuck!*[68] is told in cartoon format, with characters' dialogue appearing above them in "balloons." This is a format many children know from looking at comics in newspapers, and is one that they can handle to tell stories in a combination of art and writing. The story itself has appeal for the terrible sounding—and smelling—potions that the witches Emma and Lavinia brew, and for the poetic justice as the little witch Emma outwits these two after they have refused to let her help. The book encourages children to play with language, perhaps making their own recipes for potions, as well as exploring storywriting in cartoon format.

Building Ideas from Types of Writing.   At other times, it may be helpful to use a category system as a stimulus to finding writing activities that will extend children's responses to literature. One such category system is the type of writing: narrative, expository, persuasive, or descriptive. Narrative writing tells a story and has a plot. Children can listen to the first part of a story and then write an ending for it. They could listen to the actual ending first, then write a new one. They could use a character from a book, Curious George for instance, and tell about a new adventure he has. They might look at the structure of a specific kind of narrative, such as a folk tale with wise and foolish beasts, and write a story in that mode.

Expository writing explains how something is done. Children who have heard how the characters in a book spend their holidays might then write how their own family decides where to go on vacation. They might try writing their own recipe for stone soup after hearing how the soldiers in the book of that title made soup with the help of the villagers.

Persuasive writing is designed to influence people, to be convincing. Children can write commercials for their favorite books, using language that highlights all the good points of the book and makes it sound appealing to others. They might write a letter in defense of a book character.

Descriptive writing portrays a character or a situation. It describes how an object appears to the senses, or how someone feels, or what the scene was like. Children can write descriptions of book characters without including the names of the characters. The descriptions can be put on a bulletin board as part of a riddle game. Children read the descriptions and try to guess who the characters are.

After reading *Winnie-the-Pooh*[69] orally, one third grade teacher brought in a stuffed Winnie-the-Pooh toy and let a different child take it home each evening, along with Pooh's diary. During the evening, the child would write an entry as Pooh telling what he had seen and done that night. Children were eager to take Pooh home and equally eager to share his diary the next day.

Being Flexible in Amount of Writing.   A second way of thinking about writing is to consider the quantity of writing. Some responses to books may take the form of lists or one word answers. Children might be asked to list four places they think a cricket could be hidden in their classroom, or look out the window and list all the things they see, that they think Crow Boy would be interested in watching. Often the written response may be just one sentence. First graders answered the question at the end of *Clifford's Halloween*,[70] "What would Clifford be for Halloween?" with these responses: "He could be Santa Claus,"; "He could be a big red bird,"; "He could be a red witch,"; "He could be Superman." Because Clifford is a huge red dog, disguising him is somewhat of a problem. The children drew pictures to accompany their answers. Both the pictures and the sentences kept the bigness and the redness of Clifford in mind. Only one of the students used a suggestion that had appeared in the book.

Children may write a paragraph or more, developing an idea fully. A special writing corner or a writers' club often encourages children to write. So too will the writing and illustrating of their own books, which can be sewn together and bound in cardboard covered with cloth. These are then placed in the classroom library where other children may read them. Several companies are now producing books with cloth covers and blank pages. You might suggest these books to parents as a way of encouraging their children to write at home.

Helping Children Write Well.   As you plan writing activities related to literature, you will want to do all that you can to make the writing experience a successful one for the children. Generally this means that you will engage children in a discussion period before they begin writing. During this time, children can exchange ideas and think through their own responses so that when they begin to compose they have some notion of what they want to say. A good writing program will have children doing some writing daily, taking responsibility for choosing most of their own topics, and having regular conferences with the teacher during the writing process. These procedures will carry over when children write about literature.

According to current research, children's approach to writing changes as they mature. Children of five or six put thoughts on paper with little preplanning. Writing is like play in that the children put on paper whatever comes to mind and are not concerned with the product or with potential readers. Gradually they develop a sense of audience. Children become aware of the reaction of others to their stories, of the need for the conventions of punctuation, capitalization, and correct spelling. By the end of first grade, many children are able to postpone the immediate task of writing to do preliminary tasks such as checking the spelling of a word.

Once children begin to plan, they frequently go through a period of over-planning, wanting everything decided before they begin so that there will be no "mistakes." The period of spontaneity has given way to a period of deliberateness. Before children begin composing as a professional writer does, they must rediscover the playful aspects of writing.[71] They must combine initial personal response with their awareness of audience, composing, and then editing.

Thus your task as a primary grade teacher is to encourage and support the concept of planning, but also to work with children as they write, helping them clarify thoughts and consider whether they are writing for an audience or just for themselves. You will introduce the ideas of proofreading and of editing, both

Books may stimulate writing activities through both content and form.

in stories dictated by a group and in the writing of individuals. In this way, children learn that the first draft may or may not say exactly what they want, and that changes and corrections are not only permissible but desirable. If you are working with preschoolers, your task is to encourage the children to tell stories, to engage in oral composition, and to experiment with print, writing their stories and telling you what each says.

Try to vary the writing activities that you suggest to children. This will help maintain their interest in writing and will give breadth to their concept of content and style. Structure writing and composition activities so that they are challenging but not overwhelming, allowing the children to see growth in their own skill.

Summary

Children learn language by constructing for themselves the grammar of the language they hear. To develop mature syntax and vocabulary they need to be exposed to rich, varied, and abundant samples of language, for this is the data base from which they generalize. They need to hear stories and see print in their daily environments. They also need the opportunity to use their language for a variety of purposes and in a variety of settings.

The following long-term developmental goals are appropriate for the language growth of young children:

- Children will understand and use the mature syntax of their language.
- Children will expand their vocabularies.
- Children will enjoy the creative and aesthetic use of language.

- Children will become skilled listeners.
- Children will learn to read.
- Children will communicate effectively both orally and in writing.

Books offer opportunities for helping children achieve these goals. Table 1 suggests appropriate teaching strategies. Children can be exposed to mature language in literature, hearing varied and complex syntactical structures, figurative language, and a variety of English dialects. They can be introduced to new vocabulary in context, sometimes as part of a story and at other times in concept books which focus on language. Children should be involved in using the new words they are learning.

Children can be encouraged to enjoy the ways others use language and to play with it themselves. Some "play" is with the sound of language, rhythm, rhyme, and repetition; some with patterns, refrains in books and songs. Still other play involves both the visual aspect of language and the meaning. As children listen to and recite Mother Goose rhymes, they are being introduced to the flexibility and fun of language.

As they listen to literature children can practice attentive, critical, and appreciative listening skills. They can be guided to think analytically about what they have heard through carefully structured questions and activities. They also develop a concept of the reading process as they observe how adults use the printed page and how verses they recite orally can be preserved in print.

Finally, literature provides myriad opportunities for children to engage in both oral and written language. Story interpretations and improvisations, role play, the use of masks and puppets, written responses to books, character studies, diaries, the making of one's own book—all enhance children's appreciation of literature and strengthen children's communication skills.

Extending Your Learning

1. Have a child retell a story after you have read it orally, first without the book and then looking at the illustrations. Describe and analyze the retellings.
2. Assess the language strengths of any three of the recommended children's books listed at the end of this chapter.
3. Make a list of possible book topics for young children. Tell what vocabulary you would expect to be introduced in the books.
4. Begin a collection of riddles children tell. Classify them by the age of the teller. See if you can identify any patterns.
5. Read through a collection of Mother Goose rhymes. Select five rhymes and identify the poetic elements that are present in them.
6. Again looking through a collection of Mother Goose rhymes, find ones which lead themselves to dramatization, movement, singing, or game playing.
7. Tell how you might get a child participating in the reading or telling of any three books mentioned in the preceeding chapter.
8. Read a picture book of your own choosing to a group of classmates without showing the illustrations. Have them create "mental images" as they listen. After the reading compare the images first with one another, and then with the illustrations in the book.

9. Plan an activity in response to a book for children that will require thinking above the memory level.
10. Select a book that you feel has potential for use in dramatic activity. Suggest three different approaches for its use.
11. Have children add narration or dialogue for a wordless picture book. You might want to do the narration twice, once told in first person and once in third person.
12. Suggest two writing activities that vary in difficulty but are based on the same book.

Table 1. *Supporting Children's Language Development*

Developmental Goals	Teaching Suggestions	Recommended Literature	
Children will understand and use the mature syntax of their language.	Provide rich and varied samples of mature language.	**Ages 3–5:**	
		Gilchrist	*Halfway up the Mountain*
	Respond to the content of children's telegraphic speech with mature language.	Ryder	*A Wet and Sandy Day*
	Read regularly to children.	Rylant	*Miss Maggie*
		Turkle	*Thy Friend Obadiah*
	Encourage primary care givers to read to the children.		
	Encourage children to read on their own.	**Ages 5–8:**	
		Caudill	*Did You Carry the Flag Today, Charlie?*
	Expose children to a variety of writing styles and dialects.		
		Myers	*Mr. Monkey and the Gotcha Bird*
Children will expand their vocabularies.	Introduce new words in the context of a story. Let children explain the meaning from the context.	**Ages 3–5:**	
		Banchek	*Snake In, Snake Out*
		Beyer	*"Jump or Jiggle"*
	Let children retell a story in their own words.	Ginsburg	*The Chick and the Duckling*
	Use phrases from a story to elicit personal responses from children.	McNaught	*Baby Animals*
		Maestro	*Busy Day*
		Marshall	*George and Martha Back in Town*
	Share concept books that present vocabulary items. Have children create sentences or stories from the words and pictures given.	Yabuuchi	*Whose Baby?*
		Ages 5–8:	
		MacLochlan	*The Sick Day*
	Let children respond physically to words in a story or poem.	Sylvester	*Summer on Cleo's Island*
	Read several books on the same topic to reinforce vocabulary.		
	Have children use accurate vocabulary to tell personal experiences similar to ones presented in literature.		
	Guide children to dramatize stories so they will use the vocabulary they have heard.		

Table 1. (Cont.)

Developmental Goals	Teaching Suggestions	Recommended Literature	
Children will enjoy the creative and aesthetic use of language.	Read literature which emphasizes language play and follow up by engaging children in word play themselves.	**Ages 3–5:** Bossom	A Scale Full of Fish and other Turnabouts
	Read poetry regularly to the children.	Emberley	Drummer Hoff
		Gag	Millions of Cats
	Let children listen to and write tongue twisters.	Hutchins	The Surprise Party
		Marzallo	Close Your Eyes
	Encourage children to say refrains in books with you as you read.	Piper	The Little Engine That Could
		Sendak	Chicken Soup With Rice
	Share literature in which there is a patterning of language. Let children create short sequences themselves.	Udry	Thump and Plunk
		Westcott	I Know an Old Lady
		Yashima	Umbrella
	Present cumulative folktales.		
	Show visual games with language such as rebus writing.	**Ages 5–8:** Adler	Bunny Rabbit Rebus
	Encourage riddles and other play on the meanings of words.	Bayley	One Old Oxford Ox
	Read or recite a wide selection of Mother Goose rhymes.	Charlip	Fortunately
		Coletta	From A to Z
		Gynn	A Chocolate Moose for Dinner
		Kuskin	Roar and More
		McCord	"The Pickety Fence"
		Parish	Amelia Bedelia
		Schwartz	A Twister of Twists, A Tangler of Tongues
Children will become skilled listeners.	Give children a specific purpose for listening.	**Ages 3–5:** Hutchins	Goodnight, Owl!
	Have children participate in the telling of a story.		
	Set a pattern of asking questions that require critical thinking.		
	Model appropriate listening behavior.		
	Suggest that children create mental images as they listen.		
	Reread stories occasionally for children to check their original impressions.		

Table 1. *(Cont.)*

Developmental Goals	Teaching Suggestions	Recommended Literature	
Children will learn to read.	Share literature so that children hear language patterns which occur more frequently in writing than in speech.	**Ages 3–5:** Chorao	*The Baby's Lap Book*
	Present whole stories, giving children a broad context for comprehending meaning.	Hoban	*I Read Signs*
		Hoban	*I Read Symbols*
	Hold books so that children observe the process of reading—looking at print, turning pages.	Hoban	*I Walk and Read*
		Wildsmith	*Brian Wildsmith's Mother Goose*
	Reread children's favorite stories and poems.		
	Plan for an aide or parent to read to children individually.		
	Reinforce left to right progression in reading.		
	Present books in such a way that reading becomes desirable.		
	Set up listening centers where children can hear a story while looking at the book.		
	Make charts or individual booklets of rhymes children know.		
	Display books that contain rhymes children know.		
Children will communicate effectively both orally and in writing.	Transcribe stories that children dictate.	**Ages 3–5:** Gag	*Millions of Cats*
	Let children tell about stories they like.	Slobodkina	*Caps for Sale*
	Have children retell a story using a flannelboard.	**Ages 5–8:** Burningham	*Would You Rather . . .*
	Let children interpret stories dramatically.	dePaola	*Pancakes for Breakfast*
	Encourage use of masks and puppets for dramatization.	Most	*If the Dinosaurs Came Back*
	Have children provide the text for wordless picture books.	Roth	*Patchwork Tales*
	Tape-record children telling plot of wordless books.	Stevenson Van Allsburg	*Yuck!*
	Engage children in choral speaking.		*The Mysteries of Harris Burdick*
	Pair children for game in which one describes a picture in a book and the other tries to locate it.		

Table 1. *(Cont.)*

Developmental Goals	Teaching Suggestions	Recommended Literature
Children will communicate effectively both orally and in writing.	Allow informal conversation as children work on projects. Suggest activities that require group interaction and discussion Conference with children as they write.	

Notes

1. Marilyn Cochran-Smith, *The Making of a Reader* (Norwood, N.J.: Ablex Publishing Corp., 1984).

2. David B. Doake, "Reading-Like Behavior: Its Role in Learning to Read," in *Observing the Language Learner*, eds. Angela Jaggar and M. Trika Smith-Burke (Newark, Del.: International Reading Association, 1985): 82–98.

3. Jerome C. Harste, Virginia A. Woodward, and Carolyn L. Burke, *Language Stories & Literacy Lessons* (Portsmouth, N.H.: Heinemann Educational Books Inc., 1984): 18.

4. Courtney B. Cazden, *Child Language and Education* (New York: Holt, Rinehart & Winston, 1972): 124–28.

5. Celia Genishi and Anne Haas Dyson, *Language Assessment in the Early Years* (Norwood, N.J.: Ablex Publishing Corp., 1984).

6. Carol Chomsky, "Stages in Language Development and Reading Exposure," *Harvard Educational Review* 42 (1972): 1–33.

7. Dorothy H. Cohen, "The Effect of Literature on Vocabulary and Reading Achievement," *Elementary English* 45 (February 1968): 209–13.

8. David McNeill, "Developmental Psycholinguistics," in *The Genesis of Language: A Psycholinguistic Approach*, eds. F. Smith and G.A. Miller (Cambridge: Massachusetts Institute of Technology Press, 1966): 69.

9. Kornei Chukovsky, *From Two to Five*, Trans. Miriam Merton (Berkeley: University of California Press, 1925, 1978): 62–64.

10. From *Miss Maggie* by Cynthia Rylant. Text copyright © 1983 by Cynthia Rylant. Reprinted by permission of the publisher, E.P. Dutton, a division of New American Library.

11. Text excerpt from *Halfway Up the Mountain* by Theo E. Gilchrist. By permission of J.B. Lippincott, Publishers.

12. Text excerpt from *A Wet and Sandy Day* by Joanne Ryder. Text copyright 1977 by Joanne Ryder. By permission of Harper & Row, Publishers.

13. Brinton Turkle, *Obadiah the Bold* (New York: Viking Press, 1965).

14. Excerpted from the book *Mr. Monkey and The Gotcha Bird* by Walter Dean Myers. Illustrated by Leslie Morrill. Text copyright © 1984 by Walter Dean Myers. Reprinted by permission of Delacorte Press.

15. From *Did You Carry the Flag Today, Charley?* by Rebecca Caudill. Copyright 1966 by Rebecca Caudill. Reprinted by permission of Holt, Rinehart & Winston, Publishers.

16. Reprinted by permission of Farrar, Straus, & Giroux, Inc. Selections from *Summer on Cleo's Island* by Natalie Sylvester. Copyright 1977 by Natalie Sylvester.

17. Sylvester, *Summer on Cleo's Island*, n.p.

18. James Marshall, *George and Martha Back in Town* (Boston: Houghton Mifflin Co., 1984): 42.

19. Linda Banchek, *Snake In. Snake Out.* Illus. by Elaine Arnold (New York: Thomas Y. Crowell Publishers, 1978).

20. Betsy and Giulio Maestro, *Busy Day* (New York: Crown Publishers Inc., 1978).

21. From *Another Here and Now Story Book* by Lucy Sprague Mitchell. Copyright, 1937, by E.P. Dutton & Co., Inc. Copyright renewal, 1965, by Lucy Sprague Mitchell. Reprinted by permission of E.P. Dutton.

22. Patricia MacLochlan, *The Sick Day*. Illus. by William Pene du Bois (New York: Pantheon Books Inc., 1979).

23. Harry McNaught, *Baby Animals* (New York: Random House Inc., 1976).

24. Masayuki Yabuuchi, *Whose Baby?* (New York: Philomel, 1985).

25. Mirra Ginsburg, *The Chick and the Duckling*. Illus. by Ariane and Jose Aruego (New York: Macmillan Publishing Co., 1972).

26. Courtney B. Cazden, "Play with Language and Metalinguistic Awareness: One Dimension of Language Experience," *International Journal of Early Childhood* 6 (1976): 13.

27. Gloria T. Blatt, "Playing With Language," *The Reading Teacher* 31 (February 1978): 490.

28. Norma Kaplan, Nursery School Teacher at Jewish Community Center, Providence, R. I.

29. Maurice Sendak, *Chicken Soup With Rice* (New York: Harper & Row, Publishers Inc., 1962).

30. Jean Marzallo, *Close Your Eyes*. Illus. by Susan Jeffers (New York: Dial Press, 1978): n.p.

31. William Brighty Rands, "Godfrey Gordon Gustavus Gore," in *Time for Poetry*, ed. May Hill Arbuthnot (Chicago: Scott, Foresman and Co., 1961): 129.

32. Alvin Schwartz, *A Twister of Twists, A Tangler of Tongues*. Illus. by Glen Rounds (Philadelphia: J.B. Lippincott Co., 1972).

33. Nicola Bayley, *One Old Oxford Ox* (New York: Atheneum Publishers, 1977): n.p.

34. Janice Udry, *Thump and Plunk*. Illus. by Ann Schweninger (New York: Harper & Row Publishers, Inc., 1981).

35. David McCord, "The Pickety Fence," in David McCord, *Far and Few*. Illus. by Henry B. Kane (Boston: Little, Brown and Co., 1952).

36. Barbara Emberley, *Drummer Hoff*. Illus. by Ed Emberley (Englewood Cliffs, N.J.: Prentice-Hall Inc., 1967).

37. Taro Yashima, *Umbrella* (New York: Viking Press, 1958): 20.

38. Pat Hutchins, *The Surprise Party* (New York: Macmillan Publishing Company, 1969).

39. Watty Piper, *The Little Engine That Could*. Illus. by George and Doris Hauman (New York: The Platt & Munk Co., 1930).

40. Reprinted by permission of Coward, McCann, & Geoghegan, Inc. From *Millions of Cats* by Wanda Gag. Copyright 1928 by Coward-McCann; renewed 1956 by Robert Janssen.

41. Nadine Bernard Westcott, reteller, *I Know an Old Lady* (Boston: Little, Brown and Co., 1980).

42. Remy Charlip, *Fortunately* (New York: Parents Magazine Press, 1964).

43. David A. Adler, *Bunny Rabbit Rebus*. Illus. by Madelaine Gill Linden (New York: Thomas Y. Crowell Publishers, 1983).

44. Irene and Hallie Coletta, *From A to Z: The Collected Letters of Irene and Hallie Coletta* (Englewood Cliffs, N.J.: Prentice-Hall Inc., 1979).

45. Karla Kuskin, *Roar and More* (New York: Harper & Row, Publishers, Inc., 1956).

46. Peggy Parrish, *Amelia Bedelia*. Illus. by Fritz Siebel (New York: Harper & Row, Publishers, Inc., 1963).

47. Fred Gwynn, *A Chocolate Moose for Dinner* (New York: E.P. Dutton, Inc., 1976).

48. Naomi Bossom, *A Scale Full of Fish and Other Turnabouts* (New York: Greenwillow Books, 1979).

49. Howard Gardner and Ellen Winner, "The Child Is Father to the Metaphor," *Psychology Today* 13 (May, 1979): 82.

50. Carol J. Fisher and Margaret A. Natarella, "Of Cabbages and Kings: On What Kinds of Poetry Young Children Like," *Language Arts* 56 (April, 1979): 380–385.

51. Bernard Waber, *Lyle and the Birthday Party* (Boston: Houghton Mifflin Co., 1966): 6.

52. Pat Hutchins, *Good-Night Owl!* (New York: Macmillan Publishing Company, 1972).

53. Linda Leonard Lamme, "Reading Aloud to Children: A Comparative Study of Teachers and Aides," Unpublished Research Report, University of Florida, 1977.

54. Brian Wildsmith, *Brian Wildsmith's Mother Goose* (New York: Franklin Watts, 1968).

55. Kay Chorao, *The Baby's Lap Book* (New York: E.P. Dutton Inc., 1977).

56. Robert Emans, "Children's Rhymes and Learning to Read," *Language Arts* 55 (Nov./Dec. 1978): 938.

57. Tana Hoban, *I Walk and Read* (New York: Greenwillow Books, 1984).

58. Tana Hoban, *I Read Signs* (New York: Greenwillow Books, 1983).

59. Tana Hoban, *I Read Symbols* (New York: Greenwillow Books, 1983).

60. Esphyr Slobodkina, *Caps for Sale* (Reading, Mass.: Addison-Wesley Publishing Co. Inc., 1940).

61. Tomie DePaola, *Pancakes for Breakfast* (New York: Harcourt Brace Jovanovich Inc., 1978).

62. Gag, *Millions of Cats*.

63. Hutchins, *Good-Night Owl!*

64. Bernard Most, *If the Dinosaurs Came Back* (New York: Harcourt Brace Jovanovich Inc., 1978).

65. John Burningham, *Would You Rather . . .* (New York: Thomas Y. Crowell Publishers, 1978).

66. Chris Van Allsburg, *The Mysteries of Harris Burdick* (Boston: Houghton Mifflin Co., 1984).

67. Susan L. Roth and Ruth Phang, *Patchwork Tales* (New York: Atheneum Publishers, 1984).

68. James Stevenson, *Yuck!* (New York: Greenwillow Books, 1984).

69. A. A. Milne, *Winnie-the-Pooh*. Illus. by Ernest Shepard. (New York: E.P. Dutton, Inc., 1926).

70. Norman Bridwell, *Clifford's Halloween* (New York: Scholastic Book Service, 1966).

71. Lucy McCormick Calkins, "Children Learn the Writer's Craft," *Language Arts* 57 (February 1980): 207–13.

Recommended References

Alkema, Chester Jay. *Masks*. New York: Sterling Publishing Company, 1971.

Arnstein, Flora J. *Poetry and the Child*. New York: Dover Publications Inc., 1970 copyright 1962.

Baird, Bil. *The Art of the Puppet*. New York: Macmillan Publishing Co., 1975.

Bruner, Jerome. *Child's Talk. Learning to Use Language*. New York: W.W. Norton & Co. Inc., 1983.

Cazden, Courtney B. *Child Language and Education*. New York: Holt, Rinehart & Winston, 1972.

Chukovsky, Kornei. *From Two to Five*. Trans. by Miriam Morton. Berkeley: University of California Press, 1971 (1925).

Cochran-Smith, Marilyn. *The Making of a Reader*. Norwood, N.J.: Ablex Publishing Corp., 1984.

Currell, David. *The Complete Book of Puppetry*. Boston: Plays, Inc. 1975.

Dale, Phillip S. *Language Development*. New York: Holt, Rinehart & Winston, 1976.

Fisher, Carol J. and Terry, C. Ann. *Children's Language and the Language Arts*. New York: McGraw-Hill Inc., 1982.

Garvey, Catherine. *Children's Talk*. Cambridge, Mass.: Harvard University Press, 1984.

Genishi, Celia and Dyson, Anne Haas. *Language Assessment in the Early Years*. Norwood, N.J.: Ablex Publishing Corp., 1984.

Graves, Donald. *Writing: Teachers & Children at Work*. Exeter, N.H.: Heinemann Educational Books Inc., 1983.

Harste, Jerome C.; Woodward, Virginia A.; and Burke, Carolyn L. *Language Stories and Literacy Lessons*. Portsmouth, N.H.: Heinemann Educational Books Inc., 1984.

Heinig, Ruth Beall and Stillwell, Lyda. *Creative Drama for the Classroom Teacher*. Englewood Cliffs, N.J.: Prentice-Hall Inc., 1981.

Jaggar, Angela and Smith-Burke, M. Trika, (eds.) *Observing the Language Learner*, Newark, Del.: International Reading Association, 1985.

Lamme, Linda Leonard. *Growing Up Writing*. Washington, D.C.: Acropolis Books Ltd., 1984.

Lewis, Shari. *Making Easy Puppets*. New York: E. P. Dutton, Inc., 1967.

McCaslin, Nellie. *Creative Dramatics in the Classroom*, 2d ed. New York: David McKay Co. Inc., 1974.

Meek, Margaret. *Learning to Read*. London: Bodley Head, 1982.

Moffett, James and Wagner, Betty Jane. *Student-Centered Language Arts and Reading*. Boston: Houghton Mifflin Co., 1983.

Petty, Walter T. and Jensen, Julie M. *Developing Children's Language*. Boston: Allyn and Bacon Inc., 1980.

Way, Brian. *Development Through Drama*. London: Longman, 1967.

Recommended Children's Books

Balian, Lorna. *Humbug Potion: An A-B-Cipher*. Nashville, Tenn.: Abingdon Press, 1984.

Burningham, John. *Mr. Gumpy's Outing*. New York: Holt, Rinehart & Winston, 1971.

Domanska, Janina. *Spring Is*. New York: Greenwillow Books, 1976.

Emberley, Ed. *Klippity Klop*. Boston: Little, Brown & Co. Inc., 1974.

Graham, Lornenz. *David He No Fear*. Illus. by Ann Grifalconi. New York: Thomas Y. Crowell Publishers, 1971.

Hobzek, Mildred. *We Come a-Marching. .1,2,3*. Illus. by William Pene du Bois. New York: Parents Magazine Press, 1978.

Hoguet, Susan Ramsay. *I Unpacked My Grandmother's Trunk*. New York: E. P. Dutton Inc., 1983.

Hutchins, Pat. *Don't Forget the Bacon*. New York: Greenwillow Books, 1976.

Kellogg, Steven. *Pinkerton, Behave!* New York: Dial Press, 1979.

Kipling, Rudyard. *The Elephant's Child*. Illus. by Lorinda Bryan Cauley. New York: Harcourt Brace Jovanovich Inc., 1983.

Lindgren, Astrid. *The Tomten*. Illus. by Harald Wiberg. New York: Coward-McCann, 1961.

Lobel, Arnold. *The Rose in My Garden*. Illus. by Anita Lobel. New York: Greenwillow Books, 1984.

McCloskey, Robert. *Time of Wonder*. New York: Viking Press, 1957.

Potter, Beatrix. *The Tale of Jemima Puddleduck*. London: Warne, 1936.

Preston, Edna Mitchell. *The Sad Story of the Little Bluebird and the Hungry Cat*. Illus. by Barbara Cooney. New York: Four Winds Press, 1975.

Ryder, Joanne. *Fog in the Meadow*. Illus. by Gail Owens. New York: Harper & Row, Publishers, Inc., 1979.

Shulevitz, Uri. *Rain, Rain, Rivers*. New York: Farrar, Straus & Giroux Inc., 1969.

Stanley, Diane. *The Conversation Club*. New York: Macmillan Publishing Co., 1983.

Tresselt, Alvin. *White Snow, Bright Snow*. Illus. by Roger Duvoisin. New York: Lothrop, Lee & Shepard Books, 1947.

Wells, Rosemary. *Max's First Word*. New York: Dial Press, 1979.

Recommended Poetry

Aldis, Dorothy. *All Together: A Child's Treasury of Verse*. Illus. by Marjorie Flack, Margaret Fireman, and Helen Jameson. New York: G. P. Putnam's Sons, 1952.

Bodecker, N.M. *Snowman Sniffles*. New York: Atheneum Publishers, 1983.

Brown, Margaret Wise. *Four Fur Feet*. Illus. by Remy Charlip. New York: William R. Scott, 1961.

De la Mare, Walter. *Peacock Pie*. Illus. by Barbara Cooney. New York: Alfred A. Knopf Inc., 1913, 1961.

deRegniers, Beatrice Schenck, et al., eds. *Poems Children Will Sit Still For: A Selection for the Primary Grades*. New York: Citation, 1969.

Fisher, Aileen. *Rabbits, Rabbits*. Illus. by Gail Niemann. New York: Harper & Row, Publishers, Inc., 1983.

Hoberman, Mary Ann. *Nuts to You and Nuts to Me: An Alphabet of Poems*. Illus. by Ronni Solbert. New York: Alfred A. Knopf Inc., 1974.

Hopkins, Lee Bennett. *Me!* Illus. by Talivaldis Stubis. New York: Seabury Press, 1970.

Itse, Elizabeth M., ed. *Hey, Bug! and Other Poems About Little Things*. Illus. by Susan Carlton Smith. New York: American Hertiage Press, 1972.

Kuskin, Karla. *The Rose on My Cake*. New York: Harper & Row, Publishers, Inc., 1964.

Larrick, Nancy, comp. *When the Dark Comes Dancing*. Illus. by John Wallner. New York: Philomel, 1983.

Livingston, Myra Cohn. *Sky Songs*. Illus. by Leonard Everett Fisher. New York: Holiday House, 1984.

Lobel, Arnold. *The Book of Pigericks*. New York: Harper & Row Publishers Inc., 1983.

McCord, David. *Every Time I Climb a Tree*. Illus. by Marc Simont. Boston: Little, Brown & Co. Inc., 1967.

Merriam, Eve. *Blackberry Ink*. Illus. by Hans Wilhelm. New York: William Morrow & Co. Inc., 1985.

Milne, A.A. *When We Were Very Young*. Illus. by Ernest Shepard. New York: E.P. Dutton, Inc., 1924.

Prelutsky, Jack. *It's Snowing! It's Snowing!* Illus. by Jeanne Titherington. New York: Greenwillow Books, 1984.

Prelutsky, Jack. *The Random House Book of Poetry for Children*. Illus. by Arnold Lobel. New York: Random House Inc., 1983.

Watson, Clyde. *Father Fox's Pennyrhymes*. Illus. by Wendy Watson. New York: Thomas Y. Crowell Publishers, 1971.

Worth, Valerie. *Small Poems*. Illus. by Natalie Babbitt. New York: Farrar, Straus & Giroux Inc., 1972.

5

Supporting Children's Intellectual Development

Intellectual Development in Young Children

Young children come to school with a wealth of information. They are attempting to organize the information, to make sense of their world, to integrate their experiences. They are beginning to form concepts from isolated ideas. A concept is "a generalized idea or understanding embodying many images and memories which have been blended into a meaningful whole."[1] The advantage of developing a system of concepts is that it allows one to process new information by fitting it into a framework. Each impression, object, or event need not be assessed and remembered separately. When children have seen several round objects and have been told that each is a ball, they generalize so that new examples fit into their concept of ball. When they hear the term *heavy* used to describe a box that is difficult to lift, a desk their father cannot move, and an overweight neighbor, they begin to develop a concept of heavy.

Adults are often more aware of young children's ability to conceptualize when they are inaccurate than when they conform to expected perspectives. A four year old was told that her grandfather was in the hospital. She asked each day when he would be coming home. After nearly two weeks of frustration, she announced that she wished he could get out of the hospital soon because "I want to see the baby." This child's experiences with hospitals had been limited to expectant mothers making the trip. Her concept of hospital was that of a place where people went to have babies. If Grandpa had gone there, he should be returning with a baby. The problem with the generalization is not with the reasoning, but that it was made on the basis of insufficient examples. When the parent explained that Grandpa was in the hospital because he was sick and that doctors there were trying to help him get well, the child's concept of hospital was enlarged. The changing and enlarging of concepts as new events are experienced and new insights are gained is a continual process.

One task of the day care professional or teacher is to help young children form accurate concepts. Teachers help by providing materials for the children to manipulate, by bringing information to the classroom or center, by taking children on trips, by encouraging children to discuss what they have seen. In other words, they provide the raw data from which the children can construct their own concepts. Through questioning, teachers guide children to think about and order what they have experienced.

Simply telling children the concepts you would like them to acquire is seldom effective, for it may result in rote learning, but not in real understanding. "Concepts are constructions that must be made by each person for herself. Words, of course, can be given to others,"[2] writes Helen Robison, a specialist in early childhood education. Thus the adult may provide the conventional name, but the child must build the concept.

Young children engage in thinking processes that are fundamental in concept formation. They associate ideas, they classify, they generalize, they reach logical conclusions.[3] However, until they are seven or eight years of age, children rely more on sensory data than on logic to reach conclusions regarding physical objects. Almost all four year olds will look at two short, wide glasses of water equally filled and report that both glasses have the same amount of water. After watching the water from one of these glasses poured into a tall, narrow container, the children will report that the tall glass has more water than the short one or vice versa. The logic that no water has been added or taken away is secondary to the sensory data that after the water is poured from one glass into a taller container, it looks as if the amounts are different. Around the age of seven, children begin to rely on the logic of the situation and will report that the quantities of water remain equal. At this time, they are also able to keep more than one attribute in mind, to look at both the height and the width of the containers.

After the age of seven, children are also more likely to use the standard forms of logical reasoning. They will use deductive reasoning, which goes from the general to the particular. "All collies are dogs. This is a collie. Therefore it is a dog." They will use inductive reasoning, which goes from the particular to the general. "Collies, spaniels, boxers, beagles, and terriers all have hair, four legs, and make a barking sound. They are dogs. It is likely that all dogs have hair, four legs, and make a barking sound."

Four and five year olds sometimes use what is termed transductive reasoning.[4] They go from particular to particular, without any reference to the general. This often results in faulty conclusions. The child may connect two events in a cause and effect relationship simply because they occur together. "The dog ran away. My Daddy was late getting home from work. The dog ran away because Daddy was late."

One four year old, reasoning from particular to particular, was not concerned that Santa Claus appeared in three department stores she and her mother went into, nor that he was also stationed in the center of the shopping mall. It did not occur to her that there might be more than one. For her seven-year-old brother, however, the generalization that a man cannot be in two places at the same time led to a questioning of the ever-present Santa and the conclusion that there had to be more than one.

The Swiss psychologist Piaget has concluded that the order in which children's thinking matures remains the same for all children, but that the pace varies from child to child.[5] Particularly if you are teaching seven and eight year olds, a period of transition from one stage of intellectual development to another, you may find great variety in the logic children use as they explain what they observe.

Young children engage in intuitive and associative thought as well as the rational. An essential aspect of cognitive development is the development of the imagination. Many young children have imaginary playmates. They talk to them, play with them, reserve space for them at the table. The fantasy world may seem real to four and five year olds, and they have difficulty at times distinguishing between fantasy and reality. The teacher or day care professional helps them as they develop the ability to differentiate, but at the same time encourages them to use their imaginations.

Goals for Teaching

As in other areas, teaching goals for intellectual growth can be categorized as long term developmental goals, general goals for an age or grade level, and specific goals for individual children. The long term goals are those behaviors or competencies that are developed over time and are considered desired patterns of behavior. A long term goal for intellectual development is that children will continue to acquire new concepts and to refine old ones. Teachers and day care professionals will be helping children attain this goal throughout the preschool and primary years.

General goals for each grade level are often listed in curriculum guides. At other times they are developed by the teacher as he or she plans an outline for the year's learning. A general goal for the first grade level is that children will verbalize the criteria they use to classify various sets of objects.

At times you will have specific goals for individual children. An example for a four year old might be "Katanya will place the scissors and crayons in the appropriate boxes when she is finished using them." It is an intellectual goal because it requires classification, putting scissors with scissors and crayons with crayons. While most of the children may be doing this, it is a goal for Katanya because she is not yet cognizant of the categorization system being used.

Literature contributes to the achievement of all three types of goals. This chapter focuses on selected long term developmental goals, ones that are common to the preschool and primary years. Literature offers opportunities for you to help children grow toward the following goals for intellectual development:

- Children will continue to acquire new concepts and to refine ones already held.
- Children will develop skill in a variety of thinking processes.
- Children will expand their powers of logical reasoning.
- Children will utilize critical thinking skills.
- Children will engage successfully in problem solving.

Opportunities Books Offer

Assisting in the Acquisition and Refinement of Concepts

Young children have many concrete experiences that aid them in the process of developing and refining concepts. Books, both fiction and nonfiction, are another source of information from which children gather data necessary for generalizing and through which they assess the accuracy of concepts already held.

Giving Information.   Literature often provides information that children could not discover through their own manipulations and observations of the environment. Some is in the form of naming what they have observed. Children may know that there are three different kinds of fish in the aquarium, but no amount of watching will teach them what the fish are called. You may want to read books to the children which will provide this information, or you may want to leave the books for them to use themselves. If the children are doing work with wood, a useful book to have is *The Toolbox*[6] by Anne and Harlow Rockwell. The premise is a child looking at the tools in a toolbox. Each tool is clearly illustrated with its name and a sentence telling some fact about its use. Children can learn the names of the tools they are using and see some other tools as well.

Often names are given in the context of a story. *The Remarkable Egg*[7] opens as a coot is building her nest near a pond. She is nearly finished when she finds a huge red egg in her nest. She then begins asking other birds if the egg belongs to them. Each bird is identified by name, and the illustrations by Roger Duvoisin show the characteristics of each bird clearly. Children listening to this mystery are introduced to a variety of birds. Each bird explains that the egg does not belong to it and describes its own egg. By the time the "egg" is claimed by a boy who had lost his ball, the coot has talked with ten other birds. Young listeners can be asked to look back through the pictures and identify any birds that they have seen.

Both of these books provide labels for objects with which the children are familiar and both introduce new members of familiar categories.

Sometimes books will give information about a topic familiar to the children, but will present new facets of that topic. Children know about television heroes and heroines from having watched their fantastic exploits week after week. *The Bionic Bunny Show*[8] has as its protagonist a rabbit named Wilbur, the star of a television series about a bionic bunny. The story tells about the filming of one episode of the show, from Wilbur's arrival at the studio with only ten minutes to get his costume and make-up on and finish learning his lines, to his capturing the Robber Rats on film. In the course of the story, children see the use of a story board, of props used for his "bionic" powers, of retakes when he muffs his lines, of various camera angles. At one point the director instructs, "Set up for the bionic leap. Wilbur, you pose for three shots. Remember, just look like it's easy. The editor will put these shots together so that it looks like you did it yourself."[9] The book is good fiction as well as being informative. Wilbur, at home after his bionic day, is unable to remove a stuck jar lid.

Children can compare shows they watch on television to Wilbur's "Bionic Bunny Show"; they can categorize what is real and what is make-believe on the shows they watch; they can create story boards, composing their own television stories.

With other books, you can present ideas about people, places, and events far removed from the children's own situations. Young children have ideas about different peoples and places from television and from the conversation of the adults around them. Even though their concept of distance is vague, they can learn about different places and people. However, there should be some point of contact between the children's experiences and those presented in the book. Often this contact is in the emotions of the characters. Most American children listening to *Mary of Mile 18*[10] would never have experienced anything like the frontier living of this family of settlers in northern British Columbia. They would not know what it was like to bring water into the house in a pail, carry out the used water, go out in forty below zero weather, or watch the Northern Lights. However, they could relate to Mary's wish to keep a stray dog, and her disappointment when her father will not allow it. They know how it feels to be awaiting the birth of a new baby in the family and to be responsible for younger children. Teachers and day care professionals presenting such a book would talk with the children about the differences in the ways people live, but would stress the similarities of needs and of feelings.

As you choose books about different peoples, look for those that show the emotions and motivations of the characters. Books that emphasize only the "strange" customs or life-styles may influence children to have negative reactions to people who are different from themselves, rather than to appreciate cultural diversity. *How My Parents Learned to Eat*[11] does a superb job of presenting different customs, in this case contrasting American and Japanese eating habits. The little girl who tells the story explains that some days her family eats with chopsticks and other days with knives and forks. She goes on to tell about her parents' courtship when her father was an American sailor and her mother a Japanese schoolgirl. Both attempted to learn about the culture and customs of the other. Her father learned to use chopsticks by going to a Japanese restaurant and having the waiter show him. Her mother learned to use a knife and fork from a great uncle who had visited England. She learned to hold the utensils British style, and then had to change to American style. Both parents felt insecure with their newly acquired skills, but both cared about

Books can help children learn to appreciate cultural diversity. (Illustration by Allen Say from How My Parents Learned To Eat *by Ina R. Friedman. Text copyright © 1984 by Ina R. Friedman. Illustrations copyright © 1984 by Allen Say. Reprinted by permission of Houghton Mifflin Company.)*

the other and accepted the cultural differences. The focus of the book is the parallel experiences and feelings of the parents.

Past events can be introduced with emphasis being placed upon what happened and why it was interesting or important. As children listen to *The Glorious Flight*,[12] the story of Louis Bleriot's attempts to build an airplane and his eventual flight across the English Channel in a heavier-than-air machine, they can enjoy the humor of the story, the marvellous illustrations, the sense of success when he finally achieves his goal. They need not be concerned with understanding fully the period in which the event took place nor the exact location of the place.

You may want to share with children books that represent a variety of American settings. As a beginning step, look at the books of Robert McCloskey and Donald Carrick for settings on the northeast coast; at those of Byrd Baylor for a southwest setting; and at the work of Ezra Jack Keats, Joan Lexau, Lucille Clifton, and John Steptoe for urban settings.

Using Books as Teaching Aids.   Some books have qualities that make them visual aids in themselves. This is true of many alphabet, counting, and concept books. *What's Inside?*,[13] for example, shows pairs of photographs to illustrate "inside" and "outside," with the outside of familiar objects being shown, then what's inside them appearing when the page is turned. Three year olds can look at a photograph of socks, for example, and tell "what's inside." The book suggests questions an adult might use with children to encourage them to tell not only what they expect to see, but to describe the object inside, how it got there, and why it is there.

Often a group of books can be used. Suppose you were working on color names with a small group of children. You could being by showing Hoban's *Is It Red? Is It Yellow? Is It Blue?*[14] Following the title page there are six dots, each labeled with its color: red, yellow, blue, orange, green, purple. Children could name the ones they recognized. Then they could look at the pictures. Each is a color photograph, some with many colors, some with only a few. The colors in the picture are shown at the bottom in a series of dots. Children could match the dots to the colors in the photographs, touching each part of the picture which is the same color. They could do a variety of classification activities: objects by color; objects by shape; objects that move; objects that are alive. They might tell which of the objects pictured they have at home. There are opportunities for describing pictures, for making up stories about the pictures. You might use the book for classifying colors with one group, for language experience in storytelling with another.

Some teachers help children with color names by having them cut pictures of a certain color from magazines; some have them draw pictures using different shades of the same color; some have days when everyone wears something of a certain color, or when the snack is food of that color; some reinforce color concepts by daily reminders, such as calling children to a table by the colors they are wearing.

Suppose you had used some of these ideas. You might then want to use another book which includes color concepts, *Freight Train*. This book shows a train with each car a different color. The print matches the color of the car. Reading almost like a poem, the story names the cars, then shows the train traveling.

> Freight train.
> Moving.
> Going through tunnels.
> Going by cities.
> Crossing trestles.
> Moving in darkness.
> Moving in daylight.
> Going, going . . .
> Gone.[15]

The last illustration shows only smoke. There are strong possibilities for vocabulary development and for information about trains, as well as for color. If you were using the book for the color aspects, you might read it several times. After they had heard it once, the children could supply the name of the color as each appeared. Then they could say as much as they remembered while you read. Finally you could have them repeating the phrases in choral speaking, capturing the rhythm of a train. There is reinforcement on the color while at the same time giving enjoyment in the sound of language.

You might further involve children with books and with color by sharing *Mr. Rabbit and the Lovely Present.*[16] A little girl asks Mr. Rabbit for help in finding a birthday gift for her mother. She then tells each color that her mother likes, and the rabbit names things which are that color. Finally she has collected a basket of fruit of many different colors. Children could make suggestions for gifts of different colors, perhaps making pictures that could go on a chart. If you find several books on the same topic, you will have more opportunities for approaching that subject from a variety of perspectives and for involving children in a variety of ways.

Look at books for ways in which they can be used by the children themselves. Alphabet books can be shared by two children learning to recognize letter sounds. They take turns opening the book, seeing the letter, naming its sound or sounds, and naming the objects pictured. Counting books can be used by having a child open the book randomly, see the numeral, select that many counters, then place one counter on each object to see if he or she counted correctly. *Anno's Counting House,*[17] although it requires an introduction by an adult, can be used by pairs of children to count and categorize as different numbers of people appear in the cut-out windows of two houses.

Books need not be used in their entirety. Select those portions that fit your goals. In the preceding section a book was mentioned for naming tools. If you had used it, and were using tools in the classroom, you might share just one page from *Crash! Bang! Boom!*[18] a book that is about sounds. Each double page has fifteen to twenty objects and the sounds they make, classified by where the sounds occur. You would use only the page that shows tools and the sounds they make. Children could try naming the tools and could listen for the sounds to see if they would describe them as the author does. It might lead to their wanting to look at other pages, but if not, it would still have met your original goal.

Sharing Books That Stimulate Projects.   Books can be used as direct models for further work. Children who had seen and listened to *Wild Mouse*[19] would know what it was like to observe an animal daily and to keep a record of those observations. The author of *Wild Mouse* recorded in diary format the growth and development of a litter of three white-footed mice for a period of about two weeks. The descriptions are accompanied by sketches. Children can observe an animal or plant in the classroom, dictating their observations, or for older children, writing their own. They can make drawings to show what they are seeing. At the end of the week or two of recording, they can go back and read what they have said, see what changes they have noticed. This would be an opportunity for them to summarize what they learned through their own observation.

A simpler project could be modeled after *Where Does My Cat Sleep?*[20] by Norma Simon. Also illustrated with pencil drawings, this book shows the various places the family cat sleeps. Children might watch their own pets for a short period of time, carefully noticing their behavior. Later, they can dictate short descriptive passages, or show through illustration what they've discovered.

Books may simply suggest projects. Some you may choose deliberately to introduce areas of study or new learning centers. Perhaps you would read *Gilber-*

to and the Wind[21] as an introduction to a unit about air. Gilberto talks about the wind and describes it when it is gentle and when it is fierce. The wind is personified. You could use this to begin having children feel the wind, to make pinwheels as Gilberto does, or blow bubbles outside and watch them float. They could then begin discussing what the wind is and how it differs from day to day.

You might read *The Boy Who Didn't Believe in Spring*,[22] especially if you are teaching in an urban area. In the book, a little boy named King Shabazz does not believe there is such a thing as spring, even though his teacher and his Mama are talking about it. He and his friend Tony Polito walk just around the corner, where spring is supposed to be. Still doubting, the two stumble across some flowers in a vacant lot, then find a bird's nest in an abandoned car. King decides that it really is spring. This book could motivate children to look for spring in their neighborhoods.

Sometimes a book will catch the children's fancy even if you have not planned it as an introduction to further work. Be open to children's responses so that you can take advantage of what some have termed the *teachable moment,* that unplanned yet perfect opportunity to extend children's knowledge and thinking skill.

Both *Gilberto and the Wind* and *The Boy Who Didn't Believe in Spring* are fiction. Often you will find that fiction can be as effective as nonfiction in providing a stimulus for study.

Reinforcing Concepts.   Just as some books can be used to introduce ideas, others serve to reinforce concepts, or to add further information to a topic children have already explored through direct experience. The concept book *Over, Under & Through*[23] is excellent for reinforcing children's understanding

Books can add information to a topic children are exploring.

of these terms and the other prepositions demonstrated in the book. Only the word is given, with photographs illustrating the concepts. For *in* and *on* the pictures show a cat sitting *in* the window, *on* the sill; strawberries *in* a basket; a child putting a letter *in* a mailbox; a chick perched *on* a child's hand; a bird *on* its perch *in* a cage; two boys *in* a telephone booth. Children can look at the pictures and describe what is happening.

Reinforcement may be simply reading a book. If you read *Rosie's Walk*,[24] you would also be reinforcing these same concepts of *in, on, under,* and *through* because they are used to describe Rosie's walk around the barnyard. You would choose to read the book with no further work, knowing that once more children are hearing the terms used in context.

You can use books to answer questions that have been raised, or to give further information. If the children have walked along the seashore, watched the waves, listened to the gulls, and collected seashells, you would look for books to help coordinate what they have seen, to explain some of the phenomena. Perhaps you would read *Beach Bird*[25] because it describes one day on the beach, the animals that are there, and particularly the gulls. It is direct in its portrayal of survival, of who eats whom. You might make available on the table with the shells a copy of *Houses From the Sea*.[26] Children can match the shells they have with the ones pictured in the book. They might label their shells. Then you could read the book, for it describes the common names and tells about how the names match the appearance of the shells. Children might make up new names for their shells, ones that they think fit.

Often you will find books that describe experiences similar to ones children in your class have had. Read some of these so that your group can see how others have reacted, and compare their feelings with those of characters in books. *Momo's Kitten*[27] and *Joey's Cat*[28] would be appropriate books to read if one of the children had a cat with new kittens and if the class had been following the birth. Both books describe mother cats and how they care for their kittens, and both tell about a child's reaction. Children might listen for things they had already noticed, such as how the mother cat carries her kittens, or what the kittens do in play. They might make a chart of how to care for a mother cat. They might compare how they feel about the kittens with what Momo and Joey feel. The books and activities build on the children's own experiences and extend them through comparison with the experiences of others.

Clarifying Misconceptions.   One of the ways people learn is by expressing their ideas to others and listening to the comments and reactions that result. Teachers who are listening to what children are saying will find that children's talk often reveals misconceptions they may have. The teacher is then in a position to help the children clarify their thinking.

There are times when books are very helpful in this endeavor. There are other times when direct experience makes far more sense. One first grader commented to her teacher that "Mr. Gaddis and Mrs. Crabtree sure are good singers." The teacher was puzzled at first over the child's assessment of the musical abilities of the principal and the school secretary. Her pause was filled by further comment from the child. "I like the way they sing the carols." Then she knew. It was the week before the Christmas holiday and Christmas carols were being played on the intercom system for the last half-hour of school. The only voices which the child had heard on the intercom were those of the principal and the secretary. Therefore, if there was singing in the afternoon, they must be the ones doing it. This was one of those times when direct experience was far better than a book. The teacher explained that the singing was coming from the office, but that the secretary was playing a record, not singing herself. Then that afternoon, the teacher and several of the children went to the office to see just how it was done.

Other times, however, a book may be the better aid for clarifying concepts. A five year old came to school telling about an old movie he had seen on television. The cars were funny, he said, and nobody dressed like that. Earlier the class had been talking about *real* and *make-believe* stories. He gave his judgment of the film, saying it had to be make-believe.

There are several concepts involved in his statement. There is the distinction between realism and fantasy. He is including in realism only that which he has experienced himself and knows to be possible. Everything else is fantasy. The teacher will help him define other criteria for deciding the difference between realism and fantasy, perhaps emphasizing the aspect of impossibility within fantasy. Also involved in his statement is a lack of realization that changes are occurring continually, in cars, in clothing, in people, in himself.

Both of these involve more than a single experience and both can be explored through books. In the regular period for literature, the teacher might read a book of historical fiction, perhaps one of the Obadiah books by Brinton Turkle. She could introduce it by saying, "This story is about people who lived long ago." After comparing their lives and feelings with those of Obadiah, the children could be asked if they thought there was anything make-believe about the story.

On another day, the teacher could look for a book that deals specifically with changes over time. One such book is *The Sky Was Blue*.[29] The book opens with a little girl and her mother looking at a photo album. The little girl comments on the funny clothes her mother wore when she was a little girl. The mother explains that she thought the dress was pretty, then shows the kind of doll she had, and the kind of car the family had. The illustrations show the styles clearly. But, the mother continues, some things stay the same. The sky was blue, the sun yellow, the grass green, and her mother hugged her before she turned off the light at night. Together they turn the pages of the album, and together they see how things looked when grandmother and great-grandmother were little girls. As they close the album, the mother explains that someday the girl will show the pictures to a child of her own and tell her the same things.

Children can be encouraged to talk with their parents and grandparents about what they wore and what they liked to do when they were five and six years old. Parents and grandparents could be invited to come to the class and tell the children about their childhoods. Children might bring family snapshots to school, comparing them. Another project might be for the children to bring in pictures of themselves as babies and as toddlers, seeing how they have changed already. Many classrooms keep charts of children's growth during the year. This could be a time for seeing what growth had occurred thus far in the year.

When you hear children making comments that indicate misconceptions, you will have several decisions to make. First is whether to approach it directly, such as the teacher did with the singing on the intercom, or to make notes to provide experiences at a later time, as was suggested for the comments about the old movie. You will also have to decide how to go about giving the child some feedback. Generally speaking, it is better if you can provide first hand experience for the children. However, not all concepts lend themselves to this approach. Sometimes, also, you will need preparation time to do a good job. Literature can be particularly useful for giving information and for providing a starting point for discussion and for projects.

If you are just beginning to work with young children, books that are written for them may give you some help in gearing your expectations to the children's level of understanding. *The Sky Was Blue,* for instance, does not require any real concept of how much time has passed, only that as time passes, things change. This is in keeping with young children's concept of time, which is not clearly developed. Look at several books on the same topic, plan your presentation to be on what seems a reasonable level in terms of the books and what you know of your class, then listen carefully to the children's reactions.

Developing Skill in a Variety of Thinking Processes

Books provide the opportunity for children to engage in many thinking processes. Obviously almost any picture book you select could be used to help children improve in their observational skills. Some, however, are better than others.

Observing.   If you want children to become aware of detail, you might select a book by Peter Spier. His illustrations are filled with action and rich detail. In *Noah's Ark,*[30] the front endpaper begins the story, with Noah tending his vineyard while armies fight and cities burn. The building of the ark continues through the title page. Then the text appears, a translation of "The Flood" by Jacobus Revius. The illustrations continue the saga, with no further text. Children can look at the story once, then go back and pick out the details. Do they notice the one owl that stays awake during the day? They might do a matching game. Can they find the pairs of animals? Guide questions from you can direct their attention to patterns within the detail. For example, ask them if they can find the work that Noah is doing on each page, or have them tell what things they see outside the ark.

The color photographs in *Backyard Insects*[31] by Millicent Selsam stimulate attention to detail in a different way. The text describes protective devices, including camouflage and protective coloration. Children looking at the photos will first need to find the insect; then they can note particular devices.

If you are using a book such as this, you will want to be certain that the children can see the illustrations easily. This will mean working with a few children at a time, or using a filmstrip. Filmstrips can make it easier for children to see, and any single frame can be shown for as long as necessary.

Some books are observational guessing games. For children four to six, *Each Peach Pear Plum*[32] challenges them to find a storybook or nursery rhyme character hidden in each of the illustrations. A couplet tells about one character, then says "I spy" another one. Children can look for Bo Peep, Mother Hubbard, Jack and Jill, and others. If you have shared it with one child, you might then ask that child to choose a friend and play the game again with the friend doing the guessing. The "I spy" technique can be applied to other books. One child can look at an illustration and tell something he or she spies in the picture, and another then finds the object. This and similar guessing games can be played with *1 Hunter*,[33] a counting book in which a lone hunter walks through the jungle unaware of the many partially hidden animals, and *Pigs in Hiding*,[34] a story of trickery in which the hidden pigs are found only when food lures them into the open.

Another book that requires careful observation and involves guessing is *Look Again*.[35] Readers open the book to find that they are seeing part of something through a square hole that has been cut from a white page covering a photograph. They try to guess what they are seeing. When they turn the white page, the whole photograph shows, and they can see how accurate their guesses were. Seven and eight year olds, as well as intermediate grade children, can play the game, guessing at the zebra's stripes and the pattern on the turtle's shell. They might tell why they guess what they do before they turn the page. Some might want to make *Look Again* books of their own, cutting pictures from magazines and making cover sheets with windows showing only a portion of the picture.

Also using the technique of a hole in one page for viewing the pages before and after it is *Peek-A-Boo!*,[36] appropriate for three and four year olds. It adds the element of perspective for the left page will show the baby, with what the baby sees showing through the hole in the page on the right. When the page with the hole is turned, the viewer is now the character on the right, and it is the baby being seen.

Perspective plays a role in *Round Trip*[37] and in *The Look Again. . . and Again, and Again, and Again Book*.[38] For both, as the book is turned, and perspective altered, the illustrations also change. In *Round Trip,* the black and white illustrations show a trip from a small town, through the country, to the city. When reversed and read backwards, the story is of the trip home. The now upside-down illustrations reverse foreground and background to create new images. *The Look Again . . . Book* asks the reader to turn each page so that illustrations are viewed from all four sides. A caption tells what the graphic could be from each of the angles. Both books are intriguing and both encourage careful and flexible observation. Older children might want to create some graphics of their own.

You may want children to observe the action in a story, or the reactions of characters. Wordless picture books are excellent for this purpose, for the entire story is told through illustrations. Children can describe what is happening. In books such as *A Boy, A Dog, A Frog and a Friend,*[39] in which facial expressions play a prominent part, children could tell how a character feels. The body language of a finger in front of a closed mouth could be explained, or the boy's reaction when he falls in the water.

Keep in mind the maturity level and the experience of the children as you select books for practice in observing. The four year old will need less complex books with clearer illustrations than the seven year old. Alphabet and count-

We saw fireworks and stopped to watch.

We followed the shore past marshy inlets and summer cottages.

Foreground and background reverse to create new images. (From Round Trip *by Ann Jonas. Copyright © 1983 by Ann Jonas. By permission of Greenwillow Books, a division of William Morrow & Co.)*

ing books can be used with very young children just for looking at the objects pictured. Books such as *Anno's Journey,*[40] with more detail and a somewhat unfamiliar setting (Europe), would be better used with slightly older children, ones who can make sense of the journey through the countryside, villages, and cities, and who may recognize some familiar characters in the background. There will still be detail they will miss. In one illustration, among the many activities around the farm, three characters are attempting to pull a huge turnip out of the ground, and a rider, accompanied by a man on foot, is headed, spear in hand, for the windmill. Some but not all will know the folk tale about the enormous turnip, but doubtless it will be only the teacher who recognizes Don Quixote.

Hypothesizing. Children can be guided to hypothesize about any book being shared with them. They can look at the cover or listen to the title and make reasonable guesses about the book's possible content. They can tell what they think a character will do next, or what might happen next. Children should be taught that hypothesizing means taking into account the information one already has in order to make predictions and should be encouraged to give reasons for their conjectures. They should be taught that hypothesizing is a logical process and is not simply telling what one would like to happen, or what one thinks would be interesting. Their guess may prove to be exactly what the author has done with plot, but it may turn out to be quite different though still reasonable. The object is to suggest logical possibilities, not to match exactly the author's choice.

Some books have plots that naturally invite hypothesizing. *Mystery on the Docks*[41] is the story of Ralph, a restaurant cook who rescues Eduardo, his favorite opera singer, from kidnappers. Ralph and Eduardo are mice; the kidnappers are rats; and the entire story takes place either on the docks or on the ship where Eduardo is taken. Children who have watched television mysteries will be ready to help solve this one.

Other books have such strong characterization that this becomes the basis for children's hypotheses about what will happen next. They see the character's feelings and reactions and use these, as well as their own understanding of the emotions, for anticipating actions. After hearing any one of the George and Martha books by James Marshall, children will know that neither George nor Martha will do anything knowingly that might hurt the other, and that both are tolerant of the other's foibles.

Still other books will have an identifiable pattern to the actions within them. Folk tales, for instance, often have cumulative or repetitive plots. Children thus may use the generalizations they make about the literary form itself to suggest what will happen.

Comparing.   Literature offers the opportunity for children to engage in structured comparisons. As noted in chapter three, when you group books in pairs, or units, or webs, you are setting the stage for the children to compare and contrast one work of literature with another.

Suppose you have been talking with the children about city life and country life. The time would be ideal to have children compare books about the topics as well as the topics themselves. *Town & Country*[42] gives many specific examples of everyday experiences in a large city and in a rural area. The color illustrations add even more detail. Experiences a child might have, such as attending school, are compared and contrasted. After looking carefully at the book and listening to the text, children might compare their own life-styles with the two described in the book. Are they living in a rural or an urban area? If neither fits, how is their home like the country? How is it like the city? What sounds do they hear at night? What do they do for fun during bad weather?

The next day, you might share a much shorter and simpler book, *Tall City, Wide Country*.[43] The illustrations are uncluttered, the text consists of only one phrase per page. The book can be read forwards or backwards, for the phrases string together in a long sentence either way. When reading about the "wide country," you hold the book horizontally, and the pictures spread out like the flat farmland, with a wide expanse of land and sky. When reading about the "tall city," you hold the book vertically, and the pictures rise like the skyscrapers and elevators they depict. This book presents one basic contrast between country and city. The country is wide; the city tall.

Then you put both books side by side and ask the children how the two books are alike and how they are different. They respond immediately that both are about city and country life, and that both compare the two. They note the detail in *Town & Country* and the format of *Tall City, Wide Country*. You ask them what they think each author wanted the reader to know about country life and city life. Then you ask if the pictures for each book help the author get his or her point across. You show the illustrations for both books again, and ask what they now notice about the format in *Town & Country*, which also uses vertical

In this book life in a large city is compared with life in a rural area. (Provensen, Alice and Martin. Town & Country. *NY: Crown, 1984.)*

versus horizontal to symbolize the difference between city and country, but does so by the placement of text as well as by the shape of illustration. The city section has vertical illustrations with the text running down the side. The country section has horizontal illustrations with the text running beneath the pictures. You close by showing the endpapers for *Tall City, Wide Country.* In the front is a horizontal double page spread of farmland, and in the back is a vertical double page spread of tall buildings. Ask the children to design endpapers for *Town & Country* that would show another contrast between city and country.

Think about what topics your class is exploring, or what areas you plan to introduce. When you have several books on that topic, read through them for possibilities of activities or questions which will lead children to compare them.

Occasionally there are companion books which are excellent for children to compare. Such a set is *City in the Summer*[44] and *City in the Winter*[45] both by Eleanor Schick. Children can tell how the city looks different, how people's dress is different, what sort of activities go on in the city in the summer and in the winter as pictured in the books. They can compare the days of the boy in each story, one who spends the day with an elderly neighbor at the beach, and the other who spends the day inside with his grandmother. They might draw or paint what their house and yard look like in the summer and in winter, or dictate a story telling one thing they do only in summer and another which they do only in winter. Another interesting set of books that can be compared in this same manner is *Island Winter*[46] and *Summer Business.*[47] The same protagonist, Heather, appears in both books. *Island Winter* shows what happens on the island in winter when all the visitors have gone home, while *Summer Business* shows the activities of Heather and her friends in the summer when the island is filled with tourists.

Sometimes changes are pictured within a single book. The role of the teacher in this case is to draw attention to the changes and to the qualities which remain the same. In *The Story of an English Village*[48] John Goodall shows in watercolor illustrations the changes that take place in a village in England in each century from the fourteenth to the twentieth. He shows an outdoor scene and an indoor scene for each century, and two for the twentieth. Third grade children can flip the pages back and forth to see what has changed from one picture to the next. They might be directed to name as many changes as they see from the 14th to the 15th centuries, with the teacher listing the changes on the board. Then as they look at the illustrations for the 16th century, they can follow their list and see what is happening and continue this procedure for each set of pictures. They might be directed to look only at clothing, or transportation, or the food shown, and tell what is happening on that one subject as the time passes. Skill in comparing both builds on and strengthens skill in observing.

Classifying.   Some books lend themselves readily to experiences in classification. *Shapes and Things*[49] is one that does. The book is a collection of photograms, photographs made by placing objects directly on photographic paper and exposing them to sunlight. When the paper is processed, the result is a series of silhouettes. In this book, which has no text, the objects have been grouped by the author. Children looking at a page might first try to identify the objects—on one page, a hammer, a nail, three screws, a screwdriver, and a wrench—and then tell what the objects have in common. In doing this they are recognizing the class to which the objects belong and naming it. They might also be asked to tell one other object that would fit the ones pictured. Children can be encouraged to do some classification of their own by collecting items that they think would fit together for another page of the book. For books such as this one, the teacher should feel free to select only those pages that will have meaning for the class. There is no need to "do" every page. The teacher will also want to work with small groups of children, so that all will be involved in the thinking and discussion.

Other books have the potential if the teacher sees it. One teacher[50] had read *Frog and Toad Are Friends*[51] to her kindergarten class. At one point in the book, Toad and Frog return home from a walk and Toad discovers that he has lost a button off his jacket. He and Frog go back over all the places they have walked in an attempt to find it. Frog and several other animals find buttons, but none matches the one Toad lost. They find a black one but his was white. They find one with two holes but his had four. Attribute by attribute, it is narrowed to a white, four-holed, big, round, thick button. They cannot find it, and an angry Toad returns home to find the button on the floor of his living room. Concerned about the trouble he has caused his friend, he sews the button, and also sews all the other buttons that they have found. The next day he gives his button-covered jacket to Frog.

After the children had heard the story, the teacher produced a large box of buttons. Each child decided what kind of button he or she would look for. They used the classifications Toad used, such as thick, or white, but chose others as well. They tried to see how many they could find that would fit their classification, then compared their collections of buttons. Later some of the children made pictures of Frog wearing Toad's jacket. They used fabric from the scrap box to make jackets, then pasted buttons all over the jackets for decoration. It was an enjoyable experience for the children, in part because of the story, and in part because the teacher selected a classification activity which was challenging but not overwhelming for the children. They pasted the buttons on their pictures because the teacher knew that attempting to sew small buttons onto cloth would have been frustrating for them.

Children might be asked to classify some of the stories they have heard. If the categories are not given, children can begin to develop their own. They might divide stories into those they liked and those they did not like; they might divide them into stories that could happen and stories that were make-believe; it might be stories about animals and stories about people. The teacher guides the children to think about the content of the stories, and perhaps the format, and to find a variety of ways of classifying them.

Organizing.   Another thinking skill is that of organizing. Young children can be helped to organize by learning to sequence events. Cumulative folk tales, as well as many contemporary stories, are a rich source of material. Reconstructing the sequence of events in some tales, however, is a difficult task because knowing the order of events is a matter of straight recall. For example, the little boy in *In the Forest*[52] is followed by a series of animals who join him for his walk before his father arrives. That he happens across the elephants before the bears is of no consequence. Likewise, the animals whom the little chicken in *Chicken Forgets*[53] meets on his way to pick blackberries could be met at any time, for each distracts him with new advice. It is necessary only that the robin be the last he meets, for the robin shows him the blackberries, and he is successful in getting the basket of wild berries that his mother has requested.

Other tales have a patterned order to the events. The goats in *The Three Billy Goats Gruff*[54] get progressively larger, until the third and largest is able to crush the ugly troll. The poor villager whose house is too small with his mother, his wife, and his six children follows the rabbi's advice in *It Could Always Be Worse.*[55] He brings larger and larger animals into the house with them, from chickens to the cow. When the largest has been there for a week and the man can stand it no longer, the rabbi advises him to put all the animals out. Suddenly the house is larger and quieter, and life is sweeter. Again a pattern of increase in size makes the sequence of events easier to remember.

Sometimes the pattern is that of chronological order. In *Charlie Needs a Cloak*[56] Charlie first shears his sheep, then washes the wool, then cards it. From spring to fall Charlie proceeds with the preparation of his cloak: dying the yarn, weaving the cloth, sewing the pieces of fabric. When winter comes, he has completed his new cloak. In *The Little Red Hen*[57] the hen gets no help from the cat, the dog, or the mouse from the time she finds the grains of wheat until she has planted them, harvested them, had them ground into flour, and used the flour to bake a cake. The others are willing to help her eat the cake, but having done all the work by herself, the hen decides to eat the cake by herself. The sequence in these books reflects the way something is made. Children repeating the sequence can infer as well as recall what comes next.

Children can be given the need to sequence the events in a story by making plans to interpret it dramatically. After talking about the characters in the story, they can review what happened first, second, and so on. They may tell how they know when in the story each event happened.

You might encourage children to work with sequencing by telling the story on a flannelboard, then letting children retell it. Put all the figures in random order on a table beside the flannelboard. Children can take turns selecting the piece that should go up next and telling that part of the story.

Another technique to engage children in sequencing is to have the children draw a picture of one thing that happened in the story. Working with only three or four children, ask each to tell what is happening in his or her picture. Then ask them which of the pictures would come first in the story, which next, and so on until all are ordered. Work with small groups, in part because the more pictures there are the more complex the task becomes, and in part because children tire of listening to many children describing their pictures.

Sequencing should allow the children to be active participants, doing something that requires them to use the sequence, not just answering the question, "Then what happened?"

Applying.   Books that describe "how to do it" can be used to give children the opportunity to apply what they are hearing or reading. The directions need to be clear and the project within the capabilities of the children. Rockwell's *Look at This*[58] gives directions for making applesauce, a dancing frog from construction paper and paper fasteners, and a noisemaker of rolled paper. The directions are given in the first person as though a child who had made the objects were telling how to do it. Step by step illustrations add to an already clear text. A teacher might read one project from the book to a small group of first or second graders, then give it to them to follow the directions through looking at the pictures. They should be able to make the paper projects on their own, though the applesauce would need supervision.

A teacher of kindergarten children might read the directions, then work with the children, reading each direction again as the children complete each step. A book such as this might also be used as a model for children to dictate or write their own directions for making something. Can they describe the procedure clearly enough for another child to follow the directions? They can find out by trying it.

Expanding the Ability to Reason Logically

For young children, basic experiences with logical thinking involve working with *if . . . then* propositions. If it rains, then we will stay inside all day. If she forgets to return the permission slip, then she cannot go on the picnic. Certainly much literature involves such cause and effect relationships. Letting children predict what will happen next in a story is one technique for encouraging them to think about causality and to determine when connections between events appear reasonable.

There are also books for children that center on errors in logical reasoning, or on trickery, or on the humor of exaggeration. Reading them gives children a chance to feel superior to the book characters because they know what is going on. They recognize the absurdity and enjoy their own mastery of the situation.

In *Theodore Turtle*,[59] Theodore loses belonging after belonging, always putting one down while he searches for another. Young children see what is happening and know why he has so much trouble. Then there is Mr. Higgins in *Clocks and More Clocks*.[60] When he finds a clock in the attic he wants to know if it tells the correct time. He buys another clock to check, but when he walks from clock to clock, he notices that they always read about one minute different. After buying several more clocks and having the problem continue, Mr. Higgins invites the Clockmaker to check the clocks. As the Clockmaker goes from clock to clock and compares their time to that on his watch, he finds that they are all correct. Mr. Higgins is so impressed that he buys the watch. And, of course, there is Cully Cully, the hunter who in *Cully Cully and the Bear*[61] shoots at a bear, but only nicks its nose. A chase begins that eventually culminates with hunter and bear circling a tree, each convinced that there are several of the other.

Some books depend on the illustrations to show the absurdity of what the characters are saying. In *Nothing Ever Happens on My Block*,[62] Chester Filbert sits on the curb and complains about how dull his block is. Readers looking at the illustrations see a neighborhood alive with action. A witch appears in different windows, a robber is chased by a policeman, children play, fires burn, houses are rebuilt. Still Chester sits, oblivious to the excitement around him. In *Pea Soup and Sea Serpents*,[63] Norton and Atherton go out in their boat in a thick fog to look for sea serpents. They discuss the water, the fog, whether they can swim, all the time not seeing a mischievous pink monster. It eventual-

ly overturns their boat, then helps them back to shore. They end the day thinking that perhaps they will try again on a less foggy day. The serpent trails behind,
carrying their pail for them.

Some books show cleverness in the form of trickery. The cook in *The Perfect
Pancake*,[64] who makes perfect pancakes but serves only one to a person, is
tricked into making far more for the peddler. He tells her that there is something
slightly wrong with each pancake. As she keeps trying for the perfect one, he
keeps eating. In *Inch by Inch*[65] an inchworm agrees to measure the nightin-
gale's song to keep from being eaten, then simply inches out of sight.

Topsy-Turvies,[66] subtitled "Pictures to Stretch the Imagination," makes a
direct challenge to the reader. Each illustration in this wordless picture book
in some way plays with perspective. Second or third graders might look at the
illustrations and try to see what is strange about them. Some may be able to
verbalize the impossibilities, such as a maze where people enter right side up
but exit upside down, or a building where the inside and the outside walls seem
to shift positions.

For each of these books, the children's responses during the reading may
give you an indication of whether or not they understand the twists of logic
that the authors employ. You may want to ask children, "If you could tell Mr.
Higgins (or another character) one thing that you think would help him, what
would it be?" Children can then demonstrate their command of the situation.

Encouraging Critical Thinking

The term *critical thinking* is being used in this text to indicate thought that involves seeing relationships between events, inferring what is not stated directly, analyzing events within a story, synthesizing evidence, and evaluating both
the content and the quality of literature. It is thinking that goes beyond the
literal level. Two strategies for encouraging children to think critically are the
asking of higher level questions and the planning of questions and activities
that will elicit divergent responses.

Asking Higher Level Questions.   One widely used system for categorizing
questions is that of Sanders.[67] Based on the work of Benjamin Bloom,[68] this
system categorizes questions by the kind of thinking required to answer them.
Thus a question that asks for information directly stated in a reading is a *memory*
question because it requires recall, or memory, to answer.

The other types of questions described by Sanders and applied to literature
are as follows:

- Translation—These questions ask children to translate an idea in a book
  into a different form, such as telling part of the plot in one's own words,
  or drawing a picture of a scene that has been described.
- Interpretation—These questions ask children to draw inferences, explain
  cause and effect relationships, or compare facts. Children must process
  the information presented in a book.
- Application—These questions ask children to apply ideas from literature
  to new situations.

- Analysis—These questions ask children to respond based on a knowledge of logical reasoning processes or knowledge of literary forms.
- Synthesis—These questions ask children to combine pieces of information in a new way.
- Evaluation—These questions ask children to both develop and apply standards for judging a work.

Thinking about questions in this way is useful because it helps a teacher provide variety in the kinds of thinking he or she asks children to do and because it emphasizes forms of critical thinking.

To plan a series of questions for a discussion with young children, decide first on the focus of your questions. Then devise questions that will develop this focus and that will engage children in such processes as interpretation or synthesis or evaluation. For each of your higher level questions, think of what memory level information it encompasses. You may need to ask several memory questions to establish the children's base of literal understanding before progressing with your key questions.

Suppose you had read *Dark and Full of Secrets*[69] to a group of children. In the story, Christopher and his father are canoeing, and Christopher doesn't want to swim because he can't see what is in the water nor what might be on the bottom. He has enjoyed swimming in the ocean, but the pond is dark and full of secrets. His father laughs at first, but then brings a mask and snorkel for each of them so that Christopher can dive down, see what is there, and overcome his fears. The experiment works so well that after lunch Christopher ventures out by himself. Fascinated with what he is seeing, he is unaware that he is drifting into deep water. When he tries to stand to clear his mask, he cannot touch bottom. He tries treading water, but then something brushes his foot, causing him to gasp. His mask and mouthpiece fill with water, and he panics. He calls for his father, but it is his dog Ben who comes to the rescue. Holding onto Ben's tail, Christopher makes it to shallow water. His father has come to the water's edge, where he reminds Christopher not to out so far, and makes certain that Christopher is not hurt. Once he has caught his breath, Christopher is again enthusiastic about the fish he has seen. He also is no longer afraid of the dark pond water, even though he cannot see into it from the surface.

As you think about a focus for your discussion, you consider the theme of overcoming fear, the idea of where families go and what they do on vacations, and the topic of pond life. You decide to use the idea of fear because it is so central to the story, and because young children will be able to identify with that emotion. You decide to begin with two memory questions to establish the children's grasp of the facts of the story and then proceed to questions requiring other thinking skills. You plan to ask the following questions:

1. Why was Christopher afraid to swim in the pond?
2. What did his father do to help?
3. Do you think this was a good idea? Why? Why not?
4. What else might his father have done to help?
5. Later in the story Christopher is afraid again. How do the illustrations help you know how Christopher is feeling? (Show illustrations.)

Christopher panics when his mask and snorkel fill with water. (Illustration by Donald Carrick from Dark and Full of Secrets *by Carol Carrick. Text copyright © 1984 by Donald Carrick. Reprinted by permission of Ticknor & Fields/Clarion Books, a Houghton Mifflin Company.)*

6. How is this fear different from his fear of what might be in the pond?
7. Tell us about a time when you were afraid. What did you do? Did anyone help you?
8. When do you think it might be good to be afraid?
9. Do you think Christopher will go snorkeling again? What makes you think this?
10. Do you think there may be other times when Christopher will be afraid? Tell why you think this.

You will have guided children in a discussion about the book and about their own emotions, starting and ending with the story itself, and making your final question one that concludes the unit. In the process, children will have been asked memory (1,2,7), interpretation (6,9,10), analysis (5), synthesis (4), and evaluation (3,8) questions. After you have lead several similar discussions, categorize the kinds of questions you have been asking. If there are types that you never seem to use naturally, work in a conscious manner to develop your questioning skills in the appropriate areas.

Try to state your questions as concisely as possible so that young children don't lose the thread of meaning, or answer one part before you finish the entire question. Pace yourself to wait for answers. If the question requires thought, then you must give children time to think. Silence makes some teachers and day care professionals nervous, so they answer the question themselves, or ask another question to fill the space. You can train yourself to give children time to think.

Not every book should be followed by questions. Discussion is only one means of exploring a book's ideas more fully. You will want a balance among discussion, activities, and no follow up at all.

Planning for Divergent Responses.   Another way of classifying questions and activities is to assess the number of *correct* responses that may be offered. Convergent questions have only one best, or right, answer. Divergent questions have more than one acceptable response. The question, "What did Christopher's father do to help?" is a convergent one because the book clearly shows what his father did, and thus there is only one correct answer. The question, "When do you think it might be good to be afraid?" is a divergent one because both the answer given and the rationale behind it would vary from child to child. Sometimes a question is convergent because it is on a literal level, but at other times it may be a higher level question for which the evidence is so strong that there appears to be only one reasonable answer.

Activities, like questions, may call for either convergent or divergent responses. The book *Jumanji*[70] by Chris Van Allsburg captures children's imaginations and lends itself to many divergent activities. It is the story of Judy and Peter who are left home alone for the afternoon and get bored. They decide to take a walk in the park where they find a game titled *Jumanji: A Jungle Adventure Game,* with a notation on the box in what appears to be a child's handwriting that the game is free, and that the instructions should be read carefully. They take the game home, discovering during play that the events described on the game board really do happen. The lion actually does appear in their house and attack; the monkeys steal food; and the monsoon season arrives. When Judy finally reaches the Golden City, thus winning the game, the house is cleared of all its jungle inhabitants and order is restored. The children take the game back to the park leaving it just where they found it. The book closes with two other children picking up the box.

Children might write a new set of directions for the game, perhaps suggesting a different method of ending the game. (In the book the game could only be ended by someone winning.) They might create a story about a time when one of their board games became like *Jumanji,* or one about who would pick up the game next and what would happen. They might construct a board game using only events that they would like to see happen for each of the squares, or they might role play Judy and Peter explaining to their parents what was going on as though the parents had returned in the middle of the game. All of these activities would encourage a variety of responses.

Divergent questions and activities stimulate children to consider a broad range of possibilities, both as they think through responses themselves, and as they listen to the ideas and opinions of others. Many of the activities suggested throughout this book call for divergent responses. Look particularly at the section in chapter eight which is titled "Stimulating Creativity in Art, Music, and Movement."

Engaging in Problem Solving

You will be helping children regularly to define and solve their problems. How can Jim get a turn at jump rope? What can Susan do to keep Jill from teasing her? What could the class make as gifts for their parents?

Literature presents ample opportunities for children to define and suggest possible solutions to problems book characters have. Their solutions may not be the one or ones chosen by the book characters. It is important to help children realize that there may be many solutions to a problem, and that solutions may be evaluated according to their consequences. Some may be problems much like the ones the children themselves have; others may be totally in the realm of fantasy.

Three year olds can listen to *The Blanket*,[71] a very short story in which the boy cannot find the blanket he always takes to bed with him. His mother and father look for it, but finally he finds it under his pillow. Children can tell about any toy or object that they usually take to bed with them. Then present two problems for them to solve. First, if you could not find your toy at bedtime, where would you look? And second, if you did not find it, what could you do?

Four year olds can listen to *Ton and Pon, Two Good Friends*,[72] in which Big Ton and Little Pon are sent by their mothers to deliver a basket of apples to a friend. They try various ways of sharing the load, but each time one or the other ends up with most of the weight. The illustrations show clearly what is happening. Their solution is to eat the apples, then fill the basket with flowers, which are much lighter. However, the friend thanks them for the flowers, and presents them a basket of apples to take home to their mothers. Children can try some of the ways Ton and Pon carried the basket and can experiment with ideas of their own.

Primary children might listen to "The Squad Car."[73] In this poem, the narrator buys his older brother Woody a wind-up Dick Tracy squad car for his birthday. The boys at the birthday party play with the car, but then the key gets knocked down a hole in the wall. They try fishing it out with a magnet, but that does not work. They write the toy company for another key but the company does not answer. They try other keys, but none fit. The squad car sits on the shelf, still shiny.

Children can be asked to brainstorm ideas for what might be done about the squad car. In brainstorming they try to think of as many ideas as they can, not stopping to evaluate any of the ideas. The teacher lists their suggestions on the board or on chart paper. Once all their ideas are listed, the teacher leads a discussion in which they look at each suggestion and tell what might happen if that were done. As a group they decide on which solution they think has the most merit. Then the teacher reads "The Last Part of the Squad Car Story."[74] This tells about the family's solution to the problem. A year later, when Woody is having another birthday party, they decide to get him another Dick Tracy squad car. Then he will have two cars and one key. When the car comes, the key is welded into the keyhole. So Woody keeps the new squad car and gives the old one to his brother. The poem ends when they make a new friend who trades his key to an old squad car for three marbles. You can point out to the children that none of the solutions in the poem worked. It was the unexpected arrival of someone new with a key which made the car usable again.

Second and third graders enjoy the imaginative problem solving in humorous books such as *What If. . .?*[75] There are fourteen encounters, with the problem stated on the right hand page and the solution on the back of that page. Children can wrestle with such questions as, "What if a tiger knitted you a pair of socks forty-seven times as long as your feet?" After giving their own suggestions, they can turn the page and see the author's solution: "Call your brother and say, together, 'Clever Tiger! What a really marvelous pair of sleeping bags!' " They might then pose their own problems, giving them to classmates to find solutions.

Because most stories involve some problem that must be solved, it is possible to stop in almost any story and ask children what the problem is and what solutions they might have for it. However, doing this on a regular basis is likely to lessen their enjoyment of the literature. You will want to select only one or two books each month to use for problem solving. Look for ones where the problem is fairly clear. In *Albert's Toothache*,[76] you could stop just before his grandmother arrives. Albert has complained all day of a toothache, but no one in his family believes him. After all, he is a turtle, and since turtles have no teeth, it is difficult to believe that he has a toothache. You could ask the children, "Do you think Albert has a toothache? Why or why not? How could his mother find out what the trouble is with Albert?" When his grandmother arrives, she asks Albert *where* he had a toothache. He tells her on his left toe, because that is where a gopher bit him. The ache is from the gopher's tooth. In this case, getting more information from Albert solved the problem.

Thinking of solutions to problems of book characters can be game-like. The idea is to present alternatives, not to guess what happened in the book. For this reason, you might well do some of your problem-solving questions after a book has been completed. Questions would then ask what a character might have done other than what he or she actually did do.

Summary

Young children come to school with a wealth of information. They are attempting to organize that information, to make sense of their world, to integrate their experiences. They are actively constructing concepts and engaging in the thought processes that are fundamental in concept formation. Until they are six or seven years of age, children tend to rely more on sensory data than on logic to reach conclusions regarding physical objects. They may also engage in transductive reasoning, going from particular to particular without reference to the general, resulting in faulty conclusions. They engage in intuitive and associative thought as well as the rational, and find enjoyment in imaginative thought and play.

The following long term goals are appropriate for the intellectual growth of young children.

- Children will continue to acquire new concepts and to refine ones already held.
- Children will develop skill in a variety of thinking processes.
- Children will expand their powers of logical reasoning.
- Children will utilize critical thinking skills.
- Children will engage successfully in problem solving.

Books offer opportunities to help children in the acquisition and refinement of concepts. Table 2 suggests appropriate teaching strategies. Often information that children could not discover on their own is presented in books. Other books, particularly concept books, are in themselves teaching aids, for they organize information logically and present it with illustrations that add to children's understanding. Literature can both stimulate children to explore a topic and provide reinforcement for learnings they have acquired through direct experience.

Literature furnishes an opportunity for children to engage in many thinking processes. They may observe carefully as they look at the illustrations in picture books; they may make predictions about what will happen in a book; they may compare two books on similar topics or themes; they may classify objects portrayed in books, or classify the stories themselves; they may organize, using sequence as the organizing factor; and they may apply the information given in books, following directions which they have read themselves or which the teacher has read to them.

Much literature involves cause and effect relationships, and for this reason gives children experience in predicting outcomes, using an *if . . . then* approach to logic. There are also books that center on errors in logical reasoning or on trickery and give children the chance to show their grasp of the absurdity described.

Children can be encouraged to think critically and to engage in problem solving through carefully planned questions and activities. After establishing a firm base of literal understanding, the teacher guides the children to use higher levels of thinking, making inferences and judgments. He or she plans questions and activities that elicit divergent rather than convergent responses, praising children for new and thoughtful ideas.

Table 2. *Supporting Children's Intellectual Development*

Developmental Goals	Teaching Suggestions	Recommended Literature	
Children will continue to acquire new concepts and to refine ones already held.	Share concept and informational books. Have children compare experiential knowledge with information from books. Use books as visual teaching aids. Read several books on the same topic to provide more than one perspective. Let children use books themselves to reinforce concepts. Use books as a stimulus for further exploration. Present books that reinforce concepts already being acquired. Read books that may help clarify misconceptions.	**Ages 3–5:** Anno Burch Clifton Crews Daughtry Ets Hoban Hoban Holl Hutchins Rockwell Simon Spier Yashima Zolotow	Anno's Counting House Joey's Cat The Boy Who Didn't Believe in Spring Freight Train What's Inside? Gilberto and the Wind Is it Red? Is it Yellow? Is it Blue? Over, Under, & Through The Remarkable Egg Rosie's Walk The Toolbox Where Does My Cat Sleep? Crash! Bang! Boom! Momo's Kitten Mr. Rabbit and the Lovely Present

Table 2. (Cont.)

Developmental Goals	Teaching Suggestions	Recommended Literature	
		Ages 5–8:	
		Blades	*Mary of Mile 18*
		Brady	*Wild Mouse*
		Brown	*The Bionic Bunny Show*
		Carrick	*Beach Bird*
		Friedman	*How My Parents Learned to Eat*
		Goudy	*Houses From the Sea*
		Provensen	*The Glorious Flight*
		Zolotow	*The Sky Was Blue*
Children will develop skill in a variety of thinking processes.	Have children observe and describe detail in illustrations. Have children play observational guessing games with book illustrations. Let children tell the story in wordless picture books. Encourage children to make predictions. Engage children in structural comparisons of books. Compare changes in illustrations within a single book. Share books that classify objects. Build classification activities based on books. Dramatize stories so that children must organize by sequencing events. Let children apply the information in "how to do it" books.	**Ages 3–5:**	
		Ahlberg	*Each Peach Pear Plum*
		Ahlberg	*Peek-a-Boo!*
		Asbjornsen	*The Three Billy Goats Gruff*
		Chwast	*Tall City, Wide Country*
		Dubanevich	*Pigs in Hiding*
		Galdone	*The Little Red Hen*
		Hoban	*Shapes and Things*
		Hutchins	*1 Hunter*
		Lobel	*Frog and Toad Are Friends*
		Schick	*City in the Summer*
		Schick	*City in the Winter*
		Spier	*Noah's Ark*
		Zemach	*It Could Always Be Worse*
		Ages 5–8:	
		Anno	*Anno's Journey*
		dePaola	*Charlie Needs a Cloak*
		Gardner	*The Look Again . . . Book*
		Goodall	*The Story of an English Village*
		Hoban	*Look Again!*
		Hurd	*Mystery on the Docks*
		Jonas	*Round Trip*
		Martin	*Island Winter*
		Martin	*Summer Business*
		Mayer	*A Boy, A Dog, A Frog and A Friend*
		Provensen	*Town and Country*
		Rockwell	*Look at This*
		Selsam	*Backyard Insects*
Children will expand their powers of logical reasoning.	Let children predict what will happen next in a story. Have children discover errors in reasoning in books of trickery or humor.	**Ages 3–5:**	
		Gage	*Cully Cully and the Bear*
		Kahl	*The Perfect Pancake*
		Lionni	*Inch by Inch*

Table 2. (Cont.)

Developmental Goals	Teaching Suggestions	Recommended Literature	
		MacGregor	Theodore Turtle
		Raskin	Nothing Ever Happens on My Block
		Ages 5–8:	
		Anno	Topsy-Turvies
		Hutchins	Clocks and More Clocks
		Schroder	Pea Soup and Sea Serpents
Children will utilize critical thinking skills.	Ask questions about literature that are above the literal level. Plan questions and activities that will elicit divergent responses.	**Ages 5–8:** Carrick Van Allsburg	Dark and Full of Secrets Jumanji
Children will engage successfully in problem solving.	Let children define problems book characters have. Have children brainstorm possible solutions to problems. Encourage children to evaluate possible solutions in terms of consequences. Let children engage in imaginative and humorous problem solving.	**Ages 3–5:** Burn- ingham **Ages 5–8:** Low Neville Williams	The Blanket What If. . . ? "The Squad Car Story" Albert's Toothache

Extending Your Learning

1. Select a book by Anne and Harlow Rockwell or by an author of your choice. Tell how the book can contribute to children's concept development.
2. Read three picture books that are set in the same region of the United States. Describe the image of this part of the country that emerges.
3. Select five realistic picture books about animals. Make plans to use at least three of them with children.
4. Share with two or three children one of the books mentioned in the preceding chapter that requires the children to observe closely. Compare their responses to the book.
5. Select a picture book appropriate for first or second graders. Develop a set of questions to use when discussing it. The majority of questions should be above the memory level and all should be sequenced logically.
6. For a single picture book, describe two activities that would evoke divergent responses.
7. Select three books from the list of recommended children's books at the end of this chapter. Tell how each of these might support a child's intellectual growth.

8. Read from any two of the recommended references at the end of this chapter. Identify three central concepts related to children's development that would be useful for you as a day care professional or teacher to know.

Notes

1. Kenneth D. Wann, Mirian Selchen Dorn, and Elizabeth Ann Liddle, *Fostering Intellectual Development in Young Children* (New York: Teachers College, Columbia University, 1962), 12.

2. Helen F. Robison, *Exploring Teaching in Early Childhood Education* (Boston: Allyn and Bacon Inc., 1983), 34.

3. Wann, Dorn, and Liddle, *Fostering Intellectual Development*, 28–34.

4. J. H. Flavell, *The Developmental Psychology of Jean Piaget*, (Princeton, N.J.: Van Nostrand Reinhold Co. Inc., 1962).

5. Jean Piaget and Barbel Inhelder, *The Psychology of the Child* (New York: Basic Books Inc., Publishers, 1969).

6. Anne & Harlow Rockwell, *The Toolbox* (New York: Macmillan Publishing Co., 1971).

7. Adelaide Holl, *The Remarkable Egg.* Illus. by Roger Duvoisin (New York: Lothrop, Lee & Shepard Books, 1968).

8. Marc Brown and Laurene Krasny Brown, *The Bionic Bunny Show* (Boston: Little, Brown & Co. Inc., 1984).

9. Marc Brown and Laurene Krasny Brown, *The Bionic Bunny Show* (Boston: Little, Brown & Co. Inc., 1984), 8.

10. Ann Blades, *Mary of Mile 18* (Montreal: Tundra Books, 1971).

11. Ina R. Friedman, *How My Parents Learned to Eat.* Illus. by Allen Say (Boston: Houghton Mifflin Co., 1984).

12. Alice and Martin Provensen, *The Glorious Flight* (New York: Viking Press, 1983).

13. Duanne Daughtry, *What's Inside?* (New York: Alfred A. Knopf Inc., 1984).

14. Tana Hoban, *Is It Red? Is It Yellow? Is It Blue?* (New York: Greenwillow Books, 1978).

15. Text "Freight train. Moving . . . going . . . Gone." and illustration "a black steam engine" in *Freight Train* by Donald Crews. Copyright © 1978 by Donald Crews. By permission of Greenwillow Books (A division of William Morrow & Co.).

16. Charlotte Zolotow, *Mr. Rabbit and the Lovely Present.* Illus. by Maurice Sendak (New York: Harper & Row Publishers, Inc., 1962).

17. Mitsumasa Anno, *Anno's Counting House* (New York: Philomel, 1982).

18. Peter Spier, *Crash! Bang! Boom!* (Garden City, N.Y.: Doubleday & Co. Inc., 1972).

19. Irene Brady. *Wild Mouse* (New York: Charles Scribner's Sons, 1976).

20. Norma Simon, *Where Does My Cat Sleep?* Illus. by Dora Leder (Chicago: Albert Whitman & Co., 1982).

21. Marie Hall Ets, *Gilberto and the Wind* (New York: Viking Press, 1963).

22. Lucille Clifton, *The Boy Who Didn't Believe in Spring.* Illus. by Brinton Turkle (New York: E. P. Dutton, Inc., 1973).

23. Tana Hoban, *Over, Under & Through* (New York: Macmillan Publishing Co., 1973).

24. Pat Hutchins, *Rosie's Walk* (New York: Macmillan Publishing Co., 1968).

25. Carol and Donald Carrick, *Beach Bird* (New York: Dial Press, 1973).

26. Alice E. Goudy, *Houses from the Sea.* Illus. by Adrienne Adams (New York: Charles Scribner's Sons, 1959).

27. Mitsu and Taro Yashima, *Momo's Kitten* (New York: Viking Press, 1961).

28. Robert Burch, *Joey's Cat.* Illus. by Don Freeman (New York: Viking Press, 1969).

29. Charlotte Zolotow, *The Sky Was Blue.* Illus. by Garth Williams (New York: Harper & Row Publishers, Inc., 1963).

30. Peter Spier, *Noah's Ark* (Garden City, N.Y.: Doubleday & Co. Inc., 1977).

Notes

31. Millicent E. Selsam, *Backyard Insects*. Illus. by Ronald Goor (New York: Four Winds Press, 1983).

32. Janet and Allan Ahlberg, *Each Peach Pear Plum* (New York: Viking Press, 1979, c1978).

33. Pat Hutchins, *1 Hunter* (New York: Greenwillow Books, 1982).

34. Arlene Dubanevich, *Pigs in Hiding* (New York: Four Winds Press, 1983).

35. Tana Hoban, *Look Again!* (New York: Macmillan Publishing Co., 1971).

36. Janet and Allan Ahlberg, *Peek-A-Boo!* (New York: Viking Press, 1981).

37. Ann Jonas, *Round Trip* (New York: Greenwillow Books, 1983).

38. Beau Gardner, *The Look Again. . . and Again, and Again, and Again Book* (New York: Lothrop, Lee & Shepard Books, 1984).

39. Mercer and Marianna Mayer, *A Boy, A Dog, A Frog and A Friend* (New York: Dial Press, 1971).

40. Mitsumasa Anno, *Anno's Journey* (New York: Collins World, 1978).

41. Thacher Hurt, *Mystery on the Docks* (New York: Harper & Row, Publishers, Inc., 1983).

42. Alice and Martin Provensen, *Town & Country* (New York: Crown Publishers Inc., 1984).

43. Seymour Chwast, *Tall City, Wide Country* (New York: Viking Press, 1983).

44. Eleanor Schick, *City in the Summer* (New York: Macmillan Publishing, 1969).

45. Eleanor Schick, *City in the Winter* (New York: Macmillan Publishing Co., 1970).

46. Charles E. Martin, *Island Winter* (New York: Greenwillow Books, 1984).

47. Charles E. Martin, *Summer Business* (New York: Greenwillow Books, 1984).

48. John Goodall, *The Story of an English Village* (New York: Atheneum Publishers, 1979).

49. Tana Hoban, *Shapes and Things* (New York: Macmillan Publishing Co., 1970).

50. Sue Marshall, Living and Learning Center, Johnston, R.I.

51. Arnold Lobel, *Frog and Toad Are Friends* (New York: Harper & Row, Publishers, Inc., 1970).

52. Marie Hall Ets, *In the Forest* (New York: Viking Press, 1944).

53. Miska Miles, *Chicken Forgets*. Illus. by Jim Arnosky (Boston: Little, Brown & Co., 1976).

54. P. C. Asbjornsen and J. E. Moe, *The Three Billy Goats Gruff*. Illus. by Marcia Brown (New York: Harcourt Brace Jovanovich, 1957).

55. Margot Zemach, *It Could Always Be Worse* (New York: Farrar, Straus & Giroux, 1976).

56. Tomie de Paola, *Charlie Needs a Cloak* (Englewood Cliffs, N.J.: Prentice-Hall Inc., 1973).

57. Paul Galdone, *The Little Red Hen* (New York: Seabury Press, 1973).

58. Harlow Rockwell, *Look at This* (New York: Macmillan Publishing Co., 1978).

59. Ellen MacGregor, *Theodore Turtle*, Illus. by Paul Galdone (New York: McGraw-Hill Publishing Inc., 1955).

60. Pat Hutchins, *Clocks and More Clocks* (New York: Macmillan Publishing Co., 1970).

61. Wilson Gage, *Cully Cully and the Bear*. Illus. by James Stevenson (New York: Greenwillow Books, 1983).

62. Ellen Raskin, *Nothing Ever Happens on My Block* (New York: Atheneum Publishers, 1971).

63. William Schroder, *Pea Soup and Sea Serpents* (New York: Lothrop, Lee & Shepard Books, 1977).

64. Virginia Kahl, *The Perfect Pancake* (New York: Charles Scribner's Sons, 1960).

65. Leo Lionni, *Inch by Inch* (New York: Astor-Honor, 1960).

66. Mitsumasa Anno, *Topsy-Turvies* (New York: John Weatherhill Inc., 1970).

67. Norris Sanders, *Classroom Questions: What Kinds?* (New York: Harper & Row Publishers, Inc., 1966).

68. Benjamin S. Bloom, ed., *Taxonomy of Educational Objectives* (New York: Longmans, Green & Co., 1956).

69. Carol Carrick, *Dark and Full of Secrets*. Illus. by Donald Carrick (New York: Clarion, 1984).

70. Chris Van Allsburg, *Jumanji* (Boston: Houghton Mifflin Co., 1981).

71. John Burningham, *The Blanket* (London: Jonathan Cape, 1975).

72. Kazuo Iwamura, *Ton and Pon, Two Good Friends* (Scarsdale, N.Y.: Bradbury, 1984, © 1980).

Notes

73. Mary Neville, "The Squad Car," in *Woody & Me*. Illus. by Ronni Solbert (New York: Pantheon Books Inc., 1966).
74. Mary Neville, "The Last Part of the Squad Car Story" in *Woody & Me*. Illus. by Ronni Solbert (New York: Pantheon Books Inc., 1966).
75. Used by permission of Atheneum Publishers from *What If. . . ?* by Joseph Low. Copyright © 1976 by Joseph Low.
76. Barbara Williams, *Albert's Toothache*. Illus. by Kay Chorao (New York: E.P. Dutton, Inc., 1974).

Recommended Children's Books

Allard, Harry. *Miss Nelson is Missing*. Illus. by James Marshall. Boston: Houghton Mifflin Co., 1977.

Allen, Pamela. *Who Sank the Boat?* New York: Coward-McCann, 1983.

Ancona, George. *It's a Baby!* New York: E.P. Dutton, Inc., 1979.

Aruego, Jose and Dewey, Ariane. *We Hide, You Seek*. New York: Greenwillow Books, 1979.

Baker, Alan. *Benjamin's Book*. New York: Lothrop, Lee & Shepard Books, 1983.

Baylor, Byrd. *The Best Town in the World*. Illus. by Ronald Himler. New York: Charles Scribner's Sons, 1983.

Burningham, John. *Would You Rather. . .* New York: Thomas Y. Crowell Publishers, 1978.

Crews, Donald. *Truck*. New York: Greenwillow Books, 1980.

Goodall, John S. *An Edwardian Holiday*. New York: Atheneum Publishers, 1979.

Lobel, Arnold. *A Treeful of Pigs.*. Illus. by Anita Lobel. New York: Greenwillow Books, 1979.

Parish, Peggy. *Beginning Mobiles*. Illus. by Lynn Sweet. New York: Macmillan Publishing Co., 1979.

Rahn, Joan Elma. *Holes*. Boston: Houghton Mifflin Co., 1984.

Rockwell, Anne R. and Harlow Rockwell. *The Emergency Room*. New York: Greenwillow Books, 1985.

Ruben, Patricia. *True or False?* Philadelphia: J.B. Lippincott Co., 1978.

Ruben, Patricia. *What is New? What is Missing? What is Different?* Philadelphia: J.B. Lippincott Co., 1978.

Spier, Peter. *Fast-Slow, High-Low: A Book of Opposites*. Garden City, N.Y.: Doubleday & Co. Inc., 1971.

Tresselt, Alvin. *What Did You Leave Behind?* Illus. by Roger Duvoisin. New York: Lothrop, Lee & Shepard Books, 1978.

Van Allsburg, Chris. *The Garden of Abdul Gasazi*. Boston: Houghton Mifflin Co., 1979.

Waber, Bernard. *The Snake: A Very Long Story*. Boston: Houghton Mifflin Co., 1978.

Wildsmith, Brian. *Puzzles*. London: Oxford University Press, 1970.

Recommended References

Furth, Hans. *Piaget for Teachers*. Englewood Cliffs, N.J.: Prentice-Hall, Inc. 1970.

Furth, Hans, and Wachs, Harry. *Thinking Goes to School*. New York: Oxford University Press, 1975.

Keil, Frances. *Semantic and Conceptual Development*. Boston: Harvard University Press, 1980.

Piaget, Jean, and Inhelder, Barbel. *The Psychology of the Child*. New York: Basic Books Inc., Publishers, 1969.

Wann, Kenneth D.; Dorn, Miriam; and Liddle, Elizabeth Ann. *Fostering Intellectual Development in Young Children*. New York: Teachers College Press, 1962.

Weikart, David P.; Rogers, Linda; and Adcock, Carolyn. *The Cognitively Oriented Curriculum*. Urbana: University of Illinois Press, 1975.

6

Supporting Children's Personality Development

Personality Development in Young Children

Emotions, values, ways of perceiving, and feelings about self are all a part of personality. It is defined by Mussen as "the organization of an individual's predispositions and his unique adjustment to his environment."[1] Some aspects of personality are genetically influenced. For example, children who are physically attractive often find others reacting to them in positive ways, and this helps them to think positively about themselves. The social environment, however, plays a greater role in the development of personality than does the biological inheritance of an individual. A child raised in a society that stresses competition is more likely to become competitive than is a child raised in a society that emphasizes sharing and cooperation.

Erikson[2] seeks to explain personality growth by describing how human beings respond to potential conflicts at specific periods in their lives. He posits eight stages in a total lifespan, of which the first four are most applicable for young children. The first stage, the first year of life, is critical in that it is during this period that

children develop trust which leads to later feelings of security. The conflict is between trust and mistrust. Trust develops when the primary care giver responds
warmly and lovingly to the child.

During ages two and three, children struggle for autonomy. The conflict is between autonomy and doubt. Children want to explore, to do things for themselves,
to be in control. Children who have been encouraged by their parents to be independent at this age are more highly motivated to achieve when they reach school
than are children who were not rewarded for such behavior.[3]

At ages four and five, children have a conflict between initiative, wanting to
carry out activities on their own, and guilt over what they would like to do. For
nursery school and kindergarten teachers, this is a time when children can be encouraged to make choices, to take action on their own.

From ages six to eleven, children struggle with industry versus inferiority. Pro-
ductivity becomes important. They want to complete tasks, to learn what is expected of them, to gain recognition for their efforts. These are crucial years in
the development of self-concept and self-esteem.

Self-concept refers to individuals' ideas of their own capabilities, what they
see themselves as being able to do. Self-esteem is the value individuals put
on themselves, how worthy they feel themselves to be. Both self-concept and
self-esteem are influenced strongly by the way in which the others react to and
treat the individual. Children who know that the important people in their lives
value them think more highly of themselves. They become more confident,
and this confidence leads them to attempt difficult tasks and to anticipate success. Teachers and day care professionals can aid the development of positive
self-concepts in children by suggesting tasks that are challenging yet attainable.
They can show also that they value and support each child's efforts.

The development of the self-concept begins early at home. So too does
another learning based on children's interactions with their parents. This is the
process of identification, in which an individual accepts the characteristics and
beliefs of another as his or her own. A boy may walk just like his father, or
a girl use the mannerisms and voice inflection of her mother. This early identification with the parent of the same sex leads to sex typing, the adoption of
the sex roles considered appropriate in a particular culture. As sex roles become
far less restricted, day care professionals and teachers will want to provide
children with ways of identifying their own sexuality while remaining free from
sex role stereotypes.

Identification is a lifelong process. As children encounter a larger social world,
they begin to identify with models other than their parents. Teachers, friends,
and characters from books, movies, and television all may be emulated.
Children thus acquire a complex system of beliefs and behaviors.

Children just coming to school are learning about themselves and their emotions as well as about their physical and social environments. One may learn
that his temper tantrum which effectively provided attention at home is ignored
at school. Another may find that many of her classmates, like her, are afraid
of the dark and fear being left alone. As children begin to learn ways of expressing and of managing their feelings, they learn what is acceptable behavior
in a particular situation and what is not. In seeking to help children, the adult

will want to provide experiences that will enhance each child's self-concept, that will help each child function as independently as possible, and that will help each child deal successfully with his or her emotions.

Goals for Teaching

Teaching goals for personality development can be categorized into long term developmental goals, into general goals for each grade or age level, and into specific goals for individual children. Long term goals describe behaviors or competencies that are developed over time, and that are thought of as desired patterns of behavior. The long term goal that children will attempt new tasks willingly is reflective of personality development because the willingness to attempt something new is related both to self-concept and to the need to achieve.

General goals for each grade level are often listed in curriculum guides. Personality goals and social goals may be combined under a heading of *affective goals*, distinguishing them from the cognitive, or intellectual, goals. One such goal for kindergarten is that children will function independently in several work areas within the classroom. It is more specific than a long term goal and is keyed to the needs and abilities of children of this age. All, or nearly all, of the children in the group will be expected to reach this general goal.

Goals for individual children are even more specific. You will develop these goals as you work with a group and come to know each child. "Steve will overcome his fear of the coatroom and go in by himself to get his coat" is an individual goal, one developed by a teacher who saw Steve's need, a need that was not shared by other children in the class.

There are times when your use of books will help in the achievement of all three types of goals. This chapter focuses on long term developmental goals, ones that are common to the preschool and primary years. Books offer opportunities for you to help children grow toward the following goals for personality development:

- Children will weigh evidence and make appropriate choices.
- Children will set tasks for themselves and will complete tasks they begin.
- Children will develop positive and realistic self-concepts.
- Children will develop feelings of self-worth and self-esteem.
- Children will begin to recognize their own values and to choose from among values.
- Children will understand their emotions and will express them in socially acceptable ways.

Opportunities Books Offer

Involving Children in Choice-Making

"Would you like to hear a story?" is more often a rhetorical than a real question in a classroom or center. Children are not being asked for their preferences; they are being informed that it is story time and the adult is going to read to them. Listen to your own way of telling children about planned activities. If they have no choice, try to introduce the activity in statement rather than question form. "Today I am going to read a story about two fleas," or "Please get ready for story time. I think you'll be surprised at how this story ends."

Presenting Options.   Begin to think of ways that children can be encouraged to make choices. If you present children with a choice, you must be willing to accept their decision. This means that objectionable options should not be presented. As you share literature with children, there are many opportunities for them to make choices and ways for you to structure the choice making so that all the alternatives are acceptable. Some are very simple ones. Children may be asked which story or poem they would like to hear read or reread. Narrow the choices to two or three and have all available. Poetry especially lends itself to this sort of choice making, for poems become better liked as they become more familiar. One nursery school teacher constructed a poster board *poetry rabbit*. In its basket the rabbit had a collection of paper eggs of different sizes, colors, and designs. On each egg was a poem about spring. The three and four year olds could select an egg and the teacher would read the poem on it. After several days, the children knew which egg had the poem they particularly liked. Rereading poems helps children find poetry pleasurable, as well as giving them a chance to choose.

Sometimes the choice will be one of sequence, of what will be done first. Would they like to hear the story before or after snack time? Would they like to have art first or story time first? These choices are group ones, where each child's opinion counts, but which are decided by what the majority prefers. Many others can be individual choices, where one child makes the choice and where the decision involves only that child's behavior.

One area for choice is whether the child wants to listen to a story or not. It may be in the form of announcing that all who are ready for a story should come to the story circle, or should go in the corner where an aide is sitting with the book to be read. The principal of one elementary school reads to children during the lunch period each day. She announces as they come into the lunchroom what the book for that day will be. Children who wish to hear it go with her to another room, listening to the story as they eat their lunches. She reports that the number of listeners fluctuates, and that different children attend. The choice is theirs, each day, whether they would like to hear that story, or whether they would like to eat in the lunchroom, visiting with friends as they eat. They are responsible for their choices. Once made, they cannot change rooms that day. However, they are not asked to make a long term commitment. In a classroom or day care facility, children can be given a choice of listening or not by having a listening center set up in the room. Those who want to hear a story or poem may go to the center; those who do not can engage in other activities.

Encouraging Book Selection.   Young children can select which book they would like to take with them from the library to their room, or perhaps from the classroom or center to their homes. Some classes have periods for *Sustained Silent Reading,* a period when everyone, including the teacher, reads books of his or her choice. The purpose for sustained silent reading is to show that recreational reading is valued by the school, as well as to give each child the opportunity to read in a quiet setting. In preschool and primary classes, where some children are reading and some are not, this might be a brief period of looking at books following a trip to the library. Their choices of books become important because the children know there is a special time for looking at them.

In schools or centers where book clubs are permitted or in ones that have book fairs, children can select books not just to borrow but to keep. In these cases, they can purchase paperback books at moderate prices. The Reading is Fundamental program also provides children with books of their own.

Planning Several Activities.   If you have planned to have an activity following the reading of a book, think about having two or three independent ones and allowing each child to choose one of them. Suppose you had read *Amifika*[4] to a class of kindergarten children. In this story, Amifika overhears his mother telling Cousin Katy that his daddy is coming home from the army, and that they will have to get rid of some things to make more space. She plans to dispose of things he will not remember. Amifika hardly remembers his daddy, and he reasons that his daddy will not remember him; therefore, he is going to be one of the things which will be tossed out. After hiding several places and being in the way, he goes outside where he falls asleep. He is awakened

Children should be encouraged to make selections thoughtfully.

as he is being carried by a man who suddenly seems very familiar. "You my own Daddy!"[5], he cries, surrounded by his daddy's arms and the love of both his parents.

One activity would be for children to think of someone they have known who is now far away. They might tell what they remember about that person. Then they could dictate a letter telling about themselves, what they would like that person to remember. The teacher or aide would write what they said and each could illustrate his or her letter. Plans would be made for actually sending the letters.

Another activity might be for children to draw things they think could be disposed of in the classroom if more space were needed. They might think about what is not needed, or what would not be missed. After they have drawn their responses, they would tell why they selected the objects they did.

Children could choose one of the two activities. The teacher's time would be spent first with those dictating letters, then with those explaining what they have drawn. All of the children could be engaged in discussions of times they have felt unwanted or in the way.

Varying the Types of Choices.   You can vary the sorts of choices you provide. The choice might be variety in art media; it might be variety in oral versus written work; it might be variety in level of difficulty of the activities. In a third grade class, one activity might involve writing a paragraph. Another might be making a list. Both would engage the children in thinking about the literature that had been shared, but one would require more skill in composition than the other. This would allow children at differing skill levels to select an activity at which they would be successful.

Children can be encouraged to work together on projects for both the social and the language growth it promotes. For many children, working together makes a task more enjoyable. There are times, however, when children prefer to work alone. Some activities based on literature may be phrased so that children choose to "work with a friend or by yourself." Two children might easily look around the room together to decide what is not needed in the activity following *Amifika*, then either make separate pictures, or a composite picture. Given two activities, one group and one individual, children may choose on the basis of the type of activity or on the basis of the number of people participating in it.

Children can decide whether or not they wish to share literature activities they have completed. Their work can be displayed or their activities described. They may tell the entire class or just a few children what they have done. Giving the opportunity to show their work demonstrates that you value it; giving the option of not sharing shows that you respect the feelings of the child.

Helping Children Make Responsible Choices.   As you encourage children to make choices, try to make certain that they have the information necessary to make satisfactory choices. If they are to select their own book from the library, do they know where the picture books section is? Where they can find the poetry? How to get a librarian to help them if they cannot find what they want?

Do readers know to open the book and try reading a page or two to see how difficult the reading is? Do prereaders know to look at some of the pictures as well as the cover before taking a book?

Once they have made their choice, encourage children to stay with it long enough to give it a good try. While it is unreasonable to force a child to keep looking at a book she is tired of, or to prohibit a child from sharing his project if he has had to hear three other children before getting the courage to speak, it is equally unproductive to allow children to change their choices capriciously. A part of learning to make choices is learning to accept responsibility for them. If a child has made a poor choice, this is the time for discussing the selection process he or she used and how it could be modified for better results.

Finally, keep notes on the activities and the types of books children choose, noting if any of your pupils are in a pattern that is limiting to their growth. You can then counteract their choices through planned activities. A child who always chooses to work alone can be assigned group experiences in other classroom or center projects. Another who never chooses a writing activity may be required to write at other times, or be given a choice between two writing activities. It is possible to balance children's choices with your perception of their needs by making all options you offer valid learning experiences and by structuring other activities to compensate for areas of neglect in the ones they may choose.

Encouraging Children to Set and Complete Tasks

Children in the primary grades can set tasks for themselves with some guidance from teachers and other adults. A group sharing special toys from home gets curious about teddy bears and panda bears. Are there really animals that look like that?

Defining a Task.   The teacher helps the children define the task so that the action they need to take to answer their question is clear. Two children from the group go to the library, or to classroom references if they are available, to look in dictionaries and encyclopedias under *teddy bear* and *panda.* If they had not used these references before, this would have been an ideal time for the teacher to demonstrate their use. The children return quickly, reporting that there is indeed an animal called a giant panda, but that there is no listing under teddy bear.

At this point the teacher asks the group how they could find more about the panda, and where else they might look to find out about teddy bears. Some of the children suggest library books, but not all know how to use a card catalogue. One who does goes to the library with two others to see what they can find on pandas. As they look, two of the three children will be learning ways of using the library.

Three other children are to look under the listing for teddy bear in the card catalogue, to look in several dictionaries, and to ask the librarian for help. When the first group returns, they have found a book titled *Panda*[6] by Susan Bonners. The other group has found that teddy bears are modeled after koalas, and have returned with *Beady Bear*[7] by Don Freeman and *Koalas*[8] by Bernice Kohn.

Keeping Children Task Oriented.   The children then list, and the teacher records on chart paper, what they would like to know about these bears. "Where do they live? What do they eat? How big are they? Do they have lots of babies?" When the questions have been listed, the teacher asks for volunteers to listen especially for the answer to the first question. One by one the questions are assigned. The teacher reads the book about pandas. Children go down the list and tell what they have learned about these bears. The question, "What did you think was especially interesting about pandas?" which the teacher adds at the end allows children to tell other information they have gleaned. "They can even eat splinters without hurting their stomachs," and "They get new teeth just like we do." There are also new questions as a result of the information they have heard. "What is a takin?" and "Are pandas found in other places besides China?"

In this case the children found an appropriate book, one that is also excellent nonfiction. The watercolor and gouache illustrations in shades of aqua capture the softness of the winter landscape where the pandas live. Children looking at the pictures can see what bamboo is, how pandas mate, stages in a cub's growth. The text is clear and informative.

Helping Children Assess Their Efforts.   Sometimes children will return with books that are not appropriate to the questions being asked. This is a time for teaching children to listen critically to the content and to make judgments themselves about its value for them. They can be guided to look at the content of a book in depth in the classroom and to check content briefly as they are selecting the book.

The teacher notes that one of the books the second group found about koalas is nonfiction, the other fiction. She reads the nonfiction book first, with children listening for specific information as they did for pandas. When she has finished *Koalas,* the children answer their own questions. Again there are more questions raised. "If koalas are marsupials rather than bears, what is the difference between bears and marsupials?" There are plans for further investigation.

The teacher then reads *Beady Bear* to the class. "How is this book different from the other one about koalas?" she asks. The children answer that it is a story, that it is about a toy teddy bear rather than a real animal. "Which book is better for learning about real koalas?" she asks. Then she continues by asking what they liked about each of the books.

As you talk with children about the appropriateness of particular books, try to make it clear that appropriateness is related to purpose. Rather than books being *good* or *bad,* there are some that answer their needs and others that do not. Be careful also not to overgeneralize. It is tempting to guide children to the conclusion that informational books give facts, and that these are the books to read when information is needed. However, many fiction books include accurate informational content, and certainly they are a prime source for information about how people act and feel. The insight gained from reading fiction should not be made to sound insignificant in comparison to the factual knowledge gained from nonfiction. Nor should the categories be labeled so that nonfiction becomes associated only with work, while fiction fits under fun. This contradicts the feelings of many readers who choose nonfiction for recreational reading. It also can make fiction appear less important than nonfiction.

Judging the Appropriateness of Tasks.   You will need to judge the maturity and capabilities of your students as you help them set tasks. Some can go to the library themselves. Others may need your guidance. Some may be able to listen for answers to an entire list of questions, while others can concentrate on only one.

Both fiction and nonfiction offer opportunities for children to set tasks. The books may be needed in the completion of the task, or may be the forerunner to the task of describing a response to literature. Children who have had experience in sharing their reactions to books can decide for themselves how they would like to present their thoughts and feelings. They could tell two friends how the story begins, trying to make it interesting enough that the friends will read the book. They could create a painting which they think the main character in a book would like. Then they can tell their classmates about their painting and its appeal to the book character. They could make clay models of characters from the book. Second and third graders may want to write comments about the book for display in the book corner.

Primary children can be helped to set their own tasks by having a chart in the room which lists suggestions for sharing a book. They may use the ideas as stated, or may build on the ideas to develop a new idea. Both preschool and primary children can set tasks in consultation with the teacher.

Whether the task is set by the child or chosen from a series of alternatives, you can urge that it be completed. Successfully finishing a project makes the child feel competent and enhances his or her self-concept. You can make this completion more likely to occur by ensuring that:

1. The task is on an appropriate level for the child.
2. The standards for successful completion are reasonable.
3. The materials needed are readily available.
4. The project is feasible in terms of teacher time, that is, it will not require an inordinate amount of explanation in relation to the time the project itself takes.
5. There is a classroom pattern of giving attention to completed projects.

Suppose that you were the teacher of the class learning about pandas and koalas. After reading the three books discussed earlier, you decide to read *Corduroy*,[9] a picture book about a teddy bear living in a department store. Corduroy overhears Lisa say that he is the bear she has always wanted and also hears her mother say that they have spent too much money already, and that the bear is missing a button on the strap of his overalls. That night, after the shoppers have gone, Corduroy begins searching for his lost button. He wanders around the store, finally discovering the bedding department. As he is pulling a button off a mattress, it gives way and he falls backwards, knocking over a lamp. The watchman who hears the noise finds Corduroy and takes him back to his shelf in the toy department. The next morning Lisa is the first customer in the store. She has counted the money in her piggy bank and has come to buy Corduroy. When she gets him home, she sews a button on the strap and gives him a big hug.

You have decided to read this book because it goes back to the children's initial interest in their own toys and because it is good literature. You introduce it by saying, "Remember the story we heard about Beady Bear?" After the children have responded to this question, you continue, "This is another story written by the same author, Don Freeman. This one is about a bear also, and it is called *Corduroy*." After reading the story, you ask the children to get their own toys and come back to the reading circle. Then you have them close their eyes and imagine what their toys might like to do in their houses at night, when everyone is asleep. They imagine what their toys like, what they might say if they could talk. Children then choose one of two activities. They can create a picture which shows what their toy might do at night, or they can use their toy as a puppet and have a conversation with another toy. Those who choose to draw should be able to get the paper and crayons or paint and chalk for themselves and begin. Those who choose the conversation may work in pairs simultaneously, or may listen as pairs take turns with the dialogue. This would depend on their experience with the use of puppets in spontaneous drama and their ability to work together on their own.

You would suggest the tasks knowing that the children can do them. You might need to give help midway, perhaps joining in a conversation with a toy yourself, but children will feel good about what they have done. You will look at the thought that went into the pictures and conversations, not expecting mature artists or master puppeteers. You have planned so that the children think about the ideas before they begin to work. When they get the materials, they begin quickly. You show your interest in their tasks by talking with the children as they work and by allowing them to share their work with their classmates if they wish. Your planning and follow up are strong motivators for children to establish the habit of completing their work.

Building Self-Concept

Literature can help children develop positive self-concepts through content and theme, and also through activities which may follow the sharing of a book. One aspect of self-concept is recognizing one's strengths and one's weaknesses.

Recognizing Capabilities. There are books for young children that emphasize the many capabilities that they have. The concept book *My Hands Can*[10] shows through clear illustrations and simple text many of the things which "my hands" can do, from zipping to clapping, to both building and breaking. Children listening to the book can be thinking of all the things they can do with their hands. After hearing it, they might take turns telling one thing they can do, or perhaps demonstrating or pantomiming the skill. They might play follow the leader using their hands for each action to be imitated. Both content and activities reinforce the concept that children are capable.

They might also follow the illustrations in the wordless picture book *Sunshine*.[11] They see the little girl getting up, having breakfast with her parents, but able to brush her teeth and get fully dressed without their help. They can describe or demonstrate those tasks they can do at their own homes and take pride in being independent at the center or nursery school.

Children can be encouraged to tell how they have solved problems after they listen to *Alfie's Feet*.[12] Alfie enjoys wearing his new rubber boots, but notices that they feel funny. By himself he discovers that the right boot is on his left foot and vice versa. Although his mother paints an "R" on the right boot and an "L" on the left to help him, he can tell right from left even after the letters wear off. Children need to know that they are capable of solving certain problems by themselves.

In a format similar to *My Hands Can,* the narrator of *I Know a Lot of Things*[13] relates a somewhat random listing of what he/she knows: A cat goes meow, a dog goes bow-wow, houses are made of glass and sticks and bricks. The last page indicates that as the narrator grows, he or she will know even more. A book such as this can lead children to realize that they do indeed know many things. Try having them dictate an experience chart, telling what they know about a particular topic. This gives them a chance to show their knowledge and may well give you some insight into their needs and interests.

Seeing Oneself Realistically.   Literature can help children see themselves realistically, yet with a focus on their strong points. Phyllis Krasilovsky has several books that emphasize a special characteristic of a child. *The Very Tall Little Girl*[14] opens with a description of the tall little girl who can reach things in her mother's desk and is taller than her friends. Her doctor says she is about six inches taller than most girls her age. Then the book tells about some of the irritations. Because people often think she is older than she actually is, they expect her to act older. The desks and chairs at school are too small, and she can never play the parts of tiny elves or kittens in school plays. She tries to hunch down and even to stop eating. Then one day she notices that her parents and her brothers and sisters are all taller than their friends and that nobody seems to mind. She begins to see many good things about being tall. She is allowed in the deep end of the swimming pool, and at movies she can see over the other children's heads. She is the first little girl in her neighborhood who rode a bicycle. She decides it is fun to be tall and thus special.

As children come to see themselves in relation to others and to compare themselves physically with others, books such as these help them make realistic yet positive judgments.

You may want to present several books that describe opposing characteristics. If you had shared *The Very Tall Little Girl,* you might then read *Titch.*[15] Titch is smaller than his sister Mary and his brother Pete. They ride bicycles; he rides a tricycle. They fly kites but he has a pinwheel. In a triumph of poetic justice, they have the spade and the flowerpot, but Titch has the tiny seed which grows into a huge plant.

Recognizing Growth and Change.   These books lead into another aspect of self-concept, the realization that one is continually growing and changing. *I Know a Lot of Things* gives a direct statement about learning more as one grows older. *Zeek Silver Moon*[16] describes Zeek from his birth until he is five or six years old. Readers learn about his toys when he was two and the dog he got when he was four-and-a-half. They learn about his curiosity, about the experiences he shared with his parents. The story provides a natural base for discussions of growth and change and of increased ability to do things.

After hearing this book, children could ask their parents to tell them what they were like at age two. They could also collect photographs of themselves at various ages and use these to tell how they have changed. You might even develop your own book of photographs to share with the children, showing how you have changed.

Many children will enjoy and identify with the title character in *You'll Soon Grow Into Them, Titch,*[17] because they have worn hand-me-down clothes that older children in the family have outgrown, and that may not be the perfect fit for the next in line. Titch inherits pants from his older brother, a sweater from his sister, and socks from both of them. All are too large, but his brother and sister assure him that he will soon grow into them. Titch's parents, however, decide that he should have some new clothes. Once he is outfitted, Titch presents his old clothes to the new baby; after all, he'll soon grow into them.

Children might also dictate a list of skills that they have acquired only recently to demonstrate that changes aren't solely related to physical appearance. They could create poems using one of the forms suggested by Kenneth Koch. Children begin every odd line with "I used to _____ ," and every even line with "But now _____ ," resulting in a poem that tells about the changes in their lives.[18] They might tell stories about times when they learned to do something special: to cross the street by themselves, to ride a bicycle, to get out their own milk and cereal in the morning. They might even draw pictures in which they show what they hope to be able to do next year. After such sharing of experiences, trying reading poems such as Hoberman's "A Year Later" or Margolis' "Two Wheels."

A Year Later

Last summer I couldn't swim at all
I couldn't even float!
I had to use a rubber tube
Or hang on to a boat;
I had to sit on shore
While everybody swam
But now it's this summer
And I can![19]

Mary Ann Hoberman

Two Wheels

I told you I won't. It's too hard.
I told you I can't. It's too hard.
Didn't I tell you?

My feet, they won't reach.
My hands, they won't steer.
It's too hard.

Watch out—I'm tipping.
Don't let go—I'm falling.
Please: I give up.

> Not so fast, not so fast.
> I don't like this.
> Stop stop stop stop.
>
> Hey, I can't stop.
> Hey, I'm riding, I'm riding.
> Hey, hey, hey, hey, hey.
>
> Did you see me?
> What did I tell you?
> It was easy.[20]
>
> Richard Margolis

Both poems relate the good feeling that comes from mastering a new skill, and both show that the skill did not come automatically. Growth takes time; not all skills are acquired the moment one wants.

Some, but probably not all, primary grade children will understand the boy's feeling in *Someone New*. He thinks that something is strange, but he does not know what. He keeps feeling that someone is missing. The wallpaper he had chosen he no longer likes. His toys seem strange, and he packs them into a box along with the shells he found last summer at the beach. Then he realizes that he is becoming a new person.

> Someone's gone.
> Someone's missing
> and I know who.
> He's in that box
> with all those things
> and I—
> I am someone new.[21]

The idea is a complex one, and not all children will comprehend the theme. For some, however, it may be an opening to talk about themselves and to think about the someone new they are becoming.

Becoming Confident. Children can be helped to see themselves as generally capable and as having within themselves the resources that will help them to meet unexpected demands. Of the four basic forms of literature, two, comedy and romance, show how the protagonist overcomes problems and goes on to achieve fulfillment and success. The mood is one of hope. Most literature for young children is either romance or comedy. Thus, most of the stories you will share with children will be offering a picture of a book character who succeeds. These books show children who are able to cope with problems. Kindergarten and first grade students see Benjie in *Benjie on His Own*[22] as being somewhat like themselves. When his grandmother does not meet him after school, he is frightened, even though he had told her he was too big to be walked to and from school. He starts home, recognizing some of the places they usually pass, proceeding from landmark to landmark. Still, he is frightened by a dog, and afraid as four older boys stop him and force him to turn his pockets inside out. He does get home, though, on his own. When he goes up to the apartment, his grandmother is quite ill, and he must get help. The story continues as Benjie thinks about advice his grandmother had given him for times when he does not know what to do. Benjie shows that when he must get help, he can think of a way. The story shows that young children can be independent, that they can cope with unusual circumstances. It is not necessary to discuss the point with them. Simply by your reading the book, they are being given a model of a capable individual.

Similarly, the books by Shigeo Watanabe, appropriate for three and four year olds, show a bear cub engaged in various activities, and although he may have a few setbacks, he forges ahead confidently in such stories as *I Can Ride It!*,[23] *I Can Build a House!*,[24] and *I Can Take a Walk!*.[25]

Identifying with One's Heritage.   Self-concept involves an indentification with one's heritage. Books that present characters of varying ethnic backgrounds are discussed in chapter seven on the social development of children. Learning about children who are different from themselves is part of children's social development. The book that for one student presents a model for ethnic identification is for another student an introduction to a new group of people or to new customs. Suggested books are in the social development chapter to emphasize that teachers and day care professionals should have a variety of peoples represented in the books they choose no matter what the ethnic makeup of their class. However, you will want to be certain that you read some books whose major characters match the ethnic backgrounds of the children in your class.

Books can help children recognize their own capabilities. (Illustration by Yasuo Ohtomo reprinted by permission of Philomel Books from I Can Take a Walk! *by Shigeo Watanabe, illustrations © 1983 by Yasuo Ohtomo.)*

Developing Sex Role Expectations.   Just as books present models for ethnic identification, so too do they present models for sex role identification. When you read books to children, be aware that you are showing them one perception of how the world is structured. If you read only books which show female characters as passive and male characters as active, you are saying to them that this is the behavior expected of females and of males.

Recent books for children are breaking away from sex role stereotypes which once appeared frequently. They are including more female characters who are active, assertive, and competent. Women in some books are portrayed as career oriented and successful outside the home. Males are permitted to show tenderness, to cry. One second grade girl, involved in a discussion of appropriate sex role behaviors, pondered the question of why it had been considered acceptable for girls to cry but not for boys to do so. Her solution was simple: "Girls had more to cry about." Those who have seen their horizons expanded in recent years may well agree with her assessment.

As you select books, eliminate those which present stereotyped characters, whether the character is sexist or not. Stereotyping means that all individuals within a group are described as though they were alike. Women work in the home and wear aprons; men work in offices and wear suits. Boys play baseball; girls play dolls. Books whose characters are stereotyped are poor literature, for the author has not developed the individuality necessary for good characterization. Thus these books should be discarded on literary grounds.

Do not depend on the date of publication to tell you if a stereotype exists. Some recent books present stereotyped characters, and many old favorites do not. One could hardly ask for a more active and unique female than Madeline in the books by Ludwig Bemelmans, the first of which was published in 1939. In the list of professional references at the end of this chapter are several bibliographies of non-stereotyped books for children which you may find useful.

A second problem exists, and that is to provide a balance of types of characters in the total body of literature you share with children. To present only books that show women working at exciting careers is to create as imbalanced a picture as to present only books that show women functioning as mothers or homemakers. Assess each book for its literary value, then make a list of role models presented. See if any gaps exist, and if so, look for books to rectify omissions.

There will be opportunities to discuss with the children their attitudes toward certain behaviors of characters. One teacher read *Max*[26] and *Ira Sleeps Over*[27] to his class of first graders. In the first book, Max is on his way to a baseball game when he stops in at his sister's ballet lesson. Intrigued by the whole procedure, he joins the line of girls in doing exercises at the bar and particularly enjoys the leaps. He goes to the baseball game, plays well, and decides to warm up for each game with ballet.

Ira, in *Ira Sleeps Over,* is invited to spend the night with his friend Reggie. His sister begins needling him about his teddy bear, asking him if he plans to take it to Reggie's and reminding him that he has never slept without it. His parents reassure him that it is fine to take Tah Tah, but his sister insists that Reggie will laugh. When the time comes, Ira goes next door leaving his teddy bear behind. As the two boys tell ghost stories in bed, Reggie gets up and gets something from a drawer—his teddy bear, named Foo Foo. Ira goes home to get Tah Tah, this time convinced that Reggie will not laugh.

The teacher talked with one group of eight children. They readily described the toys they slept with. The names ranged from a bear called Fuz to a more elegant stuffed rabbit called Mr. O. Hare. None of the children had ever been to a ballet lesson. In the discussions, they all agreed that boys did sleep with stuffed animals. They did not, however, all agree on Max's dancing. Some said that dancing was fun and that anyone could do it. Others said that boys should not take ballet, but that this was okay because Max was preparing for a ball game. And still others said that ballet was for girls, not boys. The teacher did not given an opinion, but pointed out that they seemed to have different feelings about it, and asked them to think about how they knew what boys did and what girls did. This was a first step in urging children to question conventional stereotypes.

As you assess the role models in books which contribute to children's concept of their own sexual identity, plan to provide a variety of non-stereotyped characters and allow discussion of roles. If children are thinking in stereotypical terms, you may well want to introduce evidence which conflicts with their current beliefs. The teacher who read *Max* could later show news clippings of male dancers, or have all the children engage in dancing themselves. Literature allows you to provide a great variety of possible behaviors and to broaden children's conceptions of possibilities for themselves.

Building Self-esteem

Self-esteem is influenced strongly by the reactions of others to the individual. Children gain an impression of their worth from their perception of the treatment they are given by the important people in their lives. Parents, teachers, and classmates all contribute to the total picture. You as teacher can influence this directly through your relations with the children, and indirectly as you model behavior for children to use with others. You also can select curriculum materials and activities that build self-esteem.

Using Content That Reaffirms Self-worth.   Look for literature whose content reaffirms self-worth. *Big Sister Tells Me That I'm Black* gives a catchy, cheerleader beat to a poem celebrating proud feelings:

> big sister tells me
> that i'm black
> she says she knows me
> front and back . . .
> hip hip
> hip hooray
> hip hip
> i'm black today[28]

I Like to Be Me explores what else one could be from a rainbow to a birthday cake, but ends with "But most of all I like to be me."[29] These examples say directly that one can feel happy with one's own identity.

First Grade Takes a Test[30] describes a situation that is very real for many primary grade youngsters. The children are given a paper and pencil test by a lady who comes in especially for the task. On the basis of the test results, one child, Anna Maria, is chosen for a special class. The other children then begin calling each other "dummy." The teacher intervenes and explains forceful-ly that the test doesn't really tell all the things they *can* do, such as reading books, having good ideas, and helping others. Her point is strengthened when Jim figures out that they can settle an argument over which child has the larger cookie simply by weighing the cookies. Because there is typically so much em-phasis on doing well in school, it is valuable to call children's attention to the many positive qualities each possesses that may not be related directly to school work.

Presenting Themes of Individuality.   Look also for books with themes of in-dividuality. Children need to both recognize and value their own uniqueness. The theme that each of us is unique appears in books at all levels. For preschoolers there is Robert Bright's *Which is Willie?*[31] Willie is a penguin at the South Pole who wants to be different, but all the penguins look alike. When he goes to the city, he is so different that everyone stares. He buys clothes to fit into the city and again he is the same. Willie then returns to the South Pole with his top hat and tie, only to be the object of stares there. Finally Willie decides to just be himself and not to care whether he is alike or different.

A similar theme is presented for kindergarteners and first graders in *Sloppy Kisses.*[32] Emmy Lou comes from a family where everyone likes to kiss. One day Rosemary observes Emmy Lou being kissed good-bye by her father as he drops her off for school. Rosemary offers the opinion that kissing is for babies and is "yukky." Emmy Lou, in response to her friend's criticism, decides that she is now too old for kissing, and informs her family of this decision. They comply with her request that they no longer kiss her but assure her that they still love her. Emmy Lou is proud to tell Rosemary of her decision, but that night cannot get to sleep. Finally her father says he knows what she needs, picks her up, and gives her a big sloppy kiss. She goes right to sleep. The next day, as father pats Emmy Lou on the shoulder in front of the school, she calls him back for a kiss. This time when Rosemary begins with more critical com-ments, Emmy Lou states that kissing is for everybody and gives Rosemary a kiss on the cheek. A theme within the story is that one should choose behaviors that are satisfying to oneself, rather than matching behavior to the expecta-tions of others.

The need to be an individual is effectively presented in *The Other Emily.*[33] Emily loves her name and is not prepared to find another child in her class with the same name. The other Emily is not bothered, and even wants them to do Show and Tell together. Emily soon adjusts to the idea of sharing her name, but the importance of having one's own special identity comes through clearly.

For first and second graders there is *Jenny and the Tennis Nut.*[34] The tennis nut is her father, who brings Jenny a gift of a tennis racket and begins to teach her the game. He is certain she will love it because both he and her mother do. He tells her that he wants her to have a sport that she enjoys and that she does well. She responds that she already has one and demonstrates her gymnastic skill by doing cartwheels, somersaults, handstands, and walking on a tree branch. She had played circus while her parents were off playing tennis. Jenny's father agrees that she has found her sport and offers to buy some equipment for her. He also tells her that maybe when she is older she will want a second game, and he will always be willing to teach her tennis. The theme that we are each unique is reinforced by the father's acceptance of Jenny's skill and of her choice.

For second and third graders there is *Two Piano Tuners.*[35] Debbie has lived with her grandfather, Mr. Weinstock, for the two years since her parents died. He is an excellent piano tuner, but in spite of Debbie's claims that she would like to be a piano tuner too, he urges her to think of becoming a concert pianist. The two are at odds on this until a visiting pianist and friend of Mr. Weinstock listens to Debbie play on a piano she has attempted to tune. He recognizes that she is better at tuning than at playing a piano. The friends says that it is each person's responsibility to find out what he really wants to do. Debbie knows, and her grandfather relents and says he will teach her the skill of piano tuning.

All of these books, on different levels of difficulty, present a theme of the value of one's own decisions, one's own special skills, one's own preferences. You can follow the reading of these books with activities that focus on the individuality of your students. You might try one or more of the following ideas:

1. Have the children make booklets about themselves, describing in words or pictures their special skills, what they might like to learn to do, what they enjoy, what they dislike.
2. Make a bulletin board that features pictures of each child, labeled with the child's name. The children can dictate a sentence to accompany each picture, a sentence in which they tell one unique feature about themselves.
3. Tape-record the children individually telling about a pet, or their home, or their favorite food. Then play the tape for the group. As the children guess who is speaking, they learn about that child. Each child becomes the center of attention for a brief period of time. All learn that each person has a unique voice, one that others recognize even when they cannot see the speaker.

Sharing Literature That Promotes Feelings of Security. Books can help give a feeling of security to very young children. The day-care child, held on the lap of an adult, associates reading with the warmth of human contact. The nursery school child sits beside an aide and the two share a moment of understanding as they laugh together over a humorous book. Focusing attention on children in this way helps them feel that they are valued. Books such as *Whose Mouse Are You?*[36] and *The Runaway Bunny*[37] have content that reinforces this feeling. In answer to the question "Whose mouse are you?" the mouse at first says nobody's, but after rescuing his mother, father, and sister, can answer that he is their mouse, and also the mouse of his brand new brother. He belongs; he is valued. The bunny who runs away is continually reassured by his mother that no matter where he goes, she will come after him. The

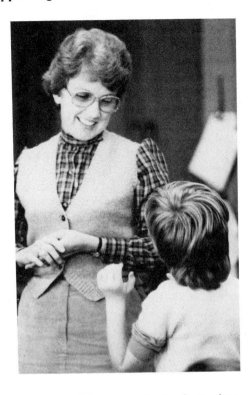

*Teachers and day care professionals can show
each child that he or she is unique and special.*

language patterns in both books invite rereading, and the message that "you are important" is one which helps build the young child's self-esteem.

Older children, particularly those from broken homes, may gain security from the sensitivity in *Always, Always,*[38] a book in which the child narrator tells about her divorced parents and her relationship with them. She loves them both and is eager to see both her father in Colorado in the summers and her mother in New York in the winters, yet she is sad to be leaving each time she begins another cross country trip. Both parents love her. Both know that some activities she enjoys with them might not be approved of by the other. When she questions her mother about why they were divorced, and then why they married in the first place, she is answered directly, then assured quietly that she is the best thing that happened to them. The book ends as she remembers that this is exactly what her father had said when asked the same question.

Suggesting Activities That Encourage Positive Feedback.   Your behavior toward each child can show that each is valued. You can also arrange activities in which children will get positive comments and treatment from their classmates and learn to give praise themselves. Some will occur naturally as children take responsibility for care of classroom pets, plants, and materials. Others may be based on books read. One teacher read *I'm Terrific*[39] to her class of second graders. When the book opens, Jason Everett Bear is giving himself gold stars for all the terrific things he does. The second graders enjoyed the story, but were unimpressed with Jason's transformation to a more modest bear. The teacher used the idea of stars by having each child make a large star, print his or her name on it, and decorate it. Then she collected the stars. Without looking, each child drew one of the stars from a basket. The children then wrote on the back three "terrific" things about the child whose star they had drawn. The teacher collected the stars again, and read the "terrific" things for each child as she gave them to their owners.

The children thought about the special attributes of their friends, and each child received praise. The teacher had built in some checks, however, to ensure that the activity went well. She used two children as examples and asked what they did well, what the children liked about them, what they liked. Thus, the class understood the sorts of comments that were expected. Then she collected the stars just before recess, glancing at the writing on each one. Had there been comments which were denigrating, she was in a position to have them changed without hurting a child's feelings and without making it common classroom knowledge. As you plan what is *right* about an activity, plan also for the *wrongs* which might occur. Those extra few minutes of thought may help children to feel a warm satisfaction about themselves.

Recognizing One's Own Values

Values are the belief system one holds about what is important. Many educators approach the study of values with children through a process called values clarification. It is an attempt to help individuals analyze the values they hold, both the ones they can verbalize and the ones which underlie their actual behavior. Through a variety of strategies children explore their beliefs and the consequences of acting on those beliefs. The goal is that children will choose from among values, choose consistently and knowingly, and develop and act upon their own value system.[40]

Children learn values from the people who are important in their lives. For preschool children, parents are of primary importance; for the school age child, teachers and peers as well as parents have influence. Values clarification is likely to be more effective in grades two and three and up than in the preschool and early primary years. Children are then being exposed to more than one set of values and are able to think about them in terms other than Mommy is right or Mommy is wrong.

Literature, in its exploration of actions and motivations for actions, presents a panorama of value systems. Books that present value conflicts clearly lend themselves to discussion and to activities by which children can judge their own beliefs. One approach is to ask students to decide which character they are more like when characters conflict over values. In *I Want to Stay Here! I Want to Go There!*,[41] two fleas are riding comfortably on a dog. One is curious and wants to see the rest of the world. The other is happy where it is and has no desire to go exploring. The curious one leaves, with the other trailing unhappily behind. Finally the home lover returns to the dog, feeling that it will know something of the world when the other returns and describes its trip.

Children refer to the fleas as "the red one" and "the blue one" because no names are given, and the fleas are not shown. Only their dialogue shows, one in a red circle and the other in a blue circle. After you have read the book, as the children, "Are you more like the red flea or the blue flea?" After each has had a chance to decide, ask the children to think of a time when they have acted either like the red flea or like the blue flea. They can share their responses through art, through writing, or through oral activities. As they explain their answers, they can be asked to tell whether they act that way often. This is one step in discovering what they value, and how consistent they are in acting on that value.

Other times you can emphasize the reasons for holding a particular value, and the consequences of acting on it. In the book titled *Frederick*,[42] a group of mice are preparing for the winter. All but Frederick are gathering corn and nuts and wheat and storing them for the winter. Frederick sits alone and explains that he is gathering sun rays for cold winter days, and colors, and words. When winter comes, the mice eat through their store of supplies. Then they call upon Frederick, who alleviates their discomfort by reciting a poem which makes them feel the sun and see the colors of summer.

Children can be asked to write down whether they think Frederick should have been permitted to share in the mice's food since he did not gather any of it. Having them write "yes" or "no" on a paper forces them to decide for themselves, not be swayed by what a friend says or by what the majority seem to feel. Those who said "yes" can be grouped together and those who said "no" together. Each group is to list all their reasons for feeling as they do. They could also be asked to select what the group thinks is the best reason.

Then you might lead a discussion in which you ask the groups to apply their beliefs to new situations. Do those who hold that only people who work should share the food think children, who do not generally hold jobs, should share in the family's food? Do those who hold that poets contribute something of value and should not have to work in the way others do feel that a poetry-writing classmate should be excused from clean-up time in order to continue writing?

Preschool as well as primary children can identify the values a book character holds if they are asked what is important to that character. They might also be asked if they agree with the character. In *Miss Rumphius*,[43] the story begins with the title character as a small girl telling her artist grandfather about her dreams. She wants to go to distant places and to live in a house by the sea when she grows up. Her grandfather says that she must do a third thing—make the world more beautiful. She agrees, but doesn't know how she will do this. The story continues with her travels and her move to a house by the sea. As an old woman, she sees the lovely lupines she had planted in her garden, then others growing where the seeds had spread. She decides she can fulfill her commitment to make the world more beautiful by scattering lupine seeds along the country lanes and walks. The story concludes as Miss Rumphius talks with her great-niece and tells her that she must do something to make the world more beautiful. Do your listeners think it is important to try to make the world more beautiful? How could they accomplish this, either now or in the future?

In these examples, children are not told what to believe, but only asked to think about their beliefs. You will find that literature often revolves around questions of values. The strategy of having students take a stand, think through their reasons for it, listen to the reasoning of those who differ, and discuss the consequences of acting on various value systems is one that can apply to many books. It opens the way for children to consider other positions and perhaps make more knowledgeable choices.

Miss Rumphius tells the children that they too should do something to make the world more beautiful. (From Miss Rumphius *by Barbara Cooney. Copyright © 1982 by Barbara Cooney Porter. Reproduced by permission of Viking Penguin Inc.)*

Helping Children Understand and Express Their Emotions

Literature highlights the role of emotions in human lives. It shows not only what happens to a character, what a character does, but how that character feels. Part of the reader's response to literature is usually a recognition of the emotions being expressed. Much of the discussion of books centers on how characters felt about one another and how their feelings influenced their actions. Reading every day to children cannot help but aid their understanding of people and of human emotions.

As you select books, it may be helpful for you to think of these four ways in which literature can contribute to young children's emotional growth. First, literature shows that many of the feelings they experience are experienced by others, and are both normal and natural. Second, it explores the feeling from several aspects, giving a fuller picture, and providing the base for the naming of that emotion. Third, literature, through the actions of various characters, shows options for ways of dealing with particular emotions. And fourth, literature makes clear that one person experiences many emotions, sometimes conflicting ones.

Finding That Others Share Similar Feelings.   To show children that others have felt as they do, look for books that describe common childhood experiences. *Will I Have a Friend?*[44] and *Shawn Goes to School*[45] both describe a boy's first day in kindergarten. Children may know what it is like to enter a new classroom, but may not have realized others shared their feelings. Here they have a chance to see one boy, wanting a friend but shy in his new environment, and another who was eager to go to school, but cries when his mother and sister are about to leave.

In *Daddy,*[46] Wendy describes her Saturdays spent with her father and his new wife. Children who regularly visit with a divorced parent know what she means when she describes the "wrinkles" in her stomach as she worries about her father. Preschoolers know the distress felt by the young boy in *The Blanket*[47] when he cannot find the blanket he always takes to bed with him. The feelings are treated seriously in these books, a recognition that children care and that their feelings matter.

A second grader bending down to pick up a crayon bumped his head on his desk as he straightened up. The teacher knew that earlier in the day he had broken his thermos. Seeing the pain on his face she commiserated by saying, "This is just a bad day for you, Tom." From the depths of his misery he answered, "All my days are bad days." The next day the teacher read *Alexander and the Terrible, Horrible, No Good, Very Bad Day*[48] in which Alexander tells all the horrible no good things that happened to him. There was no prize in his breakfast cereal, only he had a cavity, there were lima beans for supper, and there was kissing on TV. Tom thoroughly enjoyed the story, as did the rest of the class. It is quite probable, however, that it would not have been so funny to Tom on his bad day. You will need to make a judgment about children's reactions to a book, knowing when they may need time before they are ready to relive or talk about an emotion.

Books for preschoolers often concentrate on a single emotion. Jonathan in *I Don't Care*[49] has lost his balloon. After a day of saying that he does not care, he goes to his room and cries. He emerges feeling better. *His Mother's Dog*[50] is far more complicated and thus is more appropriate for primary grade children than preschoolers. The narrator is happy when his parents agree to get him a dog for his birthday and thinks he would like a Newfoundland. His father says that it would eat too much, and his mother remembers the cocker spaniel she had as a child. It was named Puck. When the gift arrives, it is a cocker spaniel. The boy likes it, but it likes his mother. It follows her around the house and sleeps on the floor by her door. The boy names it Moose, but his mother forgets and calls it Puck and that is the name that sticks. Then the mother has a baby. Both the dog and the boy feel left out. The parents put the dog outside, fearing that it might be dangerous in its jealousy. The boy is sent outside, too, after he decides to accompany his singing with cookie sheet cymbals. The dog follows the boy when the two are outside and even comes into his room. "His mother's" dog becomes his.

The feelings of both the mother and the boy are shown in this book. The boy feels ignored and somewhat jealous when the dog follows his mother. His grandmother aggravates the situation when she gives her attention to the new baby, forgetting even to say good-by to the boy when she goes home. The boy,

in a pout, asks for homemade bread, commenting that he does not like TV din-
ners. The mother is exasperated with his noise and his demands and tells him
she has just come from the hospital. What does he expect? The two reconcile
later when she comes to his room to say goodnight and tells him she will always
love him. She also hopes he will like the new baby. He says he will try, but he
doubts if he will.

For some books, you may want to discuss with the children times when they
have felt the way the character does. At other times, you may want to focus
entirely on the literature itself, drawing out how the character felt and how the
author let the reader know these feelings.

Exploring Various Aspects of an Emotion.   Reading several books in which
characters have the same or similar feelings gives children data from which
to generalize. It is also an opportunity for putting feelings into words. Suppose
you have read two books about the arrival of a new baby. Originally you chose
these because several of the children in your group have new brothers or sisters.
The two that you read, *A Baby Sister for Frances*[51] and *She Come Bringing Me
That Little Baby Girl,*[52] both describe the feelings of jealousy experienced by
the older child. To expand upon this theme, you choose two more books in
which jealousy plays an important role. One, *A Birthday for Frances*[53] has
Frances suffering again, but this time because it is her sister's birthday, not
hers. And the other, *One Frog Too Many,*[54] shows the reactions of a boy, his
turtle, his dog, and his frog when the boy is given another frog. The first three
welcome it, but the frog is not pleased. He glares at their new companion and
manages to bite it and kick it off a raft when the others are not looking. The
children tell what was similar about these feelings. They may relate times when
they have felt that way. If none of the children offers the term *jealous,* you in-
terject it into the discussion yourself. These children will begin to realize that
a single emotion may be produced by many different circumstances and will
be building a vocabulary for telling others how they feel.

You might then introduce a book in which jealousy is only one of the emotions being experienced, and give children the opportunity to describe it in a
more complex context. In *Timothy Goes to School,*[55] for example, Timothy
heads out for his first day at school full of enthusiasm. The teacher seats him
next to Claude, who immediately makes fun of the sunsuit Timothy is wearing.
The next day Timothy wears a new jacket, and Claude again criticizes his
clothes. Timothy hopes that Claude will make mistakes, or fall in a puddle, or
have some other mishap, but he never does. Timothy is jealous of Claude's
confidence and tries to dress to conform to what appear to be Claude's expectations. At the same time, he dislikes Claude's attitudes and actions. Finally
he meets Violet, who has the same feelings toward Grace that Timothy has
toward Claude. They become friends and go home together laughing about
Claude and Grace. The feelings of the characters are multidimensional. Because
all the characters are animals, the ideas, rather than the actual appearance of
the characters, are primary.

Some teachers have used the form of "Happiness is . . ." to elicit examples
of specific emotions. Children complete the sentence in as many ways as they
can. The emotion may be whatever the teacher or children select: "Love is . . ."

or "Grouchy is . . ." If you begin with this approach, you may want to read literature which approaches the emotion from this perspective. An example is Eloise Greenfield's poem entitled "Love Don't Mean,"[56] in which love is portrayed as a child keeping her mama company while her daddy is gone. Dick Gackenback's story of young Walter and his love for animals *Do You Love Me?,*[57] presents a theme that not all animals want love, at least not the kind that keeps them in a cage. It is another opening for discussing with children an emotion, and ways of showing it.

Perceiving Options for Managing Emotions.   As they see how emotions are expressed by book characters, children are given options for handling their emotions. Some may be ways they already use. Crying, as in *I Don't Care,* may not change the circumstances that produced the disappointment, but it does offer release.

Fantasizing is another way of managing feelings, from anger to longing. The title, *And My Mean Old Mother Will Be Sorry, Blackboard Bear,*[58] expresses the little boy's state of mind when he is sent to bed for getting water all over the bathroom and honey all over the kitchen. The bear on his blackboard comes to life and the boy leaves with it, not even taking his toothbrush. He will never brush his teeth again and then his mean old mother will be sorry. In his mind he spends the night in the woods with his bear, but by morning is ready to return, and his mean old mother does not seem quite so mean.

In other books, characters fantasize how they can do what they want. John, in *When I Have a Son,*[59] expresses his wishes when he tells what his son will be able to do, all the things he himself would like to do. His son will be able to talk while they are fishing, play the television as loud as he wants, wear jeans all the time.

Another book by Charlotte Zolotow, *A Father Like That,*[60] poetically tells a boy's imaginings of what his father would be like. His father would play checkers with him. His father would understand if he were in trouble at school. His father would not call him a sissy when he cried. When he has finished, his mother tells him that she likes that kind of father. And in case one like that never comes along, he should remember what he has been thinking, because he can be a father like that himself someday.

Fantasizing is not offered as a permanent escape, but as one way of sorting through feelings, one way of expressing them, if only to oneself. It is also a safe way of previewing possible actions.

Within stories that children are hearing every day, they will encounter characters who hide their feelings, who share them, who show them through their actions. They will see some characters misunderstood because they did not explain their feelings. They will experience with the characters a full range of feelings.

Exploring the Varied Emotions of a Single Character.   Some of the books you read will show the many emotions of a single character. Consider also reading a series of books about one character. The books about Frances by Russell Hoban show this "human" badger in many different situations. Two other excellent groups of books can be read so that they form a chronological story.

The ones about Everett Anderson by Lucille Clifton start with Everett's experiences for one week, *Some of the Days of Everett Anderson.*[61] Another tells about his Christmas, another about a new neighbor. Then comes *Everett Anderson's 1-2-3,*[62] when his mother decides to marry Mr. Perry. The next book is the self-explanatory, *Everett Anderson's Nine Month Long.*[63] *Everett Anderson's Goodbye,*[64] the final book in the series, tells of Everett's adjustment to the death of his father.

In the second group of books, three can form a continuing story, with the fourth being an epilogue. *Lost in the Storm*[65] by Carol and Donald Carrick shows Christopher and his dog Bodger, how they play together, how worried Christopher is when Bodger is out all night in a storm. Then in *The Accident,*[66] Bodger is killed and Christopher must cope with his grief. In *The Foundling,*[67] Christopher is not ready to replace Bodger with a new dog from the pound, but a stray puppy that follows him changes his feelings about having another dog. In a later story, *Dark and Full of Secrets,*[68] the puppy has grown to full size, and is now an integral part of the family, just as Bodger had been.

Frances, Everett Anderson, and Christopher become almost like friends as their adventures are shared. They show that one person may feel a variety of emotions and show this in a manner compatible with young children's ability to comprehend the situations.

Following the reading of books such as these, plan ways for children to verbalize emotions, either their own or those of the book characters. They may add words to wordless picture books, either in dialogue or narrative form. They could dramatize a story, following the plot but giving their own dialogue, thus expressing the feelings in their own words. Older children can role play a situation. Look for times when the children can use puppets or masks as they engage in dialogue. Children often speak more freely when they are speaking through another *person.*

Occasionally you will find books or poems with patterns children can use to express their own feelings. Karla Kuskin has something to say about her feelings in this poem:

> Okay everybody, listen to this:
> I am tired of being smaller
> Than you
> And them
> And him
> And trees and buildings.
> So watch out
> All you gorillas and adults
> Beginning tomorrow morning
> Boy
> Am I going to be taller.[69]

What might children say with a beginning of, "Okay everybody, listen to this"?

Or after having heard *The Temper Tantrum Book,*[70] children could make their own group booklet, with each contributing a picture or a sentence for "I hate it when . . ." or "I love it when . . ." Engage children in activities that will help them think about how they feel and help them develop the language to express their emotions clearly.

Overcoming Unfounded Fears.   Common fears of childhood are the themes in some books and are common occurrences in others. Characters will be frightened by animals or afraid of the dark. Sometimes children's fears are unfounded in reality, but at other times they are reflective of actual danger. Benjie, in *Benjie on His Own,* had reason to fear the older boys who wanted his money. Children talking about their fears and the fears of characters in books are gathering information that will help them determine which fears are useful for providing an awareness of dangerous situations and which inhibit them in areas where the potential danger is minimal. They are also facing their fears, the first step in overcoming them.

Literature can help children cope with fears of the unknown by providing knowledge about common objects and events and about new experiences they are about to undertake. *Holes and Peeks,*[71] for the three or four year old, simply has a child looking in various holes around the house. Bathroom fixtures become less frightening when the child sees and talks about where the pipe leads. A child who has never traveled on a bus and must make a trip alone is given valuable information by hearing about Janie's trip in *Bus Ride.*[72] The factual content—where the luggage is stored, how the seat buttons work, where the bathroom is—is given in the context of Janie's total experience. Her initial fear of and then her liking for her seating companion, Mrs. Rivers, form the basis of the story. This book gives insight into the uneasiness children may feel and arms them against it by making the experience understandable and less strange. As you learn what children in your group are facing, whether a trip to the dentist or a move to live with a new set of foster parents, you will be able to share literature with them that will make the experience less frightening.

Literature can give children the opportunity to talk about their fears. If they are responding to a book, they may say how they feel and put the fear in perspective. Children listening to *Jim Meets the Thing*[73] will be encouraged to tell about times when television monsters or horror stories have frightened them. Other tricks of the imagination are humorously but understandingly portrayed in *What's Under My Bed?*[74] After laughing at all the terrible things Grandpa describes as having seen and heard when he once stayed with his grandparents long ago, children can talk about the things they imagine lurking in the dark when they are in a strange place.

Young children are often afraid of separation, of being left alone and having no one to care for them. Three and four year olds listening to the concept book *You Go Away*[75] see many instances of the meanings of "going away" and "coming back." The early pages show "away" and "back" as games of peek-a-boo, or a father playfully tossing his child in the air. But as the book continues, the distances become greater. A mother leaves her child at school and comes back. Finally parents are shown leaving with suitcases, and the children are assured that they will come back. The book provides an opportunity for children to tell how they feel when their parents leave. The illustration showing a child crying when her mother is out of sight in a grocery store might be a good opening for discussion.

Children between five and nine are in a period of realizing that death, the ultimate separation, is permanent. Books about the death of a pet or a grandparent will give them an idea of how others feel when a death occurs. Just as

When Jim saw The Thing on television, he got scared. Maybe The Thing could come out of the TV!

After hearing this book, children may want to tell about television shows which have frightened them. (From Jim Meets the Thing *by Miriam Cohen. Ill. by Lillian Hoban. Copyright © 1981 by Miriam Cohen. By permission of Greenwillow Books. A division of William Morrow & Co.)*

adults have varied beliefs about death, so too is there a range of beliefs presented in literature. Children have a better chance of coping if adults are honest with them, admitting that separation is painful and that people have differing beliefs about death.

Over a year's time you could read several books in which a death occurs, each giving new information about people's responses to it. *Nonna*[76] describes the extended family mourning together over the grandmother's death. The child sees the funeral and the arrangements that must be made. *My Grandpa Died Today*[77] focuses on a boy as he goes on with his life, even though he misses his grandfather. The book states that after death his grandfather no longer moved, or talked, or breathed. *Annie and the Old One*[78] shows that Annie, no matter how much she wishes it, cannot prevent the death of her grandmother. She comes to accept her grandmother's teaching that death is a natural part of life. In *Nadia the Willful,*[79] it is Nadia's persistence in talking about her brother Hamed after his death that helps her father realize that talking about his son will help him ease his own grief, and that those we love live on in our memories. All four books contribute to children's understanding of emotions after a loved one's death.

To encourage children to talk about their fears and to see ways they might lessen them, read several books which include fears children commonly have. Some of the children may volunteer to talk about fears they have; others may tell about them when asked. You will learn about areas where you may be able to help, and children may give valuable advice to one another.

Summary

Emotions, values, ways of perceiving, and feelings about self are all a part of personality. Erikson seeks to explain personality growth by describing how human beings respond to conflicts at specific periods in their lives. Central to how children resolve such conflicts and to the development of self-esteem and a positive self-concept is the way in which adults and peers respond to them.

The following long term goals are appropriate for the personality development of young children.

- Children will weigh evidence and make appropriate choices.
- Children will set tasks for themselves and will complete the tasks they begin.
- Children will develop positive and realistic self-concepts.
- Children will develop feelings of self-worth and self-esteem.
- Children will begin to recognize their own values and to choose from among values.
- Children will understand their emotions and will express them in socially acceptable ways.

Books offer opportunities for helping children achieve these goals. Table 3 suggests appropriate teaching strategies. Children can be involved regularly in choice making, deciding which books they would like to hear read, which activity they wish to complete, which book they will take from the library. They can learn, also, to be responsible for the choices they make. In many instances teachers can help children set tasks for themselves and assess their own efforts in completing the tasks.

Literature, through content and through activities based on content and theme, can strengthen the development of self-concept and self-esteem. As children hear literature that shows the skills and abilities of others, they discover that they too have many skills and abilities. Comparisons aid in the ability to see oneself realistically and to recognize the process of growth and change. Books present models with which children identify. Thus, teachers will want to avoid books which stereotype characters and look for ones which present well-developed characters in a variety of roles and settings. Teachers will also share books that promote feelings of security and self-worth.

Because literature explores the actions and motivations of characters, it presents a panorama of value systems and of emotional reactions. Primary grade children can clarify their own value positions as they assess the actions of book characters. Both primary and preschool children gain experience in recognizing and talking about emotions as they participate in literary experiences. Books provide particular support for helping children overcome unfounded fears, both through giving information about new experiences and through providing a stimulus for the discussion of common fears.

Extending Your Learning

1. Select a picture book and describe three possible activities based upon it.
2. Make a list of five choices children might reasonably be asked to make during one school day, or three during a half-day of preschool.
3. Look at any two of Shigeo Wantanabe's books. How does each encourage a child to be independent?

4.   Analyze sex role models presented in ten picture books. Identify any stereotypes that may be present. Do the same for five books from one of the bibliographies of nonsexist books listed in the recommended references.

5.   Read at least one of the picture books recommended in chapter four of *Shadow and Substance* (listed in the recommended references) written primarily for Afro-American readers. Tell how it might contribute to a black child's self-concept, and to appreciation of black culture by nonblacks.

6.   Identify the values underlying the actions of the main character in five different picture books.

7.   Read several books about the same character, listing the situations and emotions they experience and assessing the range of emotions shown by the character. Recommended books include the books about Christopher by Carrick; the books about Everett Anderson by Clifton; the books about Jim and his classmates by Cohen; and the books about Frances by Hoban.

Table 3. *Supporting Children's Personality Development*

Developmental Goals	Teaching Suggestions	Recommended Literature	
Children will weigh evidence and make appropriate choices.	Give children real choices and abide by their decisions. Encourage children to choose their own books for independent perusal. Provide children with a choice of activities following the reading of a book. Vary the types of choices offered. Help children make responsible choices.	**Ages 3–5:** Clifton	*Amifika*
Children will set tasks for themselves and will complete tasks they begin.	Teach children to define the task. Library projects (7-8 years). Keep children on task by having them list questions to be answered. Have children assess their own efforts. Let children decide how to share a story. Suggest tasks attainable but yet challenging for the children.	**Ages 3–5:** Freeman **Ages 5–8:** Bonners Kohn	*Corduroy* *Panda Koalas*
Children will develop positive and realistic self-concepts.	Choose books that emphasize capabilities children have. Choose books that show characters seeing themselves positively and realistically.	**Ages 3–5:** Bemelmans Ehrlich Hoberman Holzenthaler	*Madeline* *Zeek Silver Moon* "A Year Later" *My Hands Can*

Table 3. (Cont.)

Developmental Goals	Teaching Suggestions	Recommended Literature	
	Choose literature that shows children growing and changing. Engage children in activities that demonstrate change. Read books that show children who can cope with problems. Choose books that provide models for ethnic and sex role identification. Discuss children's ideas of appropriate sex role behaviors.	Hughes	*Alfie's Feet*
		Hutchins	*Titch*
		Hutchins	*You'll Soon Grow Into Them, Titch*
		Krasilovsky	*The Very Tall Little Girl*
		Ormerod	*Sunshine*
		Rand	*I Know a Lot of Things*
		Watanabe	*I Can Build a House!*
		Watanabe	*I Can Ride It!*
		Watanabe	*I Can Take a Walk!*
		Ages 5–8:	
		Isadora	*Max*
		Lexau	*Benjie on His Own*
		Margolis	*"Two Wheels"*
		Waber	*Ira Sleeps Over*
		Zolotow	*Someone New*
Children will develop feelings of self-worth and self-esteem.	Choose literature that reaffirms self-worth. Choose literature that supports individuality. Have children make booklets and tapes about themselves. Read books that give children a feeling of security. Plan activities that promote children complimenting one another.	**Ages 3–5:**	
		Adoff	*Big Sister Tells Me That I'm Black*
		Bel Geddes	*I Like To Be Me*
		Bright	*Which is Willie?*
		Brown	*The Runaway Bunny*
		Gibbs	*The Other Emily*
		Kraus	*Whose Mouse Are You?*
		Winthrop	*Sloppy Kisses*
		Ages 5–8:	
		Cohen	*First Grade Takes a Test*
		Dragonwagon	*Always, Always*
		Goffstein	*Two Piano Tuners*
		Schulman	*Jenny and the Tennis Nut*
		Sharmat	*I'm Terrific*
Children will begin to recognize their own values, and to choose from among values.	Lead discussions about value conflicts in books. Have children decide which character they agree with when characters express differing values. Encourage children to evaluate the rationale for particular beliefs.	**Ages 5–8:**	
		Cooney	*Miss Rumphius*
		Lionni	*Frederick*
		Lionni	*I Want to Stay Here! I Want To Go There!*

Table 3. (Cont.)

Developmental Goals	Teaching Suggestions	Recommended Literature	
Children will understand their emotions, and will express them in socially acceptable ways.	Share books that show emotions common to young children. Combine books to explore several facets of a single emotion. Present children with options for dealing with emotions. Show one character experiencing many emotions. Engage children in dialogue that expresses emotion through dramatic activities such as puppetry and role play. Let children tell their feelings using the format of a specific book or poem. Provide children with knowledge about new experiences. Encourage children to talk about their fears.	**Ages 3–5:**	
		Alexander	And My Mean Old Mother Will Be Sorry, Blackboard Bear
		Breinburg	Shawn Goes to School
		Burningham	The Blanket
		Caines	Daddy
		Clifton	"Everett Anderson" books
		Cohen	Will I Have a Friend?
		Cohen	Jim Meets the Thing
		Corey	You Go Away
		Greenfield	She Come Bringing Me That Little Baby Girl
		Hoban	"Frances" books
		Jewell	Bus Ride
		Jonas	Holes and Peeks
		Kuskin	"O.K. Everybody . . ."
		Sharmot	I Don't Care
		Stevenson	What's Under My Bed?
		Wells	Timothy Goes to School
		Zolotow	A Father Like That
		Zolotow	When I Have a Son
		Ages 5–8:	
		Alexander	Nadia the Willfull
		Bartoli	Nonna
		Carrick	Books about Christopher
		Fassler	My Grandpa Died Today
		Gackenback	Do You Love Me?
		Greenfield	"Love Don't Mean"
		Mayer	One Frog Too Many
		Miles	Annie and the Old One
		Preston	The Temper Tantrum Book
		Skorpen	His Mother's Dog
		Viorst	Alexander and the Terrible, Horrible, No Good, Very Bad Day

Notes

1. Paul Mussen, *The Psychological Development of the Child* (Englewood Cliffs, N.J.: Prentice-Hall Inc., 1973), 47.
2. Erik Erikson, *Childhood and Society*, 2d. ed. rev. (New York: W.W. Norton & Co. Inc., 1963).
3. Mussen, *Psychological Development*, 68.
4. Lucille Clifton, *Amifika*. Illus. by Thomas DiGrazia (New York: E.P. Dutton, Inc., 1977).
5. Clifton, *Amifika*, n.p.
6. Susan Bonners, *Panda* (New York: Delacorte Press, 1978).
7. Don Freeman, *Beady Bear* (New York: Viking Press, 1954).
8. Bernice Kohn, *Koalas*. Illus. by Gail Haley (Englewood Cliffs, N.J.: Prentice-Hall Inc., 1965).
9. Don Freeman, *Corduroy* (New York: Viking Press, 1968).
10. Jean Holzenthaler, *My Hands Can*. Illus. by Nancy Tafuri (New York: E.P. Dutton Inc., 1978).
11. Jan Ormerod, *Sunshine* (London: Kestrel, 1981).
12. Shirley Hughes, *Alfie's Feet* (New York: Lothrop, Lee & Shepard Books, 1983).
13. Ann & Paul Rand, *I Know a Lot of Things* (New York: Harcourt Brace Jovanovich, 1956).
14. Phyllis Krasilovsky, *The Very Tall Little Girl*. Illus. by Olivia H. H. Cole (Garden City, N.Y.: Doubleday & Co. Inc., 1969).
15. Pat Hutchins, *Titch* (New York: Macmillan Publishing Co., 1971).
16. Amy Ehrlich, *Zeek Silver Moon*. Illus. by Robert Andrew Parker (New York: Dial Press, 1972).
17. Pat Hutchins, *You'll Soon Grow Into Them, Titch* (New York: Greenwillow Books, 1983).
18. Kenneth Koch, *Wishes, Lies, and Dreams* (New York: Random House, Vintage Books, 1970), 156–74.
19. Mary Ann Hoberman, "A Year Later," in *Hello and Good-by*. Reprinted by permission of Russell & Volkening, Inc. as agents for the author. Copyright ©1959 by Mary Ann Hoberman.
20. Reprinted with permission of Macmillan Publishing Company from *Secrets of a Small Brother* by Richard J. Margolis, Donald Carrick.
21. Charlotte Zolotow, *Someone New*. Illus. by Erik Blegvad (New York: Harper & Row, Publishers, Inc., 1978), 31–32.
22. Joan Lexau, *Benjie on His Own*. Illus. by Don Bolognese (New York: Dial Press, 1970).
23. Shigeo Watanabe, *I Can Ride It!* Illus. by Yasuo Ohtomo (New York: Philomel, 1982).
24. Shigeo Watanabe, *I Can Build a House!* Illus. by Yasuo Ohtomo (New York: Philomel, 1983).
25. Shigeo Watanabe, *I Can Take a Walk!* Illus. by Yasuo Ohtomo (New York: Philomel, 1984).
26. Rachel Isadora, *Max* (New York: Macmillan Publishing Co., 1976).
27. Bernard Waber, *Ira Sleeps Over* (Boston: Houghton Mifflin Co., 1972).
28. From *Big Sister Tells Me That I'm Black* by Arnold Adoff. Reprinted by permission of Holt, Rinehart & Winston.
29. Barbara Bel Geddes, *I Like to Be Me* (New York: Young Readers Press, 1963), 32.
30. Miriam Cohen, *First Grade Takes a Test*. Illus. by Lillian Hoben (New York: Greenwillow Books, 1980).
31. Robert Bright, *Which Is Willie?* (New York: Young Readers Press, 1962).
32. Elizabeth Winthrop, *Sloppy Kisses*. Illus. by Anne Burgess (New York: Macmillan Publishing Co., 1980).
33. Gibbs Davis, *The Other Emily*. Illus. by Linda Shute (Boston: Houghton Mifflin Co., 1984).
34. Janet Schulman, *Jenny and the Tennis Nut*. Illus. by Marylin Hafner (New York: Greenwillow Books, 1978).
35. M. B. Goffstein, *Two Piano Tuners* (New York: Farrar, Straus & Giroux Inc., 1970).
36. Robert Kraus, *Whose Mouse Are You?* Illus. by Jose Aruego (New York: Macmillan Publishing Co., 1970).
37. Margaret Wise Brown, *The Runaway Bunny*. Illus. by Clement Hurd (New York: Harper & Row, Publishers, Inc., 1942).
38. Crescent Dragonwagon, *Always, Always*. Illus. by Arieh Zeldich (New York: Macmillan Publishing Co., 1984).

39. Marjorie Weinman Sharmat, *I'm Terrific*. Illus. by Kay Chorao (New York: Holiday House Inc., 1977).

40. Louis E. Raths, M. Harmin, and Sidney B. Simon, *Values and Teaching* (Columbus, Ohio: Charles E. Merrill Publishing Co., 1966).

41. Leo Lionni, *I Want to Stay Here! I Want to Go There!* (New York: Pantheon Books Inc., 1977).

42. Leo Lionni, *Frederick* (New York: Pantheon Books Inc., 1967).

43. Barbara Cooney, *Miss Rumphius* (New York: Viking Press, 1982).

44. Miriam Cohen, *Will I Have a Friend?* Illus. by Lillian Hoban (New York: Macmillan Publishing Co., 1967).

45. Petronella Breinburg, *Shawn Goes to School*. Illus. by Errol Lloyd (New York: Thomas Y. Crowell Publishers, 1973).

46. Jeannette Caines, *Daddy*. Illus. by Ronald Himler (New York: Harper & Row, Publishers, Inc., 1977).

47. John Burningham, *The Blanket* (London: Jonathan Cape, 1975).

48. Judith Viorst, *Alexander and the Terrible, Horrible, No Good, Very Bad Day*. Illus. by Ray Cruz (New York: Atheneum Publishers, 1972).

49. Marjorie Weinman Sharmat, *I Don't Care*. Illus. by Lillian Hoban (New York: Macmillan Publishing Co., 1977).

50. Liesel Moak Skorpen, *His Mother's Dog*. Illus. by M. E. Mullin (New York: Harper & Row, Publishers, Inc., 1978).

51. Russell Hoban, *A Baby Sister for Frances*. Illus. by Lillian Hoban (New York: Harper & Row, Publishers, Inc., 1964).

52. Eloise Greenfield, *She Come Bringing Me That Little Baby Girl*. Illus. by John Steptoe (Philadelphia: J.P. Lippincott Co., 1974).

53. Russell Hoban, *A Birthday for Frances*. Illus. by Lillian Hoban (New York: Harper & Row, Publishers, Inc., 1968).

54. Mercer and Marianna Mayer, *One Frog Too Many* (New York: Dial Press, 1975).

55. Rosemary Wells, *Timothy Goes to School* (New York: Dial Press, 1981).

56. Eloise Greenfield, "Love Don't Mean" in *Honey I Love*. Illus. by Diane and Leo Dillon (New York: Thomas Y. Crowell Publishers, 1978).

57. Dick Gackenback, *Do You Love Me?* (New York: Seabury Press, 1975).

58. Martha Alexander, *And My Mean Old Mother Will Be Sorry, Blackboard Bear* (New York: Dial Press, 1974).

59. Charlotte Zolotow, *When I Have a Son*. Illus. by Hilary Knight (New York: Harper & Row, Publishers, Inc., 1967).

60. Charlotte Zolotow, *A Father Like That*. Illus. by Ben Schecter (New York: Harper & Row, Publishers, Inc., 1971).

61. Lucille Clifton, *Some of the Days of Everett Anderson*. Illus. by Evaline Ness (New York: Holt, Rinehart & Winston, 1970).

62. Lucille Clifton, *Everett Anderson's 1–2–3*. Illus. by Ann Grifalconi (New York: Holt, Rinehart & Winston, 1977).

63. Lucille Clifton, *Everett Anderson's Nine Month Long*. Illus. by Ann Grifalconi (New York: Holt, Rinehart & Winston, 1978).

64. Lucille Clifton, *Everett Anderson's Goodbye*. Illus. by Ann Grifalconi (New York: Holt, Rinehart & Winston, 1983).

65. Carol Carrick, *Lost in the Storm*. Illus. by Donald Carrick (New York: Seabury Press, 1974).

66. Carol Carrick, *The Accident*. Illus. by Donald Carrick (New York: Seabury Press, 1976).

67. Carol Carrick, *The Foundling*. Illus. by Donald Carrick (New York: Seabury Press, 1977).

68. Carol Carrick, *Dark and Full of Secrets*. Illus. by Donald Carrick (New York: Clarion Books, 1984).

69. Karla Kuskin, untitled poem in *Near the Window Tree* (New York: Harper & Row, Publishers, Inc., 1975), 21.

70. Edna Mitchell Preston, *The Temper Tantrum Book*. Illus. by Rainey Bennett (New York: Viking Press, 1969).

71. Ann Jonas, *Holes and Peeks* (New York: Greenwillow Books, 1984).
72. Nancy Jewell, *Bus Ride*. Illus. by Ronald Himler (New York: Harper & Row, Publishers, Inc., 1978).
73. Miriam Cohen, *Jim Meets the Thing*. Illus. by Lillian Hoban (New York: Greenwillow Books, 1981).
74. James Stevenson, *What's Under My Bed?* (New York: Greenwillow Books, 1983).
75. Dorothy Corey, *You Go Away*. Illus. by Lois Axeman (Chicago: Albert Whitman & Co., 1976).
76. Jennifer Bartoli, *Nonna*. Illus. by Joan E. Drescher (New York: Harvey House, 1975).
77. Joan Fassler, *My Grandpa Died Today*. Illus. by Stewart Kranz (New York: Human Sciences Press, 1971).
78. Miska Miles, *Annie and the Old One*. Illus. by Peter Parnall (Boston: Little, Brown & Co., Inc., 1971).
79. Sue Alexander, *Nadia the Willful*. Illus. by Lloyd Bloom (New York: Pantheon Books Inc., 1983).

Recommended References

Adell, Judith, and Klein, Hilary Dole. *A Guide to Non-Sexist Children's Books*. Chicago: Academy Press Limited, 1976.

Coller, A. R. "The Assessment of 'Self-Concept' in Early Childhood Education." Urbana, Ill.: ERIC Clearinghouse on Early Childhood Education, 1971.

Coopersmith, Stanley. *The Antecedents of Self-Esteem*. San Francisco: W. H. Freeman and Company, 1967.

Davis, Enid. *The Liberty Cap: A Catalogue of Non-Sexist Materials for Children*. Chicago: Academy Press Limited, 1977.

Erikson, Erik. *Childhood and Society*. 2d ed. New York: W. W. Norton & Co. Inc., 1963.

Medeiros, Donald C.; Porter, Barbara J.; and Welsh, I. David. *Children Under Stress*. Englewood Cliffs, N.J.: Prentice-Hall Inc., 1983.

Muller, Phillipe. *The Tasks of Childhood*. New York: McGraw-Hill Inc., 1969.

Mussen, Paul. *The Psychological Development of the Child*. Englewood Cliffs, N.J.: Prentice-Hall Inc., 1973.

Schmidt, Velma E., and McNeill, Earldene. *Cultural Awareness, A Resource Bibliography*. Washington, D. C.: National Association for the Education of Young Children, 1978.

Sims, Rudine. *Shadow and Substance: Afro-American Experience in Contemporary Children's Fiction*. Urbana, Ill.: National Council of Teachers of English, 1982.

Recommended Children's Books

Adoff, Arnold. *Where Wild Willie*. Illus. by Emily Arnold McCully. New York: Harper & Row, Publishers, Inc., 1978.

Alexander, Sue. *Dear Phoebe*. Illus. by Eileen Christelou. Boston: Little, Brown & Co. Inc., 1984.

Aliki. *Feelings*. New York: Greenwillow Books, 1984.

Aliki. *The Two of Them*. New York: Greenwillow Books, 1979.

Cohen, Miriam. *No Good in Art*. Illus. by Lillian Hoban. New York: Greenwillow Books, 1980.

Corey, Dorothy. *Tomorrow You Can*. Illus. by Lois Axeman. Chicago: Albert Whitman & Co., 1977.

Ets, Marie Hall. *Just Me*. New York: Viking Press, 1965.

Gray, Nigel. *It'll Come Out in the Wash*. Illus. by Ed Frascino. New York: Harper & Row, Publishers, Inc., 1979.

Hazen, Barbara Shook. *The Me I See*. Illus. by Ati Forberg. Nashville: Abingdon Press, 1978.

Hoban, Lillian. *Arthur's Honey Bear*. New York: Harper & Row, Publishers, Inc., 1974.

Hutchins, Pat. *Happy Birthday, Sam*. New York: Greenwillow Books, 1978.

Iverson, Genie. *I Want to Be Big*. Illus. by David McPhail. New York: Unicorn/Dutton, 1979.

Kherdian, David. *Right Now*. Illus. by Nancy Hogrogian. New York: Alfred A. Knopf Inc., 1983.

Kraus, Robert. *Leo the Late Bloomer.* Illus. by Jose Aruego. New York: Windmill, 1971.

Rice, Eve. *Oh, Lewis!* New York: Macmillan Publishing Co., 1974.

Schuchman, Joan. *Two Places to Sleep.* Illus. by Jim LaMarche. Mineapolis: Carolrhoda Books, 1979.

Tobias, Tobi. *The Quitting Deal.* Illus. by Trina Schart Hyman. New York: Viking Press, 1975.

Varley, Susan. *Badger's Parting Gifts.* New York: Lothrop, Lee & Shepard Books, 1984.

Wells, Rosemary. *Noisy Nora.* New York: Dial Press, 1973.

Zhitkov, Boris. *How I Hunted the Little Fellows.* Trans. by Djemma Bider. Illus. by Paul O. Zelinsky. New York: Dodd, Mead & Co., 1979.

7

Supporting Children's Social and Moral Development

Social and Moral Development in Young Children

Five-year-old Holly came running into the classroom, telling her teacher in indignant tones that Ralph kept chasing her on the playground. The teacher asked Holly what had happened. Holly explained that Ralph was standing near the swings, and that when she approached him he started after her. "What did you do when he started toward you?" asked the teacher. "I ran away," answered Holly. "What do you suppose might have happened if you had kept walking toward him, or perhaps stood still?" probed the teacher. There was a long silence. Then Holly's face showed that she had grasped the idea and with a decisive "Oh" she turned and walked back to the playground.

Holly was just beginning to learn that her behavior toward others could affect their behavior toward her. It is but one of many social lessons that Holly will learn as she matures.

Social Development

Much of children's social development, their ability to relate to other people, is correlated with their ability to see from the viewpoint of another. Piaget describes children who are in the preoperational stage of intellectual development, usually from about two to about six or seven years of age, as being egocentric. They are unable to consistently put themselves in someone else's place because they consider their own point of view the only possible one. Social workers and day care professionals are finding that many preschool youngsters whose parents are divorced see themselves as the cause of the separation. They are not able to view the problems from their parents' perspectives, to comprehend that they may not be the center around which all actions revolve. They may also reason from particular to particular. If Daddy left home, and if they had misbehaved, then Daddy must have left *because* they misbehaved.

Young children may misinterpret other people's feelings. Flapan[1] found that the six year olds in her study were aware of dramatic incidents but did not look at sequences of action to make inferences about people's feelings. The nine year olds, however, tended to give more causal explanations for people's actions and to take intentions into account. This means that young children will often need help in seeing that other people have feelings that matter and that may differ from their own, as well as in learning to interpret the emotions of others. Being able to see from another's viewpoint and to interpret another person's response are developments central to the ability to interact successfully in social relationships.

Mussen and Eisenberg-Berg were concerned with conditions under which children exhibited prosocial behavior, actions that were intended to aid another person and for which no rewards were expected. When would a child volunteer to give her toy to someone who did not have one, or help a classmate who was injured or crying? After analyzing hundreds of studies, they concluded:

> To act in accordance with learned or internalized norms, the child must first perceive the other person's needs, interpret them accurately, and recognize that he or she can be helped. In addition, the child must feel competent in this situation, that is, capable of providing what is needed, and the cost or risk entailed in helping must not be prohibitive. Unless these preconditions are met, even the child who knows the norm of social responsibility is not likely to render aid.[2]

Thus, it requires more than simply telling children to help others in order for them to actually provide help when it is needed. The authors write that experiences such as seeing prosocial behavior modeled and having participated in role playing will enhance prosocial behavior.

The models of behavior that children see are a powerful force in their learning. According to prosocial learning theorists, children observe how behaviors are performed and in what situations.[3] If they see a teacher treating children courteously and kindly, they are likely to adopt this behavior toward one another. They are also influenced by the rewards that follow behaviors, both when the reinforcement comes directly to them and when they observe its being given to someone else.[4] If one child is praised for completing a task, both that child and the observers learn that completing tasks is a behavior that will be rewarded. Likewise, negative reinforcement identifies behavior to be avoided.

Children observe a wide variety of models and use these, along with their perceptions of the reinforcement given, to determine acceptable behaviors for themselves. Sometimes they will make mistakes from an adult's perspective. Kelly knew from kindergarten that at snack time each child received an equal share of the food. She listened at home as her parents planned a dinner party, estimating the number of hors d'oeuvres needed for the guests. On the evening of the party, Kelly greeted the guests by explaining, "You each get five shrimp, three little sandwiches, and three meatballs." From her perception, that was acceptable behavior. The reaction of her parents, a look of distress, and that of the guests, amused laughter, indicated to Kelly that the behavior in a kindergarten setting was not appropriate in this setting. Much social learning involves determining when and where behaviors are likely to be condoned, as well as learning the behaviors themselves.

Children are influenced by observing adults interacting with peoples of varying ethnic and national backgrounds. Parents and other significant adults who either denigrate those who differ from themselves or totally avoid them contribute to children's distrust of peoples of different races, religions, or nationalities. Recent evidence has indicated children as young as four are aware of racial differences,[5] and that they have ideas about many foreign countries and peoples.[6]

In an extensive study of children's views of foreign peoples involving children from eleven groups in ten countries, Lambert and Klineberg [7] found that six year olds tended to focus on differences more than similarities among peoples and generally withheld affection from foreign peoples more than did the ten and fourteen year olds also interviewed. The young children disliked what seemed to them to be strange or exotic. However, the younger children gave facts about the physical features, clothing, language, and habits of foreign peoples and did not stereotype groups or give subjective evaluations of personality characteristics as did the older youngsters. The younger ones did stereotype their own nationality, almost always positively. The authors postulate that how children learn about their own group membership may be a factor in how they perceive others. If differences among groups are emphasized, a feeling of "we" and "they" seems more likely to develop. Children are helped to value those who differ from themselves if they see this attitude modeled and if they learn similarities as well as differences among groups.

Some knowledge of children's social development results from experimental studies while other learnings arise simply from observing children. Preliminary data from observational studies on the social growth of children under two years of age show that even infants tend to react positively to their peers.[8]

Friendships are important for children for several reasons. First, they provide opportunities for children to learn and practice social skills. Adults will often interpret a child's unclear request, or stop conflict the minute it begins, but children engage with one another as equals, thus requiring that communication be clear to be effective, and that techniques of handling conflicts or making requests be learned. Second, friendships give children a context in which they can compare themselves with others. Who is the taller of the two?

Who can run faster? This sort of social comparison helps children develop a valid sense of their own identity. Finally, friendships foster a feeling of group belonging, a security that differs from that achieved within the family. However, friendships may have undesirable as well as desirable effects. They may be the cause of jealousy, rejection of others, or antisocial behavior as well as security, self-acceptance, and trust. In writing about children's friendships, Rubin states, "The fact of the matter is that children's closest friendships manifest all of the prominent features of close relationships among adults, including their destructive as well as their constructive elements. Perhaps the biggest difference between children's and adults' interactions is that children tend to be more straightforward."[9]

As children mature, their concept of friendship changes. The three year old is likely to describe a friend in terms of physical attributes. He or she may say, for example, "Carlos is the same size as me." Children at this age will often consider those who are playing with them at the moment to be their friends. Two to three years later the description of a friend will include observations about behaviors as well as physical features, such as "Carlos wears a red coat. He can make people laugh whenever he wants." Friendship is determined by what that person does for the child, and is generally tied to specific episodes. By age eight or nine, children describe the traits they like or dislike, and are beginning to see friendship as a relationship that lasts over time. At this stage, a child might say, "Carlos is my friend because we like each other, and he will help me even when he's busy. He's my friend even when he's away visiting his grandmother." Thus the shift is from viewing people as physical entities to seeing them as psychological beings as well, and from thinking of friendship as a momentary encounter to seeing it as a lasting relationship.[10]

It is likely that children develop part of their concept of friendship from observing adult friendships. However, it appears that the major portion of their understanding comes from their own encounters with others and the way they integrate what they have learned. Thus children need to have the experience of working with each other in both large and small groups. It is necessary, however, to recognize that children vary in their social needs and in their social styles, and to respect these differences.

Moral Development

Moral, as well as social, development is related to intellectual development. Jean Piaget and Lawrence Kohlberg see the growth of moral reasoning as developing in stages which coincide with stages of cognitive growth. Piaget[11] describes two broad stages of moral development. In the first, children cannot see from another's point of view and perceive acts as either totally right or totally wrong. They judge an act on the basis of consequences and not on intention. The child who broke the cookie jar into many pieces trying to dry it is guiltier than the child who only cracked the jar while trying to sneak a cookie. They follow rules set down by adults not because of a belief in the need for a particular rule, but because the adult who gave it wields authority.

In the second stage, children can see another's point of view. They are less absolutistic in judgments and will assess acts more by intentions than by consequences. They also begin to favor less punishment for wrongdoers. Piaget sees this shift in stages as occurring when the child is around eight or nine years old.

Kohlberg[12] based his studies on Piaget's model of moral development. He describes a total of six stages of development, each keyed to the individual's sense of justice and to the reasoning used to solve moral dilemmas. Children ages four to ten reason at the first two stages, at the *preconventional* level. In stage 1, punishment and obedience orientation, they obey rules in order to avoid punishment. In stage 2, instrumental purpose and exchange, they conform to rules out of self-interest and do things for others in order to get things in return. As they mature, they will pass through further stages. Stage 3 is one of doing what *good boys* or *good girls* do and stage 4 one of respecting the law as a way of maintaining society. In the last two stages, personally developed moral principles take precedence over concern with authority. Kohlberg believes that most Americans operate at about stage 4.

Children develop their ability in moral reasoning through consideration of moral problems and through contact with the moral reasoning of others. Reasoning just one stage above their own is more meaningful to them than reasoning that is several stages higher. And the stage at which children as well as adults reason about moral questions is not always a predictor of their actual behavior in a situation involving a moral question.

Social learning theorists emphasize the importance of models of moral behavior and the use of rewards and punishment in children's moral development. Children who have internalized the standards of their parents may feel guilty when they do not comply with the standards, even if the parent is not in a position to punish them. The theorists note also that children's responses to moral questions can be changed by their listening to or observing a model who holds the opposite opinion.[13] After being given directions for one set of behaviors, then observing other behaviors being modeled, children are likely to imitate the model. "Do as I say and not as I do," is often ignored.

Although the theories of moral reasoning and of social learning have different key elements, they are not contradictory when applied to young children. A child reasoning at Kohlberg's stage 1, that of behaving in a particular way to avoid punishment, will be greatly influenced by rewards and punishments and by the behavior he sees modeled and the consequences it brings.

Both theories are useful in guiding young children's moral development. Piaget and Kohlberg illustrate the need for children to discuss the reasons behind moral decisions and help teachers understand the kinds of reasoning common among young children. Social learning theories remind teachers of the importance of the models of behavior they present, both through their own actions and through vicarious sources introduced into children's learning environments.

Goals for Teaching

Once again the goals for teaching can be described as long term developmental ones, general ones for a particular age or grade level, and specific ones for individual children. A long term goal for social and moral development is that children will become sensitive to the feelings and intentions of others. This ability to empathize with others and to understand their motivations will help children interact successfully with both peers and adults. Teachers and day care professionals will be helping children achieve this goal throughout the preschool and primary years.

A general social goal for preschoolers is that in a small group, each child will tell about an experience, or perhaps share an object, and will listen to others tell about their experiences. The children are learning the social skills of taking turns and of listening to others, as well as developing their own speaking skills. The amount of waiting time in relation to the amount of action time is kept low by limiting the number of children in the group.

A general social goal for second grade is that children will work in small groups on specific tasks for ten to fifteen minutes without the teacher's immediate presence and will make progress toward completing the task. It is expected that by the end of the year, nearly all of the children in each of these levels will have achieved the general goals set for them.

In addition, there will be goals for individual children that teachers develop as they come to know their classes. A social goal for a third grader could be that Peter will volunteer to help Robin and Chris with their reading. The teacher knows that Peter is capable of the task, but wants him to recognize both his own competence and the needs of others and then engage in prosocial behavior.

Literature can contribute to the achievement of all three types of goals. This chapter focuses on long term developmental goals. Books offer opportunities for you to help children grow toward the following goals for social and moral development:

- Children will make inferences about the feelings and intentions of others.
- Children will view a situation from more than one perspective, seeing the viewpoint of another person.
- Children will engage in prosocial behavior.
- Children will judge the appropriateness of specific behaviors and predict the possible consequences of particular behaviors.
- Children will know about others who differ from themselves and value this diversity.
- Children will engage competently in group activities.
- Children will evaluate various solutions to moral problems and ethical questions.

Opportunities Books Offer

Giving Children Experience in Making Inferences About the Feelings and Intentions of Others

Books provide a rich source of data from which children can begin to gain information as well as to make inferences and to check the validity of inferences. As stories unfold, characters reveal more and more of their feelings and more and more of their reasons for acting as they do. Children can make hypotheses at several points in a story and as the story progresses see if their hypotheses were accurate. The situation is nonthreatening, one in which there is no penalty if their predictions are not what actually happens in the story. Children simply explore whether there was ample evidence to support their guesses or whether they missed some important clues to the feelings of the characters.

Interpreting Nonverbal Language in Illustrations.   The illustrations in books give children experience in reading and interpreting body language and facial expressions. Because these illustrations are static, catching a moment in time, they give children a chance to study them and to talk about specific aspects. Marie Hall Ets's book *Talking Without Words*[14] focuses on the use of body language to communicate. Sometimes actions take the place of words. Holding out a bag of cookies or candy to someone else is a way of offering the sweets to them. A finger in front of the lips means to be quiet. At other times the body expresses a reaction to an event, a mood, or an emotion. Holding the nose usual-ly means the presence of an unpleasant odor—real or metaphoric—and stick-ing out the tongue expresses dislike for someone. Ets shows these actions and others in illustrations and uses a brief text to say what they mean. The use of children and their mother in these explanations helps children relate to what is being communicated. The book provides an excellent point of departure for having children pantomime messages, with others telling what is being said. You could have the children take turns, demonstrating one of the gestures shown in the book. Then they could begin to think of other body messages that were not shown. Children from preschool through the primary grades can understand this book and enjoy using their bodies to show meanings.

Wordless picture books are an excellent source of material in which body language and facial expressions are emphasized. In *Frog Goes to Dinner*[15] the expressions range from the pleasure of the parents as the family goes into a restaurant, to the surprise of one of the patrons when the boy's frog lands in her salad, to the haughtiness of the head waiter as he expels the family, to the disdain and anger of parents and sister as they glare at the boy and his frog on the way home. The final surprise of the story happens as the boy and frog are sent away in disgrace. The boy, with head bowed, carries an unhappy frog to his room. But as soon as the door is closed, boy and frog convulse with laughter. The variety of emotions, as well as the changes in emotions, provide much material for drawing inferences. Children can tell the story in their own words, perhaps by one recalling just what happened and the next suggesting how the characters feel. Another technique is for the children to take the part of one of the characters and speak in appropriate dialogue. It is useful to give children a card with the name or the picture of their character on it. This avoids confusion about who has which part, and if you want to have different children play the parts, you can help them remember by simply changing the cards. It eliminates arguments about who was to do what.

Wordless picture books vary in difficulty just as do other picture books. *Frog Goes to Dinner* is most appropriate for children in the primary grades or higher. For kindergarten and younger children, look for books with fairly simple plots, and in which the action is straightforward. A book such as *Out! Out! Out!*[16] is appropriate for young children because the plot is uncomplicated and easy to follow. A pigeon flies into the kitchen, encouraged by the baby who held out a spoonful of food to it as it sat on the windowsill. It comes in and begins eating from the baby's bowl. The mother, then the grocery man, and then the cus-todian all try to shoo the bird away. Finally the little boy in the family leads the pigeon back to the window and outside by leaving a trail of corn flakes for it to follow. The somewhat exaggerated expressions and actions of the characters are easy to read.

Books with text may have illustrations that are as explicit as to the characters' actions and feelings as those in wordless picture books, but the listeners, or watchers, do not have to make the interpretations themselves. Children can still be given the opportunity to discuss the illustrations. They may be asked to tell what they can about a character from the early illustrations. The end-papers for Sam[17] show Sam stretched out on the floor, looking rather wistful, his head resting on his crossed arms. On the title page, Sam's back faces the readers, but his head is turned so that his facial expression can be seen. Once again, he is looking uncertain. Children can be shown these two pictures before the reading begins and asked to say how they think the boy feels. They should be encouraged to give their reasons for their judgments. Then the story can be shared. Sam wants to play, but all the other members of his family are busy. He tries to join them, picking up one of his brother's books, and then joining his sister as she cuts clothes for her paper dolls. Each person suggests that he do something else. Finally, in frustration, he sits down and cries. The family realizes how he feels, and his mother asks him to help her in the kitchen. After the children have heard the story, go back and look again at some of the illustrations. Ask the children to tell how Sam feels in selected pictures, and how they know. Have children sit or walk like one of the characters. Have them show with their bodies and faces what the characters were feeling.

In some instances, you will want to ask the children to interpret some of the illustrations and to make predictions about what may happen next as you read a story. At other times, you may want to complete an entire story before engaging the children in any discussion. You can decide how to approach the story and the discussion by remembering that enjoyment and understanding of the story are the central purposes for your reading. Thus, if interrupting the narrative would destroy the story, wait until it is completed before talking about illustrations. But if the children seem confused, or if discussion throughout the story heightens interest for them, then go ahead with discussions at various points in your reading.

Look for illustrators who are particularly adept at showing facial expressions and body language. Symeon Shimin, Lillian Hoban, Mercer Mayer, and Donald Carrick are just a few whose work almost always captures easily recognizable emotions in physical expressions.

Relating Voice Inflection to Meaning. Children can gain experience in relating voice inflection to meaning and to the feelings of the speaker. The facets of language which linguists call *suprasegmentals* add meaning to speech. These are pitch, the high and low tones; stress, the emphasis with which a particular word or syllable is said; and juncture, the pause between syllables, words, or sentences. Variations in these tell the listener whether the sentence is a question or a statement; whether the phrase is "ice cream" or "I scream;" whether the speaker is being sincere or sarcastic.

Children do not need to know the terms or even to isolate pitch, stress, and juncture. They do need to hear expressive speech so that they can begin making generalizations for themselves about the speaker's meaning. You can provide many examples through your skillful reading. For example, your voice should reflect the change in Sam's father from his angry statement of "SAM, get your hands off that typewriter. . . . How many times must I tell you—that typewriter is not a toy for children," to his concerned question, "What in the world is the matter with Sam?"[18]

Going Beyond a Literal Interpretation of Dialogue.   Children can be given the opportunity to analyze when dialogue can be accepted at face value, and when a meaning other than or beyond a literal interpretation of the words is intended. Preschool children can recognize the hidden agenda in Charlie's first four questions in the poem "Charlie's Bedtime."

> Can you bring me a glass of water?
> Can I have a little juice?
> Can I say goodnight to Daddy again?
> Will you read me Dr. Seuss?

They can look for the reason Charlie wants to avoid going to bed as they listen to the last lines.

> Will I see you in the morning, Mommy?
> Can I keep on the light?
> Oh—
> If only I'd find a real way
> To chase away the night.
>
> Lee Bennett Hopkins[19]

After hearing the poem, they might tell what they do when they want to stay up later and whether their strategies work or not. They might also share how they feel about bedtime, perhaps making pictures of their bedrooms, or telling what sounds they hear after they have gone to bed.

Try reading Yolen's *No Bath Tonight*[20] to four or five year olds. In this story, Jeremy announces each evening that there is to be no bath for him, each time because of a minor injury. He has hurt his foot, or skinned his nose sliding into first base, or gotten stung by a bee. His parents acquiesce, and it is not until his grandmother comes to visit and makes "kid tea" in the bathtub so that she can read the "kid leaves" left in the tub that Jeremy decides to bathe. After reading about Jeremy's first injury, ask the children why he says no bath tonight on Monday. If they give Jeremy's answer, just continue reading. If they think he is trying to avoid a bath, tell them to see if they still think that when they have heard more of the story. When you have read through a week of excuses, ask again why Jeremy keeps saying no bath tonight. This time they should see the pattern.

Primary children will comprehend the more subtle nuances of the language used by Clancy and his friend Tippitt in *Clancy's Coat*.[21] The two have been angry with each other ever since Tippitt's cow trampled the vegetables in Clancy's garden. Tippitt looks out one day to see Clancy approaching, a package under his arm. He has brought a coat that needs turning, and tells Tippitt he has brought it to him "for the reason that you're the best tailor in Crossgar, and not for the sake of old friendships."[22] Clancy rubs his hands together and

Children can be asked to describe a character's feelings as they look at an illustration. (From Everett Anderson's Goodbye *by Lucille Clifton with illustration by Ann Grifalconi. Text copyright © 1983 by Lucille Clifton. Illustrations copyright © 1983 by Ann Grifalconi. Reprinted by permission of Holt, Rinehart and Winston Publishers.)*

comments on how cold it is outside, all the while eyeing the steaming teapot. Tippitt ignores the hints, and informs Clancy that the coat will be ready the next Saturday.

During the week, Tippitt goes to the barn on an extra cold night and, looking for something to keep his cow warm, spies Clancy's coat. He forgets about using the coat as a blanket until Clancy arrives, then invites him in to soothe the expected annoyance. When Clancy asks for his coat, Tippitt replies, "It's not ready yet. It's been over my. . .over. . .overlooked."[23] He assures Clancy it will be ready the next Saturday, and gives him a cup of tea. For several weeks, Tippitt uses the coat for emergencies, telling Clancy such things as "There's good work being done on it, I'll promise you that"[24] when his hen is laying eggs on it.

Little by little the two friends mend their differences, and when Tippitt remarks to Clancy that it was a lucky thing his coat needed turning, Clancy winks and says, "I told you there was a lot of use left in it."[25] The meaning of the dialogue goes far beyond the literal.

Following a Sequence of Action.   The meaning behind some dialogue is related to an entire sequence of action. Only if the readers know what has happened earlier are they able to interpret the statements of various characters accurately. In *Could Be Worse*[26] Grandpa relates an adventure at the breakfast table. He was pulled out of bed by a large bird, had an encounter with an abominable snowman, was chased across the desert by a huge blob of marmalade, met up with a squid and a giant sea turtle, and finally returned to his bed by getting a ride on a piece of toast and an airplane made out of newspaper. The readers know that Grandpa has not become insane or senile, but is reacting to his grandchildren's comments about him that he had overheard. They think the reason he never says anything interesting is because nothing interesting ever happens to him. Readers who have heard Grandpa respond to all the problems his grandchildren have by saying "Could be worse" are ready and waiting for the response that Grandpa gets when he asks the children what they think of his adventure: "Could be worse!"

Children who have had to defend their toys from being taken over by jealous younger brothers or sisters recognize the sequence of events in *Peabody*[27] as Annie opens her birthday present and finds a large teddy bear. Her younger brother Robert immediately announces that he wants it. Children recognize the cleverness, and the lack of accuracy, in Annie's response, "Peabody bites." After they have seen Robert gazing longingly at Peabody, they also can appreciate Annie's telling Robert that the red wool string that makes a fence around Peabody is an electric fence, something not to be touched.

Following the sequence of action is as helpful in making inferences about feelings and intentions of characters as it is for fully understanding dialogue. Young children develop an understanding of action and reaction in human relationships when they see an entire drama played out in book form.

Observing Patterns of Behavior.   Some youngsters, like Holly mentioned earlier, are just beginning to learn that their actions influence the actions of others. It was a new thought that Ralph may have chased her because she had been running herself. Other children, like six-year-old Rob, have learned how to control the behavior of others in certain situations. "Want to see my mommy get mad?" he asked his uncle and cousins who were visiting. Before they could answer, he opened a gate to the kitchen and put the cat in where his mother was working. Within seconds the angry words of his mother could be heard. "How did that cat get in here! I told you to keep the gate closed." Rob just grinned.

Children vary in their comprehension of the total situation in which action occurs. To help them see specific behaviors in a broader context, share books in which the action-reaction pattern is fairly clear and use these books as the basis for dramatization. One such book is *The Quarreling Book*.[28] When the book opens, Mr. James has just left the house on a rainy morning and has forgotten to kiss his wife good-bye. She is then cross and becomes critical of Jonathan when he comes down for breakfast. He thinks her criticism unfair and so when Sally appears, he asks why she cannot ever be on time. The pattern continues, with each character having his or her mood spoiled, becoming irritable, and managing to ruin someone else's day in turn. The chain is broken when Eddie shoves his dog off the bed, but is licked into better humor by the dog who has interpreted the action as an invitation to play. Once Eddie feels better, he reacts to his sister's search for her pencil by giving her his best one. The pattern then reverses, with each character cheering another and apologizing for earlier actions. By five o'clock the sun has come out, and all is complete when Mr. James returns home and kisses his wife hello.

If children are lined up in the order in which the characters appear, they can dramatize this story fairly easily. Each knows that first someone will say something sharp or unkind to them, and that feeling angry, they will then do the same thing to someone else. When the pattern is reversed, the action moves back up the line.

Another story which has only two characters but repeated action, and lends itself to dramatization, is *The Winter Picnic*.[29] Adam wants to have a picnic even though it is winter. His mother wants to finish cleaning the closet. Thus he continues preparations, stopping several times to ask her to join him, and she stops her cleaning long enough to tell him that she wants to finish the job. In the end he convinces her to take a look, and she does join him. In the meantime, listeners can see how the buildup of action, and particularly Adam's repeated requests, cause his mother to answer more sharply. The first time he asks, she tells him picnics are for summer not winter and concludes with, "In winter you can play in the snow. Why don't you go play in the snow?" The second time he tells her about his plan, she says. "Fine. Just let me finish what I'm doing." By his third visit, Adam's mother is tired of the interruptions. "Adam, please! Can't I be allowed to finish one thing I start. Just once. That's all I ask. Just once!"[30] Seen in context, within a total situation, her irritation makes sense, and children can see how one person's behavior can affect another's. This may be a time for children to dramatize not only this story, but to develop some scenes of their own, ones in which they show what they can do that will make their mothers answer sharply, or what they can do that will make their mothers happy. They might also show what their mothers can do to make them either pleased or unhappy. The emphasis is on how one person's behavior may affect another's.

Empathizing with a Book Character.   As children come to be able to read the feelings of another, they also become more sensitive to the feelings of others. You can ask them to empathize with a character by having them think about how they would feel if something similar happened to them. They might each tell about pets they have, or have had, prior to your reading of *When Lucy Went Away*.[31] The child narrator tells about the family's pet cat, Lucy. One summer when the family is ready to leave the summer place and return to the city, Lucy is missing. She does not return and the family must leave without her. They never find out what happened to her, and the child reminisces rather sadly. Children who have described their own pets can tell about how they would feel if their pet went away. Others who do not have pets might tell how they would feel if they lost one of their favorite toys. From "How would *you* feel if. . ." to "How do you think (book character) felt when. . ." is a transformation from a question that is centered on the child to a question that is centered on the book character, but both ask the child to imagine feelings.

You can use a book such as *How Do I Feel*[32] by reading the descriptions of each situation with children imagining that it is happening to them. Let them tell how they feel when someone laughs at their clothing, or when grandmother gives them a bag of groceries to carry, or when the adults around them are arguing. Then read another book and ask them how they think the character feels. For example, they might listen to *Keep Running, Allen!*[33] and respond to "How do you think Allen feels about going places with his older brothers and sisters?" Allen spends his time either running to keep up or being told to run to keep up. He longs to have time to look at things, to go at his own speed. Ask the question just before the page on which Allen lays on the grass and just stays there, watching a caterpillar crawl over his hand and looking at the clouds. Allen's frustrations, as well as those of his brothers and sister who have to wait for him, are fairly clear. Then ask how Allen's feelings have changed when you read the last few pages. His older brothers and sister have come back to check on him, and when Mike demonstrates in jest how Allen looks stretched out on the grass, he too discovers that the grass is soft and smells good. All three join Allen on the grass, looking at the sky and feeling dreamy.

One step further in the process of identifying and empathasizing with a character is for children to be asked to tell about times when they have felt the way they think the character feels. Thus children who have heard *Keep Running, Allen!* might tell about times they have gone shopping with their mothers and been forced to walk faster than they wanted, or when they have been playing and had to come in for dinner even if they preferred to keep playing. They might relate to Allen's satisfaction at finally getting to do what he wanted rather than what others wanted. When did they make the choices, decide to play in the mud or to eat only popcorn for dinner? They are making a connection with another person, increasing their awareness of others' feelings, when they share an emotion, even though the stimuli for that emotion may differ.

You might also share literature in which one character shows empathy for another. The mother in *Katie Did!*[34], for example, learns that the feelings of one child cannot be ignored when that child is asked to be considerate of another. In the book, Mary Rose is told to be quiet and let her baby brother sleep. While being quiet, she manages to spill some juice, take pots and pans outside to the sandbox, and create various other messes. When confronted by her mother, she explains that her doll Katie did all those things, including putting the turtle in the fishbowl because the turtle's mother didn't have time to play with him. The mother readily understands the child's feelings, and she takes time right then to be with her.

The narrator of this poem shows through his actions that he understands how his brother is feeling.

> His Dog
> My Brother shuffles through the door
> carrying little Sandy in his arms.
> His tears make Sandy's fur wet.
> When I try to pet her head,

he pulls away. "Don't," he says.
"She's dead."
Then I pet my brother's head.
She was his dog.[35]

Richard J. Margolis

Children thus can be given the opportunity to empathize with a book character and to see characters within literature empathasizing with one another.

Fostering Children's Ability to See from the Viewpoint of Others

When children de-center, that is, recognize that not everyone thinks as they do, they are ready to see from the viewpoint of another. The books and activities which help give children experience in recognizing how others feel provide a base for developing skill in taking various perspectives. Children can talk first about how the character may have felt or how they would have felt under the same circumstances and then begin to take the role of a character, reacting as that character would, telling what that character thinks, doing what they think that character would do in a new situation.

Sharing Books That Present Several Viewpoints.   You can help children recognize different viewpoints by reading to them several books in which different points of view are clearly illustrated. One such book, The Pain and the Great One,[36] is written in two parts. In one part, a boy of six describes life with The Great One, his older sister. In the other part, the sister describes life with her younger brother, The Pain. The same feelings of jealousy are described by both, and the reader sees several incidents told from two different viewpoints.

In another book with two narrators, The Day I Was Born,[37] Alexander and his brother take turns describing the day of Alexander's birth. Their memories of the event differ. Alexander says that his father and older brother went to a restaurant to celebrate his birth; the brother says that he and his father went out to eat because if they hadn't, they would have to have eaten reheated creamed cauliflower. In both of these books, children can see that the story differs when the teller changes.

These books with multiple narrators are unusual. Generally a story will have just one narrator, either a participant in the story who relates events from his or her point of view or an omniscient narrator who describes the thoughts and reactions of several characters.

An example of a book with an omniscient narrator is John Brown, Rose and the Midnight Cat.[38] Rose is a widow who lives with her dog, John Brown. The two are very close, keeping each other company and looking after one another. Then one night Rose sees something moving in the garden. She is sure it is a cat, but John Brown refuses even to look. After Rose has gone to bed, John Brown goes outside and tells the cat to stay away. For several nights Rose sees the cat and puts milk out for it. For the same nights, John Brown tips over the bowl. Readers see Rose's desire for the cat to join them and John Brown's wish to keep it away. Children might be asked to give all the reasons they can think of for why Rose might want the cat. They could tell why John Brown does not. They might pretend they are either Rose or John Brown and talk to the cat as they peer out the window, or role play the two characters as they sit by the fire talking about the cat. They could also role play the two characters as they talk about the cat after John Brown, recognizing Rose's need, has let it in. They can tell each other why they acted as they did.

Sometimes the story may be in first person, with the "I" who tells the story discovering that his or her view is not shared by everyone. The narrators in *Why Couldn't I Be An Only Kid Like You, Wigger?*[39] and *If It Weren't For You*[40] have similar views of family life. Both have other children in the family and both think it would be marvelous to be the only child. In the first book, the narrator invites his friend Wigger into his room and describes the awful things about a large family. He has to stand in line for the bathroom, he has to wear hand-me-down clothes, he gets blamed for things he did not do. If he were an only child, he could eat out, go places with his parents. Wigger, however, when asked why he comes over, says that it is lonely being an only child, an entirely new thought to the narrator. The illustrations show two viewpoints, for as the narrator thinks of eating out, he pictures himself eating ice cream. As Wigger sees it, eating out is being uncomfortably dressed up and facing an artichoke on the plate.

In the second book the pattern of *If it weren't for you*[41] is used as the narrator thinks of all that could be done without the interference of a younger sibling. He would get all the presents, could watch what he wanted on television, would have a room of his own, and would never have to set an example. On the last page, though, he realizes, that if it weren't for the younger child, he'd be alone with the grown-ups.

After hearing one or both of these stories, children can make their own lists. What are all the bad things about having brothers and sisters as they see it, or all the unpleasant things about being an only child? What are all the positive aspects of the two situations? If they could change from the pattern of their family now, would they?

Observing Book Characters Whose Perspective Is Limited.   In some books, one character's lack of understanding of the viewpoint of another is central to the story. In *The Happy Lion,*[42] the lion does not understand why all the people who greeted him so pleasantly when he was at the zoo run from him as he wanders down the street. After all, on all previous occasions on which they met, the people were polite and friendly.

The fish in *Fish is Fish*[43] cannot imagine the land creatures that his friend the frog describes to him. He sees everything as a sort of fish mutation, so that birds become fish with many colored wings, two legs, and fins, and cows are fish with udders, horns, four legs, and fins.

Children can take on the limited perspective of the character, drawing how cars, or buildings, or various animals might appear in the mind of the fish. After hearing *The Happy Lion* they could dictate what the lion would write if he kept a diary. In both cases, they can see a broader perspective than the one they are taking.

Taking the Viewpoint of Another.   Children can be asked to take the viewpoint of someone who is far different from themselves if the literature gives some point of contact, or if you as teacher can establish this contact. Young children can imagine what it is like to be much older than they are. They can share with each other what their grandmothers and grandfathers like and dislike, how they behave. They can listen to stories such as *My Noah's Ark*[44] in which the narrator is a ninety-year-old lady who is describing the ark her father made for her as a child. She has kept it all her life, shared it with all her family. Now she is alone, but the ark brings back memories. One second grader who had heard this story wrote his own story about his grandfather:

> I know why my grandfather paints. It is because he is old. He paints what he remembers.

Knowing that memories are important to many older people is one step in understanding a different perspective.

Engaging in Role Play and Puppetry. Children can enjoy and benefit from taking the perspective of first one character and then another. Children who have listened to *Katharine's Doll*[45] could dramatize parts of the story with one child being Katharine and the other Molly, then dramatize it again with the roles reversed. In the story, the two girls are friends, playing together often, even wearing the same shoe size. Then Katharine gets a new doll named Charlotte. Both girls play with the doll, but Katharine finds it difficult to share and Molly feels left out. At one point Katharine is so busy with the doll that she forgets to say good-bye to Molly when she leaves. At another time, Katharine asks Molly whom she came to play with, her or Charlotte, and Molly replies Charlotte. Children could work in pairs, with several pairs dramatizing simultaneously. They could create situations of their own in which one has a new toy and the other comes to play with it. They might conclude by discussing how they felt in each role and when they have played those roles in real life.

They can also engage in role play where the roles are not ones that they themselves might play on different occasions. In *Eliza's Daddy*,[46] they might first be Eliza, waiting for the Saturday visit of her divorced father, wanting to see his new home and new wife, his new family. They could decide how they would ask to visit his new home if they were Eliza and how they would feel. They could then play the role of Eliza's father, trying to imagine how he feels as he comes to pick her up. In the book, he agrees to take her to his house if she really wants to spend her Saturday there, but never says why he had not taken her there before. Children might extend the dialogue, with Eliza asking what his home is like, or what he thinks of his new daughter and new baby. Her father can answer and also explain why he had not suggested that she come to visit.

Try using puppets or masks to stimulate children to take different roles. As they change puppets, they change characters. They must switch from one outlook to another, from one set of characteristics to another. You will also see whether children are able to de-center as you listen to their use of puppets. Some may never take the character's role, but rather hold the puppet and say what they think. Others may begin as a different character, but midway revert to their own outlook, unable to sustain another perspective. This gives you valuable insight into the children's development.

With puppets children can take the perspective of first one character, then another.

As you plan your literature selections, and especially as you are developing language acitivities that extend the books, think about ways in which children can be given the opportunity to take the perspective of another person. Role play and puppets provide natural situations for this to happen. You can also set up special activities. One child may be the book character, and the others interviewers for a television station. The interviewers ask questions, and the child answers as the character would. What would Rose say when asked about her pets, or the old lady when asked about the toy ark she keeps on her bedside table?

Or suppose that the book character kept a scrapbook, or a photo album. The children can make pages for the book or album, then describe what is in it, and why it is important to them as that book character. They might dictate captions for items in the books. What would the lion save as mementos of his trip away from the zoo, or given snapshots of his stroll through the main street of town, how would he label the reactions of various people upon seeing him? Give children the opportunity to share their books, explaining to classmates what they have included and why it is important.

Providing Models of Prosocial Behavior

Literature that portrays characters engaged in social behavior shows children not only a way of acting, but also the ingredients necessary for prosocial behavior to occur. That is, the character is able to recognize that another needs help or that there is something that could be done for him or her, feels confident that he or she can provide that help, and sees the risk as not too great to get involved. When you share stories that include prosocial behavior, you might call attention to these aspects individually as well as looking at the action as a whole.

Reading Books That Demonstrate Prosocial Behavior.   Suppose you read *The Bravest Babysitter*[47] to your class. In this story, Heather comes to babysit with Lisa, and soon after her arrival it begins to rain. Heather says nothing, but is unable to concentrate, and covers her ears with each clap of thunder. Lisa makes a series of suggestions of what they can do, reading together, playing dress up, dancing. Heather allows Lisa to stay up until the rain stops. Children could demonstrate what Heather did which let Lisa, and the listeners, know that she was afraid of the thunder. One child might cover her ears, and another be Heather telling Lisa that she could stay up even though it was past her bed-time. They are identifying the feelings of a character through words and actions. Then ask, "If your babysitter were afraid of thunder, what could you do to help?" Again, they might demonstrate their strategies. The assumption is made that they are indeed capable of helping in a situation such as this. Your seeing them as capable helps them to see themselves in that light.

After sharing and discussing one book on prosocial behavior, simply read another so that children view various models of such behavior. *David and Dog*[48] would be an excellent choice, for in this story David's older sister Bella recognizes David's unhappiness at having lost his stuffed dog and his frustration when he finds it at a school sale only to have a little girl purchase it before he can. Bella is quick to change her approach after the girl refuses to sell David's dog back to them. She offers to trade the huge teddy bear she has won in a raffle for David's toy. The ploy is successful, and David's hug for Bella says thank you. Bella even assures him that she will not miss the teddy bear, and that with all her other toys in bed, the teddy bear would have meant no room for her.

Preschool children will identify with Alfie's feelings in *Alfie Gives a Hand*.[49] He attends a backyard birthday party and has to adjust to a rather obstreperous host. He is timid and wants to cling to his blanket. However, when he must choose between the blanket and giving a comforting hand to another child, he is willing—and able—to release the blanket. Helping others may not always be easy, but it is within the capabilities of even the youngest.

Discussing Ways of Providing Help.   Once you have read several books that have instances of prosocial behavior, have children tell or role play what they could do in specific problem situations. Give them the setting and the problem. For example:

- You are walking home by yourself and you see a little boy standing on the sidewalk crying. He tells you he is lost. What would you do?
- A friend of yours tells you on the playground that she feels sick. She is holding her stomach. What would you do?

Planning Prosocial Behavior.   Consider also grouping books that show social behavior so that children can make some generalizations. One grouping would be to read books in which the child character does something for a family member. In *Evan's Corner*,[50] Evan helps his younger brother Adam make a special corner for himself. In *Ask Mr. Bear*,[51] Danny goes from animal to animal, looking for a gift for his mother's birthday. Mr. Bear has the answer—a bear hug. In *Sunflowers for Tina*,[52] Tina thinks that her grandmother's life has few bright spots left, and so dressed in her yellow dress, dances for her, bringing forth the first laughter Tina has ever heard from her grandmother. In *Do You Know What I'll Do?*,[53] a little girl tells her baby brother all the good things she will do for him. *Ask Mr. Bear* and *Do You Know What I'll Do?* are particularly good for preschool children because of the highly appealing repetition of language and because the emotions are less subtle in these than in the other two books. Children can be lead to generalize that there are many ways of giving to and helping others, and that children can be helpful. After reading two, or three, or all four of the books, ask children to select one member of their family. Then have them make a catalog of all the good things they could do for that person. Have them think of realistic actions. They might help a younger sister get dressed, or share a toy with a brother, or help mother by making a bed. They can take their booklet home and let the family member choose one item which the child will then give. Another time, have them think of imaginative things they would like to do for another person, things that they might not be capable of really doing. "I'll get him all the cotton candy he wants," or "I'll take her to beach every day," or 'I'll buy him a car that starts even on cold mornings."

Comparing Themes of Helping. This could lead into talking about how it feels to help someone without being asked. Children can give examples of their own. Follow the discussion by reading a book such as *A Special Trade*.[54] Nelly is very small and her neighbor and good friend old Bartholomew pushes her in her carriage, telling her to hang on if there is a bump. As she grows older, he helps her learn to walk and to skate. But as she grows older, so does he. Now sometimes Bartholomew needs a helping hand, which Nelly offers. After a fall on the stairs, he is in a wheelchair, and Nelly pushes him around the neighborhood. Nelly says that first it was her turn to sit and his to push, and now it is his turn to sit and hers to push—a kind of trade.

Children can identify this theme of helping one another by comparing books. A book with very different characters, but a similar theme, is *Amos and Boris*.[55] In this fantasy, Boris the whale befriends Amos the mouse when Amos falls off his boat. Years later Boris is washed ashore and it is Amos who gets two elephants to push him back into the ocean. The language of the book is so evocative that it is likely you will want to concentrate on this aspect of the book. However, asking, "How is this book like *A Special Trade?*" shows children that two very different books may express a common theme, and focuses their attention on the idea of helping one another.

A book character is just one model among many to which children are exposed. Some books that you present will show behavior that you would not choose to have children emulate. Often the problem to be solved in the book results from the behavior of one of the characters, behavior that may not reflect values that you condone. It would be dangerous to select only those books in which characters exhibit prosocial behavior. You would be eliminating excellent literature that may portray humans in some of their very human but not so lovable thoughts and actions, and you would be exercising a kind of censorship, a screening of literature based on the values presented. Rather than eliminating these books, add them to the collection of books that show children engaged in prosocial behavior. Help children see that they too are capable of aiding others in given situations and that there are internal rewards for such behavior.

Encouraging Children to Judge the Appropriateness of Particular Behaviors

Learning when a behavior is appropriate requires generalizing about types of situations and types of behaviors. A social encounter is not likely to be repeated in exact form. Children can be helped to generalize about the appropriateness of behaviors by seeing many examples of both behaviors and their consequences. Some examples will come from direct observation or participation, but others will come from vicarious experiences such as literature.

Preschoolers hearing John Burningham's The Cupboard[56] see a young child taking pots and pans from a kitchen cupboard and playing with them. When his mother suggests that he think of something else to do, he does, but as he walks away she asks him to please come back and put the pots and pans away. The last illustration shows the two of them placing the utensils in the cupboard. Young children hearing the story can be asked to recall times when they are expected to put things away. It is probably a safe generalization for them to say that they should put away anything that they have finished playing with and are no longer using.

However, not all situations are as easily assessed. Children hearing a story and knowing the full context of a situation can be asked to make judgments about a character's behavior, noting the circumstances that may have influenced it. Second and third graders who have heard The Washout[57] can be asked what they think the boy in the story, Christopher, could have done when he saw that the logs and rocks he usually used to cross the brook were gone. Christopher and his mother had just come to the family's summer cottage. A storm during the night had washed away a part of the road, and at other places fallen trees had made it impassable. They had neither food nor telephone. Christopher's mother had told him he could explore but that he was to stay out of the brook. Christopher, however, is by the brook when he discovers a new row boat that has broken loose from its mooring. In a somewhat dangerous fashion he poles the boat around the lake and then walks to a small grocery store. Once there the grocer gives him a food supply and a man at the store takes him home, cutting the trees out of the way as they go. Christopher's mother has been extremely worried about him. He apologizes, then asks her if she is glad he made the trip. She agrees that she is.

Children can describe what else he could have done, and postulate consequences for each of the suggested behaviors. They might relate what their own parents' reaction would be if they behaved as Christopher did. Ask questions that will focus children's attention on the relationship between the situation and the behavior. For The Washout, such a question would be, "Do you think Christopher's mother would have said the same thing to him if he had taken the boat when nothing special had happened? What makes you think this?"

As children become more accustomed to viewing single incidents within broader contexts, and as they become more able to predict the reactions of others, they will be able to assess more accurately the sorts of behaviors that are most likely to be appropriate in any given situation.

Helping Children Learn About and Value Differences Among People

Basic to being open to others is feeling good about oneself. Thus, many of the activities designed to enhance the self-concept of young children aid in their acceptance of others. As they explore what they can do, they see also what their classmates can do; as they tell what they like, they hear what their classmates like. Thus, they are beginning to see the diversity within their own small group and to value both themselves and their friends. The differences add interest.

Selecting Literature That Values Diversity.   Literature can focus attention on how individuals vary and emphasize the value of this variance. In *A Mitzvah Is Something Special*,[58] Lisa interacts with her two grandmothers. Grandma Esther is proud of having her own teeth. She is a good cook and baker, she makes her own quilts, and she remembers her husband Nathan as "the best." The other grandmother, Dorrie, contrasts with Esther. She wears tinted contacts and has both a long wig and a short wig. She will play dress-up with Lisa, and she is good for cheering people up, with her love of music and the good times with her friend Gus. She remembers her husband Al as "mean" and says that it was "good riddance when he left."[59] Lisa likes both her grandmothers, enjoying different things about each one, recognizing that each is special in certain ways. Children can compare people they know, telling what is special about each. It may be grandmothers, but it could just as well be neighbors or friends. The discussion can be focused on what is liked about each to emphasize positive feelings.

The theme of valuing others different from oneself, or from the norm, appears in literature at all levels. Young children hearing *Oliver Button Is a Sissy*[60] see Oliver being teased because he takes tap dancing lessons, and because he neither enjoys playing ball nor is good at it. When he loses a talent show, he comes back to school doubly dejected, but is surprised to find that the graffiti on the wall proclaiming him a sissy has been changed, with "sissy" marked out and "star" written in. Children might think about what makes their friends "stars," what their special talents are. Some classrooms in the primary grades have graffiti walls, bulletin boards where youngsters can write messages. A wall such as this could be used to write positive comments about classmates, with the teacher providing several examples and making clear the nature of acceptable comments.

Read books to your students that reflect positive attitudes toward others. Preschool children listening to *What Does the Rooster Say, Yoshio?*[61] see two children who do not speak the same language visiting a play farm. As they see the animals, each imitates the sounds of that animal, with the sound being written as it is symbolized in their own languages. Thus, dog is "Wan, Wan" for Yoshio and "Bowwow" for Lynn. When they see a cow, both go "Moo, moo" to their mutual delight. They run to their mothers mooing in unison. Although they cannot communicate with each other through language, they accept and enjoy each other and are able to overcome their communication barrier. The book introduces the concept that people may speak different languages, but that they are still able to get along with one another.

Focusing on Similarities.   Share several books that picture a particular people, or race, or religion so that one book does not become representative of that group in the minds of the children. You might look over your literature curriculum to see if you could be fostering any misconceptions. If, for instance, all the books you have selected which have black characters have urban settings, you should add several books with black characters that are set in suburban or rural areas.

To avoid a "we-they" approach, focus on individuals within groups rather than on the groups themselves and focus on similarities. Thus, you could assemble several books by themes or central idea, ones in which the protagonists represent several different backgrounds and group classifications. *Amigo,*[62] *Chin Chiang and the Dragon's Dance,*[63] and *Howie Helps Himself*[64] all feature a child with a special wish or goal. In *Amigo,* a little Mexican boy wants a dog, but his family is poor and they cannot afford to feed a pet. Told in poetry, the story develops the friendship between Francisco and a prairie dog. Each plans to win the other for a friend, and each is successful. In *Chin Chiang and the Dragon's Dance,* Chin Chiang must learn to dance the dragon's dance with his grandfather for the first day of the Year of the Dragon. He wants to do well but is fearful. An old woman, Pu Yee, who used to dance the dragon's dance helps Chin Chiang by dancing it with him for practice. His grandfather pulls him into the dance and he does fine—pulling Pu Yee into the dance as well. In *Howie Helps Himself,* Howie attends a special class, and although he has learned how to do many things, his strongest wish is to be able to move his wheelchair by himself. He practices and practices, at times almost giving up. Then one afternoon when his father comes to pick him up, he tries once more and this time is successful in wheeling himself all the way to the door of the classroom where his father is waiting.

In each of the books, the protagonist is a member of a group that could be studied for itself. By grouping the stories according to the feelings of the characters, children see the human qualities that they share and that they themselves understand. This helps them to see the similarities among people who may differ from them in some ways, but who share common emotions and needs.

Reading Literature from Other Countries.   Finally, share with children literature from other countries. Foreign folk tales are especially plentiful. When you introduce one, tell the country or at least the continent where it originated. If you are going to read *Oh, Kojo! How Could You!,*[65] you might say, "This story is called *Oh Kojo! How Could You!,* and it is a tale that was first told in the Sudan, a country in Africa." Young children have not yet developed clear concepts of distance nor of the meaning of *country,* and learning where Africa is would add little to their literary experience. However, telling them that the story comes from another country introduces the idea that many countries have literature, and that stories from many places can be enjoyed. There is a list of recommended folk tales at the end of this chapter.

Howie's wish is to be able to move his wheelchair by himself. (Illustration by Joe Lasker from Howie Helps Himself, *by Joan Fassler, Copyright 1975. By permission of Albert Whitman and Co.)*

The same procedure can be used with books that were first published in another country. Tell children the title of the story and the name of the author, and then tell where the author lives or lived. For example, you might read *Pettranella*[66] by Betty Waterton, and explain that the author lives in Canada, and has written a book about a family that moved to that country a long time ago. Children will see similarities between this family homesteading in the Canadian wilderness and episodes they have seen on television of American homesteaders. They will also be able to relate to the story's emotional content. In the book, a little girl has to leave the grandmother she loves, and the grandmother gives her a special gift for her new home.

Some foreign authors whose work is appropriate for young children are Edward Ardizzone, Nicola Bayley, Raymond Briggs, John Burningham, Shirley Hughes, Pat Hutchins, Helen Oxenbury, Brian Wildsmith, Mitsumasa Anno, Jean de Brunhoff, Max Bollinger, Alois Carigiet, C. Hans Fischer, Astrid Lindgren, and Svend Otto. Activities can be based on the literary content of the stories, but also stress the idea that people of other countries write stories that American children enjoy.

Engaging Children in Group Activities

Children develop social skills only in a context where they have the opportunity to practice them. Day care centers and schools are natural places for this to happen. As you plan the presentation of literature and related activities, capitalize on the opportunities to help children be a part of the group.

Children will feel like a part of the group in activities where all are working together, especially if an attitude of cooperation permeates the endeavor. This activity may be simply listening to a story, being quiet so others can hear, laughing along with others at humorous passages. It might be a group response to the literature, participating as the book is read a second time, singing the words to the song illustrated as a picture book, engaging in choral speaking, or doing finger plays. The enjoyment of activities such as these is enhanced when each child feels secure in his or her own group membership.

As you plan ways of extending books, develop activities that require the children to work together. For those preschoolers who are working side by side but not *with* one another, suggest projects where they will need to share materials or space. They could make a collage of mushroom shapes after hearing *Mushroom in the Rain.*[67] The brightly colored mushrooms used in the book illustrations suggest to children the possibilities for various shapes, colors, and patterns. Paper, fabric, yarn, foil, magazines, and other materials should be placed in a central location. Children are grouped around the materials, thus encouraging conversation as they work. They can comment about each other's work or perhaps tell others about their collages. They become engaged in social interaction because of the way the activity is structured. Other activities that

Children learn to share space and materials in day care centers and schools.

promote the development of social skills are those that require some joint planning. Creative dramatics, puppetry, pantomiming, writing group stories, dancing with partners, and making murals all require children to participate and to listen to the ideas of others in order to be successful.

Begin with small groups, only two or three children, and enlarge the groups as the children become more adept at handling the situation. Pairs of children could work together to create pictures showing some of Grandpa's adventures in *Could Be Worse!*[68] Those children who worked well in pairs could then be put in larger groups for other activities. Four could work together to create a mural showing how the fish in *Fish Is Fish*[69] might imagine a highway filled with traffic. Vary group membership so that the children learn to cooperate with many different people and so that you can better assess the causes of any difficulty groups may experience. Try to structure the activities and the groups so that the children will not only gain practice in social interaction but also will feel successful about their participation.

Stimulating Children to Explore Moral Problems and Ethical Questions

Whether you plan to or not, it is likely that you will read to children stories which represent various levels of moral reasoning or the part of the characters.

Presenting Examples of Moral Reasoning.   In some books such as *The Elephant Who Liked to Smash Small Cars,*[70] the character reasons at Kohlberg's stage one, the avoidance of punishment. As the title suggests, the elephant does like to smash small cars, and he exercises this predilection by jumping on all the small cars in a new car lot that opens on his street. The salesman replaces his damaged stock with big cars, good for smashing elephants. After several bashings by the large cars, the elephant agrees not to smash the small ones if the salesman goes back to selling that kind. When the lot is once more filled with small cars, the elephant still would like to crumple them but he does not. His behavior is governed by his desire to avoid punishment.

In the folk tale *Under the Shade of the Mulberry Tree,*[71] the character reasons at stage two, where personal reward determines ethical decisions. A poor man asks to sit in the shade of a rich man's tree, but his request is refused. Then he offers to buy the shade, and the greedy rich man assents. However, once the poor man owns the shade, he then has the right to follow it as the sun moves, so that eventually he moves into the rich man's house. Trickery is a common motif in folk tales. In this particular tale, the trickery is justified because it brings pleasure to the poor man, and because the rich man was selfish in not sharing his shade.

Moral reasoning at stage three is widely represented in the decisions book characters make. At this stage, right is determined by what *good girls* or *good boys* do. For example, in *Angelo the Naughty One,*[72] Angelo conforms to the expectation that good boys are clean, and is proud to be a *good boy* once he has overcome his fear of water. He will now wash and stay clean because that is what good children do.

Children grow in their ability to reason about moral questions as they hear the reasoning of others. In general, they understand the reasoning at their own stage, the stages below their own, and one stage above theirs. Hearing various stages of reasoning expressed by book characters and by classmates expands their own reasoning power and is instrumental in their movement from one stage to another.

Engaging Children in the Reasoning Process.   With preschool children, a first step is to read stories in which characters are faced with a decision to be made and in which there is no clear cut answer. Read half of *Finders Keepers*[73] and ask the children who should get to keep the bone, Nap, the dog who saw it first, or Winkle, the dog who touched it first. As in many questions of justice, there is reasoning for more than one decision. What makes some ethical decisions so difficult is that the conflict is between two values both of which seem to represent morality. Should people tell their friends the truth if the truth will be hurtful? Should people lie if in so doing they could save a friend's life? Even young children can be asked to suggest and defend a solution to a problem in which the *right* answer is debatable.

At other times children may be asked to tell about instances when they act in accordance with the reasoning a book character is using. Is there anything they would really like to do, but like the elephant, do not because of the unpleasantness that would result?

Read some books that present questions about behavior and ask students to decide which behavior they think is right and why. If you read the story about split pea soup in *George and Martha*,[74] you could discuss the theme of the story, that friends should always tell each other the truth. Martha has made an enormous quantity of split pea soup which she serves to George. He does not care for it, but does not want to hurt her feelings. When he has eaten all he can, he pours what is left in his bowl into his loafer. Martha sees him from the kitchen and wants to know why he did not tell her that he did not like the soup. When he has explained his reason, Martha responds that friends should always tell each other the truth, and that he will not have to eat split pea soup again.

You might read another book that presents the same question. In *Towser and Sadie's Birthday*,[75] Sadie the cat is crying because she has not gotten birthday presents for the last few years. Towser, a terrier, offers to get her whatever she wants, and she says she wants the moon. When he cannot get it for her, Towser blows up a large white balloon and tells her it is the moon. She is delighted and takes her present everywhere with her. She even listens to Towser's explanation that what appears to be the moon in the sky is simply the hole where the moon was. The next day the wizard asks Sadie why she is holding an old balloon. She tells him to speak quietly because Towser might hear. After all, he thinks it's the moon, and he'd be upset to find out it's only a balloon. The wizard leaves thinking how nice Sadie is.

Primary grade children can write their opinions on slips of paper to answer the question of whether friends should *always* tell each other the truth. Have them share their responses and their reasons for agreeing or disagreeing with Martha's position that friends should always tell one another the truth. Ask the group to decide which reasons they think are the best ones. The emphasis is on the reasoning given, and there is no attempt to reach a consensus on a final "yes" or "no" to the question.

Looking at the Same Issue in Several Books.   Children might look at a single moral question, such as honesty, through a comparison of several books. After reading *George and Martha,* read *A Bargain for Frances.*[76] When Frances starts over to visit Thelma, her mother tells her to be careful, reminding her that on previous occasions when she played with Thelma, she got the worst of things. Frances says it will be safe because they are just going to have a tea party. Once at Thelma's, Frances explains her plan to buy a new blue china tea set. Thelma convinces her that those sets are not made anymore and offers to sell her red plastic set to Frances. When the deal is completed, Thelma insists on "no backsies." After she returns home, Frances learns from her sister that blue china sets are still made, that they are in the stores, and that Thelma was shown one a day earlier in the candy store. Frances runs to the candy store in time to see Thelma buying a new blue tea set and returns home without being seen. After some thought, Frances puts a penny in the sugar bowl of the set she bought from Thelma and calls her.

"Remember," said Thelma, "no backsies."
"I remember," said Frances. "But are you sure you really want no backsies?"
"Sure I'm sure," said Thelma.
"You mean I never have to give back the tea set?" said Frances.
"That's right," said Thelma. "You can keep the tea set."
"Can I keep what is in the sugar bowl too?" said Frances.
"What is in the sugar bowl?" said Thelma.
"Never mind," said Frances. "No backsies. Good-bye."
Frances hung up. Frances waited for the telephone to ring, and when it rang she said, "Hello."
"Hello," said Thelma. "This is Thelma."
"I know," said Frances.
"I just remembered," said Thelma, "I think I had something in the sugar bowl. I think it was a ring. Did you find a ring?"
"No," said Frances. "And I don't have to tell you what is in the sugar bowl because you said no backsies."
"Well," said Thelma, "I just remembered that I put some money in the sugar bowl one time. I think it was some birthday money. I think it was two dollars, or maybe it was five dollars. Did you find money?"
"You said no backsies," said Frances. "So I don't have to tell you. I don't have to say how much money is in the sugar bowl."[77]

With Thelma now eager to make a deal, Frances offers to return the tea set for the money. Thelma must explain that she has purchased another tea set and then offers to trade her new tea set plus a dime for her old one. When the exchange is made and Thelma discovers the penny, and consequently the trick, she says it was not nice, and now she will have to be careful when she plays with Frances. The two decide that it is better to be friends than to be careful, and Frances shares the dime with Thelma.

After the children have enjoyed the story, catching on to the trick in time to relish Thelma's entrapment, ask if Frances told a lie to Thelma. Reread parts of the dialogue as the discussion progresses so that the children can listen with this purpose clearly in mind. They might offer opinions about whether deliberately misleading someone is lying. Then ask them if they think it was

Frances is not outdone by Thelma's trickery. (Illustration by Lillian Hoban from A Bargain for Frances *by Russell Hoban. Pictures copyright © 1970 by Lillian Hoban. By permission of Harper & Row, Publishers, Inc.)*

all right for Frances to trick Thelma. Did she deserve what she got? Did Thelma's behavior justify Frances'?

Next read *Sam, Bangs & Moonshine.*[78] Sam makes up tales, "moonshine" her father calls them. Moonshine is not real. But when she tells her friend Thomas, who goes wherever she tells him, that her baby kangaroo is visiting her mermaid mother in a cave behind Blue Rock, her moonshine causes trouble. The tide comes up, covering the road to the Blue Rock. Sam tells her father in time for him to go after Thomas in a boat. When he returns, Sam's father tells her that there is good moonshine and bad moonshine, and that she must learn to tell the difference. Children can draw what for them is good moonshine, the use of their imaginations. Then they can explain what the terms "good moonshine" and "bad moonshine" mean to them. Ask whether they think there is any difference between "bad moonshine" and "lying" or "fibbing."

By reading several books concerning the issue, added dimensions are given. Children begin to look at situations in which the answer to what is right requires them to weigh possible actions themselves, to use their own reasoning power. The purpose is not to recommend specific actions, but to encourage children to reason about moral questions.

Summary

Much of children's social development, their ability to relate to other people, is correlated with their ability to see from the viewpoint of another. Realizing how another feels and understanding the intent of another person's response are central to the ability to interact successfully in social relationships. These are also key elements in determining whether children will engage in prosocial behavior.

Children learn socially acceptable behavior through observing a wide variety of models, and through positive and negative reinforcement. Children develop their ability to reason about moral questions partially in relation to their stage of intellectual development, and partially as a result of rewards and punishment that have been given for particular actions.

The following long term goals are appropriate for the social and moral development of young children.

- Children will make inferences about the feelings and intentions of others.
- Children will view a situation from more than one perspective, seeing the viewpoint of another person.
- Children will engage in prosocial behavior.
- Children will judge the appropriateness of specific behaviors and predict the possible consequences of particular behaviors.
- Children will know about others who differ from themselves and value this diversity.
- Children will engage competently in group activities.
- Children will evaluate various solutions to moral problems and ethical questions.

Books offer opportunities to give children experience in making inferences about the feelings and intentions of others. Table 4 suggests appropriate teaching strategies. Children can interpret nonverbal language as shown in illustrations in picture books; they can relate voice inflection to meaning as they listen to the dialogue from books; they can go beyond a literal interpretation of dialogue, inferring what is really meant; and they can follow sequences of action and observe patterns of behavior in stories.

Literature fosters children's ability to see from the viewpoint of others. Some books will describe an event from several perspectives; others will present a story with a character who has a more limited viewpoint than does the reader. Children can be encouraged to take the perspective of another in discussions, and in dramatic activities such as role play or puppetry.

Children can begin to assess behavior and the consequences that may follow by discussing what happens to book characters in particular situations. Sometimes that character may provide a model for prosocial behavior, with the children seeing that they too would be capable of helping someone else. At other times, the children may generalize about what behaviors are appropriate in specific situations.

Literature provides children with information about people who differ from themselves, and by emphasizing the humanity of individual members of a group, helps children develop positive attitudes toward others and value diversity.

Teachers will read books about many ethnic and cultural groups, including folk tales from many regions.

Finally, literature can stimulate children to explore moral problems and ethical questions. Characters in books will demonstrate various levels of moral reasoning and will be faced with moral dilemmas. Children can reason themselves about the questions facing the characters and may compare how different characters have reacted to the same question.

Table 4. *Supporting Children's Social and Moral Development*

Developmental Goals	Teaching Suggestions	Recommended Reading	
Children will make inferences about the feelings and intentions of others.	Have children interpret the body language of characters in illustrations.	**Ages 3–5:** Bulla	*Keep Running, Allen!*
	Let children interpret the meaning of voice inflections in portions of dialogue you have read.	Ets	*Talking without Words*
	Encourage interpretation of dialogue beyond the literal level.	Galbraith Scott Simon Weber Wells Yolen Zolotow	*Katie Did! Sam How Do I Feel? The Winter Picnic Peabody No Bath Tonight The Quarreling Book*
	Help children relate sequences of action to feelings and intentions of book characters.		
	Encourage children to relate their own feelings to those of book characters.	**Ages 5–8:** Alexander Bunting Mayer	*Out! Out! Out! Clancy's Coat Frog Goes to Dinner*
		Ross	*When Lucy Went Away*
		Stevenson	*Could Be Worse*
Children will view a situation from more than one perspective, seeing the viewpoint of another person.	Read books that present several viewpoints.	**Ages 3–5:** Fatio Hazen	*The Happy Lion Why Couldn't I Be An Only Kid Like You, Wigger?*
	Let children analyze the limited perspective of certain characters.		
	Have children imagine being someone else.	Thomas Winthrop Zolotow	*Eliza's Daddy Katharine's Doll If It Weren't for You*
	Let children role play more than one role in a single situation.		
		Ages 5–8: Blume	*The Pain and the Great One*
		Goffstein Lionni Sharmat	*My Noah's Ark Fish is Fish The Day I Was Born*
		Wagner	*John Brown, Rose and the Midnight Cat*

Table 4. (Cont.)

Developmental Goals	Teaching Suggestions	Recommended Reading	
Children will engage in pro- social behavior.	Share books that present models of prosocial behavior. Discuss the kinds of help children can provide others. Compare themes of helping.	**Ages 3–5:** Flack Greenberg Hughes Zolotow	Ask Mr. Bear The Bravest Babysitter Alfie Gives a Hand Do You Know What I'll Do?
		Ages 5–8: Baldwin Hill Steig Wittman	Sunflowers for Tina Evan's Corner Amos and Boris A Special Trade
Children will judge the ap- propriateness of specific behaviors and predict possible consequences of such behaviors.	Ask children to evaluate the behaviors of book characters. Have children suggest other possible behaviors for book characters.	**Ages 3–5:** Burn- ingham **Ages 5–8:** Carrick	The Cupboard The Washout
Children will know about others who dif- fer from themselves and value this diversity.	Present literature in which diversity among people is valued. Focus on the similarities rather than the differences among peoples. Read more than one book about a particular group of people. Focus on individuals within groups rather than on the groups themselves. Share literature from other countries.	**Ages 3–5:** Battles Fassler **Ages 5–8:** Aardema de Paola Eisenberg Schweitzer Wallace Wateron	What Does the Rooster Say, Yoshio? Howie Helps Himself Oh Kojo! How Could You! Oliver Button is a Sissy A Mitzvah is Something Special Amigo Chin Chiang and the Dragon's Dance Pettranella
Children will engage com- petently in group ac- tivities.	Engage children in choral speaking. Structure activities so that children must work together. Begin with groups of two or three, enlarging the member- ship as children become more adept in group work.	**Ages 3–5:** Ginsburg **Ages 5–8:** Lionni Stevenson	Mushroom in the Rain Fish is Fish Could Be Worse

Table 4. (Cont.)

Developmental Goals	Teaching Suggestions	Recommended Reading	
Children will evaluate various solutions to moral problems and ethical questions.	Read books in which characters engage in various stages of moral reasoning.	**Ages 3–5:** Garrett	Angelo the Naughty One
	Invite children to suggest and defend solutions to moral or ethical problems presented in books.	Lipkind Marshall Merrill	Finders Keepers George and Martha The Elephant Who Liked to Smash Small Cars
	Have children select the "best" reason for particular solutions to problems.	Ross	Towser and Sadie's Birthday
	Let children compare the presentation of a single moral issue in several books.	**Ages 5–8:** Demi	Under the Shade of the Mulberry Tree
		Hoban	A Bargain for Frances
		Ness	Sam, Bangs & Moonshine

Extending Your Learning

1. Find ten specific illustrations in picture books that show a character's feelings. See if your classmates can identify the emotion from looking at the illustration without knowing the story line.
2. Find a book in which the meaning of the dialogue extends beyond the literal level. Then share the book with a child to see if he or she can interpret the meaning.
3. Read a picture book to a small group of primary children. After you have finished, ask them to retell the story from the viewpoint of a particular character.
4. Select five books that would lend themselves to role play or puppetry. Tell why each is appropriate for this type of activity.
5. Make a list of at least ten activities in which children could take the perspective of another person.
6. Suppose you had read several books to children in which the characters exhibited prosocial behavior. Write five situations you now could share with the children in which you give a setting and a problem and ask the children what they could or would do to help.
7. Select three books from those by any of the foreign authors listed in the section *Reading Literature From Other Countries* that you think the children you know would enjoy.
8. For each of five books, plan one activity that could be done by an individual child and one that would require group cooperation.

Notes

1. Dorothy Flapan, *Children's Understanding of Social Interaction* (New York: Teachers College Press, 1968).

2. Paul Mussen and Nancy Eisenberg-Berg. *Roots of Caring, Sharing, and Helping* (San Francisco: W. H. Freeman and Co., 1977), 5–6.

3. Albert Bandura, *Social Learning Theory* (Englewood Cliffs, N.J.: Prentice-Hall Inc., 1977).

4. Bandura, *Social Learning Theory.*

5. Mary Ellen Goodman, *Race Awareness in Young Children* (Reading, Mass.: Addision-Wesley, 1952).

6. Kenneth Wann, Miriam Dorn, and Elizabeth Liddle, *Fostering Intellectual Development in Young Children* (New York: Teachers College Press, 1962).

7. Wallace E. Lambert and Otto Klineberg, *Children's Views of Foreign People: A Cross-National Study* (New York: Appleton-Century-Crofts, 1967).

8. C. Ekerman, J. Whatley, and S. Kutz, "Growth of Social Play With Peers During the Second Year of Life." *Developmental Psychology 11* (1975): 42–49.

9. Zick Rubin, *Children's Friendships* (Cambridge, Mass.: Harvard University Press, 1984), 11.

10. Ibid., pp 37–39.

11. Jean Piaget, *The Moral Judgment of the Child* (New York: Macmillan Publishing Co., 1932, 1955).

12. Lawrence Kohlberg, "Moral Development and the New Social Studies," *Social Education 37* (1973): 369–75.

13. Bandura, *Social Learning Theory.*

14. Marie Hall Ets, *Talking Without Words* (New York: Viking Press, 1968).

15. Mercer Mayer, *Frog Goes to Dinner* (New York: Dial Press, 1974).

16. Martha Alexander, *Out! Out! Out!* (New York: Dial Press, 1968).

17. Ann Herbert Scott, *Sam.* Illus. by Symeon Shimin (New York: McGraw-Hill Inc., 1967).

18. Scott, *Sam,* n.p.

19. From *Charlie's World* by Lee Bennett Hopkins (Copyright 1972 by the Bobbs-Merrill Co. Inc. Reprinted by permission of the publisher.)

20. Jane Yolen, *No Bath Tonight.* Illus. by Nancy Winslow Parker (New York: Thomas Y. Crowell Publishers, 1978).

21. From *Clancy's Coat* by Eve Bunting. Illustrated by Lorinda Bryan Cauley. Copyright © 1984 by Eve Bunting. Reprinted by permission of Viking Penguin Inc.

22. Bunting, *Clancy's Coat,* n.p.

23. Bunting, *Clancy's Coat,* n.p.

24. Bunting, *Clancy's Coat,* n.p.

25. Bunting, *Clancy's Coat,* n.p.

26. James Stevenson, *Could Be Worse* (New York: Greenwillow Books, 1977).

27. Rosemary Wells, *Peabody* (New York: Dial Books for Young Readers, 1983).

28. Charlotte Zolotow, *The Quarreling Book.* Illus. by Arnold Lobel (New York: Harper & Row, Publishers, Inc. 1963).

29. Robert Welber, *The Winter Picnic.* Illus. by Deborah Ray (New York: Pantheon Books, a division of Random House, 1970).

30. Welber, *The Winter Picnic,* n.p.

31. G. Max Ross, *When Lucy Went Away.* Illus. by Ingrid Fetz (New York: E. P. Dutton Inc., 1976).

32. Norma Simon, *How do I Feel?* Illus. by Joe Lasker (Chicago: Albert Whitman & Co., 1970).

33. Clyde Robert Bulla, *Keep Running, Allen!* Illus. by Satomi Ichikawa (New York: Thomas Y. Crowell Publishers, 1978).

34. Kathryn Galbraith, *Katie Did!* Illus. by Ted Ramsey (New York: Atheneum Publishers, 1983).

35. Reprinted with permission of Macmillan Publishing Company from *Secrets of a Small Brother* by Richard J. Margolis, Donald Carrick.

36. Judy Blume, *The Pain and the Great One*. Illus. by Irene Trivas (New York: Bradbury Press Inc., 1984).

37. Marjorie and Mitchell Sharmat, *The Day I Was Born*. Illus. by Diane Dawson (New York: E. P. Dutton Inc.,, 1980).

38. Jenny Wagner, *John Brown, Rose and the Midnight Cat*. Illus. by Ron Brooks (Scarsdale, N.Y.: Bradbury Press Inc., 1977).

39. Barbara Shook Jazen, *Why Couldn't I Be an Only Kid Like You, Wigger?* Illus. by Leigh Grant (New York: Atheneum Publishers, 1975).

40. Charlotte Zolotow, *If It Weren't For You*. Illus. by Ben Shecter (New York: Harper & Row, Publishers, Inc., 1966).

41. Zolotow, *If It Weren't For You*, 31–32.

42. Louise Fatio, *The Happy Lion*. Illus. by Roger Duvoisin (New York: McGraw-Hill Inc., 1954).

43. Leo Lionni, *Fish is Fish* (New York: Pantheon Books Inc., 1970).

44. M. B. Goffstein, *My Noah's Ark* (New York: Harper & Row, Publishers, Inc., 1978).

45. Elizabeth Winthrop, *Katharine's Doll*. Illus. by Marylin Hafner (New York: E. P. Dutton Inc., 1983).

46. Ianthe Thomas, *Eliza's Daddy*. Illus. by Moneta Barnett (New York: Harcourt Brace Jovanovich, 1976).

47. Barbara Greenberg, *The Bravest Babysitter*. Illus. by Diane Paterson (New York: Dial Press, 1977).

48. Shirley Hughes, *David and Dog* (Englewood Cliffs, N.J.: Prentice-Hall Inc., 1977).

49. Shirley Hughes, *Alfie Gives a Hand* (New York: Lothrop, Lee & Shepard Books, 1984).

50. Elizabeth Starr Hill, *Evan's Corner*. Illus. by Nancy Grossman (New York: Holt, Rinehart & Winston, 1967).

51. Marjorie Flack, *Ask Mr. Bear* (New York: Macmillan Co., 1932).

52. Anne Norris Baldwin, *Sunflowers for Tina*. Illus. by Ann Grifalconi (New York: Four Winds Press, 1970).

53. Charlotte Zolotow, *Do You Know What I'll Do?* Illus. by Garth Williams (New York: Harper & Row, Publishers, Inc., 1958).

54. Sally Wittman, *A Special Trade*. Illus. by Karen Gundersheimer (New York: Harper & Row, Publishers, Inc., 1978).

55. William Steig, *Amos & Boris* (New York: Farrar, Straus & Giroux Inc., 1971).

56. John Burningham, *The Cupboard* (London: Jonathan Cape, 1975).

57. Carol Carrick, *The Washout*. Illus. by Donald Carrick (New York: Seabury Press, 1978).

58. Phyllis Rose Eisenberg, *A Mitzvah Is Something Special*. Illus. by Susan Jeschke (New York: Harper & Row, Publishers, Inc., 1978).

59. Eisenberg, *A Mitzvah Is Something Special*, 26.

60. Tomie de Paola, *Oliver Button is a Sissy* (New York: Harcourt Brace Jovanovich, 1979).

61. Edith Battles, *What Does the Rooster Say, Yashio?* Illus. by Roni Hormann (Chicago: Albert Whitman & Co., 1978).

62. Byrd Baylor Schweitzer, *Amigo*. Illus. by Garth Williams (New York: Macmillan Publishing Co., 1963).

63. Ian Wallace, *Chin Chiang and the Dragon's Dance* (New York: Atheneum Publishers, 1984).

64. Joan Fassler, *Howie Helps Himself*. Illus. by Joe Lasker (Chicago: Albert Whitman & Co., 1975).

65. Verna Aardema, *Oh Kojo! How Could You!* Illus. by Marc Brown (New York: Dial Books for Young Readers, 1984).

66. Betty Waterton, *Pettranella*. Illus. by Ann Blades (Vancouver: Douglas & McIntyre, 1980).

67. Mirra Ginsburg, *Mushroom in the Rain*. Illus. by Jose Aruego and Ariane Dewey (New York: Macmillan Publishing Co., 1974).

68. Stevenson, *Could Be Worse*.

69. Lionni, *Fish Is Fish*.

70. Jean Merrill and Ronni Solbert, *The Elephant Who Likes to Smash Small Cars* (New York: Pantheon Books Inc., 1967).

71. Demi, *Under the Shade of the Mulberry Tree* (Englewood Cliffs, N.J.: Prentice-Hall Inc., 1979).

72. Helen Garrett, *Angelo the Naughty One*. Illus. by Leo Politi (New York: Viking Press, 1944).

73. William Lipkind and Nicolas Mordvinoff, *Finders Keepers* (New York: Harcourt Brace Jovanovich, 1951).

74. James Marshall, *George and Martha* (Boston: Houghton Mifflin Co., 1972).

75. Tony Ross, *Towser and Sadie's Birthday* (New York: Pantheon Books Inc., 1984).

76. Russell Hoban, *A Bargain for Frances*. Illus. by Lillian Hoban (New York: Harper & Row, Publishers, Inc., 1970).

77. Hoban, *A Bargain for Frances*, 41–47.

78. Evaline Ness, *Sam, Bangs & Moonshine*. (New York: Holt, Rinehart & Winston, 1966).

Recommended References

Ambrose, Edna, and Miel, Alice. *Children's Social Learning*. Washington, D.C.: Association for Supervision and Curriculum Development, 1958.

Bandura, Albert. *Social Learning Theory*. Englewood Cliffs, N.J.: Prentice-Hall Inc., 1977.

Damon, William. *The Social World of the Child*. San Francisco: Jossey-Bass Inc., Publishers, 1977.

Flapan, Dorothy. *Children's Understanding of Social Interaction*. New York: Teachers College Press, 1968.

Gurion, Anita and Formanek, Ruth. *The Socially Competent Child*. Boston: Houghton Mifflin Co., 1983.

Hearn, D. Dwain. ed. *Values, Feelings and Morals: Part I, Research and Perspectives*. Washington, D.C.: American Association of Elementary-Kindergarten-Nursery Education, 1974.

Hess, Robert D., and Torney, Judith V. *The Development of Political Attitudes in Children*. Chicago: Aldine Publishing Co., 1967.

Kohlberg, Lawrence. "Moral Stage and Moralization," in Lickona, T. ed. *Moral Development and Behavior*. New York: Holt, Rinehart & Winston, 1976.

Mussen, Paul, and Eisenberg-Berg, Nancy. *Roots of Caring, Sharing and Helping*. San Francisco: W. H. Freeman and Company, 1977.

Piaget, Jean. *The Moral Judgment of the Child*. New York: Macmillan Publishing Co., 1955, 1932.

Rubin, Zick. *Children's Friendships*. Cambridge, Mass.: Harvard University Press, 1980.

Schmidt, Velma E., and McNeill, Earldene. *Cultural Awarenes, a Resource Bibliography*. Washington, D.C.: National Association for the Education of Young Children, 1978.

Shaftel, Fanny R., and Shaftel, George. *Role-Playing for Social Values*. Englewood Cliffs, N.J.: Prentice-Hall Inc., 1967.

Tanyzer, H., and Karl, Jean. eds. *Reading, Children's Books, and Our Pluralistic Society*. Newark, Del.: International Reading Association, 1972.

Recommended Children's Books

Adoff, Arnold. *Black Is Brown Is Tan*. Illus. by Emily McCully. New York: Harper & Row, Publishers, Inc., 1973.

Aruego, Jose. *Look What I Can Do*. New York: Charles Scribner's Sons, 1971.

Brooks, Ron. *Timothy and Gramps*. Scarsdale, N.Y.: Bradbury Press Inc., 1978.

Cohen, Miriam. *See You Tomorrow, Charles*. Illus. by Lillian Hoban. New York: Greenwillow Books, 1983.

Corey, Dorothy. *Everybody Takes Turns*. Illus. by Lois Axeman. Chicago: Albert Whitman & Co., 1980.

Delton, Judy. *Lee Henry's Best Friend*. Illus. by Jack Faulkner. Chicago: Albert Whitman & Co., 1980.

Duvoisin, Roger. *Snowy and Woody*. New York: Alfred A. Knopf Inc., 1979.

Farber, Norma. *How Does It Feel to Be Old?* Illus. by Trina Schart Hyman. New York: E. P. Dutton, Inc., 1979.

Freeman, Don. *Dandelion*. New York: Viking Press, 1964.

Goffstein, M. B. *Neighbors*. New York: Harper & Row, Publishers, Inc., 1979.

Hazen, Barbara Shook. *Tight Times*. Illus. by Trina Schart Hyman. New York: Viking Press, 1979.

Lewin, Hugh. *Jafta—The Town*. Illus. by Lisa Kopper. Minneapolis: Carolrhoda Books Inc., 1984.

Mayer, Mercer and Mariana. *Mine*. New York: Simon & Schuster Inc., 1970.

Rockwell, Anne and Harlow. *Can I Help?* New York: Macmillan Publishing Co., 1982.

Rylant, Cynthia. *Miss Maggie*. Illus. by Thomas DiGrazia. New York: E. P. Dutton, Inc. 1983.

Sharmat, Marjorie. *Bartholomew the Bossy*. Illus. by Normand Chartier. New York: Macmillan Publishing Co., 1984.

Simon, Norma. *We Remember Philip*. Illus. by Ruth Sanderson. Chicago: Albert Whitman & Co., 1979.

Weiss, Nicki. *Maude and Sally*. New York: Greenwillow Books, 1983.

Wells, Rosemary. *Stanley and Rhoda*. New York: Dial Press, 1978.

Zolotow, Charlotte. *The Hating Book*. Illus. by Ben Schecter. New York: Harper & Row, Publishers, Inc., 1969.

Recommended Folktales

Aardema, Verna. *Oh Kojo! How Could You!* Illus. by Marc Brown. New York: Dial Books for Young Readers, 1984. (Sudanese)

Aruego, Jose. *A Crocodile's Tale: A Philippine Folk Story*. Illus. by Jose and Ariane Aruego. New York: Charles Scribner's Sons, 1972.

Bang, Betsy. *The Cucumber Stem: Adapted from a Bengali Folktale*. Illus. by Tony Chen. New York: Greenwillow Books, 1980.

Berson, Harold. *Kassim's Shoes*. New York: Crown Publishers Inc., 1977. (Moroccan)

Brown, Marcia. *The Bun: A Tale From Russia*. New York: Harcourt Brace Jovanovich, 1972.

Cooper, Susan. *The Silver Cow: A Welsh Tale*. Illus. by Warwick Hutton. New York: Atheneum Publishers, 1983.

dePaola, Tomie, *Strega Nona*. Englewood Cliffs, N.J.: Prentice-Hall Inc., 1975. (Italian)

Domanska, Janina. *King Krakus and the Dragon*. New York: Greenwillow Books, 1979. (Polish)

Ginsburg, Mirra. *Two Greedy Bears*. Illus. by Jose Aruego and Ariane Dewey. New York: Macmillan Publishing Co., 1976. (Hungarian)

Grimm, Jakob Ludwig Karl. *Little Red Riding Hood*. Illus. by Trina Schart Hyman. New York: Holiday House, 1983. (German)

Grimm, Jakob and Wilhelm. *Snow White and the Seven Dwarfs*. Trans. by Randall Jarrell. Illus. by Nancy Ekholm Burkert. New York: Farrar, Straus & Giroux Inc., 1972. (German)

Hogrogian, Nonny. *The Contest: An American Folktale*. New York: Greenwillow Books, 1976.

Jameson, Cynthia. *The Clay Pot Boy*. Illus. by Arnold Lobel. New York: Coward-McCann, 1973. (Russian)

Lexau, Joan. *It All Began With a Drip, Drip, Drip . . .* Illus. by Joan Sandin. New York: McCall, 1970. (Indian)

McDermott, Gerald. *Anansi the Spider: A Tale from the Ashanti*. New York: Holt, Rinehart & Winston, 1972.

Mosel, Arlene. *The Funny Little Woman*. Illus. by Blair Lent. New York: E. P. Dutton Inc., 1972. (Japanese)

Rockwell, Anne. *Poor Goose: A French Folktale*. New York: Thomas Y. Crowell Publishers, 1976.

Steptol, John. *The Story of Jumping Mouse*. New York: Lothrop, Lee & Shepard Books, 1984. (Native American)

Williams, Jay. *The Surprising Things Maui Did*. Illus. by Charles Mikolaycak. New York: Four Winds Press, 1979. (Hawaiian)

Zemach, Harve. *Duffy and the Devil: A Cornish Tale*. Illus. by Margot Zemach. New York: Farrar, Straus & Giroux Inc., 1973.

8

Supporting Children's Aesthetic and Creative Development

Aesthetic and Creative Development in Young Children

Aesthetic development denotes a person's increasing sensitivity to and appreciation of beauty in art and in nature. This ability to respond to the beautiful is sometimes termed a skill of *impression*. It is paired with the skill of *expression*, the ability to create. Broudy, in an article supporting the need for aesthetic education, writes that "performance activity in various media is probably a necessary condition for acquiring the skills of impression, because so much of proper aesthetic perception depends on familiarity with the expressive potentialities of paint, clay, sound, gesture, etc."[1] Performance, or creative, activity thus provides a base for children's aesthetic development, as well as being a valid educational experience itself.

Art and music, including dance and movement, are indispensable elements of any curriculum for young children. The arts give children a choice of ways in which they can express their thoughts and feelings. Children may also find that they can understand an idea expressed through music, art, or drama that

221

they might not have understood through words alone.[2] Day care professionals and teachers should work to help children enjoy participating in the arts, use their imaginations and creative potential, and progress toward more complexity in aesthetic values. A succsssful arts program introduces new forms to children, expanding their skills of both expression and impression, but does so gradually, allowing the children to accommodate the new information and gain control over new techniques. It also encourages children to use their creative potential.

Creative Potential

Torrance has defined creativity as "a special kind of problem solving."[3] It is a process in which the learners first become aware of personal gaps in knowledge, problems, or disharmonies, and then set about resolving inconsistencies. They look for new relationships among existing information. They make, test, modify, and perfect hypotheses, and finally communicate their results to others. Torrance believes that a sensitivity to problems may be aroused either through self-initiated activities or through a structured sequence of activities. Creative learning can take place in any subject area.

In the arts, creative learning is exhibited as a four year old attempts to make a snake from modelling clay only to have it separate in segments as he rolls it out. He has encountered a problem. The teacher helps, not through telling him what to do or through doing it for him, but by asking questions that stimulate his thinking. "Where is it breaking? Why do you suppose that's the place it breaks? What could you do differently?" The child then hypothesizes that keeping the clay thicker, or not rolling it so rapidly, or using both hands to roll, or moving his hands along the snake as he works might help. He tries his ideas and reports to the teacher when his snake is finished.

Creativity has been characterized by Guilford[4] and others as involving divergent thinking, fluency in the production of ideas, flexibility, originality of ideas, and elaboration. Teachers and day care professionals can encourage creative thinking by establishing an atmosphere of acceptance in the classroom and by asking questions and structuring activities that permit a variety of responses. Creativity is viewed as a process as well as a product, and as a quality that all people have to some degree. As you plan activities in the arts, you will need to provide opportunities for children to use creative thinking. You will also need to know the general capabilities of the children you are teaching.

Development in Art

There is a sequence of development in art that is fairly predictable, although as with other developmental sequences, the age levels that correspond with each stage are approximations. Most children first begin scribbling at about two years of age, although some may start a few months earlier. Their activities with crayon on paper are basically a physical activity. Lowenfeld[5] divides the scribbling stage into three segments. The first is *disordered scribbling*. Children simply move the crayon or pencil in wide sweeps across the paper. About six months after they have begun scribbling they move into *controlled scribbling*. Now they are beginning to gain some control over their markings and to experience the outcome visually. They may repeat motions resulting in patterns of lines or circles and often become engrossed in the activity. At about three-and-a-half years of age, they move into *naming of scribbling*. As the title implies, they begin telling what the scribble signifies—"This is my mommy," or "I'm eating lunch." This is an important step in their development because they have begun to think in terms of pictures rather than motions. The drawings themselves, however, may differ little from earlier scribbles.

By age four, most children can create shapes which resemble round or rectangular objects. Size relationships are more likely to be determined by the order in which they created each object and the medium they are using than by any attempt for accurate representation. They may also exaggerate size to show what is important to them. Color, also, is not chosen for accuracy. It may be determined by preference, or simply the colors available for use.[6]

Around four-and-a-half or five, children reach the *early expressive* stage. They begin to develop their ideas for drawings or paintings before they begin the actual work. They may look to adults for guidance and use their own previous work or that of peers as models. They may practice a skill to gain mastery over it, sometimes repeating a picture or sculpture. Generally they are able to tell about their work and may include more detail in the work if they are encouraged to reenact an experience or discuss a theme.

In the early elementary grades children begin to develop more complexity in their work. In pictures they frequently place all figures along a base line, but by the end of third grade are beginning to use overlapping shapes to show distance. They begin to be aware of relative size, being dissatisfied now if their flowers are as tall as their houses. They often use the stereotyped notion of proper colors, green leaves, brown tree trunks, although they will respond to structured observations and opportunities to mix colors. They enjoy art activities based on imaginative themes.

Teachers and day care professionals can help children develop artistic ability in several ways. They can provide a variety of media and give children ample time to experiment. Children need to see how paint runs together before they can begin to master its use. They need to try several ways to put legs on their clay figures or to use the sides as well as the points of their crayons.

Adults can give suggestions that encourage children to solve their own problems. This means refusing to draw the dog for the child who complains of being unable to do it and instead asking what elements make up the dog, or what is special about the dog that the child might want to emphasize.

As children show their work, teachers and day care professionals can comment objectively upon what has been done. "You've used thick, straight lines and then wavy ones which contrast with one another," or "You've mixed several interesting new shades of color." This introduces vocabulary for talking about art and allows the adult to show that all efforts are valued. Differences in style of art are to be expected and are desirable.

Adult art can be shared with children. Seeing different styles reinforces the idea that one style is not better than another and introduces children to art they might not see otherwise. Professional art can be used for talking about the process employed, but should not be used as a model for children to copy.

Development in Music

In music and movement, as in art, some abilities and responses are governed by the children's physical and motor development. Young children sing between middle C and G or A, the middle range on a piano. Gradually they add a tone or two below C, and by age eight will have added a tone or two above G. From initial stages of not matching melodic tones at all, children move to a stage where they engage in directional singing. They approximate the tones, moving in the direction of the melody. Then with practice they become more accurate in singing tunes within a range of four or five notes. McDonald writes that "Not surprisingly, the most tuneful young singers come from home and/or caregiving environments that have provided many experiences and opportunities for singing and listening to music."[7]

Children respond to music from very early ages and seem to respond most markedly to music with strong rhythm or melody. At ages three and four, children can respond to music through walking, running, clapping, and other physical movements. At first they may repeat the same movement throughout the rhythmic experience, but gradually will begin to experiment. Often a day care professional or teacher will use a drum or other instrument to follow the rhythm of the children's actions rather than as the impetus for rhythmic movement.

Children of four and five are developing in coordination and can add hopping and skipping to their repertoire of movement. They enjoy using rhythm instruments such as triangles, bells, blocks, and rhythm sticks. They can use these instruments in response to music and may also use them to illustrate stories, making judgments about appropriate pitch, rhythm, and tempo.

As children mature and engage in musical experiences, they move more accurately with the rhythm and can also develop more self-control in the use of rhythm instruments. With instructions that help them explore body movements, they use space, time and weight variations in their response to music and in dramatizations. Teachers and day care professionals help children gain these concepts by engaging them in directed movement activities. For example, to explore space, children can be instructed to find a space where they will not touch anyone else when arms are outstretched. Then they make themselves use as little of the space as possible, then as much as possible. Adding the element of time, they can move slowly, using all their space; move rapidly, using the lower half of their space; be a frightened mouse moving in their space; be an angry bear moving in their space.

Many of the teaching strategies that support development in art apply to development in music and movement also. Just as children need time to experiment with a variety of media, they also need time to experiment with singing, with instruments, and with movement. There should be an area where children can use rhythm instruments and tone bars in an unstructured setting, where they can listen to the sounds, try different rhythms or melodies, sing. Some teachers provide such an area for use during times when other "sound producing" activities will be in progress. Others have special rooms for musical experimentation. There should also be times when children use rhythm instruments in a group response to music or literature.

Children should have the opportunity to sing often, both for enjoyment and for learning to reproduce a melody. Songs to be taught should be within the vocal range of the children. The most easily learned songs have repetition of melodic lines or refrains. Teachers can help children recognize the directionality of the music and introduce the concept of musical notation by moving their hands to indicate the movement of the melody, or by showing the movement with lines on the chalkboard. Duration of notes can be shown by hand movements or written symbols, with a long motion or line indicating a note to be held, and short motions or lines indicating eighth or quarter notes.

There should be a variety of musical selections for listening activities. Interest in listening to music can be maintained by having children respond rhythmically as they listen and by sharing selections several times so that children become familiar with them.

Day care professionals and teachers can give children the vocabulary to talk about music and movement just as they can with art. They may comment objectively on children's responses—"You are marching in a steady rhythm," or "The tones you are using all have a high pitch." They may also use the vocabulary as they share adult music. Many vocabulary items are appropriate for use in several of the arts, and as children seem them used in more than one context, they gain a clearer conception of the meaning of the terms.

Teachers of young children have the opportunity to engage pupils in activities that will foster their aesthetic and creative development, and will build self-confidence in both expression and impression. The satisfaction that children experience as they participate in such activities is a reward for the teacher as well as the pupils.

Goals for Teaching

As in other areas, teaching goals for aesthetic and creative development can be categorized as long term developmental goals, general goals for an age or grade level, and specific goals for individual children. The long term goals are those behaviors or competencies that are developed over time and are considered desired patterns of behavior. A long term goal for aesthetic and creative development is that children will use, experiment with, and gain control over a variety of art media. It is a goal that will take several years to be achieved.

A general goal for second grade is that children will identify at least three different musical instruments by engaging in a special pattern of movement for each of the instruments as they listen to selections such as "Peter and the Wolf." Schoolwide curriculum guides may well suggest specific materials. In the absence of curriculum guides, or in addition to them, teachers develop their own general goals for their classes.

An even more specific goal is one for an individual child. "Raoul will use sand blocks to match the rhythm of John's movement." At age five, Raoul is becoming aware of the rhythms around him. He is beginning to explore the use of rhythm instruments, though he still needs to develop self-control in using them. Experiences in matching the rhythm of another child's movement will develop his awareness of rhythm and will give him reason to control his use of rhythm instruments such as sand blocks.

Literature contributes to the achievement of all three types of goals. This chapter focuses on selected long term developmental goals, ones that are common to the preschool and primary years. Literature offers opportunities for you to help children grow toward the following goals for aesthetic and creative development.

- Children will respond favorably to diverse styles of art and music.
- Children will exhibit a sensory awareness of their environment.
- Children will use, experiment with, and gain control over a variety of art media.
- Children will sing in tune within their vocal range and will respond to music and literature with movement and rhythm instruments.
- Children will use their imaginations as they participate in art, music, and movement.
- Children will enjoy experiencing the work of others and participating in the arts themselves.

The first two goals are for skills of impression, the next three are for skills of expression, and the last combines the two.

Opportunities Books Offer

Helping Children Develop Favorable Attitudes Toward Diverse Styles of Art

For children of preschool and primary school age, art appreciation is basically a favorable attitude toward various art forms and various styles in art. It is not expected that children, any more than adults, will like all forms equally. However, it is important that they be open to art that is new to them, and that they recognize the validity of different modes of expression. You can help children achieve this openness by presenting the idea that art is a personal form of expression, by exposing children to a wide range of art, and by involving children with art in ways that give them a basis for relating to it.

Presenting Art as Personal Expression.   One way to show art as personal expression is to share books that demonstrate the concept directly. *Bear's Picture*,[8] for example, relates how bear decided to paint a picture, set up his easel, and began adding colors that pleased him. Two gentlemen appeared on the scene and not only said that bear could not paint, but also stated that it was a silly picture because they could not tell what it was supposed to be. Bear responded that he could tell and continued to paint happily as the gentlemen tried to guess the subject of his work. When they finally asked what it was, he described the forest, and the hollow where a bear could spend a warm winter, and the sun, but they said it did not look like those things. Bear leaned confidently against his easel and explained that it did not have to because it was his picture.

There are several themes relating to art in this book. One is that anyone who wishes to can engage in art; another is that paintings need not *look like* something; a third is that it is the perogative of the individual to decide how his or her work of art should look; and a fourth is that artists often paint those things that are important to them. All these themes are worth sharing with children. Follow up on the ideas. Ask children, "Have you ever felt like bear? Tell us about the time." This will open the floor for children to talk about times when others could not recognize the subject of their art or when someone told them how their picture should look. Have children look back over some of their own paintings and drawings to see if what they drew was important to them. Then let them look at one or two paintings by well-known artists and tell what they think might have been important to that artist at that time.

A week or two later, you could share *Paint All Kinds of Pictures*[9] by Arnold Spilka. This is a picture book about painting that shows contrasts between pictures: a large picture or a small one; one in color or one in black and white; a scary one or a funny one or an exciting one. It shows a difference in the mood of a painting by contrasting a painting of a city done in bright colors with a muted scene of islands surrounded by water. It shows different styles in several pictures of houses and of fish, and in designs. Its theme is that pictures reflect how the artist feels, and that the readers can paint any kind of pictures they want. It is an excellent book for introducing vocabulary that will help children talk about painting and other arts. Children might look at the "quiet" pictures in the book and try to find other quiet ones from their own work, or look at designs and find designs on objects in their homes or classroom. While *Bear's Picture* can be used successfully with children from four or five on (when they have begun to decide what they will draw before beginning), *Paint All Kinds of Pictures* is more appropriate for second and third graders who are gaining more control over their use of media.

A second way of showing art as personal expression is to compare the work of two or more artists when they are using the same or similar subject matter. Songs and folk tales often have several illustrated versions. *Over in the Meadow* has been illustrated by Feodor Rojankovsky[10] and by Ezra Jack Keats.[11] *Hush Little Baby* has been illustrated by Aliki[12] and by Jeanette Winter.[13] After children have participated in the telling or singing of the rhyme or song, let them look at the pictures in the books, holding the books side by side so that the text matches. Children can see how each of the illustrators chooses to portray the characters and the action. Having children tell which they prefer will demonstrate that not only do artists portray subjects differently, but others react to their work differently.

Occasionally let children make images of book characters in their own minds before showing the illustrations in the book. Have them describe what they imagined then show how the illustrator portrayed those same characters. If you did this with the Everett Anderson books, you could show how two illustrators portrayed the same character. In *Some of the Days of Everett Anderson*[14] and in *Everett Anderson's Christmas Coming,*[15] the illustrations were done by Evaline Ness. In *Everett Anderson's Year,*[16] *Everett Anderson's Friend,*[17] *Everett Anderson's 1-2-3,*[18] *Everett Anderson's Nine Month Long,*[19] and *Everett Anderson's*

Goodbye[20] the illustrations were done by Ann Grifalconi. The books about Frances by Russell Hoban also have two illustrators: *Bedtime for Frances*[21] was illustrated by Garth Williams, the others by Lillian Hoban. Second and third graders could compare the two Arthurs in the books by Russell Hoban, the one drawn by James Marshall in *Dinner at Alberta's*[22] with the one drawn by Byron Barton for *Arthur's New Power*.[23]

You and the children could select one animal and then see how that animal is shown in several books of fiction. If you choose frogs, you might look at the familiar frog of *Frog and Toad Are Friends*.[24] See how Arnold Lobel's illustrations compare with the line drawings of Mercer Mayer in *Frog Goes to Dinner*,[25] the crayon and soft pencil of Rojankovsky in *Frog Went A-Courtin'*,[26] the watercolor of Enos Keith in *Rra-ah*,[27] and the collage of Duvoisin in *The Old Bullfrog*.[28] All the books you choose should be appropriate to the age level of the children. Generally with young children it is better to compare only two books at a time. A third, fourth, and fifth may be added later, one at a time. Children can see that artists use different media and different styles to show these different frog characters. Let the children use a variety of media themselves to create frogs of their own, perhaps making a mural of a frog pond.

Exposing Children to a Wide Range of Art.   Helping children see the diversity in the art in picture books and encouraging them to select different media and different styles in their own art demonstrates that differences are expected and valued. It also introduces the children to a range of two-dimensional art forms. As you select literature to share, keep a record of methods of illustration children are seeing. You may want to select from this list several books for comparison. If there are some forms that have not been presented, you will want to find good literature that fills the gap. Some illustrators are known for their work with certain media or with certain styles. Others vary considerably according to the text they are illustrating. As a beginning, look at some of the following books to familiarize yourself with media and styles of art found in books for young children.

Media:

Collage—Keats, Ezra Jack. *The Snowy Day*. New York: Viking Press, 1962.

Pencil drawings—Rylant, Cynthia. *Miss Maggie*. Illus. by Thomas DiGrazia. New York: E.P. Dutton Inc., 1983.

Woodcut—Emberley, Barbara. *Drummer Hoff*. Illus. by Ed Emberley. Englewood Cliffs, N.J.: Prentice-Hall Inc., 1967.

Cardboard cut—Hodges, Margaret. *The Wave*. Illus. by Blair Lent. Boston: Houghton Mifflin Co., 1964.

Scratchboard—Cooney, Barbara. *Chanticleer and the Fox*. New York: Thomas Y. Crowell Publishers, 1958.

Photography—Hoban, Tana. *I Walk and Read*. New York: Greenwillow Books, 1984.

Crayon—Lionni, Leo. *Fish Is Fish*. New York: Pantheon Books Inc., 1970.

Pastels—Steptoe, John. *Stevie*. New York: Harper & Row, Publishers, Inc., 1969.

Gouache—Wildsmith, Brian. *Brian Wildsmith's Mother Goose*. New York: Franklin Watts Inc., 1964.

Watercolor—Potter, Beatrix. *The Tale of Peter Rabbit*. London: Frederick Warne & Co. Inc., 1902.

Opaque paint—Ginsburg, Mirra. *Mushroom in the Rain*. Illus. by Jose Aruego and Ariane Dewey. London: Hamish, 1974.

Style of Art:

Representational—Turkle, Brinton. *Deep in the Forest*. New York: E. P. Dutton, Inc., 1976.
Carrick, Carol. *Dark and Full of Secrets*. Illus. by Donald Carrick. New York: Clarion Books, 1984.

Impressionistic—Burningham, John. *Mr. Gumpy's Motorcar*. New York: Macmillan Publishing Co., 1975.
Zolotow, Charlotte. *Mr. Rabbit and the Lovely Present*. Illus. by Maurice Sendak. New York: Harper & Row, Publishers, Inc., 1970.

Expressionistic—Ehrlich, Amy. *Zeek Silver Moon*. Illus. by Robert Andrew Parker. New York: Dial Press, 1972.
Keeping, Charles. *Joseph's Yard*. New York: Franklin Watts Inc., 1970.

Cartoon—Geisel, Theodore. *Horton Hears A Who*. New York: Random House Inc., 1940.
Stevenson, James. *Yuck!* New York: Greenwillow Books, 1984.

Abstract—Delaunay, Sonia. *Sonia Delaunay's Alphabet*. New York: Thomas Y. Crowell, Publishers, 1972.
Stone, A. Harris. *The Last Free Bird*. Illus. by Sheila Heins. Englewood Cliffs, N.J.: Prentice-Hall Inc., 1967.

Stylized—Aerdema, Verna. *Why Mosquitoes Buzz in People's Ears*. Illus. by Leo and Diane Dillon. New York: Dial Press, 1975.
Goble, Paul. *Star Boy*. New York: Bradbury Press Inc., 1983.

Surrealistic—Ionesco, Eugene. *Story Number 1*. Illus. by Etienne Delessert. New York: Harlin Quist, 1968.
Lines, Kathleen. *Lavender's Blue*. Illus. by Harold Jones. New York: Franklin Watts Inc., 1954.

Let children react to the art in picture books. As they look at the illustrations in *From the Hills of Georgia*,[29] tell them that the illustrator, Mattie Lou O'Kelley, is a self-taught artist who began painting late in her life. Let them express their opinions about the stylized, folk-art quality of her paintings. Share some illustrations that you anticipate the children will like immediately, then share some examples of more complex styles of art. The illustrations for *Ben's Trumpet*[30] are almost art deco, more abstract than most art for children. The story line is slight; a little boy hears the music from a nearby club and longs to play the trumpet himself. Children could be asked to tell whether or not seeing the illustrations made the story better for them than just listening to it. They might look at specific pictures as they respond, calling attention to what they liked or telling why the illustrations were not helpful to them. They should be guided to look at the illustrations carefully, but not guided into saying they like whatever is presented.

Involving Children with Art. Make a practice of involving children with art in ways that will enable them to relate to it personally. As they look at a painting or drawing, or an illustration in a book, have them imagine themselves someplace in the picture. What can they see from where they are standing? Do they hear any sounds? If so, what do they hear? If they could move around inside the painting, where would they go?

Another technique for encouraging careful observation and personal involvement is to show a picture for a brief period of time. Then let children tell about what they saw and tape their descriptions or reactions. Show the pictures as you play back the tape. You might use this technique with the illustrations in the books by Shirley Glubok. The text in these books about the art of different countries and cultures is for intermediate grade children. However, the photographs of actual art objects can be observed and discussed by primary grade children.

Showing films about illustrators of children's books can help primary grade children see the artists as real people. Weston Woods Studios has produced several such films. One that seems to be popular with children is about Ezra Jack Keats.[31] They are fascinated as he demonstrates the technique he used in preparing the background for the illustrations in two of his books. Many want to explore the process themselves.

Consider involving children in an art project before showing them a book that uses certain ideas or techniques. For example, let children decorate a plain white paper cup and paper plate, dishes that they may use at lunch or snack time if they choose. Talk with them about what they might do, whether making designs or drawing pictures. When the project is complete, share with them *When Clay Sings*[32] by Byrd Baylor. Her poetic description of the art on prehistoric Indian pottery is illustrated by Tom Bahti. He based his illustrations on designs found on the pottery of the Anasazi, Mogollon, Hohokam, and Mimbres cultures. The children will find that other peoples also drew animals, birds, fish, all sorts of designs, and even monsters. They have a point of reference for looking at the art of another person, another culture.

As children see and become involved with a variety of artistic styles and media, both through their own work and through observations and discussion of the work of others, they are learning that diversity in art is to be both valued and enjoyed.

Sharpening Children's Awareness

Much of literature, especially poetry, provides readers with a verbal description of authors' perceptions of their environments. Individuals who are sensitive to the world around them share with evocative language their insights and their reactions. Reading such literature to children fosters a sharpened aware-

The illustrations in this book introduce children to the art of several Native American cultures. (Used by permission of Charles Scribner's Sons from When Clay Sings *by Byrd Baylor, illustrated by Tom Bahti. Copyright © 1972 by Byrd Baylor. Illustrations copyright © 1972 by Tom Bahti.)*

ness. Children see a model of keen observation. They hear a detailed description, or a mood captured in metaphor. As a teacher, you can select books which present the sensory awareness of the author. You can also select books that describe activities the children can repeat, and others that can be a stimulus for activities that will enhance sensory awareness.

Sharing in the Awareness of Others.   Look both at prose and at poetry for finding books in which authors write in sensory terms and in which illustrators show the beauty they observe. An example of a book in which an author-illustrator has shown the wonder and beauty of a commonplace event is *Dawn*[33] by Uri Shulevitz. A small boy and his grandfather sleep on the shore of a lake through the night under the light of a full moon. At dawn they break camp, with the mist still over the water, and row out into the middle of the lake. There they see the sunlight begin to bring color to the world, until finally the sun bursts from behind the mountain and bathes the entire scene in brilliant light. The text is sparse, the very simplicity of the words focusing attention on the magnificence of the scene. The illustrations show the subtle changes as dawn comes. Sharing the book with children brings to them a quiet sense of wonder.

Lucy and John Hawkinson's *Birds in the Sky*[34] conveys a feeling of joy as the person in each illustration describes the special qualities of various birds.

> Ducks are swift and sure. They beat their wings fast as they rise and turn, silhouetted against the sky. Then down to the pond they go, to land together with a single splash.[35]

The movement of the birds is captured in language, the sight in the illustrations. The book is accurate enough to be used as a guide for bird identification, but it does far more than that, for it says to the reader that birds have beauty and grace which can be enjoyed by all.

Both of these books focus on the sense of sight. Look for literature that uses the other senses as well. *The Cloud*[36] tells about Nina and her mother as they hike to the top of a mountain, so high that they may walk into a cloud, her mother says. Nina thinks it will be fun. "Maybe it would be as soft as lying under Mama's quilt."[37] However, when they are actually walking through the low-lying cloud, Nina finds that it is cold and damp, and she doesn't like it. It doesn't look like a fairyland and it doesn't feel soft. Once they reach the tree line the air is warmer, and as the cloud dissipates into mist, Nina sees its beauty. She admits that she was frightened earlier. By describing tactile as well as visual impressions, the book shows the contrasting moods Nina experiences as her environment changes.

Eve Merriam's "A Matter of Taste" asks questions that children will answer even before *you* ask.

> What does your tongue like the most?
> Chewy meat or crunchy toast?
>
> A lumpy bumpy pickle or tickly pop?
> A soft marshmallow or a hard lime drop?
>
> Hot pancakes or a sherbet freeze?
> Celery noise or quiet cheese?
>
> Or do you like pizza?
> More than any of these?[38]

The onomatopoeia in the following two poems, "Mud" and "Poem to Mud," adds to children's delight in the message as two poets explore the feel of mud.

> Mud is very nice to feel
> All squishy-squash between the toes!
> I'd rather wade in wiggly mud
> Than smell a yellow rose.
>
> Nobody else but the rosebush knows
> How nice mud feels
> Between the toes.
>
> Polly Chase Boyden[39]

Poem to mud—
Poem to ooze—
Patted in pies, or coating your shoes.
Poem to slooze—
Poem to crud—
Fed by a leak, or spread by a flood.
Wherever, whenever, whyever it goes,
Stirred by your finger, or strained by your toes,
There's nothing sloppier, slippier, floppier,
There's nothing slickier, stickier, thickier,
There's nothing quickier to make a grown-up stickier,
Trulier coolier
Than a wonderful mud.

Zilpha Keatley Snyder[40]

Often poems about the weather or seasons will include sensory descriptions, and certain poets use such descriptions regularly. The work of Aileen Fisher is filled with portrayals of and reactions to the natural world. The following seven selections are appropriate for young children:

- *Cricket in a Thicket*. Illus. by Feodor Rojankovsky. New York: Charles Scribner's Sons, 1963.
- *Feathered Ones and Furry*. Illus. by Eric Carle. New York: Thomas Y. Crowell Publishers, 1971.
- *Going Barefoot*. Illus. by Adrienne Adams. New York: Thomas Y. Crowell Publishers, 1960.
- *I Like Weather*. Illus. by Janina Domanska. New York: Thomas Y. Crowell Publishers, 1963.
- *In the Middle of the Night*. Illus. by Adrienne Adams. New York: Thomas Y. Crowell Publishers, 1965.
- *In the Woods, In the Meadow, In the Sky*. Illus. by Margot Tomes. New York: Charles Scribner's Sons, 1965.
- *Out in the Dark and Daylight*. Illus. by Gail Owens. New York: Harper & Row, Publishers, Inc., 1983.

Experiencing One's Own Environment.   Some books describe experiences that the children can try for themselves. Jane, in *The Paint Box Sea*,[41] is using her new watercolors to paint a picture of the sea. When her brother tells her that water is blue, not red as she is painting it, she tells him that it did look red-gold and now is the color of tea. Throughout the summer they make a game of watching the colors of the sea. They go out in different weather and at different times of the day. They see the sea at night, the water looking shiny and black in the moonlight. Look around the environment where you are teaching. What is there that you and the children can observe over a period of time, in different conditions, to see the colors and the moods? Perhaps you are close to a pond or stream, or want to watch a grassy field, or the pavement in bright sunlight, on a gloomy day, or glistening wet from rain water. Help children record what they have seen. List their reactions after each observation, then read over what they have dictated after several entries and help them put their thoughts together into a single experience chart.

After reading *The Listening Walk*,[42] take the children on a listening walk of their own. See how many different sounds they hear. Listening walks can be taken indoors as well as outdoors and in both large and small groups. Preschool children going in guided groups can stop and all listen to the different sounds together, discussing each sound as it is heard. Older children might go in pairs around the school, each pair noting either with words or pictures what they hear. When all have returned to the classroom, the groups compare their experiences. You will know how much responsibility your students can handle, whether they can go unaccompanied by an adult within limits, or whether the experience is more likely to be successful if you or an aide go along.

Adapt the experiences to fit your environment. *We Walk in Sandy Places*[43] describes tracks of various animals in the desert sand. You do not need to be living in a desert to use the idea of the book. Think about where tracks can be found near your school or center. It may be in sand, but in beach sand. It may be in the dust, or in mud, or in snow. All will suffice for children to observe the markings left by birds and insects, by dogs or chipmunks, and to see the patterns and perhaps make some guesses about who was there and what was happening.

Using Books as Stimuli for Sensory Activities.   Many books and poems provide stimuli for activities that require children to use their senses in discovery or exploration. As you select books think about any possibilities there may be for using sight, sound, touch, taste, and smell. Here are some examples:

Sight.   Read *Goggles*,[44] in which Peter and Archie look through an old pipe as they search for the dog Willie while hiding from some older boys. Then let children make spyglasses of their own by rolling paper into a tube. Have them look around the room through the tube, perhaps viewing it from the floor, or standing on a chair to look down. They can draw what they see in this limited field of vision from several perspectives.

Share *My Back Yard*[45] and have children observe their own back yards, or the center or school play area, and describe what they see, just as Rockwell has done in the book. Then read *All Upon a Sidewalk*,[46] an ant's eye view of a city sidewalk as Lasius Flavus searches for food for her queen. The illustrations show the ants' world as though seen through a magnifying glass. What do children discover as they explore with a magnifying glass? Let them tell about it, or dictate a story, or record it with crayon or paint.

Sound.   Read poems that describe sounds with strong use of onomatopoeia, poems such as "Our Washing Machine"[47] by Patricia Hubbell. After they hear the clicks and whirrs of this machine, have them describe the sounds of other machines. Or after looking at Peter Spier's *Gobble, Growl, Grunt*[48] have them tell how they would make the sound of various animals. This is an excellent time for children to use a tape recorder, capturing a sound and listening to it several times, perhaps having others guess what it is.

Read *The Tiniest Sound*,[49] poetic descriptions of quiet happenings that conclude with the question of whether there could be a tinier sound than the one described. Have children draw what for them is the tiniest sound.

Touch.   After preschoolers have played with *Pat the Bunny*,[50] make a class booklet of materials to be felt and decide together what words they will use to describe each one.

Use just one quotation from Marcia Brown's *Touch Will Tell.* "Have you hugged a tree lately? Try it and feel its coat."[51] Let children "hug" several trees, seeing if they all feel alike. Using crayons and medium weight paper, let the children make rubbings of some of the bark. Let them see how the rubbings differ. Perhaps they will want to continue the project by making rubbings of other surfaces.

Read *The Seeing Stick*[52] to primary grade children. In this modern literary folk tale, the emperor promises a fortune in jewels to anyone who can help his blind daughter see. An old man hears of this and sets out with his walking stick and whittling knife. He carves the stick and shows the princess how to trace likenesses with her fingers, feeling her own face and then his carving of it. He stays, carving and telling stories for the princess and helping her grow "eyes on the tips of her fingers." The story says that this is as true as the idea of a seeing stick. It is not until the conclusion of the story that readers learn that the old man is blind too. Let children see what they can recognize through touch. Can they identify objects? Can they touch a classmate's face and recognize the person?

Taste.   Read *Bread and Jam for Frances*,[53] in which Frances refuses to eat anything but her favorite food, bread and jam. Let children talk about their favorite foods. Then have a taste festival, encouraging children to try several kinds of fruit, two or three kinds of cheese, perhaps white bread, rye bread, and raisin bread. Let each child record his or her favorite food in each of the categories in a booklet. See if any class favorites emerge.

Smell.   Leave two or three of the *Scratch-and-Sniff* books in the book area where children can experience them individually. Then have the children list odors by categories: ones they like, ones they dislike, ones from school, ones associated with particular holidays. Let children begin their own *Sniff* area, bringing in substances whose smells they like. The substances can be kept in baby food jars with the lids on them but not screwed or pressed down tightly. This will help preserve the odor while still allowing easy access.

In these activities, the children are using their senses to explore their own environments. Literature helps heighten sensory awareness both through providing an impetus for such exploration and through showing children how another person has experienced a part of the world.

Giving Children Experience with a Variety of Art Media

Children who are familiar with a variety of media are in a position to choose that medium which will best express their ideas and to select ones that they enjoy or feel most successful in using. As well as experimenting with many forms of two and three dimensional art materials, children need time to use each repeatedly so that they can gain mastery and can explore variations for its use.

Experimenting with Media Used by Illustrators.   Allowing children to experiment with art materials does not mean that the teacher never gives assistance. One child may need help in learning how to hold scissors. Another may benefit from the teacher's suggesting that the pieces of a collage be arranged before the child begins pasting any of them onto the paper. Help is given in technique, but the work is not done for the child.

One way that picture books can stimulate children to explore various media is for you to call attention to the medium used by the illustrator and to have materials available for any children who would like to try using them. Lionni's *Let's Make Rabbits*[54] calls attention itself to the media in use, for the story is of two rabbits, one made with a pencil and the other with scissors. The tools and the actual construction processes are shown as the pencil and scissors first decide to make rabbits and then later make carrots for the rabbits they have created.

With other books, you may turn back to certain pages and ask the children how they think the artist made the picture. In *Swimmy*,[55] for example, children looking closely at the illustration of the "forest of seaweeds" will see that the seaweeds are constructed of imprints made by covering lace doilies with paint and then pressing them on the paper. Children can make their own object imprints by painting one side of an object, then pressing it onto paper, or by using an ink or tempera paint pad or brayer to coat the object with paint. They can begin collecting objects themselves to add to the objects provided by the teacher. There is no attempt to copy the *work* of the illustrator, only the *method*.

Getting to Know Artists and Illustrators.   Children might learn about an artist while they are enjoying the literature and exploring techniques, particularly if you select several books in which an illustrator has used different media in different books. After *Swimmy*, share several other books by Leo Lionni. *Little Blue and Little Yellow*[56] would lead to explorations in mixing paints; *Inch by Inch*[57] to collage made from cutting the images out of paper that has been colored with crayon or paint, allowing patterns to be created before the shapes are cut. Children can see that some artists use a variety of techniques, just as they do.

Media in picture books that are appropriate for young children to use include crayon, colored pencil, chalk, pastels, scratchboard (use crayon resist with children), paints (tempera for all children, watercolor for primary children), pencil, photography (for primary children), torn paper, collage, and combinations of these.

Illustrating One's Own Work.   As children explore various media, they can be encouraged to illustrate stories that they are writing or dictating. They see the pattern of picture and text in the books they hear read to them. They also see the endpapers, the first and last pages in a book that are attached to the cover. As they see how illustrators have prepared endpapers, they can make their own for booklets that they write.

Picture books can stimulate children to explore various media. (From Let's Make Rabbits *by Leo Lionni. Copyright © 1982 by Leo Lionni. Reprinted by permission of Pantheon Books, a division of Random House, Inc.)*

Some endpapers are simply designs. In *Keep Running Allen!*[58] a blue and tan plaid covers both back and front endpapers. Children can make such designs with crayons or paint, or might use cardboard cutouts or vegetable prints to make repetitive patterns.

Some books have endpapers that relate to the story by showing a scene from it. *Hide and Seek Fog*[59] has a scene of children on a beach in the fog; *Noah's Ark*[60] shows Noah at peace on his farm while armies fight and the city burns on the front endpaper, and Noah planting vegetables under a sky filled with doves and a rainbow on the back endpaper. *Summer on Cleo's Island*[61] has a map showing where the island is.

Still other endpapers symbolize the story or picture things related to it. *Crow Boy,*[62] in which Chibi goes from frightened first grader ignored by classmates to confident sixth grader imitating crows in a talent show, features a butterfly and a blossom on the endpapers. *The Little House,*[63] in which the house experiences a city growing up around it, shows a cartoon sequence in which the mode of transportation undergoes changes, from the first small picture of a horse and rider passing the little house to the last of a horse van going by. *Time to Get Out of the Bath, Shirley,*[64] in which Shirley imagines wild adventures while she takes her bath to the monotone of her mother asking who has used the towel and commenting on Shirley's dirty clothes, shows a scene of pipes around which all sorts of activities occur. Plants grow, a girl rides in a swing suspended from one of the pipes, two knights ride through a pipe.

Children will need to decide which type of endpaper they want to make. They might also create endpapers for books that do not have illustrated endpapers. The activity is one of deciding what is essential about a story, or what would symbolize it, as well as an activity in the actual creation of a picture. The design of book jackets can involve this same kind of thinking, and can often be used on paper booklets that are not going to be bound in cardboard covers.

Listening to Descriptions of Techniques.   Share books with children that describe techniques they might try themselves. Some are casual in approach, giving the idea and telling the child to try it and see what happens. One such book is *Splodges*[65] by Malcolm Carrick. Written in first person, the text tells what the author did and the illustrations show the results. Suggestions include blowing paint on wet paper with a straw, painting with the edge of a ruler, using two crayons or two brushes tied together, making leaf prints, and folding paper over dabs of paint. After hearing it read aloud, preschool or primary children, individually or in small groups, could decide which idea they would like to try. It is not necessary to read the entire book at once, and choice making might be easier if only two or three ideas are presented at a time. The choice would be what they wanted to try first, not a choice that would eliminate the ideas not immediately selected.

Other *how-to* books are more direct in their presentation of techniques. *Pastels Are Great!*[66] by John Hawkinson shows how the sticks should be held and how various strokes can be made with them. It is most appropriate with second or third graders (or older students) who are especially interested in using pastels and in learning technique. The book encourages the reader to experiment. It might work well in a learning center where several children would read a page or two and then try out and talk about the ideas.

Representing Stories Through Art.   Books and book characters can be the subject of art activities. Children can be encouraged to respond to books through art. They may translate the images of the words, or of the two dimensional art, to three dimensional art. Characters can be made from clay, play dough, wire, pipe cleaners, styrofoam, boxes. Shadow boxes or dioramas can be constructed. Mobiles can be made using coat hangers or sticks as suspension rods.

Children are most likely to use many media in art, and to gain mastery over many, if they have the opportunity to work in art as one of their own choices and if the materials are readily available. It is useful to have a storage area for materials, one that children use, getting the materials they need and being responsible for returning materials when they are finished. Many teachers label the storage containers so that children are soon reading words such as *scissors* and *paste* and are seeing functional reading demonstrated. You will need to introduce new materials and their care either to the class as a whole, or to the children in a series of small groups, before you put them out for general use.

New materials and new techniques should be introduced gradually, so that children are not overwhelmed, and so that the art area is constantly changing. If children know what materials are needed, they can bring many of them from home. String, yarn, ribbon, sticks, toothpicks, straws, milk cartons, boxes, old wrapping paper, and a variety of other *beautiful junk* can be brought to school for art projects rather than being thrown away. It is one way children contribute to their classroom and make it theirs.

Giving Children a Variety of Musical Experiences

Literature can give added dimension to children's musical experiences in the early years, contributing to their participation in singing, listening, using rhythm instruments, and movement. Several songs that are commonly taught to and enjoyed by young children are available in picture book format and on sound filmstrips and motion pictures. You have the option of sharing these songs as motion pictures, as filmstrips, as books, or as only a listening experience if you play the cassette without showing the accompanying filmstrip. Teachers who are somewhat nervous about their own singing or piano playing often begin musical experiences for the children with records rather than singing themselves. The records and cassettes are especially useful for placing in listening centers so that children can hear the words and tune again to learn it themselves or to sing along with the record and gain practice in matching tones while engaged in an activity that for them is just fun.

Sharing Picture Books of Songs.   In selecting picture books of songs that you plan to teach the children, use the same criteria you would use for selecting other songs. Look for ones that are within the range of the children's voices, have some repetition of words or melody, and do not have large melodic intervals. "Go Tell Aunt Rhody" fits these criteria. Then judge the quality of the illustrations. Two excellent versions of "Go Tell Aunt Rhody" are available, one with illustrations by Aliki[67] and the other with illustrations by Robert Quackenbush.[68] You might use the music at the back of the book as you play the song on piano or autoharp and sing it for the children. You can point out to them that the book tells you what notes to play and sing. Present the song as a whole, not line by line. It is often helpful to show the direction of the notes with your hand, or by drawing lines on the board, such as

___   ___

___

___   ___

for the first phrase of "Go Tell Aunt Rhody." One first grader showed that she had grasped the concept of notation when she looked at six window blinds, all raised to a slightly different level, and reported, "We can sing the shades." As well as giving an introduction to notation, hand movements or lines drawn help children visualize the direction of the melody.

After you have taught the song, sing it with the children as you show the illustrations in one of the books. Children will see the words to the song on each page as they sing and will see that they are singing about the pictures also. If both books are shared, they will see that different artists can interpret a song differently and perhaps will want to illustrate other songs themselves. Four artists or editors who have each produced several picture books of songs are Robert Quackenbush, Aliki, Peter Spier, and John Langstaff. You may want to look for their work.

You might also want to purchase a book or two of collections of songs for regular use with the children. *Singing Bee!*[69] has songs for young children with simple guitar chords and piano accompaniments provided. *Music for Ones and Twos: Songs and Games for the Very Young Child*[70] has finger plays and games as well as songs. *Father Fox's Feast of Songs*[71] adds music to selections from earlier verses by Clyde Watson. All are well-illustrated.

Sharing Literature in Audiovisual Format.   Literature in audiovisual format can provide musical listening experiences for children. They often enjoy listening to songs that may be too complex for them to sing themselves. Preschoolers can listen to *The Fox Went Out on a Chilly Night*[72] and *Clementine*,[73] looking at the filmstrip or turning the pages of the books. After listening to "Peter and the Wolf"[74] they might look through the book or attempt to follow the story in pictures as it unfolds in the music, and as the various instruments indicate the character and the action. Many of the stories transferred to film have musical accompaniments. *Peter Penny's Dance*,[75] the story of a sailor who loved to dance so much that he said he could dance around the world in five years, is

Many songs are available as picture books and in audiovisual format. (Illustrations from The Fox Went Out on a Chilly Night *by Peter Spier. Used by permission of Doubleday and Co., Inc.)*

narrated with the help of flamenco guitars and African drums. *A Story, A Story*[76] builds the rhythm of the tale with drums and other rhythm instruments. Each is a combined literary and musical experience.

Using Rhythm Instruments with Literature.   Rhythm instruments can be used in conjunction with literature, with the children using drums, triangles, sand blocks, or rhythm sticks. Children can add rhythmic accompaniment to nursery rhymes that have a strong beat, ones such as "Ride a Cock Horse" and "A Bear Went Over a Mountain;" use tone bars with ones such as "Rain, Rain Go Away;" or make an ostinato, a background of steady pitch and rhythm, for ones such as "Hickory Dickory Dock." They may use the instruments to capture the rhythm of children sneaking up as elves after hearing *Long Ago Elf*,[77] or perhaps set a rhythm for creeping, changing it from a slow, steady one to one with rapid spurts of scurrying with intermittent pauses.

Older children may be stimulated to make rhythm instruments of their own after hearing *City Rhythms*,[78] in which Jimmy Peters begins listening to the sounds around him after his father tells him that the city has a rhythm of its own. Younger children may simply want to experiment, as Max does in *Max the Music Maker*,[79] with making sounds with pan lids, or with sticks against fences, or by tapping on glasses filled with water.

Moving in Response to Literature.   Movement is a natural response to music and to poetry and prose that has a strong rhythmic beat. Three year olds, still responding to their own rhythms, might move to stories or songs by adding motions rather than keeping time. Listening to *Drummer Hoff*,[80] for example, they might show what each of the soldiers carried as they prepared to fire the cannon. Four and five year olds can keep the rhythm with soft drumming, or by marching, or by striking their thighs with their hands.

Teach children several action games played while singing. *London Bridge Is Falling Down*[81] and *Skip to My Lou*[82] are both games children learn quickly, and both are in book form. After they play the games, let children look through the books.

Help children explore contrasts in music. After reading *Mama Don't Allow*,[83] in which Miles, an opossum, gets a saxophone from Uncle Waylon for a birthday present and eventually starts his own band, teach children the song "Mama Don't Allow." The words and music are in the book. Play it in the loud and rollicking way the Swamp Band plays it. Let the children dance to the music. In the book, Miles and his band get a job playing for a group of alligators on a river boat trip. At last they have found an audience that appreciates their playing. However, after an evening of music and dance, both the band and the alligators are ready for dinner. It is then that the band discovers that *it* is the dinner as well as the entertainment. The band offers to play one more song before dinner. They play a soft Lullaby of Swampland; the alligators all fall asleep; the band escapes. When Miles returns home, still playing the lullaby softly on his sax, his mother is pleased with the music she hears. Play some soft music, or lullabies, for the children. Let them move to this music and respond to the different rhythms and varying intensities of the songs. Encourage them to talk about the differences.

Think of all the books you have read that could provide a stimulus for children to move to music. They could be *Little Toot*,[84] devising their own motions as the little tug boat who disliked hard work, preferring instead to glide around the harbor making fancy figure eights in the water. They could do the spinning, whirling, free floating motions of the caterpillar clinging to his leaf boat in *Down the River Without a Paddle*.[85] They could be Willie, the wind-up mouse in *Alexander and the Wind-up Mouse*.[86] Each activity allows the children to create their own movements for a familiar character and each can be matched to appropriate music. As you share literature with children, make notes for yourself of the musical possibilities of the stories and poems, possibilities for singing, for listening, for rhythmic response and movement.

Stimulating Creativity in Art, Music, and Movement

If creativity does indeed involve the ability to restructure information in new ways, to see inconsistencies or gaps in knowledge and generate and test hypotheses to fill these gaps, to enage in divergent thinking, to be open and flexible, and to be able to elaborate on ideas, then certain approaches to teaching, and certain materials, are more likely than others to foster such behavior. Three that apply to literature as a stimulus for creativity in the arts are the use of questions and activities that lead to divergent responses, the use of books that are inventive, and the practice of encouraging children to give more than one response.

Evoking Divergent Responses.   When you make suggestions for activities to expand on literature, or when you pose questions about literature, structure these so that they lead to many different responses on the part of the children. For example, questions that ask children "What would happen if. . .?" or "Tell us one thing you would do if. . .?" or "What else could this character have done. . .?" can be answered in a variety of ways. There is no one right answer, though you will require that the children be able to support their ideas.

Activities too should have more than one acceptable response. Several children may show their answers about where an elephant could hide after hearing how Morris the elephant solved that problem in the book *Where Can an Elephant Hide?*[87] Their answers will reflect their own thinking, however, and may well draw on the book's information about protective coloration. Some may show in drawing or painting the places that they recommend; others may use three dimensional materials. The object is to develop a unique idea, not to remember an answer from a book.

If you are engaging the children in movement, allow them to choose the motions themselves. *Seven Little Monsters*[88] is a brief book by Maurice Sendak with monsters reminiscent of those in *Where the Wild Things Are*.[89] Each monster has a movement, such as going up, or creeping, or eating, or sleeping, and the seven are lined up in a row "making trouble." Children dramatizing this brief text can add their own interpretations to the movements. They can decide on a rhythmic accompaniment to the text and to their movements. Your reading of the text gives a structure to their responses, but you do not tell them how to move.

The criterion of providing for divergent responses is one that can be applied to any activity designed to extend a book or poem. This does not mean an excuse for a child to do whatever he or she pleases, disrupting everyone else. It does mean your acceptance of their ideas, even if they are not ones you had thought of or expected. Children using rhythm instruments to make the sounds of the Wild Things can decide on which instruments give the sounds they think fit, how they should be put together, when they should be loud and when soft, how fast they should be played. It is their interpretation that is important, their feel for the book, for the mood of the "rumpus" that is the climax of the book. Allowing children to continue to play the instruments when the group is beginning a new activity or to damage the instruments from using them inappropriately is neither developing their creativity nor helping them to accept responsibility.

Presenting Books That Are Inventive.   Select books in which the authors and illustrators have been inventive themselves and use these to suggest inventiveness on the children's parts. Some of these books are told in the first person, with the lead character describing his or her actions. *Sometimes I Dance Mountains*[90] combines poetry and dance, as the girl tells of her love of dancing and the illustrations show her whirling and rhythmic movements. She talks of her thoughts as she dances and presents dance as a mode of free expression, not one of learned steps or routines. How do children dance? Some third graders talked about enjoying moving to "fast" music; others looked at the movements and told about classes in gymnastics. Some wanted to demonstrate how they could dance when they felt happy. None attempted to copy the movements caught in the illustrations.

Preschoolers can add their own fantastic stories of what they might see on the way to school after they hear what Marco saw on the way home in *And to Think That I Saw It on Mulberry Street.*[91] Each adds a new element, just as Marco's story became more and more elaborate as he retold it.

Children can explore making words look like the ideas they represent after seeing *Carousel*[92] by Donald Crews. In this book, the carousel is empty at first; then riders get on; the music starts; and all go round faster and faster. Then the music ends; the carousel slows and stops; and the ride is over. The text is sparse, with concise phrases rather than sentences. The illustrations show the increased blurring of colors to capture the increased speed of the carousel. The music, shown by words such as "toot" and "boom," also becomes blurred as the description changes from music "playing" to music "blaring."

Look for books that help children see things in new ways. *It Looked Like Spilt Milk*[93] and *Clouds*[94] talk about the shapes cloud formations may take, prompting children to look at the clouds themselves. What do they see? Children can use chalk to record the formations, then describe them. In *All In Free But Janey,*[95] Janey daydreams while playing hide and seek, resulting in her getting caught, but letting readers in on a rich imaginative world. Can they look in the dark places under a porch and see the goblins and gnomes that Janey saw, not just mushrooms and small plants?

Let children expand ideas that authors and illustrators have begun. The premise of Lion[96] is that there is an animal factory in the sky where animals are invented, first being drawn and named by four artists. One day the foreman, who has not drawn for some time, thinks up a name for a animal, "lion." Deciding to create the animal himself, he circulates among the drawing tables, noting what the other artists are sketching. Inspired, he creates his lion, a small, fat animal with both fur and features and having each of the artist's colors someplace on its body. He goes to each artist in turn, asking them to say one word about what is wrong with his animal. Eventually, having made all the changes they've suggested, he gets the answer "NOTHING" and his lion looks like a real lion. Children can begin with a name they make up, then create an animal. Will it have fur? Feathers? Scales? What size will it be? What color? What sound will it make?

Ed Emberley's ABC[97] shows each letter being formed in a series of four panels. The F, for instance, is formed as fireflies gather on a screen, observed by two frogs and fiddles. By the fourth picture the lighted fireflies form the letter. Children can make letters of their own this way, first thinking of something which begins with the letter, and then creating a series of pictures to show the letter being made.

The Biggest House in the World,[98] in which the snail's house becomes increasingly more elaborate until eventually it is so heavy that the snail cannot move, begs to be emulated. Changes, Changes,[99] a wordless picture book in which a man and woman move their blocks around to construct whatever they need each time disaster strikes, can provide the stimulus for children to try new constructions in the block corner, perhaps seeing how many different objects they can make from one set of blocks.

Encouraging Multiple Responses.   Finally, encourage children to give several responses. They might create several animals after hearing Lion; replay Seven Little Monsters, each time adding new movements; or make the biggest house for a bird, the biggest house for a snake, or the biggest house for themselves. Changing ideas, adding new elements, being flexible in approach all encourage children to use their creative abilities.

Making Aesthetic and Creative Experiences Enjoyable for Children

If you enjoy aesthetic and creative activities and show that you do, this will influence children to enjoy such activities, for your behavior provides a model for them. You show that you value aesthetic experiences when you give projects such as listening to a composition your full attention, listening to the cassette with the children, responding to the music yourself.

Planning for Enjoyable Creative Experiences.   You can also plan so that the experiences will be enjoyable for you. For example, you know that if you are to teach a song to young children, you will need to sing it (or play it) many times, and you will probably sing it with the children throughout the year. Therefore it makes sense to select songs you like and that you do not think you will tire of readily. Most teachers find that they vary the songs they teach if they

have taught for several years and also select different themes or topics to explore in depth or to use in learning centers.

Organize art projects so that they operate smoothly both for you and for the children. Teach children to clean up themselves, washing out brushes and storing scissors and paste in their specified places. Children learn responsibility when they must care for the equipment they use and develop independence as they become more and more able to get what they need and to replace it when they are finished.

Show your enjoyment of the products children produce. Display them, with the children's consent, on a regular basis. Comment on what they have done, and are doing, however, in a way that emphasizes the process rather than the product. "I see you found a way to make all the pieces lay flat," or "How did you feel while you were the troll waiting for the Billy Goats Gruff to start across the bridge?" Let children talk about their work when they seem eager to share.

Helping Children Feel Successful.   Help children gain satisfaction from their experiences by selecting books and suggesting activities that match the children's developmental level. The song "Yankee Doodle" is one you could use with children of various ages. It appears in a book illustrated with woodcuts by Ed Emberley[100] and containing both a history of the song and the music for it. "Yankee Doodle" is also available from Weston Woods Studios in both motion picture and sound filmstrip formats, this time with illustrations by Steven Kellogg.[101] The music is performed by The Colonial Williamsburg Fife and Drum Corps.

If you were working with three year olds, you might sing just the first verse and the chorus for the children rather than all the verses. They could listen to it several times and join in on any phrases they remembered. You would not expect them to match the tones accurately, nor to learn all the words. You might have them follow actions for the song or walk to the rhythm of the music on the cassette that accompanies the filmstrip. Again, it is likely that while most of them will be keeping a steady rhythm, their movement will not synchronize exactly with the music.

If you were teaching five and six year olds, you could present an entire song. Most of these children would be able to learn the first verse and chorus. They could be drummers with their hands keeping time as they sing, or could use rhythm instruments. They could march like soldiers, using arm motions as well as leg movements. After looking at the Emberley illustrations, they could use a similar printing technique of their own, perhaps making a cardboard cut with a masking tape loop on the back. They could then repeat the print of their figure, lifting it from the paper by the loop. They might talk about how Emberley used the print to show many soldiers and decide what they could show.

If you were teaching eight year olds, you might read the history of the song to them, and what some of the words in the lyrics mean. They too would enjoy singing and moving to the song. If they made prints, they could use overlapping cuts as Emberley did. They might make up new lyrics to the tune, trying out each suggestion to make certain that it fit the rhythm. For this age level, you might include activities from earlier stages. Eight year olds enjoy marching, even though they were able to do it when they were six.

The essential factor is that children be able to feel themselves successful in the activity. Thus, the three year old singing two phrases off tune will enjoy it and will be learning about matching tones as long as you let him or her know that this is acceptable behavior. If, however, you expect all tones to be matched and all of the words to be learned, the child may well become frustrated and decide that singing is an activity to be avoided. One parent cleverly maintained her son's good feelings about his own art when a teacher might have damaged both his interest in drawing and his self-confidence. The teacher, dissatisfied with the kindergartener's crayoning, had written "POOR" across his paper. He came home and showed the paper to his mother, beaming. She looked at it, looked at him, and asked him to tell her about the picture. "My teacher thought it was great," he said. "How do you know?" his mother asked. "Because she put a one hundred on it, and that means it's perfect. See the O's." The mother decided that such a good paper should go on the refrigerator door for the family to enjoy for that week. The teacher's written comment was inappropriate, both for its implication that art should be graded and for the damage it could have done to that child's image of himself and his artistic ability.

Presenting Books That Promote Understanding and Appreciation of the Arts. Some books you may choose to present will have children as protagonists engaged in the arts; others will focus on adults. Both types are useful to present to children for together they show that creative and aesthetic endeavors are not limited to any one age group. Both Julie in *A Piano for Julie*[102] and Rosa in *Music, Music for Everyone*[103] have found that music brings them pleasure. Julie is delighted when her parents decide to get a piano for their own house. She had wished for one as she listened to her father play at the home of her grandparents. Rosa plays the accordian and is able to bring musical entertainment to others while making money for herself by performing with three friends at a party. Both girls are supported in their love of music by close family members.

Begin at the Beginning[104] explores difficulties one may encounter in creating a work of art. Amy has been chosen to paint a picture to represent the second grade class in a school art show. She is excited as she plans to create a painting that will have *everything* in it. However, she finds that it is not an easy task and that the advice she is given by various members of her family is not helpful. Finally her mother talks with her, saying that she should begin with what she knows. So she begins with the tree outside her window. Books such as these provide excellent starting points for children to discuss their own art work, their own reactions to the creative process.

Stories with adults engaged in artistic pursuits often, but not always, show a more philosophical attitude toward the arts than do those that feature children as central characters. Two by M. B. Goffstein discuss the importance and purpose of art. In *Goldie the Dollmaker*,[105] Goldie, the artist who makes wooden dolls, is contrasted with Omus, the practical one who makes wooden crates. The value of both engaging in and appreciating art is presented clearly. In *An Artist*,[106] Goffstein begins her thesis with the opening statement, "An artist is like God, but small."[107] In concise and poetic language she describes how an artist creates with his paints, trying to bring order to what he sees, trying to capture his own thoughts and feelings. Both books are for quiet and thought-ful times.

Kuskin takes a more lighthearted approach in *The Philharmonic Gets Dressed.*[108] Just as the title implies, this book describes how the members of the orchestra begin to prepare for a concert, starting as they get dressed at home and concluding as they begin to play. In the course of the story, the reader learns about an orchestra. Share books such as these with children to show that many people gain deep satisfaction from participation in and observation of the arts.

Sustaining an Atmosphere of Acceptance.   Give children a wide variety of media from which to choose and allow children to decide for themselves on many occasions what materials they wish to use in art or which movements they wish to use in response to music. Variety maintains interest and allows children to find activities that they particularly enjoy. The choice builds inde-pendence and allows for preferences and for creative responses.

Finally, let children work together in response to music or literature. Many like to work with their friends, especially in the primary grades. They might make a mural of cats in stories they have heard, with each child contributing one character. They talk about their contribution and also plan how the mural will look when finished. At other times, working together is simply sharing materials or being in the same vicinity, but feeling free to converse with their neighbors if they like. An atmosphere of trust and friendship transfers positive reactions to the activity being undertaken. If you can help children enjoy their aesthetic and creative activities, you will be giving them the necessary attitude for continuing to develop their skills of impression and their skills of expression.

Summary

Children's growth in creative expression through art, music, and movement is in part developmental as they gain more physical and motor control, and in part environmental as they have opportunities to engage in artistic and musi-cal experiences. Performance skills of singing, using rhythm instruments, draw-ing, painting, and dramatizing appear to provide a base for aesthetic appreciation by helping children become familiar with the techniques involved.

The following long term goals are appropriate for the aesthetic and creative growth of young children.

- Children will respond favorably to diverse styles of art and music.
- Children will exhibit a sensory awareness of their environment.
- Children will use, experiment with, and gain control over a variety of media.
- Children will sing in tune within their vocal range and will respond to music and literature with movement and with rhythm instruments.
- Children will use their imaginations as they participate in art, music, and movement.
- Children will enjoy experiencing the work of others and participating in the arts themselves.

Books offer opportunities for helping children achieve these goals. Table 5 suggests appropriate teaching strategies. Children are likely to develop favorable atttudes toward diverse styles of art if they recognize that art is personal expression, if they see a wide range of styles of art in picture books, and if they relate personally to the art they are viewing. Children become aware of the sensory qualities of their environment when they hear literature in which authors give descriptions written in sensory terms and in which illustrators show the beauty they observe. Books also may provide the stimulus for children to explore their environment taking special note of sensory qualities.

Children become familiar with a variety of media when they are given the opportunity to experiment with art materials. They may explore techniques used by illustrators of picture books; they may make illustrations for their own writing; they may try artistic techniques or projects described in books. Children need both initial help in learning about the media available in their classroom and time on their own to use the media.

Literature can give added dimension to children's musical experiences in the early years, contributing to their participation in singing, listening, using rhythm instruments, and movement. Children listen to songs illustrated in picture books either read or sung; they enjoy hearing in audiovisual format songs too complex for them to sing themselves; they use rhythm instruments in conjunction with literature; and they move in response to poetry and prose that has a strong rhythmic beat or actions which can be dramatized.

Finally, children's creativity and their appreciation of the creativity of others can be fostered through literature. Questions and activities which are based on books should evoke divergent responses, should be enjoyable for the child,

Children can listen to recordings of songs illustrated in picture books.

and should allow the child to be successful. An atmosphere of acceptance and a general pattern of encouragement for multiple reactions and responses to a single book or question are key elements in developing children's creativity and aesthetic appreciation.

Table 5. *Supporting Children's Aesthetic and Creative Growth*

Developmental Goals	Teaching Suggestions	Recommended Literature	
Children will respond favorably to diverse styles of art.	Show children that art is one form of personal expression.	**Ages 3–5:**	
		Aliki	*Hush Little Baby*
	Show how more than one artist has interpreted the same song or tale or character.	Clifton	Books about *Everett Anderson*
		Hoban	Books about *Frances*
	Let children compare how one animal appears in several books of fiction.	Keats	*Over in the Meadow*
		Langstaff	*Over in the Meadow*
	Help children see the diversity in artistic styles in picture book illustrations.	Pinkwater	*Bear's Picture*
		Winter	*Hush Little Baby*
	Encourage careful observation of illustrations.	**Ages 5–8:**	
		Baylor	*When Clay Sings*
	Involve children in art projects related to techniques used or portrayed in books.	Freschat	*The Old Bullfrog*
		Hoban	*Arthur's New Power*
		Hoban	*Dinner at Alberta's*
		Isadora	*Ben's Trumpet*
		Keith	*Rrra-ah*
		Langstaff	*Frog Went A-Courtin'*
		Lobel	*Frog and Toad Are Friends*
		Mayer	*Frog Goes to Dinner*
		O'Kelley	*From the Hills of Georgia*
		Spilka	*Paint All Kinds of Pictures*
Children will exhibit a sensory awareness of their environment.	Read prose and poetry by authors who write in sensory terms.	**Ages 3–5:**	
		Boyden	*"Mud"*
		Fisher	*In the Middle of the Night*
	Let children try sensory experiences described in books.	Hoban	*Bread and Jam for Frances*
	Use literature as a stimulus for activities that require children to use their senses in discovery or exploration.	Keats	*Goggles*
		Kunhardt	*Pat the Bunny*
		Merriam	*"A Matter of Taste"*
		Rockwell	*My Back Yard*
		Showers	*The Listening Walk*
		Shulevitz	*Dawn*
		Snyder	*"Poem to Mud"*
		Spier	*Gobble, Growl, Grunt*

Table 5. (Cont.)

Developmental Goals	Teaching Suggestions	Recommended Literature	
		Ages 5–8:	
		Baylor	*We Walk in Sandy Places*
		Brown	*Touch Will Tell*
		Evans	*The Tiniest Sound*
		George	*All Upon a Sidewalk*
		Hawkinson	*Birds in the Sky*
		Lund	*The Paint Box Sea*
		Ray	*The Cloud*
		Yolen	*The Seeing Stick*
Children will use, experiment with, and gain control over a variety of art media.	Let children experiment with selected media used by illustrators of children's books. Encourage children to illustrate stories and poems they dictate or write. Help children try artistic techniques described in books. Have children respond to books through art, both two and three dimensional.	**Ages 3–5:**	
		Bulla	*Keep Running, Allen!*
		Lionni	*Inch by Inch*
		Lionni	*Let's Make Rabbits*
		Lionni	*Little Blue and Little Yellow*
		Lionni	*Swimmy*
		Spier	*Noah's Ark*
		Tresselt	*Hide and Seek Fog*
		Ages 5–8:	
		Burningham	*Time to Get Out of the Bath, Shirley*
		Burton	*The Little House*
		Carrick	*Splodges*
		Hawkinson	*Pastels are Great!*
		Sylvester	*Summer on Cleo's Island*
		Yashima	*Crow Boy*
Children will sing in tune within their vocal range and will respond to music and rhythm instruments.	Share picture book editions of songs. Present literature in audiovisual format for children to hear musical accompaniment and songs too complex for them to sing. Let children use rhythm instruments in conjunction with literature. Encourage children to move in response to poems or stories, either adding motions or moving to the rhythm.	**Ages 3–5:**	
		Aliki	*Go Tell Aunt Rhody*
		Emberley	*Drummer Hoff*
		Emberley	*London Bridge Is Falling Down*
		Gramatky	*Little Toot*
		Quackenbush	*Go Tell Aunt Rhody*
		Quackenbush	*Skip to My Lou*
		Smith	*Long Ago Elf*
		Stecher	*Max, the Music Maker*
		Weston Woods	*The Fox Went Out On a Chilly Night*
		Weston Woods	*Clementine*
		Wiest	*Down the River Without a Paddle*

Table 5. (Cont.)

Developmental Goals	Teaching Suggestions	Recommended Literature	
		Ages 5–8:	
		Grifalconi	City Rhythms
		Hurd	Mama Don't Allow
		Lionni	Alexander and the Wind-up Mouse
		Weston Woods	Peter Penny's Dance
		Weston Woods	A Story, A Story
Children will use their imaginations as they participate in art, music, and movement.	Plan activities that will lead to divergent responses. Present books that are inventive. Encourage children to give more than one response.	**Ages 3–5:** Geisel	And to Think That I Saw It on Mulberry Street
		Hutchins	Changes, Changes
		Johnson	All in Free But Janey
		McPhail	Where Can an Elephant Hide?
		Sendak	Seven Little Monsters
		Sendak	Where The Wild Things Are
		Shaw	It Looked Like Spilt Milk
		Ages 5–8: Baylor	Sometimes I Dance Mountains
		Crews	Carousel
		du Bois	Lion
		Emberley	Ed Emberley's ABC
		Lionni	The Biggest House in the World
		Niizaka	Clouds
Children will enjoy experiencing the work of others and participating in the arts themselves.	Organize art projects so that they operate smoothly. Show your own enjoyment of the work children produce. Talk with children while they work, emphasizing the artistic process in your comments. Suggest activities that match the children's developmental level. Give children frequent opportunities to choose the media or type of response they wish to use.	**Ages 3–8:** Kellogg Shackburg **Ages 5–8:** Goffstein Goffstein Kuskin Schick Schwartz Williams	Yankee Doodle Yankee Doodle An Artist Goldie the Dollmaker The Philharmonic Gets Dressed A Piano for Julie Begin at the Beginning Music, Music for Everyone

Table 5. (Cont.)

Developmental Goals	Teaching Suggestions	Recommended Literature
	Present books that promote understanding and appreciation of the arts.	
	Let children work together on music and art projects.	

Extending Your Learning

1. Select one animal and compare how at least three illustrators have drawn it.
2. Select five picture books and identify as best you can the media and the style of illustration.
3. Preview two of the films about illustrators produced by Weston Woods Studios. Tell what primary children might learn from each of them.
4. Start a section of your poetry collection for children in which poets use sensory descriptions.
5. Plan a field trip in your area that would encourage children to observe their environment carefully.
6. Select three picture books in which the illustrator has used media that children could try themselves.
7. Design endpapers for any three picture books that have unillustrated endpapers.
8. Find three songs in picture book format that are appropriate for young children.
9. Select three picture books that lend themselves to interpretation through music or movement. Describe how you would engage children in the activity.
10. Select a filmstrip of a song. Tell how you might share this with three year olds, with six year olds, and with eight year olds.

Notes

1. H. S. Broudy, "How Basic is Aesthetic Education? or Is ART the Fourth R?" *Language Arts* 54 (September, 1977): 635.
2. Arthur D. Efland, "Excellence in Education: The Role of the Arts" *Theory Into Practice*, Vol. XXIII, No. 4 (Autumn, 1984): 267–272.
3. E. Paul Torrance, *Encouraging Creativity in the Classroom* (Dubuque, Iowa: Wm. C. Brown Group, 1970), 2.
4. J. P. Guilford, "A Psychometric Approach to Creativity," in *Creativity in Childhood Adolescence,* Harold H. Anderson, ed. (Palo Alto, Calif.: Science and Behavior Books, 1965), 1–19.
5. Viktor Lowenfeld and W. Lambert Brittain, *Creative and Mental Growth,* 5th ed. (New York: Macmillan Publishing Co., 1970).
6. Laura H. Chapman, *Approaches to Art in Education* (New York: Harcourt Brace Jovanovich, 1978).

7. Dorothy T. McDonald, *Music in Our Lives: The Early Years* Copyright © 1979 National Association for the Education of Young Children, 1834 Connecticut Avenue N.W. Washington, D.C. 10029. Reprinted by permission, p. 25.

8. Manus Pinkwater, *Bear's Picture* (New York: Holt, Rinehart & Winston, 1972).

9. Arnold Spilka, *Paint All Kinds of Pictures* (New York: Henry Z. Walck, 1964).

10. John Langstaff, *Over in the Meadow.* Illus. by Feodor Rojankovsky (New York: Harcourt Brace Jovanovich, 1957).

11. Ezra Jack Keats, *Over in the Meadow* (New York: Four Winds Press, 1972).

12. Aliki, *Hush Little Baby* (Englewood Cliffs, N.J.: Prentice-Hall Inc., 1968).

13. Jeanette Winter, *Hush Little Baby* (New York: Pantheon Books Inc., 1984).

14. Lucille Clifton, *Some of the Days of Everett Anderson.* Illus. by Evaline Ness (New York: Holt, Rinehart & Winston, 1970).

15. Lucille Clifton, *Everett Anderson's Christmas Coming.* Illus. by Evaline Ness (New York: Holt, Rinehart & Winston, 1971).

16. Lucille Clifton, *Everett Anderson's Year.* Illus. by Ann Grilfalconi (New York: Holt, Rinehart & Winston, 1974).

17. Lucille Clifton, *Everett Anderson's Friend.* Illus. by Ann Grifalconi (New York: Holt, Rinehart & Winston, 1976).

18. Lucille Clifton, *Everett Anderson's 1-2-3.* Illus. by Ann Grifalconi (New York: Holt, Rinehart & Winston, 1977).

19. Lucille Clifton, *Everett Anderson's Nine Month Long.* Illus. by Ann Grifalconi (New York: Holt, Rinehart & Winston, 1978).

20. Lucille Clifton, *Everett Anderson's Goodbye.* Illus. by Ann Grifalconi (New York: Holt, Rinehart & Winston, 1983).

21. Russell Hoban, *Bedtime for Frances.* Illus. by Garth Williams (New York: Harper & Row, Publishers, Inc., 1960).

22. Russell Hoban, *Dinner at Alberta's.* Illus. by James Marshall (New York: Thomas Y. Crowell Publishers, 1973).

23. Russell Hoban, *Arthur's New Power.* Illus. by Byron Barton (New York: Thomas Y. Crowell Publishers, 1978).

24. Arnold Lobel, *Frog and Toad Are Friends* (New York: Harper & Row, Publishers, Inc., 1970).

25. Mercer Mayer, *Frog Goes to Dinner* (New York: Dial Press, 1974).

26. John Langstaff, *Frog Went a-Courtin'.* Illus. by Feodor Rojankovsky (New York: Harcourt Brace Jovanovich, 1955).

27. Eros Keith, *Rrra-ah* (Englewood Cliffs, N.J.: Bradbury Press Inc., 1969).

28. Berniece Freschet, *The Old Bullfrog.* Illus. by Roger Duvoisin (New York: Charles Scribner's Sons, 1968).

29. Mattie Lou O'Kelley, *From the Hills of Georgia* (Boston: Atlantic/Little, 1983).

30. Rachel Isadora, *Ben's Trumpet* (New York: Greenwillow Books, 1979).

31. Weston Woods Studios, Ezra Jack Keats. Signature Collection #410.

32. Byrd Baylor, *When Clay Sings.* Illus. by Tom Bahti (New York: Charles Scribner's Sons, 1972).

33. Uri Shulevitz, *Dawn* (New York: Farrar, Straus & Giroux Inc., 1974).

34. Lucy and John Hawkinson, *Birds in the Sky* (Chicago: Children's Press, 1965).

35. Hawkinson, *Birds in the Sky,* n.p.

36. Deborah Kogan Ray, *The Cloud* (New York: Harper & Row, Publishers, Inc., 1984).

37. Ray, *The Cloud,* n.p.

38. "A Matter of Taste," by Eve Merriam from *There Is No Rhyme for Silver.* Copyright © 1962 by Eve Merriam. Used by permission of Atheneum Publishers.

39. Polly Chase Boyden, "Mud," in *Time for Poetry,* May Hill Arbuthnot ed. (Chicago: Scott, Foresman & Co., 1971), p. 157.

40. From *Today is Saturday* by Zilpha Keatley Snyder. Copyright © 1969 by Zilpha Keatley Snyder. Used by permission of Atheneum Publishers.

41. Doris Harold Lund, *The Paint-Box Sea*. Illus. by Symeon Shimin (New York: McGraw-Hill Inc., 1973).

42. Paul Showers, *The Listening Walk*. Illus. by Aliki (New York: Thomas Y. Crowell Publishers, 1961).

43. Byrd Baylor, *We Walk in Sandy Places*. Illus. by Marilyn Schwitzer (New York: Charles Scribner's Sons, 1976).

44. Ezra Jack Keats, *Goggles* (New York: Macmillan Publishing Co., 1969).

45. Anne and Harlow Rockwell, *My Back Yard* (New York: Macmillan Publishing Co., 1984).

46. Jean Craighead George, *All Upon a Sidewalk*. Illus. by Don Bolognese (New York: E. P. Dutton, Inc., 1974).

47. Patricia Hubbell, "Our Washing Machine," in *The Apple Vendor's Fair*. Illus. by Julia Maas (New York: Atheneum Publishers, 1963).

48. Peter Spier, *Gobble, Growl, Grunt* (New York: Doubleday & Co. Inc., 1971).

49. Mel Evans, *The Tiniest Sound*. Illus. by Ed Young (New York: Doubleday & Co. Inc., 1969).

50. Dorothy Kunhardt, *Pat the Bunny* (Racine, Wis.: Western Publishing Co. Inc., 1962).

51. Marcia Brown, *Touch Will Tell* (New York: Franklin Watts Inc., 1979).

52. Jane Yolen, *The Seeing Stick*. Illus. by Remy Charlip and Demetra Maraslis (New York: Thomas Y. Crowell Publishers, 1977).

53. Russell Hoban, *Bread and Jam for Frances*. Illus. by Lillian Hoban (New York: Harper & Row, Publishers, Inc., 1969).

54. Leo Lionni, *Let's Make Rabbits* (New York: Pantheon Books Inc., 1982).

55. Leo Lionni, *Swimmy* (New York: Pantheon Books Inc., 1963).

56. Leo Lionni, *Little Blue and Little Yellow* (New York: Astor-Honor, 1959).

57. Leo Lionni, *Inch by Inch* (New York: Astor-Honor, 1962).

58. Clyde Robert Bulla, *Keep Running, Allen!* Illus. by Satomi Ichikawa (New York: Thomas Y. Crowell Publishers, 1978).

59. Alvin Tresselt, *Hide and Seek Fog*. Illus. by Roger Duvoisin (New York: Lothrop, Lee & Shepard Books, 1965).

60. Peter Spier, *Noah's Ark* (New York: Doubleday & Co. Inc., 1977).

61. Natalie G. Sylvester, *Summer on Cleo's Island* (New York: Farrar, Straus & Giroux Inc., 1977).

62. Taro Yashima, *Crow Boy* (New York: Viking Press, 1955).

63. Virginia Lee Burton, *The Little House* (Boston: Houghton Mifflin Co., 1942).

64. John Burningham, *Time to Get Out of the Bath, Shirley* (New York: Thomas Y. Crowell Publishers, 1978).

65. Malcolm Carrick, *Splodges* (New York: Viking Press, 1976).

66. John Hawkinson, *Pastels are Great!* (Chicago: Albert Whitman & Co., 1968).

67. Aliki, *Go Tell Aunt Rhody* (New York: Macmillan Publishing Co., 1974).

68. Robert Quackenbush, *Go Tell Aunt Rhody* (Philadelphia: J. B. Lippincott Publishing Co., 1973).

69. Jane Hart, *Singing Bee!* Illus. by Anita Lobel (New York: Lothrop, Lee & Shepard Books, 1982).

70. Tom Glazer, *Music for Ones and Twos: Songs and Games for the Very Young Child*. Illus. by Karen Ann Weinhaus (Garden City, N.Y.: Doubleday & Co. Inc., 1983).

71. Clyde Watson. *Father Fox's Feast of Songs*. Illus. by Wendy Watson (New York: Philomel, 1983).

72. Weston Woods Studios, *The Fox Went Out on a Chilly Night*, SF59C, PBC58.

73. Weston Woods Studios, *Clementine*, SF168C, HBC168.

74. Serge Profofiev, *Peter and the Wolf*. Translated by Maria Carlson. Illus. by Charles Mikolaycak (New York: Viking Press, 1982).

75. Weston Woods Studios, *Peter Penny's Dance*, SP231C.

76. Weston Woods Studios, *A Story A Story*, SF123C.

77. Mary and R. A. Smith, *Long Ago Elf* (Chicago: Follett Publishing Co., 1968).

78. Ann Grifalconi, *City Rhythms* (New York: Bobbs & Merrill, 1965).

79. Miriam B. Stecher and Alice S. Kandell, *Max, the Music Maker* (New York: Lothrop, Lee & Shepard Books, 1980).

80. Barbara Emberley, *Drummer Hoff*. Illus. by Ed Emberley (Englewood Cliffs, N.J.: Prentice-Hall, Inc., 1967).

81. Ed Emberley, *London Bridge Is Falling Down* (Boston: Little, Brown & Co. Inc., 1967).

82. Robert Quackenbush, *Skip to My Lou* (Philadelphia: J. B. Lippincott Co., 1975).

83. Thacher Hurd, *Mama Don't Allow* (New York: Harper & Row, Publishers, Inc., 1984).

84. Hardy Gramatky, *Little Toot* (New York: G. P. Putnam's Sons, 1939).

85. Robert and Claire Wiest, *Down the River Without a Paddle* (Chicago: Children's Press, 1973).

86. Leo Lionni, *Alexander and the Wind-Up Mouse* (New York: Pantheon Books Inc., 1969).

87. David McPhail, *Where Can An Elephant Hide?* (New York: Doubleday & Co. Inc., 1979).

88. Maurice Sendak, *Seven Little Monsters* (New York: Harper & Row, Publishers, Inc., 1975).

89. Maurice Sendak, *Where the Wild Things Are* (New York: Harper & Row, Publishers, Inc., 1963).

90. Byrd Baylor, *Sometimes I Dance Mountains*. Illus. by Kenneth Longtemps (New York: Charles Scribner's Sons, 1973).

91. Theodore Geisel, *And To Think That I Saw It on Mulberry Street* (New York: Vanguard Press, 1937).

92. Donald Crews, *Carousel* (New York: Greenwillow Books, 1982).

93. Charles G. Shaw, *It Looked Like Spilt Milk* (New York: Harper & Row, Publishers, Inc., 1947).

94. Kazou Niizaka, *Clouds* (Reading, Mass.: Addison-Wesley Publishing Co. Inc., 1975).

95. Elizabeth Johnson, *All In Free But Janey*. Illus. by Trina Schart Hyman (Boston: Little, Brown & Co. Inc., 1967).

96. William Pene du Bois, *Lion* (New York: Viking Press, 1955).

97. Ed Emberley, *Ed Emberley's ABC* (Boston: Little, Brown & Co. Inc., 1978).

98. Leo Lionni, *The Biggest House in the World* (New York: Pantheon Books Inc., 1968).

99. Pat Hutchins, *Changes, Changes.* (New York: Macmillan Publishing Co., 1971).

100. Richard Shackburg, *Yankee Doodle*. Illus. by Ed Emberley (Englewood Cliffs, N.J.: Prentice-Hall Inc., 1965).

101. Weston Woods Studios, *Yankee Doodle*, SF173C.

102. Eleanor Schick, *A Piano for Julie* (New York: Greenwillow Books, 1984).

103. Vera B. Williams, *Music, Music for Everyone* (New York: Greenwillow Books, 1984).

104. Amy Schwartz, *Begin at the Beginning* (New York: Harper & Row, Publishers, Inc., 1983).

105. M. B. Goffstein, *Goldie the Dollmaker* (New York: Farrar, Straus & Giroux Inc., 1969).

106. M. B. Goffstein, *An Artist* (New York: Harper & Row, Publishers, Inc., 1980).

107. Goffstein, *An Artist,* n.p.

108. Karla Kuskin, *The Philharmonic Gets Dressed*. Illus. by Marc Simont (New York: Harper & Row, Publishers, Inc., 1982).

Recommended References

Andress, Barbara. *Music Experience in Early Childhood.* New York: Holt, Rinehart & Winston, 1980.

Arnheim, Rudolph. *Art and Visual Perception: A Psychology of the Creative Eye.* Berkeley: University of California Press, 1971.

Aronoff, Frances Webber. *Music and Young Children.* New York: Holt, Rinehart & Winston, 1969.

Chapman, Laura H. *Approaches to Art Education.* New York: Harcourt Brace Jovanovich, 1978.

Eisner, Elliott W. *Reading, the Arts, and the Creation of Meaning.* Reston, Va.: National Art Education Association, 1978.

Haines, B. Joan, and Gerber, Linda L. *Leading Young Children to Music: A Resource Book for Teachers.* Columbus, Ohio: Charles E. Merrill Publishing Co., 1980.

Lowenfeld, Viktor, and Brittain, W. Lambert. *Creative and Mental Growth.* 5th ed. New York: Macmillan Publishing Co., 1970.

Lynch-Fraser, *Dance Play.* New York: Walker & Co., 1982.

McDonald, Dorothy T. *Music in Our Lives: The Early Years.* Washington, D.C.: National Association for the Education of Young Children, 1979.

Robison, Helen F. and Schwartz, Sydney L. *Learning at an Early Age.* vols. 1 and 2. Englewood Cliffs, N.J.: Prentice-Hall Inc., 1972.

Romen, Betty. *Learning Through Movement.* New York: Teachers College Press, 1982.

Russell, Joan. *Creative Dance in the Elementary School.* London: Macdonald and Evans, 1965.

Sheehy, Emma. *Children Discover Music and Dance.* New York: Teachers College Press, 1977.

Smith, Nancy R. *Experience and Art.* New York: Teachers College Press, 1983.

Torrance, E. Paul. *Encouraging Creativity in the Classroom.* Dubuque, Iowa: Wm. C. Brown Group, 1970.

Recommended Children's Books

Asch, Frank. *Sand Cake.* New York: Parents Magazine Press, 1979.

Barrett, Judith. *Animals Should Definitely Not Wear Clothing.* Illus. by Ron Barrett. New York: Atheneum Publishers, 1970.

Bryan, Ashley. *The Dancing Granny.* New York: Atheneum Publishers, 1977.

Cohen, Miriam. *No Good in Art.* Illus. by Lillian Hoban. New York: Greenwillow Books, 1980.

Crews, Donald. *Parade.* New York: Greenwillow Books, 1983.

DePaola, Tomie. *Flicks.* New York: Harcourt Brace Jovanovich, 1979.

Heide, Florence P. *Sound of Sunshine, Sound of Rain.* New York: Parents Magazine Press, 1970.

Jeffers, Susan. *All the Pretty Horses.* New York: Macmillan Publishing Co., 1974.

Langstaff, John. *Oh, A-Hunting We Will Go.* Illus. by Nancy Winslow Parker. New York: Atheneum Publishers, 1974.

Lionni, Leo. *Geraldine, the Music Mouse.* New York: Pantheon Books Inc., 1979.

MacAgy, Douglas and Elizabeth. *Going for a Walk with a Line.* Garden City, N.Y.: Doubleday & Co. Inc., 1959.

MacLochlan, Patricia. *Through Grandpa's Eyes.* Illus. by Deborah Ray. New York: Harper & Row, Publishers, Inc., 1980.

Oakley, Graham. *Magical Changes.* New York: Atheneum Publishers, 1980.

Pearson, Tracey. *Old Macdonald Had a Farm.* New York: Dial Books for Young Readers, 1984.

Raskin, Ellen. *Spectacles.* New York: Atheneum Publishers, 1968.

Rauch, Hans-Georg. *The Lines Are Coming.* New York: Charles Scribner's Sons, 1978.

Shannon, George. *Dance Away.* Illus. by Jose Aruego and Arianl Dewey. New York: Greenwillow Books, 1982.

Stevens, Bryna. *Ben Franklin's Glass Armonica.* Illus. by Priscilla Kiedrowski. Minneapolis: Carolrhoda Books Inc., 1983.

Todd, Kathleen. *Snow.* Reading, Mass.: Addison-Wesley Publishing Co. Inc., 1982.

Ueno, Noriko. *Elephant Buttons.* New York: Harper & Row, Publishers, Inc., 1973.

9

Planning Your Program

As you begin to plan the literature program for your class or group of children, you will first need to familiarize yourself with the actual literature. Spend several afternoons or evenings in the library reading picture books and browsing through poetry for children. Look up and read any of the books mentioned in this text that seem to you to have promise for your students. Make notes about those you plan to use. Some teachers and day care professionals use index cards; others use loose leaf notebooks. The important thing is that whatever method you choose, select one that allows you to find the books again easily and to remember what strengths you saw in them.

Seeing the Possibilities

Choose books for their literary value, the quality of the text and of the illustrations. Then think about the ways in which the literature itself, or extensions of it, support goals of early childhood education and of your curriculum in particular. You will find that often one book has many possibilities. *Freight Train,*[1] for example, was cited in chapter five as a book that can aid concept development. The brief text reinforces color recognition in its labeling of freight cars of different colors. *Freight Train* could support many other goals as well, however. Here are some examples:

Language Development

Goal. "Children will expand their vocabularies." The meaning of "freight" is shown in the cars that make up the train and in the fact that no people are being transported. After reading the book, a teacher might call attention to this by asking children why they think some trains are called freight trains and others are called passenger trains. What is freight? If children show an interest in the different kinds of cars, they might continue the discussion by talking about where a caboose is on a train, and what tank cars or box cars are. Vocabulary growth involves language development and concept development.

Goal. "Children will enjoy the creative and aesthetic use of language." Here is a time when the adult's reading of the text may determine children's appreciation of the language. The rhythm of the prose should be emphasized. As the words that describe the train's travel are read, the pace can be quickened, building to the climax of "Going, going . ." a pause, and the final, quiet, "gone."

Aesthetic and Creative Development

Goal. "Children will exhibit a sensory awareness of their environment." Children having seen and heard *Freight Train* might follow up on the idea of how smoke looks as it moves in the wind, or on the sounds of vehicles, especially as they draw nearer, then pass by. If the children watch smoke from chimneys, or exhaust from cars, they can capture the path with crayons or paint or chalk. If they observe traffic in their area, they can note the sounds of the vehicles. How do the sounds of cars differ from those of trucks? What is special about the sound of an airplane? What are the different kinds of sounds that a train makes?

Goal. "Children will use, experiment with, and gain control over a variety of art media." Children who have made pictures of smoke will be using at least one medium. They might try rubbing chalk to blur the lines after they have watched wind thin out a stream of heavy smoke until nothing remains but soft wisps, gradually becoming indistinct against the sky. They might make cars for a train of their own, using boxes or styrofoam. Which materials work best for a cattle car? Which for the rounded tank car?

Goal. "Children will respond to literature and music with movement and with rhythm instruments." Children listening to the day care professional's reading of the text can add rhythm themselves with the use of sand blocks and rhythm sticks. They might match the beat of the text. They might use the instruments to show the rhythm of a train they have heard, with the adult matching their rhythm with his or her reading. The text is so brief and simple that children can learn it easily after hearing it a few times and may join in with the teacher.

A single book offers opportunities to support many of the goals of early childhood education. (Illustration "a black steam engine" in Freight Train *by Donald Crews. Copyright © 1978 by Donald Crews. By permission of Greenwillow Books, A Division of William Morrow & Co.)*

Once they know it, they can work with the rhythm in choral speaking. They might also move to the beat, maintaining the tempo before and after the reading of the text.

Goal. "Children will use their imaginations as they participate in art, music, and movement." Children will be using their imaginations as they construct new trains or work with the sound of the text. The teacher can encourage them to continue doing so by asking questions to stimulate further thinking. "How could you show what you like about that car?" "Decide how you will move your arms to the rhythm of the sand blocks. When the sound begins, show us your idea." "Now let's see if anyone can think of another way to make the sound of a train."

Personality Development

Goal. "Children will set tasks for themselves and will complete tasks they begin." The task may vary from a quick drawing to a rather elaborate construction. Teachers help children attend to their tasks by talking with them occasionally as they work, giving the children time to tell about their projects. They praise them for work completed. If the project is lengthy, and the child is getting restless, teachers may suggest that the child put it away for a while and complete it later in the day, or perhaps the following day.

Goal. "Children will weigh evidence and make appropriate choices." Children can be given several choices following the reading of *Freight Train*. If they are going to make freight cars themselves, what type of car would each like to make? Would they like to work by themselves or with a friend? If they are going to draw cars and find objects that match the color of the car, which color would they like their car to be? Would they prefer to cut objects from magazines, or to draw their own?

Social Development

Goal. "Children will engage competently in group activites." If the teacher or day care professional wishes to emphasize group work, he or she will not give children the choice of working alone or with someone else, but rather will state that this time two or three children will work together. They might be cutting blue, red, and yellow objects from magazines, then sorting the pictures according to color. They will then make a car for each set of objects. They might work together to make a train of their own, either on paper or with three dimensional materials. They might work in the block corner, setting up the tracks and the countryside so their train can travel. They might coordinate their efforts with rhythm instruments.

Selecting Activities

Many of these goals and activities are compatible with one another, though not all are. Given these possibilities, your task as teacher now becomes one of deciding which, if any, you wish to pursue. Here are three general suggestions for determining the merit of specific activities for extending books.

First, the activity should enhance the literature, not detract from it. Children who move to the sound and rhythm of the words of *Freight Train* enjoy the physical activity while also becoming aware of the effectiveness of the language. They are likely to want to hear the book again and to think positively about literature. If, however, you require the children to recognize the words *tunnel*, *trestle*, *tracks*, and *tender* when they see them on flash cards, it is likely that many of the children will see literature as a source of frustrating work. They will not be eager to have you read more books, nor to repeat *Freight Train*. They will not have gained any deeper understanding of or appreciation for the literature.

Second, the activity should emerge naturally from the book. Because *Freight Train* builds on the use of color, on motion, and on sound, activities relating to these concepts have a direct relationship to the book. Working with ideas or with themes central to the book draws attention to the literature instead of away from it. Suppose, however, you look at the illustrations and see the rails and supporting ties. You decide to talk with the children about the weight of trains and the necessity of carefully laid tracks. You find that you have to strain to tie the idea back to the book once you have finished and that rereading the book to the children has no new meaning resulting from your endeavors.

Third, the activities should match both the needs and the abilities of your students. *Freight Train* is particularly appropriate for use with preschool and kindergarten children. The activities suggested for it all relate to goals for early childhood education. Deciding which ones are most appropriate means knowing your children well, being able to assess and rank their needs, and knowing which needs will be met in other ways. It also means recognizing that there will be a range of needs and abilities in any group of children, so that you will be planning activities for small groups or for individuals much of the time. Some preschoolers are able to cut pictures from magazines; others still need practice controlling scissors and benefit more from cutting large, less detailed shapes. Some of your children may need help in learning to work cooperatively with others. Some may need to work alone before they are ready to contribute to a group project. Being able to determine which activities should be suggested to which children is a professional skill of teaching.

As you select individual books and as you plan your curriculum, group some of the books into units or webs. Ideas for grouping may emerge as you look at the literature, a particular author or illustrator's work for instance, or several books expressing a similar theme. Sometimes you may need to use reference guides to children's literature to help you find books that fit the topics you intend to develop. With *Freight Train,* you might look for other books about trains, or perhaps other color books, or other books by Donald Crews. You could follow the presentation of *Freight Train* with *The Little Engine That Could*[2] for extension of the language sounds and rhythm, or for comparing one book in which a train is described with another in which the engine is personified. You could share the sound filmstrip of *Casey Jones.*[3] The literature, combined with activities for its extension, would be about a five or six day unit.

You will sequence some units within the school year, those whose placement is a factor in their success. Other units and books you will have in mind but will be flexible in your planning of when they will be presented. The train unit might come at any convenient time, whereas holiday books obviously need to be scheduled to coincide with the event. You will check your general plan to make certain that you are developing a balanced literature curriculum, one that has both prose and poetry, fantasy and realism, classic and modern stories.

Evaluating Your Literature Program

You will evaluate your literature curriculum on a daily basis and at the close of the year. Daily evaluation will be based on the specific goals and objectives of each lesson. Did the children find at least three hidden objects in each picture? Could each child think of at least two activities Curious George might do if he were in the classroom? Did the children state two ways in which two books were alike, and two ways in which they were different? Did the children repeat the refrain with you as you read a book for the second time?

Evaluation at the close of the year will involve an assessment of the program and the children's development. Was the program balanced? Were the books and activities appropriate for the children? Were you using the best literature available? As you look at the children's behavior, you will discern changes that have occurred over the year and will find patterns of behavior that indicate the children's response to literature. A successful literature program should result in some or all of these behaviors:

- Children will reread or look at the illustrations in books you have read to them.

- Children will choose to read or look at books in their free time or as work choices.
- Children will recommend books and book related activities to one another.
- Children will choose to respond to literature through art, music, movement, and drama.
- Children will talk about book characters and happenings in new situations.
- Children will ask you to read to them.

You will also be evaluating goals for your students in their language, intellectual, personal, social, moral, aesthetic, and creative development. Your literature program will have supported growth in all of these areas.

Extending Your Learning

1. Select one book. List the goals of early childhood education that it supports, listing your rationale for why it supports each one. Then suggest several possible units for use of the book.
2. Evaluate a literature experience you have had with children. List specific criteria and describe how well each was met.

Notes

1. Donald Crews, *Freight Train* (New York: Greenwillow Books, 1978).
2. Watty Piper, *The Little Engine That Could.* Illus. by George & Doris Hauman (New York: The Platt & Munk Co., 1930).
3. Weston Woods Studios, *Casey Jones,* SF118C.

APPENDIX

THE CALDECOTT MEDAL

The Caldecott Medal is awarded annually to the illustrator of the most distinguished American picture book for children. The winner is selected by a committee of the Association for Library Services for Children of the American Librarian Association.

1938 *Animals of the Bible* by Helen Dean Fish, ill. by Dorothy P. Lathrop, J. B. Lippincott Co.
Honor Books: *Seven Simeons* by Boris Artzvbasheff, Viking Press; *Four and Twenty Blackbirds* by Helen Dean Fish, ill. by Robert Lawson, Stokes.

1939 *Mei Li* by Thomas Handforth, Doubleday & Co. Inc.
Honor Books: *The Forest Pool* by Laura Adams Armet, Longmans, Green & Co.; *Wee Gillis* by Munro Leat, ill. by Robert Lawson, Viking Press; *Snow White and the Seven Dwarfs* by Wanda Gag, Coward-McCann; *Barkis* by Clare Newberry, Harper & Row, Publishers, Inc.; *Andy and the Lion* by James Daugherty, Viking Press.

1940 *Abraham Lincoln* by Ingra and Edgar Parin D'Aulaire, Doubleday & Co. Inc.
Honor Books: *Cock-A Doodle Doo* by Berta and Elmer Hader, Macmillan Publishing Co.; *Madeline* by Ludwig Bemelmans, Viking Press; *The Ageless Story,* ill. by Lauren Ford, Dodd, Mead & Co.

1941 *They Were Strong and Good* by Robert Lawson, Viking Press.
Honor Book: *April's Kittens* by Clare Newberry, Harper & Row, Publishers, Inc.

1942 *Make Way For Ducklings* by Robert McCloskey, Viking Press.
Honor Books: *An American ABC* by Maud and Miska Petersham, Macmillan Publishing Co.; *In My Mother's House* by Ann Nolan Clark, ill. by Velino Herrera, Viking Press; *Paddle-to-the-Sea* by Holling C. Holling, Houghton Mifflin Co.; *Nothing at All* by Wanda Gag, Coward-McCann.

1943 *The Little House* by Virginia Lee Burton, Houghton Mifflin Co.
Honor Books: *Dash and Dart* by Mary and Conrad Buff, Viking Press; *Marshmallow* by Clare Newberry, Harper & Row, Publishers, Inc.

1944 *Many Moons* by James Thurber, ill. by Louis Slobodkin, Harcourt Brace Jovanovich.
Honor Books: *Small Rain: Verses from the Bible* selected by Jessie Orton Jones, ill. by Elizabeth Orton Jones, Viking Press; *Pierre Pigeon* by Lee Kingman, ill. by Arnold E. Bare, Houghton Mifflin Co.; *The Mighty Hunter* by Berta and Elmer Hadar, Macmillan Publishing Co.; *A Child's Good Night Book* by Margaret Wise Brown, ill. by Jean Charlot, W. R. Scott; *Good Luck Horse* by Chih-Yi Chan, ill. by Piao Chan, Whittlesey.

1945 *Prayer for a Child* by Rachel Field, ill. by Elizabeth Orton Jones, Macmillan Publishing Co.
Honor Books: *Mother Goose,* ill. by Tasha Tudor, Walck; *In the Forest* by Marie Hall Ets, Viking Press; *Yonie Wondernose* by Marguerite de Angeli, Doubleday & Co. Inc.; *The Christmas Anna Angel* by Ruth Sawyer, ill. by Kate Seredy, Viking Press.

1946 *The Rooster Crows* (traditional Mother Goose), ill. by Maud and Miska Petersham, Macmillan Publishing Co.
Honor Books: *Little Lost Lamb* by Golden MacDonald, ill. by Leonard Weisgard, Doubleday & Co. Inc.; *Sing Mother Goose* by Opal Wheeler, ill. by Marjorie Torrey, E. P. Dutton, Inc.; *My Mother Is the Most Beautiful Woman in the World* by Becky Reyher, ill. by Ruth Gannett, Lothrop, Lee & Shepard Books.

1947 *The Little Island* by Golden Mac-Donald, ill. by Lenord Weisgard, Doubleday & Co. Inc.
Honor Books: *Rain Drop Splash* by Alvin Tresselt, ill. by Leonard Weisgard, Lothrop, Lee & Sheperd Books; *Boats on the River* by Marjorie Flack, ill. by Jay Hyde Barnum, Viking Press; *Timothy Turtle* by Al Graham, ill. by Tony Palazzo, Viking Press; *Pedro, the Angel of Olivera Street* by Leo Politi, Charles Scribner's Sons; *Sing in Praise: A Collection of the Best Loved Hymns* by Opal Wheeler, ill. by Marjorie Torrey, E. P. Dutton, Inc.

1948 *White Snow, Bright Snow* by Alvin Tresselt, ill. by Roger Duvoisin, Lothrop, Lee & Shepard Books.
Honor Books: *Stone Soup* by Marcia Brown, Charles Scribner's Sons; *McElligot's Pool* by Dr. Seuss, Random House Inc.; *Bambino the Clown* by George Schreiber, Viking Press; *Roger and the Fox* by Lavinia Davis, ill. by Hildegard Woodward, Doubleday & Co. Inc.; *Song of Robin Hood* ed. by Anne Malcolmson, ill. by Virginia Lee Burton, Houghton Mifflin Co.

1949 *The Big Snow* by Betta and Elmer Hader, Macmillan Publishing Co.
Honor Books: *Blueberries for Sal* by Robert McCloskey, Viking Press; *All Around the Town* by Phyllis McGinley, ill. by Helen Stone, J.B. Lippincott Co.; *Juanita* by Leo Politi, Charles Scribner's Sons; *Fish in the Air* by Kurt Wiese, Viking Press.

1950 *Song of the Swallows* by Leo Politi, Charles Scribner's Sons.
Honor Books: *America's Ethan Allen* by Stewart Holbrook, ill. by Lynd Ward, Houghton Mifflin Co.; *The Wild Birthday Cake* by Lavinia Davis, ill. by Hildegard Woodward, Doubleday & Co. Inc.; *The Happy Day* by Ruth Krauss, ill. by Marc Simont, Harper & Row, Publishers, Inc.; *Bartholomew and the Oobleck* by Dr. Seuss, Random House Inc.; *Henry Fisherman* by Marcia Brown, Charles Scribner's Sons.

1951 *The Egg Tree* by Katherine Milhous, Charles Scribner's Sons.
Honor Books: *Dick Whittington and His Cat* by Marcia Brown, Charles Scribner's Sons; *The Two Reds* by Will, ill. by Nicolas, Harcourt Brace Jovanovich; *If I Ran the Zoo* by Dr. Seuss, Random House Inc.; *The Most Wonderful Doll in the World* by Phyllis McGinley, ill. by Helen Stone, J.B. Lippincott Co.; *T-Bone, the Baby Sitter* by Clare Newberry, Harper & Row, Publishers, Inc.

1952 *Finders Keepers* by Will, ill. by Nicolas, Harcourt Brace Jovanovich.
Honor Books: *Mr. T.W. Anthony Woo* by Marie Hall Ets, Viking Press; *Skipper John's Cook* by Marcia Brown, Charles Scribner's Sons; *All Falling Down* by Gene Zion, ill. by Margaret Bloy Graham, Harper & Row, Publishers, Inc.; *Bear Party* by William Pene du Bois, Viking Press; *Feather Mountain* by Elizabeth Olds, Houghton Mifflin Co.

1953 *The Biggest Bear* by Lynd Ward, Houghton Mifflin Co.
Honor Books: *Puss in Boots* by Charles Perrault, ill. and tr. by Marcia Brown, Charles Scribner's Sons; *One Morning in Maine* by Robert McCloskey, Viking Press; *Ape in a Cape* by Fritz Eichenberg, Harcourt Brace Jovanovich; *The Storm Book* by Charlotte Zolotow, ill. by Margaret Bloy Graham, Harper & Row, Publishers, Inc.; *Five Little Monkeys* by Juliet Kepes, Houghton Mifflin Co.

1954 *Madeline's Rescue* by Ludwig Bemelmans, Viking Press.
Honor Books: *Journey Cake, HO!* by Ruth Sawyer, ill. by Robert McCloskey, Viking Press; *When Will the World Be Mine?* by Miriam Schlein, ill. by Jean Charlot, W.R. Scott; *The Steadfast Tin Soldier* by Hans Christian Andersen, ill. by Marcia Brown, Charles Scribner's Sons; *A Very Special House* by Ruth Krauss, ill. by Maurice Sendak, Harper & Row, Publishers, Inc.; *Green Eyes* by A. Birnbaum, Capitol.

1955 *Cinderella, or the Little Glass Slipper* by Charles Perrault, tr. and ill. by Marcia Brown, Charles Scribner's Sons.

Honor Books: *Book of Nursery and Mother Goose Rhymes*, ill. by Marguerite de Angeli, Doubleday & Co. Inc; *Wheel on the Chimney* by Margaret Wise Brown, ill. by Tibor Gergely, J.B. Lippincott Co.; *The Thanksgiving Story* by Alice Dalgliesh, ill. by Helen Sewell, Charles Scribner's Sons.

1956 *Frog Went A-Courtin'* ed. by John Langstaff, ill. by Feodor Rojankovsky, Harcourt Brace Jovanovich.

Honor Books: *Play with Me* by Marie Hall Ets, Viking Press; *Crow Boy* by Taro Yashima, Viking Press.

1957 *A Tree is Nice* by Janice May Udry, ill. by Marc Simont, Harper & Row, Publishers, Inc.

Honor Books: *Mr. Penny's Race Horse* by Marie Hall Ets, Viking Press; *1 Is One* by Tasha Tudor, Walck; *Anatole* by Eve Titus, ill. by Paul Galdone, McGraw-Hill Inc.; *Gillespie and the Guards* by Benjamin Elkin, ill. by James Daugherty, Viking Press; *Lion* by William Pene du Bois, Viking Press.

1958 *Time of Wonder* by Robert McCloskey, Viking Press.

Honor Books: *Fly High, Fly Low* by Don Freeman, Viking Press; *Anatole and the Cat* by Eve Titus, ill. by Paul Galdone, McGraw-Hill Inc.

1959 *Chanticleer and the Fox* adapted from Chaucer and ill. by Barbara Cooney, Thomas Y. Crowell Publishers.

Honor Books: *The House That Jack Built* by Antonio Frasconi, Harcourt Brace Jovanovich; *What Do You Say, Dear?* by Sesyle Joslin, ill. by Maurice Sendak, W. R. Scott; *Umbrella* by Taro Yashima, Viking Press.

1960 *Nine Days to Christmas* by Marie Hall Ets and Aurora Labastida, ill. by Marie Hall Ets, Viking Press.

Honor Books: *Houses from the Sea* by Alice E. Goudey, ill. by Adrienne Adams, Charles Scribner's Sons; *The Moon Jumpers* by Janice May Udry, ill. by Maurice Sendak, Harper & Row, Publishers, Inc.

1961 *Baboushka and the Three Kings* by Ruth Robbins, ill. by Nicolas Sidjakov, Parnassus Imprints.

Honor Book: *Inch by Inch* by Leo Lionni, Obolensky.

1962 *Once a Mouse. . .* by Marcia Brown, Charles Scribner's Sons.

Honor Books: *The Fox Went Out on a Chilly Night* by Peter Spier, Doubleday & Co. Inc.; *Little Bear's Visit* by Else Holmelund Minarik, ill by Maurice Sendak, Harper & Row, Publishers, Inc.; *The Day We Saw the Sun Come Up* by Alice E. Goudey, ill. by Adrienne Adams, Charles Scribner's Sons.

1963 *The Snowy Day* by Ezra Jack Keats, Viking Press.

Honor Books: *The Sun Is a Golden Earring* by Natalia M. Belting, ill. by Bernarda Bryson, Holt, Rinehart & Winston; *Mr. Rabbit and the Lovely Present* by Charlotte Zolotow, ill. by Maurice Sendak, Harper & Row, Publishers, Inc.

1964 *Where the Wild Things Are* by Maurice Sendak, Harper & Row, Publishers, Inc.

Honor Books: *Swimmy* by Leo Lionni, Pantheon Books Inc.; *All in the Morning Early* by Sorche Nic Leodhas, ill. by Evaline Ness, Holt, Rinehart & Winston; *Mother Goose and Nursery Rhymes* ill. by Philip Reed, Atheneum Publishers.

1965 *May I Bring A Friend?* by Beatrice Schenk de Regniers, ill. by Beni Montresor, Atheneum Publishers.

Honor Books: *Rain Makes Applesauce* by Julian Scheer, ill. by Marvin Bileck, Holiday House Inc.; *The Wave* by Margaret Hodges, ill. by Blair Lent, Houghton Mifflin Co.; *A Pocketful of Cricket* by Rebecca Caudill, ill. by Evaline Ness, Holt, Rinehart & Winston.

1966 *Always Room for One More* by Sorche Nic Leodhas, ill. by Nonny Hogrogian, Holt, Rinehart & Winston.

Honor Books: *Hide and Seek Fog* by Alvin Tresselt, ill. by Roger Duvoisin, Lothrop, Lee & Shepard Books; *Just*

Me by Marie Hall Ets, Viking Press; *Tom Tit Tot* by Evaline Ness, Charles Scribner's Sons.

1967 *Sam, Bangs & Moonshine* by Evaline Ness, Holt, Rinehart & Winston.

Honor Book: *One Wide River to Cross* by Barbara Emberley, ill. by Ed Emberley, Prentice-Hall Inc.

1968 *Drummer Hoff* by Barbara Emberley, ill. by Ed Emberley, Prentice-Hall Inc.

Honor Books: *Frederick* by Leo Lionni, Pantheon Books Inc.; *Seashore Story* by Taro Yashima, Viking Press; *The Emperor and the Kite* by Jane Yolen, ill. by Ed Young, World.

1969 *The Fool of the World and the Flying Ship* by Arthur Ransome, ill. by Uri Shulevitz, Farrar, Straus & Giroux Inc.

Honor Book: *Why the Sun and Moon Live in the Sky* by Elphinstone Dayrell, ill. by Blair Lent, Houghton Mifflin Co.

1970 *Sylvester and the Magic Pebble* by William Steig, Windmill.

Honor Books: *Goggles!* by Ezra Jack Keats, Macmillan Publishing Co.; *Alexander and the Wind-Up Mouse* by Leo Lionni, Pantheon Books Inc.; *Pop Corn & Ma Goodness* by Edna Mitchell Preston, ill. by Robert Andrew Parker, Viking Press; *Thy Friend, Obadiah* by Brinton Turkle, Viking Press; *The Judge* by Harve Zemach, ill. by Margot Zemach, Farrar, Straus & Giroux Inc.

1971 *A Story—A Story* by Gail E. Haley, Atheneum Publishers.

Honor Books: *The Angry Moon* by William Sleator, ill. by Blair Lent, Atlantic/Little; *Frog and Toad Are Friends* by Arnold Lobel, Harper & Row, Publishers, Inc.; *In the Night Kitchen* by Maurice Sendak, Harper & Row, Publishers, Inc.

1972 *One Fine Day* by Nonny Hogrogian, Macmillan Publishing Co.

Honor Books: *If All the Seas Were One Sea* by Janina Domanska, Macmillan Publishing Co.; *Moja Means One: Swahili Counting Book* by Muriel Feelings, ill. by Tom Feelings, Dial Press;

Hildild's Night by Cheli Duran Ryan, ill. by Arnold Lobel, Macmillan Publishing Co.

1973 *The Funny Little Woman* retold by Arlene Mosel, ill. by Blair Lent, E.P. Dutton, Inc.

Honor Books: *Anansi the Spider* adapted and ill. by Gerald McDermott, Holt, Rinehart & Winston; *Hosie's Alphabet* by Hosea, Tobias and Lisa Baskin, ill. by Leonard Baskin, Viking Press; *Snow White and the Seven Dwarfs* translated by Randall Jarrell, ill. by Nancy Ekholm Burkert, Farrar, Straus & Giroux Inc.; *When Clay Sings* by Byrd Baylor, ill. by Tom Bahti, Charles Scribner's Sons.

1974 *Duffy and the Devil* by Harve Zemach, ill. by Margot Zemach, Farrar, Straus & Giroux Inc.

Honor Books: *Three Jovial Huntsmen* by Susan Jeffers, Bradbury Press Inc.; *Cathedral: The Story of Its Construction* by David Macaulay, Houghton Mifflin Co.

1975 *Arrow to the Sun* adapted and ill. by Gerald McDermott, Viking Press.

Honor Book: *Jambo Means Hello* by Muriel Feelings, ill. by Tom Feelings, Dial Press.

1976 *Why Mosquitoes Buzz in People's Ears* retold by Verna Aardema, ill. by Leo and Diane Dillon, Dial Press.

Honor Books: *The Desert Is Theirs* by Byrd Baylor, ill. by Peter Parnall, Charles Scribner's Sons; *Strega Nona* retold and ill. by Tomie de Paola, Prentice-Hall Inc.

1977 *Ashanti to Zulu: African Traditions* by Margaret Musgrove, ill. by Leo and Dianne Dillon, Dial Press.

Honor Books: *The Amazing Bone* by William Steig, Farrar, Straus & Giroux Inc.; *The Contest* retold and ill. by Nonny Hogrogian, Greenwillow Books; *Fish for Supper* by M.B. Goffstein, Dial Press; *The Golem* by Beverly Brodsky McDermott, J. B. Lippincott Co.; *Hawk, I'm Your Brother* by Byrd Baylor, ill. by Peter Parnall, Charles Scribner's Sons.

1978 *Noah's Ark* by Peter Spier, Double-day & Co. Inc.
Honor Books: *Castle* by David Macaulay, Houghton Mifflin Co.; *It Could Always Be Worse* by Margot Zemach, Farrar, Straus, & Giroux Inc.

1979 *The Girl Who Loved Wild Horses* by Paul Goble, Bradbury Press Inc.
Honor Books: *Freight Train* by Donald Crews, Greenwillow Books; *The Way to Start a Day* by Byrd Baylor, ill. by Peter Parnall, Charles Scribner's Sons.

1980 *Ox-Cart Man* by Donald Hall, ill. by Barbara Cooney, Viking Press.
Honor Books: *Ben's Trumpet* by Rachel Isadora, Greenwillow Books; *The Treasure* by Uri Shulevitz, Farrar, Straus & Giroux Inc; *The Garden of Abdul Gasazi* by Chris Van Allsburg, Houghton Mifflin Co.

1981 *Fables* by Arnold Lobel, Harper & Row, Publishers, Inc.
Honor Books: *The Bremen-Town Musicians* by Ilse Plume, Doubleday & Co. Inc.; *The Grey Lady and the Strawberry Snatcher* by Molly Bang, Four Winds Press; *Mice Twice* by Joseph Low, Atheneum Publishers; *Truck* by Donald Crews, Greenwillow Books.

1982 *Jumanji* by Chris Van Allsburg, Houghton Mifflin Co.
Honor Books: *A Visit to William Blake's Inn: Poems for Innocent and Experienced Travelers* by Nancy Willard, ill. by Alice and Martin Provensen, Harcourt Brace Jovanovich; *Where the Buffaloes Begin* by Olaf Baker, ill. by Stephen Gammell, Frederick Warne & Co. Inc.; *On Market Street* by Anita Lobel, Greenwillow Books; *Outside Over There* by Maurice Sendak, Harper & Row, Publishers, Inc.

1983 *Shadow* by Blaise Cendrars, ill. by Marcia Brown, Charles Scribner's Sons.
Honor Books: *When I Was Young in the Mountains* by Cynthia Rylant, ill. by Diane Goode, E.P. Dutton, Inc.; *A Chair for My Mother* by Vera Williams, William Morrow & Co. Inc.

1984 *St. George and the Dragon* retold by Margaret Hodges, ill. by Trina Schart Hyman, Little, Brown & Co. Inc.
Honor Books: *Hansel and Gretel* retold by Rika Lesser, ill. by Paul Zelinsky, Dodd, Mead & Co.; *Have You Seen My Duckling?* by Nancy Tafuri, Greenwillow Books; *The Story of Jumping Mouse* by John Steptoe, Lothrop, Lee & Shepard Books.

Joan I. Glazer is a professor of education at Rhode Island College, where she teaches courses in children's literature, language arts, and film for children. She has taught at the elementary school level, served as a Head Start supervisor, and worked as an educational consultant for numerous school districts. She is a member of the Commission on Literature for the National Council of Teachers of English, and serves on the Poetry Award Selection Committee and the Outstanding Trade Books in the Language Arts Committee for that organization. In 1982 Dr. Glazer was honored with the Distinguished Teacher Award from the School of Education and Human Development at Rhode Island College.

Subject Index

Movement, 241–42, 245
Music
  development in, 224–25
  involving children with, 239–42, 244–47

Nonfiction
  definition, 9
  evaluating, 14–15
Nonverbal communication, 191–92

Observing
  developing skill in, 128–30
  patterns of behavior, 195–96
Onomatopoeia, 89–91, 232–33
Oral response to literature, 100–103
Organizing, developing skill in, 134–35

Paperback books, 4
Parents
  reading aloud, 23–24
  selecting books, 21–23
Participation books, 4
Personality
  definition, 149
  development of, 149–51
Picture books, definition, 6–8
Picture story books, 6–7
Plot, 10–11
Poetry
  definition, 8–9
  evaluating, 15–17
  examples of, 15, 52, 53, 86, 89, 160,
    161, 174, 232, 233
  preferences of young children, 20, 51–52
  recommended books of, 23, 115–16
Poets, recommended, 9
Preferences in literature, children's 19–20
Problem solving, 141–42
Prose, definition, 9
Prosocial behavior
  models for, 186–87, 201–4
  research, 186
Puppets
  for taking roles, 200
  in story interpretation, 102
  in storytelling, 36

Questioning
  convergent questions, 140
  for discussion, 58–59
  divergent questions, 140
  for encouraging critical listening, 97
  for guiding literary understanding, 58–60
  levels of questions, 137–38

"Read Alone" books, 7

Reading
  aloud, 23–24, 30–34, 43–44
  how children learn, 76, 98
  interests of children, 19–20
  observing the process, 98–99
  relation of literature to comprehension
    in, 78
Reasoning
  expanding children's ability in, 136–37
  forms of, 118–19
Realism, defintion, 9
Rebus writing, 91–92
Reference materials, 155–56
Refrains, 90–91
Response to literature, 20–21, 54–55
Reviews
  of audiovisual materials, 39
  of books, 23, 30
Rhyme
  authors who write in, 89
  in poetry, 16
Rhythm, in poetry, 15–16, 88–89
Rhythm instruments, 241, 245
Riddles, 93–94
Role play, 101–2, 200–201

Security, books promoting feelings of,
  166–67
Self-concept
  definition, 150
  enhancement of, 158–64
Self-esteem
  definition, 150
  enhancement of, 164–68
Sensory awareness, 230–35
Sequencing, 135
Setting, 11
Sex-role identification, models for, 150,
  163–64
Social development, children's, 185–88
Songs
  in audiovisual format, 240–41, 245
  in picture book format, 239–40
Stereotyping, 13, 163–64, 187
Storytelling
  by adults, 34–39
  by children, 102–3
  recommended titles for, 47
Style of writing
  definition and examples, 13
  relations to comprehension, 52–54
Styles of art, in picture books, 229
Suprasegmentals, 192
Sustained silent reading, 152
Syntax, 77–78, 81

Tasks, setting and completing, 155–58

Author/Illustrator/ Title Index